Little Ship, Big War

The Big E
The Far and the Deep
Sun, Earth and Man

Little Ship, Big War

THE SAGA OF DE343

Commander
Edward P. Stafford,

USN (Ret.)

WILLIAM MORROW AND COMPANY, INC.

NEW YORK   1984

Library of Congress Catalog Card Number: 84–60482

ISBN: 0–688–03253–2

Printed in the United States of America

First Edition

1 2 3 4 5 6 7 8 9 10

BOOK DESIGN BY BERNARD SCHLEIFER

This book is for all Destroyer-escort sailors everywhere,
a special breed of stalwart men who sailed
to war in little ships and held the seas for freedom
when the need was there.

Acknowledgments

To TELL A TRUE sea story about a real ship, the first thing the storyteller must have is her deck log. It forms the skeletal structure of the story, providing not only her precise itinerary, but the dates and times of all important events, and even what the weather was like. In the relation of the story it must be constantly referred to. *Abercrombie*'s log is rightfully in the custody of the National Archives in Washington, and is available to be inspected there. But it may not be removed from the premises, a decided disadvantage to someone attempting to write a book about her, sixty-five miles away. By some near-miracle of interest, influence, initiative and ingenuity, my friend William W. Watkins, formally an *Abercrombie* radarman, was able to provide me with my own working copy of *Abercrombie*'s log, and for that I am hugely in his debt.

A source nearly as essential as the deck log is the log of incoming and outgoing visual (flashing-light and semaphore) signals. It provides a wealth of information and detail, formal and informal, available nowhere else, and helps to put flesh on the bare bones of the deck log. For that most valuable document I am indebted to former signalman (later Master Chief Quartermaster) Raymond J. Shiel, who in a true labor of love copied the voluminous official document in his own hand while *Abercrombie* was being decommissioned back in early 1946, and then highlighted, color coded and annotated it for my benefit.

Details of combat with the enemy, and the forces involved, are contained in the Action Reports and War Diaries submitted at the time. For those reports, for *Abercrombie* as well as for the other ships mentioned in the text, I am indebted (for the third time since 1958) to Dr. Dean C. Allard, Director of the Operational Archives Branch of the Naval Historical Center in Washington, D.C., and to his extremely efficient, helpful and courteous staff.

The book, as an intimate, detailed account of one small ship engaged in a very big war, could not have been written without the active help of the men who manned and fought her. Seventy-six of the former ship's company returned my questionnaires, thirty submitted to lengthy interviews either in person or by phone, sixteen furnished personal (and illegal) "logs" or diaries, and eleven sent me tape cassettes detailing their memories of those eventful twenty months nearly forty years ago. In addition, the forty-nine former crewmen who gathered in Knoxville, Tennessee, in the spring of 1983 cheerfully responded to a list of questions I had prepared for the occasion, and thus straightened out a number of facts, anecdotes and incidents which otherwise would have been lacking in the accuracy which is so essential to a book like this. Special thanks is due to Thomas M. Rutters for coming up with an old address book from his time in DE343, which in a kind of geometrical progression has enabled us to locate 129 of *Abercrombie*'s crew plus another thirty-one who, sadly, have not survived. Special thanks is also due former chief gunner's mate James A. Ramsey, who, bless him, apparently never threw away anything relating to the *Abercrombie*. He furnished me crew lists, watch bills, orders to gunnery ranges ashore, a series of amusing anecdotes, and even the official notice of the passing of Butch the mascot.

I am grateful to the following gentlemen for taking the time to share with me their experiences on *Abercrombie*'s sister DEs: Francis Kilchenstein of the *Suesens;* John E. "Red" Harrington, Robert "Mel" Harden, Jack K. Moore, Jack Yusen, Lloyd A. Gurnett and William S. Burton of the *Roberts;* Abbott M. Gibney and John F. Murphy of the *Oberrender;* and William A. Rogers of the *Wann.* Mr. Benjamin D. Hyde, former Commanding Officer of the APD *Bunch,* also was kind enough to furnish me details of the loss of *Dickerson* (APD21) and of the subsequent rescue of her people by UDT21 embarked in his ship. Rear Admiral T. C. Phifer, former Commander of *Abercrombie*'s Escort Division 69, was kind enough to send me his excellent tape describing at first hand the battle off Samar, as well as answer a number of questions for me by phone.

For the Prologue, William A. Tunstall, formerly of the USS *Hornet* and plane captain of William W. Abercrombie's TBD Devastator at Midway, provided his unique memories of Ensign Abercrombie and Bernard Phelps, his radioman, on the morning of the battle.

And for the Epilogue, I am grateful to Mr. John Riley, who is writing a comprehensive book about destroyer escorts in World War II for the Naval Historical Center, for coming up with documents that led me to Rear Admiral Kenneth C. Wallace, former skipper of the *Long Beach,* and to Captain Robert S. Salin, former C.O. of Attack Squadron 93, who in turn described the final hours of the hulk which had once been DE343.

In the fall of 1982 I made a trip to Galveston, Texas, to refresh my memory by visiting the USS *Stewart* (DE258), which is, as far as I know, the only remaining DE. The *Stewart* is preserved on land in Sea Wolf Park in Galveston, and the man in charge of her is Charles "Chuck" Fulmer. Chuck Fulmer saved what was a largely wasted trip from Baltimore to Galveston by opening up all the very many *Stewart* compartments, including the pilothouse and wardroom, which are not open to visitors, and by spending several hours accompanying me on a tour of his ship. I am most appreciative.

Finally I am indebted to my good friend master chief gunner's mate Gale Habets for 1944–1945-vintage ordnance and gunnery publications and for training manuals that helped me immeasurably in describing the operations of *Abercrombie*'s guns, and for his ready and obliging availability as my expert, consultant and adviser in gunnery matters.

Contents

12   CONTENTS

Little Ship, Big War

Prologue

IT ALL BEGAN, oddly enough, with a lumbering, obsolescent airplane which on Thursday, the fourth of June 1942, should never have been where it was, or doing what it was doing. The plane's pilot was a big, quiet, twenty-five-year-old ensign who had been an officer and a Naval Aviator for less than a year. He was proud to be from Kansas City, and each day when his carrier's noon position was posted, he had the same question, "How far is that from Kansas City?" His name was William Warner Abercrombie, and he was known to his fellow pilots of Torpedo Squadron Eight on the carrier USS *Hornet* as "Abbie."

Now Abercrombie's plane, along with fourteen others of his squadron, was 135 miles northwest of Midway Island. They were attacking, without fighter escort, four of the biggest and best aircraft carriers in the Imperial Japanese Navy—all veterans of the Sunday attack at Pearl Harbor six months before. In the rear seat of his venerable TBD Devastator torpedo plane, facing aft over a pair of .30-caliber machine guns, sat Bernard Phelps, aviation radioman second class, a feisty young farmer from Moultrie County, Illinois, who dreamed of becoming a civil engineer. The evening before, Phelps had won forty dollars from his shipmates at poker. He had wanted to send it home "just in case," but there had not been time.

The four carriers under attack by Abercrombie, Phelps and the rest of Torpedo Eight were the *Akagi, Kaga, Hiryu* and *Soryu.* The carriers were protected by a surface antiaircraft screen of two battleships, three cruisers and eleven destroyers. Above the carriers circled a Combat Air Patrol (CAP) of some fifty Zero fighters.

Torpedo Eight was sighted when it was still eight miles from the carriers. To be effective, the torpedoes had to be dropped less than half a mile from the target. With the 2,000-pound, 14-foot-long torpedoes slung externally between the protruding tires of their only partially retractable landing gear, the TBDs at full throttle could make only 160 knots.

The Zeros were more than twice as fast and infinitely more agile, and there were three Zeros to each Devastator. Because the enemy ships had unexpectedly turned away from the American force, Torpedo Eight's flight, launched at maximum range, had been longer than predicted. As a result, at the time of sighting, the fuel gauges in the TBDs already showed less than half of the original supply remaining. Even without torpedoes it was doubtful that they could return to land on the *Hornet.* A full-throttle attack would make it impossible, although at least one pilot thought there was a chance he might make it back to Midway.

The fifteen Devastators bunched up for mutual protection, and slanted down to their attack altitude of one hundred feet with throttles full forward.

The carriers turned away from their attackers at twenty-five knots. The range closed with agonizing slowness, about two miles each minute. And for every second of those long minutes the Zeros swarmed over the lumbering Devastators, slashing in from all directions, often almost colliding in their eagerness to make a kill. They went for the lead planes first, finding the range with twin 7.7-millimeter machine guns firing through the prop and then opening up with twenty-millimeter cannons in the wings. The TBD gunners swung their twin thirties and fired back, and when an incautious Zero crossed ahead, the torpedo pilots got off a few rounds from their single, fixed, forward-firing .30-caliber "peashooters."

But it was a fatally unequal fight. One after another the TBDs began to go down. At least one exploded in midair. Some slanted burning into the sea. Some rolled over out of control and crashed on their backs. As the range closed, the ships opened up and the sky blossomed with jarring black bursts of AA while heavy shells sent up columns of solid water, and the tracer streams from heavy, then light machine guns laced horizontally across the surface, shifting and intersecting among the planes. The approach to the turning carriers was marked by splotches of skidding orange flame and black smoke, and long, tearing splashes. Occasionally a tumbling wing tip with a white star showed for a moment and vanished. Long before they could reach their torpedo release points, most of the TBDs were gone. The aggressive, determined squadron commander himself, leading the formation, had been one of the first to go. He was last seen standing upright in his flaming cockpit as his Devastator slammed into the sea.

No one would have blamed them if the remaining pilots had jettisoned their torpedoes and tried to run for home. Not one did. Not one even dropped his torpedo at long range and turned away. Every Torpedo Eight pilot pressed the attack as long as he was alive and his plane would fly.

Ensign Abercrombie's TBD, being toward the rear of the ragged little formation, was one of the last to go down, only a mile from his target, and very far indeed from Kansas City.

Only one of the fifteen pilots lived to reach his torpedo release range of one thousand yards, and both pilot and plane were so shot up that it is not known whether he actually released the torpedo or, if he did, where it went.

What is known is that there were no hits. Not one plane returned to the *Hornet*. Of the thirty young men who took off that morning, only one survived.

Immediately behind Torpedo Eight came Torpedo Six from the carrier *Enterprise*. Ten of those fourteen planes went down. Next came Torpedo Three from the *Yorktown*, boring in as though they didn't know that two squadrons had been slaughtered before them. Even with an escort of six Wildcat fighters, Torpedo Three lost ten of its twelve planes.

Thirty-five out of forty-one TBDs were shot down—and not one torpedo exploded against a Japanese hull.

Yet Abercrombie and Phelps, their squadron mates and their peers from the other carriers, opened the doors for victory. Their determined attack against all odds disrupted Japanese flight operations and kept the enemy fighters busy at sea level while, high above, two squadrons of bombers approached their dive points unopposed.

Six minutes after the last torpedo attack and only an hour after the death of Ensign Abercrombie, the dive bombers sent three of the enemy carriers to the bottom. Before that fateful day was out, the fourth carrier had joined her sisters.

Thus did the United States Navy avenge Pearl Harbor, and thus did the Empire of Japan lose four of its first-line carriers with all their planes and most of their pilots—a blow from which it was never able to recover. Of greater significance was the fact that while the biggest naval war in history was only six months old, it had reached its turning point.

Ensign William Warner Abercrombie, with his fellow pilots of the fourth of June off Midway, was posthumously awarded the Navy Cross "for extraordinary heroism and distinguished service beyond the call of duty. . . ." The citation that eventually came to his parents in Kansas with the gold medal on its ribbon of Navy blue and white also had the following to say:

> Grimly aware of the hazardous consequence of flying without fighter protection, and with insufficient fuel to return to his carrier, Ensign Abercrombie, resolutely, and with no thought of his own

life, delivered an effective torpedo attack against violent assaults of enemy Japanese aircraft and against an almost solid barrage of anti-aircraft fire. His courageous action, carried out with a gallant spirit of self-sacrifice and conscientious devotion to the fulfillment of his mission, was a determining factor in the defeat of the enemy forces and was in keeping with the highest traditions of the United States Naval Service.

To honor the Midway torpedo pilots further, and to inspire other men with their examples of courage and devotion to duty, the Navy in late 1943 began to assign their names to new warships. Ensign Abercrombie was one of the pilots so honored, and the keel of the USS *Abercrombie* (DE343) was laid on 8 November 1943.

DE343 was launched at Orange, in eastern Texas, on 14 January 1944. Ensign Abercrombie's mother smashed the netted champagne bottle on the sharp, high bow, and the new ship splashed stern first into the narrow Sabine River, bobbed two or three times and then steadied up, riding high in the muddy water, for she was still just an empty hull.

But that empty hull held a lot of promise. Exactly 306 feet long, and 36 feet 8 inches wide, with a mean draft of 9½ feet, in a few short months it would become the home of ten officers and some two hundred crewmen. When manned and equipped, the hull would become one of the first of a new class of warships, a destroyer escort, but faster, better armed, more versatile than any DEs then operating—in effect, it was a "poor man's destroyer," capable of relieving the faster, more heavily armed, far more expensive destroyers of such chores as convoying slow transports, merchant ships or landing craft, screening the smaller and slower escort carriers, and performing antisubmarine patrols and searches. The destroyers thus relieved would then be available to join the growing first-line task forces of new attack carriers, cruisers and battleships.

To perform such a wide variety of missions, the hull which one day would be the USS *Abercrombie* would be fitted with twin oil-fired boilers and steam turbines capable of driving it through the oceans of the world at twenty-four knots. Its main battery would be two power-operated five-inch guns in enclosed mounts, one forward and one aft, both capable of engaging either air or surface targets. The five-inchers would be backed up by two rapid-firing forty-millimeter twin mounts, also positioned fore and aft and also able to fire at anything on the sea or in the air. For close-in work there would be ten 20-millimeter guns, designed primarily for antiaircraft defense but also capable of being depressed to counter surface threats.

To locate enemy submarines the DE would have the latest sonar equipment, and to kill them there would be a "hedgehog" forward, which could throw a circle of rocket-propelled, fast-sinking, contact-firing explosive charges far out over her bow, and aft there would be four K-guns on each side to hurl conventional depth charges and racks to roll more over her stern. At her masthead, the most advanced radars would be able to scan the sea and sky in any weather, day or night. The latest communications gear would keep her in touch with fleet and force commanders, shore stations and the other men-of-war with which she would be operating.

The process of transforming the empty hull of DE343 into such a warship was delayed only briefly by the speeches, flags and ceremony of launching. The Sabine was still roiled from the splash of the new ship when two small tugs came alongside and with tooting whistles, roaring diesels and churning water at their sterns, nudged her up against the shipyard dock. Her lines had barely been made fast when metal brows were lowered into place and hard-hatted workers swarmed aboard to begin a three-shift, seven-day, all-out crash effort to get her ready for sea.

BOOK · I

1. Orange, Texas

In the early months of 1944, the war was being waged on a global basis. And since the surface of the earth is nearly three-fourths water, United States naval forces were everywhere committed and engaged. In the English Channel ports, masses of ships were assembling and rehearsing for the long-awaited invasion and liberation of Europe. Along the ocean lifelines supporting Allied forces in Italy and North Africa, other ships and planes were battling the U-boats and Axis bombers. On the opposite side of the globe, fast carrier task forces were suppressing and neutralizing the main enemy base of Truk, "the Gibraltar of the Pacific," and supporting the capture of Kwajalein and Eniwetok. In the South Pacific, landing craft and their escorts were putting troops ashore to occupy Manus in the Admiralty Islands with its magnificent Seeadler Harbor. At the same time, final preparations were going forward for the recapture of Guam, Saipan and Tinian, an operation requiring more than 500 ships to deliver 127,000 troops to hostile islands 3,500 miles from the nearest major U.S. base.

During those same months, shipyards on all three U.S. coasts, and even plants far inland, were cranking out ships by the dozens to meet those commitments. Seventeen coastal shipyards and a score of inland fabricators were building and assembling destroyer escorts. One such shipyard, the Consolidated Steel Corporation building yard in Orange, Texas, was turning out a new destroyer escort about every eight days.

When I reported to Orange on 16 March, five DEs in various stages of completion were moored to the company's long wooden dock on the Sabine. The dock smelled of creosote and dry wood, and a faint odor of still, muddy water wafted up between the heavy planks. Railroad tracks ran the length of the dock about ten feet from the water. Across the dock from the line of ships was a two-story, shedlike building with a peaked roof and a line of windows in the upper story. The lower story had four wide doors opening onto the dock and a huge, hangarlike opening at one end.

23

A sign on the corner of the building read "Supply Department" and under that "Building 118."

Sailors in dungarees and undress blues, and chiefs and officers in khakis and the new grays, crossed back and forth between ships and shed. Most of the officers carried clipboards and gray, Navy-issue flashlights or rolled blueprints or plans. One of the ships was already in her "dazzle" warpaint of black, gray and white irregular, sweeping curves and blotches. Another was in the process of being painted, with spray guns hissing and the smell of paint in the air. The cross-dock traffic was heavier at those ships and it moved faster. There was a feeling of organized urgency.

The ships themselves were draped with a spaghettilike tangle of electrical cables, compressed-air lines, oxygen and acetylene hoses, ropes and rigging. They rang with riveting and flashed with blue showers of welding sparks. Dockside cranes swung large, heavy objects aboard and lowered them gently into place—twenty-millimeter guns, chestlike ready-ammunition lockers, long loops of anchor chain, crates, bales and boxes.

I walked down the dock in the thin spring sun, stepping over the lines and cables, trying to stay clear of the cross-dock traffic, anxious for my first look at the ship in which I would go back to the war. It was one of those moments that are clearly of huge personal significance. The orders I carried in a large official envelope were specific: "Report to the Supervisor of Shipbuilding, Consolidated Steel Corporation, Limited, for temporary duty commissioning and fitting out USS *Abercrombie* (DE343) and duty aboard that vessel when commissioned." When aboard I was to be First Lieutenant (the First Lieutenant on a DE is third in command after the Captain and the Executive Officer). He is in charge of the deck force, responsible for the maintenance and integrity of the hull and all its fittings, and for damage control and fire fighting, should those be necessary. All that was known. What was not known was what kind of a ship *Abercrombie* would be. Every ship has its individual personality: competent, lackadaisical or incompetent; aggressive or reluctant; homelike or barrackslike; lucky or unlucky, happy or unhappy. That personality derives both from the quality of her construction and equipment, and from the officers and men of her crew. What would *Abercrombie*'s men be like? For better or for worse they would be married to her for years, years in remote and hostile seas, years of danger, discomfort and deprivation. Two hundred men and a dozen officers, each highly individual, would go to war in *Abercrombie*. Would they mesh into an efficient fighting machine which would enable *Abercrombie* to accomplish the missions for which she was designed, and incidentally improve the chances of her men's survival? Or would they be merely 212 assorted young men operating a sterile seagoing machine without character or focus? What relationships would develop among those men, jammed under the pressure of war into a 306- by 37-foot steel hull for no one knew how long? Lifelong friendships? Bitter hostilities? Simple, fraternal companionships? All of the above?

It would of course be impossible to answer any of those questions by simply looking at the new ship for the first time. But it was a place to start.

The DE sparkling in her completed coat of dazzle paint was, according to the lettering across the stern, the *John C. Butler,* and the white numbers on her bow were 339. She was the first of this new class of warship, with 12,000-hp geared steam turbines, dual-purpose five-inch guns and a new, low, clean silhouette. It was obvious that when the tangle and mess of the yard were cleared away, the DE would be beautiful in a clean-cut, deadly, efficient way. The big guns fore and aft, poking out of enclosed mounts raised above the narrow decks, looked competent and formidable. One level up in the superstructure behind each 5"/38, the twin forty-millimeters with their heavy recoil springs and flash-shield cones on their muzzles, capable of hammering out 160 explosive rounds a minute, were comfortably menacing. The short, raked single stack amidships just abaft the mast added a touch of dash, and just aft of that, high on the boat deck where it could launch over either side, the triple torpedo mount was an exciting reminder that in a pinch the *Butler* could give pause to any enemy ship afloat. The clean, straight sweep of the deck from the anchors at her high, sharp bow to the depth-charge racks low on her fantail and the ordered symmetry of her armament made her as graceful as a yacht. Her appearance inspired a feeling of pride and promise, an itch to stand on her bridge and feel her take the sea.

The partially painted ship was the *O'Flaherty,* number 340, and behind her lay the *Raymond,* number 341, still spotted and pale yellow in zinc chromate primer. *Raymond* looked raw and naked with her guns not yet aboard and the holes in her deck fore and aft where the 5"/38s would go. Astern of *Raymond* lay *Richard W. Suesens,* number 342, obviously still farther from completion, since even her mast had not yet been stepped.

Then suddenly there she was, a mastless, gunless yellow hull with empty hawsepipes and gaping holes in her decks. Through a huge opening toward the stern, a crane was lowering heavy machinery; parts of her engineering plant were still being installed. But on her yellow bow the neat white numbers stood out clearly—343—and evenly spaced across her broad transom the single, unforgettable long name: *A b e r c r o m b i e.*

I stood for a long time looking at her, thinking how very well I would get to know every inch of this now unfamiliar hull, wondering what distant seas and lands I would see from her decks, what kinds of storms and skirmishes and battles we would face together, and what would be the circumstances of our eventual homecoming. And as I stood staring at this potent new entity in my life, I felt the first stirrings of affection. She seemed so vulnerable in her unfinished state, like a premature infant. I knew she was just a steel hull in the final phases of fabrication, yet I felt a touch of embarrassment for her with that heroic name on her stern yet still only half a ship, high and ungraceful in the brown river, her innards open to the sky, no mast for symmetry and vision, no weapons for defense, and dressed in that callow coat of blotched and faded yellow. She seemed to be pleading for completion, for her mast and guns and warpaint and crew so that she might get to sea where she belonged.

Through one of the big doors across the dock, in a makeshift office surrounded by crates and boxes, I found the beginnings of her crew, two officers and a chief yeoman. Art Hellman, the Stores Officer, had been in Orange since 3 March, and Gus Adams, the Engineering Officer, had arrived only four days ago. Art was an affable, outgoing reservist not long out of a flourishing paint business in Ohio. Gus was a rather taciturn, no-nonsense regular Navy officer who had earned his commission the hard way, up from fireman through chief and warrant officer. The Chief Yeoman, expertly clattering away on a big manual typewriter, was Jim Larkin from New Orleans, young for a CPO, with dark hair and brown eyes. Larkin would be responsible, under the Executive Officer, for all the paper work—records, reports, files and correspondence—that would flow from Abercrombie's little ship's office during her active life.

Both Hellman and Adams were Lieutenants (junior grade)— "jaygees." I was a Lieutenant, period, so I found myself in charge.

When the introductions were over, Larkin pulled the paper out of his machine and handed me a copy. It was the current crew list. It showed that a total of twenty-eight men had reported thus far, including three chiefs, five first class and seven second class petty officers—a nucleus of experts in engineering, gunnery, communications, navigation, seamanship, administration, medical matters and food service.

Both Hellman and Adams reported Abercrombie progressing on schedule, with roughly half her allowance of stores and equipment already in Orange and more gear arriving every week. Commissioning was scheduled for late April.

I found it hard to believe that that half-empty yellow hull across the dock could be transformed into a man-of-war in less than six weeks. But that was because I had no conception of the ever-increasing tempo of activity during that time. *Abercrombie*'s crew worked from 8:00 A.M. to 6:00 P.M. and later, when required by the arrival of a large shipment of gear to be inventoried, logged, lugged aboard and, in some cases, installed. That was seven days a week. The yard worked around the clock, also seven days a week. While the yard literally put the ship together, the nucleus crew put together the organization that would make her functional when she was complete. But the crew also carried, stowed, tested, calibrated and kept continuous track of what had arrived and what was still required.

I was not "Officer-in-Charge, Precommissioning Detail, USS *Abercrombie* (DE343)" for long. On 24 March the Captain arrived.

Lieutenant Bernard H. Katschinski, USNR, was a well-built, slightly florid man in his early thirties, about five feet ten inches tall, with a receding hairline and a manner which alternated between geniality and severity. He could be an amiable and urbane dinner companion ashore in the evening, and a tyrant with a temper aboard in the morning. But he knew his business. His questions were probing and pertinent, and when he got the wrong answers he knew what to do. He came to *Abercrombie* from command of a DE of an earlier class. Before the war he had been the manager of a packing company in San Francisco. Before that he had graduated from the University of California at Berkeley with a commission as ensign from the NROTC unit there.

For two weeks after the Captain's arrival, *Abercrombie*'s nucleus crew remained essentially the same—Katschinski, Stafford, Hellman, Adams and thirty-odd men. During those days the skipper and I lived with our wives in furnished apartments in Beaumont, and car-pooled the twenty-eight miles back and forth to Orange. Hellman and Adams lived in bachelor officers' quarters, and the enlisted men in barracks in Orange, about five miles from the yard, riding battleship-gray buses back and forth to the ship.

And every day we watched the *Abercrombie* grow. Each day more equipment was lugged or lowered aboard and bolted, welded or wired into place. Each day before our eyes she became more a warship and less a hull. Day by day she settled more deeply in the river with the weight of her arms and stores. One by one the holes in her deck were sealed. She acquired a funnel and a mast. By mid-April her five-inch guns were in place, covering the last openings in her weather deck. She was still that awful yellow, still cluttered and tangled in the webs of the workmen, but we could see the warship breaking through and we no longer felt embarrassed for her.

On 14 April there were five officers and thirty-five men. Lieutenant (j.g.) Keith Wheeling had reported as Communications Officer and two more chiefs had arrived. Keith was about the skipper's age but his opposite in temperament, quietly competent, steady, warm and kind with frequent flashes of contagious humor.

A week later our little nucleus was joined by the main body of *Abercrombie's* crew, 160 men and five officers. There were only ten days left before commissioning. The tempo of activity aboard the nearly completed ship, on the dock and in the hugely expanded office ashore accelerated until it was just short of frenetic. It had to be. There was a nearly inconceivable amount of work to be done in that time.

First, 195 men had to be organized into departments and divisions, each with its own leading petty officer and division officer. Within each division the men had to be assigned to watches—three watches for Condition III when a third of the armament would be manned and a man would stand four hours on and eight hours off, and two watches for Condition II when half the weapons would be ready and the crew stood four on and four off. Every officer and man had to be assigned a battle station for Condition I—when all the armament would be fully manned. Within each division ("O" for ordnance and gunnery, "E" for engineering, "C" for communications, "S" for supply, and the First and Second Divisions of the deck force), each man would be assigned a bunk, a locker and a cleaning station. Bills had to be drawn up so that each man would know where to go, what to bring and what to do in case of fire, man overboard, plane crash, rescue of survivors, fueling at sea, abandon ship and other emergencies. Each man had to be assigned a station for entering or leaving port or maneuvering in restricted waters (Special Sea Details). Then each department and division had to test and inspect each of the hundreds of items of equipment, from ammunition hoists to rescue breathing apparatus (RBA) to radar, sonar and the galley ranges.

In the ship's office, personnel and correspondence files had to be set up, typewriters and mimeograph machines acquired, desks and file cabinets lugged aboard and bolted into place.

On the navigation bridge, charts of half the world had to be acquired, corrected to date and stowed; sextants, chronometers, stopwatches, navigational tables to be checked; signal flags to be sorted and arranged in the flag bags; halyards to be rigged; signal searchlights installed and checked out.

In the radio shack, transmitters, receivers, speakers, microphones, headphones and special communications typewriters called "mills" had to be installed.

On the fo'c'sle, two hundred fathoms of anchor chain would have to be painted and marked, the capstan and anchor windlass and pelican hooks and stoppers tested. Mooring lines, heaving lines and messengers had to be made up, and fenders acquired, rigged for use and stowed.

At the opposite end of the ship in the steering engine room, the big electric motors and rams which controlled the rudders had to be tested along with backup control systems with different power sources and even chain falls for moving the twin rudders by hand if all else failed.

The five-inch guns forward and aft had to be worked out in director, local and even manual control, the hoists for bringing up projectiles and case assemblies tested, the recoil and gas ejection systems checked.

The two twin 40-millimeter guns and the ten 20-millimeter guns had to be cleaned of the Cosmoline with which they had been coated for preservation and shipment, then lubricated and tested.

In firerooms and engine rooms, an assortment of blowers, burners, pumps, generators, air compressors, condensers, evaporators, valves and gauges had to be tested, checked and calibrated.

From bow to stern, from bilges to bridge, fire hoses with fog and foam nozzles, fire extinguishers, and battle lanterns had to be inspected, tested and stowed, ready for use.

A life jacket for every officer and man had to be brought aboard, equipped with a light, dye marker and shark repellent, and stowed where it would be readily available. A steel helmet for every man had to be stowed near his battle station.

Down aft in sick bay, there were sterilizers which had be hooked up to steam lines; medicines and instruments to be inventoried, checked and put away; records to be set up; bunks to be readied. A large sterilizer had to be installed, and packages of instruments and dressings located in the wardroom, which would be the primary battle dressing station in combat.

In every department, but especially in engineering, there was crate after crate of spare parts and tools to be unpacked, cataloged and located ready for use.

And everywhere in the brand-new ship, the watertight doors and hatches came in for special attention. What made them watertight was a rubber gasket on the moving part which met a steel lip, or knife-edge, on the stationary part. But unless both parts were clean and even, water could get through. So now began the endless battle of the knife-edges and gaskets, which seemed to have a dogged affinity for rust and paint, respectively.

And that was only the smallest sampling.

While all this was taking place, the gray buses each day took scores of sailors to the nearby firing range, where they learned or relearned to fire revolvers, automatic pistols, carbines, rifles and even twenty- and forty-millimeter guns. Other gray buses took teams of conning officers, sonarmen and helmsmen to the antisubmarine "attack teacher," where, to the reverberating pings of a simulated sonar, they practiced attacks on simulated subs maneuvered by instructors who watched the lighted, flat-iron shapes of DE and sub perform their deadly adagios on a vertical glass screen.

Somehow the pressures of the ordered rush of those final ten days, the close cooperation required to get things done and the long hours working toward the same goals drew the hodgepodge of officers and men together and began to shape them into a crew, a unique one formed and tailored to fit the now clearly recognizable new warship, the *Abercrombie*.

In the course of that process the five officers of the old nucleus crew began to become acquainted with the five who had arrived on 21 April. One was *Abercrombie's* Executive Officer and Navigator, John Hicks. Hicks was a fat man in his middle to late twenties with heavy jowls and thin, slicked-back brown hair. Like the Captain he was a Californian, although he came from Los Angeles and was a bachelor. At work he attempted earnestly, if somewhat obsequiously, to get things done the way the Captain wanted them done. Ashore he laughed loudly and often and frequently carried a small case with a couple of bottles of whiskey. It was hard to envision him working closely with the demanding and somewhat fastidious Katschinski.

Two of the new arrivals were the officers of *Abercrombie's* gunnery department, Tom Parlon, the Gunnery Officer, and Red Bond, his assistant. Tom was from Pennsylvania, slim and short with direct blue eyes and a high forehead. He knew his gunnery, and knew how he wanted to run his department. And he ran it that way. Red Bond was out of rural Illinois, tall, quiet and steady, a few years older than most of us, with a knowledge of weaponry that went right down to the smallest pawl, cam, sear and spring. Both Tom and Red had had previous sea duty as Armed Guard officers on merchant ships. Tom had been sunk and machine-gunned in the water by a Japanese submarine off Suva in the Fiji Islands, an experience which perhaps accounted for his evident dedication to his job as *Abercrombie's* "Gun Boss."

Since one of *Abercrombie's* primary functions would be to counter enemy submarines we were glad to see her Antisubmarine Warfare (ASW) Officer report. His name was Cyrus C. DeCoster III. Cy was literally "a gentleman and a scholar," polite, considerate, intelligent, with a master's degree in romance languages and on his way to a doctorate when the war interrupted his studies. He had been Communications Officer and then skipper of a small patrol boat in Panama. It was Cy who immediately arranged the daily sessions on the attack teacher.

The last of the five new arrivals was Ensign Otto Braunsdorf, assigned as Assistant Engineer under Gus Adams. He was young and inexperienced in the ways of the Navy and the sea, but bright with a good engineering school and a year of work in a boiler factory behind him. It was obvious that salty, pragmatic Gus Adams and intelligent, educated Otto Braunsdorf would make an effective engineering team for the new ship.

In fact it began to be apparent, even in the maelstrom of activity leading to commissioning, that either by design or chance or a combination thereof, the ten *Abercrombie* officers with their differing backgrounds, experience and personalities were fitting together to form a kind of mosaic of workable leadership.

At the top was bright, professionally competent but volatile and impatient Katschinski. Some of the volatility and impatience was filtered out as his orders and policies passed through Hicks for implementation, leaving the rest of us with an impression of sharp if demanding professionalism that instilled confidence and was easy to follow. As third in line, in charge of the deck force and damage control, I had a year of wartime command behind me, had grown up around boats and the sea, and had just completed damage control and fire fighting schools. In gunnery, Tom Parlon, the quietly hard-nosed administrator and Red Bond, the steady, hands-on supervisor and troubleshooter, made as effective a team as Adams and Braunsdorf in engineering. Cy DeCoster's considerable intellect was challenged by the theory and practice of ASW, and he responded with an energy and enthusiasm that inspired his young sonarmen. Keith Wheeling's orderly, incisive mind was ideal for his communications job with its strict security and inventory requirements, and Art Hellman, the likable, extroverted former paint salesman, was natural and successful as Stores Officer.

There is an often-quoted saying that it is the chiefs who really run the Navy, and it is true that they provide the day-to-day, man-to-man leadership, along the lines established by the Captain and implemented by his officers, which every crew requires. It is the chiefs who have the technical experience and expertise in their fields and with those, the respect of their petty officers and nonrated men. The same is true to a lesser degree of the first class petty officers, especially in departments and divisions where there are no chiefs and the first class is effectively acting chief.

Abercrombie's nucleus crew was blessed with five chiefs and five leading first class petty officers. There was chief water tender Jim Elliot to organize and operate the firerooms, chief machinist's mate Ralph Schoeneman to do the same for the engine rooms, chief electrician's mate Rus Benedict to monitor and supervise the electrical installations and electricians, chief quartermaster Ellis "Zeke" Marmon to run the bridge gang, and chief yeoman Jim Larkin in charge of the ship's office. Doing the jobs of chiefs and soon to be wearing the uniforms of chiefs as well were radioman first class Wallace Doty, bo'sun's mate first class Albert Lee Murphy Holloway, pharmacist's mate first class Charles Holston, gunner's mate first class Jim Ramsay, and ship's cook first class Roy Glidewell. In firerooms and engine rooms, the chiefs were backed up by first and second class petty officers. Chief electrician's mate Benedict was supported by a second class and a third class petty officer. In gunnery there were also a third class firecontrolman and a third class torpedoman. Under Chief Marmon on the bridge was a second class signalman; in supply, a store keeper second class; and in my area of construction and repair, a second class shipfitter and carpenter's mate. In the ship's office, Chief Larkin was assisted by college-educated yeoman first Earl Evans. To help set up and operate the wardroom mess, there was a steward's mate second class.

It was these experienced specialists who under their officers had to organize, train and lead the rest of the crew in all the multiplicity of tasks the new ship would be assigned, and in the ultimate test of action with the enemy for which she was built and manned. That was a big job. Because most of the rest of the crew were alert and patriotic but largely inexperienced kids from cities, towns, villages, hamlets and farms all over America. The majority were under twenty and right out of boot camp. Some had been to special technical schools—radar, sonar, signal, refrigeration, fire control, torpedo, gunnery, radio, cooking and baking—and would be putting their new skills to use for the first time in *Abercrombie*.

But with long hours, hard work and a dash of good luck, the necessary organizing and training were accomplished and the final installations in the ship completed.

On 21 April, under the scrutiny of Gus Adams, Otto Braunsdorf and a team of yard and naval engineers, *Abercrombie*'s engineering plant was fired up for the first time—the Navy Special fuel oil ignited and flared in her two boilers, turning the water there to steam, which hissed through the new valves and piping to spin the big turbines, and by means of reduction gears, turned the twin shafts and propellers. Each shaft was run ahead and astern for one hour while the engineers recorded steam pressure, steam temperature, main condenser vacuum and bearing temperatures, and the mooring lines drew taut against the pressure of the turning screws. When it was over, *Abercrombie* had passed her Preliminary Acceptance Trials.

On the twenty-sixth, a fleet of the gray buses pulled up alongside the ship, and the crew, sea bags on their shoulders, filed aboard to take up indefinite residence. One man, electrician's mate second class Harry

Miles, carried a nondescript black-and-white puppy under his left arm.

Then on the twenty-ninth, another team of engineers and naval officers came aboard with flashlights and checklists on clipboards. They divided into parties of two or three to each department and, accompanied by *Abercrombie*'s officers and leading petty officers, spent almost all day inspecting every inch of the new ship, operating every piece of equipment from windshield wipers and whistle to main engines and five-inch mounts. The next day was the longest and busiest yet as the discrepancies they had found were corrected; but at quitting time the Captain announced that *Abercrombie* had been formally accepted by the Navy of the United States.

On the first day of May 1944, *Abercrombie* was commissioned.

We had been peripherally aware of other commissionings during the weeks in Orange—*John C. Butler* on 31 March, *O'Flaherty* on 8 April, *Raymond* on 15 April, *Suesens* on 26 April—but we had been too busy to notice more than some strains of music from down the dock, the flash of white uniforms and summer dresses, and periodic ripples of applause.

Now *Abercrombie* was at center stage. On the morning of the the first of May, work began as usual, but toward noon the yard workers, male and female, began to leave the ship, taking their tools and equipment and reeling in their lines, power cords and hoses as they went. For the first time ever, *Abercrombie* was without that obscuring and disorderly tangle, and it was as though she had been suddenly unveiled. Her crew turned to with brooms and swabs; and by early afternoon, in her bright new paint with the Texas sun full on her, she was as handsome a warship as ever saw the sea.

The short ceremony began promptly at three o'clock. On *Abercrombie*'s broad fantail, officers and crew stood at attention in silent, white-clad ranks. On the dock in rows of folding chairs sat the invited guests, mostly the wives, sweethearts and families of the crew, my own wife and father among them. In the center of the front row were Mr. and Mrs. C. W. Abercrombie of Kansas City.

Adjacent to the guests, in other folding chairs, a band played Sousa marches, the musicians having put aside welders' masks, pneumatic drills and paint guns for drums, trumpets and bass horns.

A few minutes after three, the band quieted and a little procession of dignitaries stepped up to the podium on the fantail. First, the vice president and manager of Consolidated Steel Corporation formally turned over the new ship to the U.S. Navy. Second, the supervisor of shipbuilding at Orange, representing the Commandant, Eighth Naval District, read the orders empowering him to do so and then formally accepted the ship for the Navy. At the conclusion of his remarks, he ordered, "Hoist the colors!" Forward, a sailor broke out the Union Jack, with its white stars on a Navy blue field, at the jack staff. Aft, another sailor ran the national ensign up the short, aft-slanting flag staff. And amidships, a third sailor sent a fluttering sliver of red, white and blue soaring to the truck—the commission pennant. *Abercrombie* became in that instant the United States Ship *Abercrombie,* a commissioned warship.

Then the new warship was turned over to her Captain, and Katschinski, now wearing the gold oak leaves and two-and-a-half stripes of a lieutenant commander, read his orders, assumed command and ordered Hicks to "Set the watch." At three-thirty exactly, the watch was set, and the positions manned on quarterdeck, bridge and engineering spaces, which would be occupied continuously in port as long as *Abercrombie* remained in commission.

The ceremony ended with the playing of the national anthem. Then there were cake and punch in wardroom and mess hall followed by informal tours of the shining new ship by the invited guests. For another hour, *Abercrombie*'s gray passageways and compartments and the apple-green staterooms of "officers' country" were on display, felt the tap of high heels, lilted with female voices and were fragrant with perfume, an experience never to be repeated. And an experience that was only slightly marred when a party of officers and their families peered into the handling room of the forward five-inch gun expecting to see casing and powder hoists, but were startled to see instead a sailor and his girl in an advanced state of undress and amorous activity. (The party quickly moved on while a petty officer was left behind to assure the couple's departure and to record the man's name for appropriate disciplinary action.)

By four-thirty all guests had left the ship and the yard workers were back aboard, because although *Abercrombie* was now a commissioned man-of-war, much work still had to be done before she would be ready for sea.

The deck log for that first day of *Abercrombie*'s life listed 10 officers and 195 enlisted men "attached to this vessel on date of commissioning." The entry for the 16–20 (4:00 P.M. to 8:00 P.M.) watch read:

> USS *Abercrombie* moored portside to City Docks, Orange, Texas, with six wire hawsers to the dock. Ships present USS *Richard W. Suesens,* SOPA (Senior Officer Present Afloat), and other ships as listed in log of SOPA. Receiving telephone service from the dock.

The 20–24 (8:00 p.m. to 12:00 midnight) entry read simply "Moored as before." Both watches were signed by Tom Parlon. The day's log was signed "Examined" by J. R. Hicks, Navigator and "Approved" by B. H. Katschinski, Commanding Officer.

The following morning a naval message clattered out of a teletype in New Orleans and was instantly received in Washington. It was from the Commandant, Eighth Naval District, and addressed to the Chief of Naval Operations:

USS *Abercrombie* DE343 ACCEPTED 29 APRIL COMMISSIONED 1 MAY LTCMDR BERNARD H. KATCHINSKI USNR COMMANDING.

A warship had been born.

2. Galveston

ON THE EVENING OF 8 May the yard workers once more coiled up their lines, picked up their tools and crossed the short metal brow to the dock. This time they did not come back. At 0600 the next morning with the sun not yet risen, those of us who had been living ashore came aboard with our last few pieces of gear, overnight bags, toilet kits and last-minute gifts and packages. At 0700 a party of thirty-five officer, enlisted and civilian specialists in electronics, engineering and gunnery came aboard to witness and assist with the day's operations. Then at 0730 the bo'sun's pipe shrilled throughout the ship, demanding attention, and the gruff voice of the Bo'sun's Mate of the Watch rasped from speakers topside and below, "Now go to your stations, all the Special Sea Details." On weather decks and through passageways, through doors and hatches and scuttles, up the ladders to the superstructure and down other ladders to firerooms and engine rooms, *Abercrombie*'s crew began to move. Within minutes the bridge talker began to relay reports to Cy DeCoster, Officer of the Deck at Special Sea Details:

"Fo'c'sle manned and ready, sir."

"Fantail manned and ready, sir."

"Amidships manned and ready, sir."

"Bridge manned and ready, sir."

"Engineering spaces manned and ready, sir."

"Signal bridge manned and ready, sir."

"Radar manned and ready, sir."

"Lookouts manned and ready, sir."

At 0740 Cy saluted Katschinski, who was pacing back and forth on top of the pilothouse forward of the bridge, the highest horizontal surface on the ship. "All stations report manned and ready, sir; all departments ready for getting under way." The Captain returned Cy's salute, fingers barely touching the visor of his blue ball cap. "Very well. Single up your lines." Down on the fo'c'sle, my talker repeated the order and heard it acknowledged by the line handlers on the fantail and amidships. On the dock, line handlers from the yard cast off one part of each of the six double lines leading from the ship to tall iron bollards ashore, and as they did so, *Abercrombie*'s sailors pulled those lines aboard. Now *Abercrombie* was held to the dock with six slim strands of springlay—a bastard blend of manila and wire which rusted and tore men's hands but had to suffice, since the enemy now held the source of manila hemp in the Philippines.

Although the Captain could see it clearly from the port side of the pilothouse top, the fo'c'sle talker duly reported, "All lines singled up, sir." Without hesitation the order came down: "Take in one, two and four. Heave round on six."

It was apparent that the stocky, energetic officer in the blue ball cap, peering down at shore and river from high in the ship, knew exactly what he was doing. With *Abercrombie*'s port side to the dock and the sluggish Sabine current coming from ahead, he was going to pull in the stern, swing the bow out and let the current take her out into the stream. Number one was the bow line; numbers two and four tended aft and would prevent forward motion unless removed. Number six, with a dozen sailors now heaving on it, was the stern line. Numbers three and five tended forward from ship to dock and would go slack as she moved ahead. He had left them secured momentarily as insurance, to bring her back alongside if something went wrong with this first-ever maneuver.

Nothing went wrong. *Abercrombie*'s bow swung gently to starboard as the current caught it. There was a sudden wash and eddying under her stern as the screws began to turn. The ship eased ahead. "Take in all your lines." The line handlers ashore flopped the three remaining springlay eyes off the bollards into the river, and at that instant the jack forward and the ensign aft came down, the little steaming colors soared to the gaff at the masthead, and the USS *Abercrombie* was under way.

How many more times? From how many more places? Bound for how many more destinations?

The muddy river widened between ship and dock. With a jingling of bells from the engine control telegraph on the bridge and a swirling of water at her stern, *Abercrombie* turned cleanly on her heel, straightened out and stood smoothly downstream. In a few minutes the familiar docks and sheds of Orange were out of sight around a bend of the Sabine.

Many of *Abercrombie*'s young sailors had mixed feelings about leaving. The people of Orange had been good to them, in marked contrast to the treatment they had received in Norfolk where the crew was formed. While public buses ran from the gate of the Consolidated yard into town, it was unusual for a sailor to have to take one because normally a passing motorist would provide a ride before the bus arrived. Nor was it unusual for the motorist to invite the sailor to his home to meet his family and share a meal. And there was a brand-new, well-equipped and staffed USO in Orange, a spacious, comfortable refuge where the sailors could read or write letters, or play pool or Ping-Pong or cards away from the austere and crowded shipboard environment. Every Friday evening there was a dance at the USO, and on alternate Fridays the dances were formal, requiring dress whites and long dresses. One of DE343's men, radioman first Wallace Doty, had even been married in Orange, with her leading firecontrol-man, Ralph Rice, as his best man. So although *Abercrombie*'s crew was anxious to see new places and to get on with the job they had enlisted for, the men felt a twinge of sadness at leaving the town that had welcomed them so warmly.

All that morning, with "the Captain at the conn and the Navigator on the bridge" as required by Navy Regulations when in restricted waters, and with her best-qualified people at helm, throttles and all key positions, the new ship followed the winding Sabine toward the sea. Around noon she steamed past Port Arthur with its miles of sprawling, malodorous refineries and clustered oil storage tanks. In early afternoon she passed between Louisiana Point and Texas Point and out into the Gulf of Mexico.

It was a calm, clear afternoon when *Abercrombie* first felt the touch of the ocean. There was just enough ground swell to give a little lift to her bow and roll her just enough so that a man could tell he was at sea. Many of her green young crew could tell only too well. Some turned pale and took to their bunks, other rushed to the lifelines (not always to leeward) to lean over and retch. There was one, a slight, sandy-haired, eighteen-year-old from northern Georgia, who turned pale like the others but sought neither his sack nor the lifelines. Instead, from the nearest cleaning locker he appropriated a galvanized bucket, which he carried with him as he went unfailingly about his duties. When he found he needed two hands to do his job, he devised a lanyard and hung the bucket around his neck.

Once well clear of the land, the ship rang with the insistent electric clanging of the general alarm, accompanied by the equally insistent voice of the Bo'sun's Mate of the Watch. "General Quarters! General Quarters! All hands, man your battle stations!" Now there was no walking to stations as for Special Sea Details. Now *Abercrombie*'s decks and ladders thumped and rattled with running feet. Most of the men moved as they had been trained, forward and up on the starboard side, down and aft to port, but there were a few who forgot or were confused by athwartship passageways or ladders near the center line. There were the inevitable collisions, curses and delays. Some topside sailors arrived at their battle stations without helmets or without lifejackets, others in skivvy shirts or with sleeves rolled up. The kid from northern Georgia clambered into the forward five-inch mount with his bucket clanging against the hatch, still green and coldly sweating, but at his station and duty on time. His name was Jack Reuben Bowers, but from that day he was known as "Buckets," and it was a term not of derision but of respect.

Once again the reports poured into the bridge talker's headset:

"Mount fifty-one [five-inch mount number one] manned and ready."

"Mount forty-two [forty-millimeter mount number two] manned and ready."

"Director one manned and ready."

"All repair parties manned and ready."

"Main engine control manned and ready."

"Torpedo tubes manned and ready."

"Gun twenty-one [twenty-millimeter gun number one] manned and ready."

"Sonar manned and ready."

"Radar manned and ready."

"Depth charges manned and ready."

"Battle dressing station manned and ready."

For five, six, seven minutes the reports streamed in, with Katschinski scowling and looking at his watch, and Hicks fidgeting nervously and looking at his. It was eight and a half minutes after the sounding of the general alarm before Cy DeCoster was able to report, "All stations manned and ready, sir."

Katschinski didn't even bother to acknowledge the report. Instead, he turned to his Executive Officer. "Goddamnit, Hicks, that is way the hell too slow, even if it *is* the first time under way. Christ! We'd be blown to hell before we could get off a round! I want it down to two minutes before we get to Bermuda. Understand? And I don't give a damn if you have to hold drills all day and all night to do it. Just get it done. And no goddamn excuses!"

Abercrombie stayed at General Quarters (GQ) for two hours. One at a time she test-fired all her guns, first the five-inchers, then the forties and finally each of the ten 20-millimeters. She worked out her air-search and surface-search radars, the bedspring-shaped air-search antenna rotating at the masthead. Pilothouse and bridge echoed with the long pings of sonar as its narrow, invisible underwater beam probed out ahead, searching from beam to bow, then from the opposite beam back to the bow. On the superstructure deck the torpedo tubes trained out on either side and all circuits and sights were tested. *Abercrombie* swung in tight foaming circles with hard-over rudder, leaning away from the turns, brown haze chuffing from her stack. Steering control was shifted back to the quartermaster in after steering, and watching his gyro compass repeater, he steered courses ordered from the bridge two hundred feet away. The Captain took her up to eighteen knots and then backed emergency full. The engineers below spun their throttle wheels, shutting off steam to the ahead turbine blades and blasting it into those that drove her astern, and the ship shuddered and pounded and lost way with a welter of white water along her sides. The main propulsion machinery was cross-connected as it might have to be in case of damage, with number one boiler feeding steam to number two engine, and number two boiler to number one engine. The ship's service steam-driven generator was shut down, simulating a casualty, and the two diesel generators cut in to take the electrical load. Repair parties ran out their hoses, connected fog and foam nozzles, fired up gasoline-powered portable pumps called "handy-billies," broke out and connected submersible electric pumps, practiced with RBAs and asbestos suits. Even the twenty-six-foot motor whaleboat was swung out over the port rail, manned and lowered to the water's edge and its diesel engine started, then returned to its stowage on the boat deck.

At the end of those busy two hours, GQ was secured, the Special Sea Details remanned, and *Abercrombie* reentered Sabine Pass to tie up at the small base just inside the entrance on the Texas side. The approach and mooring were the last evolution of a day of firsts, and it looked as though they would be flawless. Katschinski brought her in at a narrow angle to the dock, backed down on the outboard engine until she lay parallel, the monkey fists of her heaving lines thumped onto the dock, and the mooring lines quickly pulled over and secured. As ship and dock drew together, the order came down, "Get over your fenders," and over went the canvas-wrapped balls of scrap manila to protect *Abercrombie*'s unblemished new paint. Except that one of the four fenders went over all the way to splash noisily in the river, an eager young seaman having neglected to make it fast and his bo'sun's mate having missed the error.

As soon as the gangplank was over, the party of technicians from Orange filed off the ship and boarded buses for home. Liberty on the base was authorized for half the crew that evening, and a few dozen men changed to undress whites, showed their liberty cards, saluted the Officer of the Deck and the quarterdeck, and went ashore. There wasn't much to do. Most had a beer or two, went to the base movie and were back aboard early. Three quarters of *Abercrombie*'s men simply stayed aboard, writing letters, playing cards or acey-deucey, or just shooting the breeze with their shipmates. When at 2200 (10:00 P.M.) the word was passed, "Taps. Lights out. Maintain silence about the decks. The smoking lamp is out in all berthing spaces," most of the young sailors in DE343 were already sound asleep.

Two days later, Special Sea Details were stationed at 0830, and *Abercrombie* was under way at exactly nine o'clock. At 0915 she slipped once more between the two low, marshy points of Sabine Pass, with Louisiana to port and Texas to starboard, and stood out into the Gulf. From *Abercrombie*'s bridge her men could see for miles in both directions across the flat marsh grass so gradually did the land yield to the shallow sea.

When the Special Sea Details were secured, Condition II was set, with half the crew, the port watch, at their stations and half the armament (one 5-inch, one 40-millimeter and five 20-millimeters) manned. After an hour the starboard watch relieved the port. An hour later the Captain ordered Condition III set with Section I of the three sections on deck and one third of the armament manned. Section II relieved Section I and was relieved in turn by Section III. No sooner were the officers and men of Section III settled into their duties topside and below than the general alarm was sounded, and once more all hands ran to battle stations. This time there were fewer collisions, more complete uniforms and less confusion. Time to man all stations—seven minutes and thirty-five seconds.

The Captain made no comment.

While still at battle stations the speakers came alive again. "This is a drill. Fire! Fire in the chiefs' quarters!" The chiefs' quarters were the responsibility of Repair I, stationed in a nearby compartment with the leading bo'sun's mate in charge of eight men. As Damage Control Officer, this was my problem and I left my battle station at Repair II amidships and ran forward to see how it was handled. I needn't have worried. By the time I arrived, the bo'sun's mate, whose name was Albert Lee Murphy Holloway, had four men and two hoses in the compartment with pressure at the nozzles, fog nozzles ready, a man in an RBA ready to work in smoke, and a pharmacist's mate, Victor "Doc" Bour, standing by with his medical kit to treat burns and smoke inhalation. Time to arrive, ready, with all gear—two and a half minutes.

I complimented Holloway, but he just grinned, a big man in dungarees with carefully exaggerated bellbottoms held up by a wide handmade belt of white Belfast cord which also supported a modest pot, an apparent prerogative of seniority. He was standing there, feet wide apart, with a brass all-purpose nozzle in his hands, the hose bulging with pressure. I had the feeling he enjoyed the drill—and would have enjoyed a fire even more.

With the "fire" out and Repair I back on station, the word was passed, "Away the boarding and salvage party, muster on the boat deck." In a few minutes a dozen men were lined up opposite the motor whaleboat, machinist's mates and water tenders to get a crippled steamship or motorship under way; a quartermaster to steer; a signalman with an Aldis lamp and a radioman for communications; a carpenter's mate and a shipfitter to make repairs—with handy-billies, submersible pumps, suction hoses, fire extinguishers, bolt cutters, plugs, wedges and sledgehammers; and Otto Braunsdorf in charge, looking almost swashbuckling with a .45 automatic on a web belt over his khaki trousers.

With the boarding and salvage party mustered, checked, secured and back at their battle stations, the next call was for the visit and search party, for use when required to board a suspicious vessel and determine her identity, cargo and destination.

I was in charge of that party with Cy DeCoster as interpreter (because of his romance-language expertise, Cy was always interpreter), both of us carrying .45s. Also with us were a signalman, a radioman, and six of the biggest, toughest petty officers in the crew, armed with carbines and hand grenades and equipped with grapnels and climbing lines for getting aboard, and with bolt cutters and axes for quick access to locked cargo holds.

With *Abercrombie* circling the suspicious ship, guns and torpedo tubes trained out, we didn't expect a lot of opposition if it were necessary to visit and search, but we intended to be ready.

Finally, the word was passed. "This is a drill. Abandon ship! Abandon ship!" *Abercrombie* had four big life rafts, five flotation nets designed to float free when the ship went down, three rubber boats and the motor whaleboat. Every man was assigned to one or the other with an officer or a chief in charge. All rafts, nets and boats were stocked with fresh water, emergency rations, and first-aid kits, but certain men were required to bring additional gear to their abandon-ship stations—signal flags, Very pistols and flares, navigational instruments, the ship's log, binoculars, pay accounts and records. The Captain, Marmon, Holloway and a yeoman with the ship's records were assigned the whaleboat. Hicks and Adams were in charge of rafts. DeCoster, Parlon and Braunsdorf were in charge of nets. I had one of the rubber boats, reserved for the repair parties, which would be last to leave. The damage control organization was under orders to remain aboard when everyone else had left, attempt to control fire and flooding, and get way on the ship. In the repair parties were men qualified to operate engines, firerooms, steering gear and even guns, as well as restore power, fight fires and repair damage.

That was the last drill of the day. At three o'clock the Special Sea Details were stationed, and at 1530 *Abercrombie* nosed in past old Fort San Jacinto at the entrance to Galveston Bay, swung to port into the narrow channel between Galveston proper and Pelican Island, with the low barracks of the Quarantine Station on its seaward tip, and headed for her assigned berth at the Todd Shipyard on Pelican Island.

The approach was similar to the one at Sabine Pass, and the ship eased in parallel to the dock about twenty yards off. This time the fenders were put over in advance and hung smartly at equal levels halfway between deck and waterline. Again the monkey fists whirled in vertical, underhand circles, then looped across and thudded on the dock to be grabbed by the line handlers on shore. After their eyes were secured to the heaving lines, the mooring lines were snaked across and dropped over the bollards. Aboard ship, three or four sailors held each line and awaited orders. The fo'c'sle talker duly reported, "Bridge, fo'c'sle, all mooring lines to the dock." *Abercrombie* was still moving very slowly ahead parallel to the dock.

"Roger," came the reply. And in another moment, "Take in the slack on all lines. Hold number two."

Number two line tended aft from well forward on the starboard side. To "hold" a line means to secure it firmly so that no more slack can pay out, even if it parts. Holding number two line, and using a few degrees of right rudder would snub in *Abercrombie* neatly and gently against the dock. But now trouble began. The sailor on number two either did not hear the hold order or he did not understand its meaning. He took a couple of figure-eight turns around the bitts, but when the line grew taut, he let the turns slide around to ease the strain. This is called "checking" a line, it is not "holding." The ship moved closer to the dock, but continued her forward motion, sliding slightly beyond her assigned berth. On top of the pilothouse, the Captain's face turned a deep scarlet. Ignoring his talker, he leaned out dangerously over the starboard side of the pilothouse directly above the guilty seaman. "You goddamn imbecile!" he yelled. "I said *hold* two! For Chrissake, don't you know the difference? Hold means *secure* the son of a bitch! Goddamnit, *hold* it! Now!!"

But the eighteen-year-old sailor, overwhelmed by this sudden torrent of abuse from on high, went into a momentary paralysis, looking up in terror at the yelling red face, while number two line coiled out around the bitts like an escaping boa, and *Abercrombie* continued to move placidly ahead ten yards off the dock. Katschinski, watching the line run out and wordless now with rage, stripped the blue ball cap from his head with a backward sweep of his right hand, hurled it to the deck at his feet, and while his entire topside force of officers and men and the line handlers on the dock looked on in embarrassed disbelief, stomped on it repeatedly with his right foot.

Holloway was loping aft from the fo'c'sle, but Pete Kish, the bo'sun's mate in charge amidships, had already taken the line from the frightened sailor with surprising gentleness and quickly made it fast. Number two line became rigid, squeaking in protest, and *Abercrombie* nestled in smoothly against the dock, half a length beyond her assigned berth.

When I entered the wardroom after the in-port watch had been set, Hicks was sitting at the green covered table with a cup of coffee before him. He squinted up at me, his head a little to one side. "Cap'n wants to see you in his cabin." His tone and manner said, "We both know you're in trouble and why, and you probably deserve to be."

But I found Katschinski seated at his desk, his face its normal color, calm and composed but not happy.

"Ed," he said, "I'm not at all satisfied with the performance of your deck force. Yesterday the fender thrown overboard, today that cretin on number two. It makes the ship look bad. We're a brand-new ship and, like it or not, we're establishing a reputation. We don't want to get one for sloppy seamanship. I'm holding you responsible for getting those guys on their toes and keeping them there. Kick some fannies if you have to, but no more foul-ups."

Except for the use of the term "cretin," it was a fair and reasonable order. It was hard to connect this mildly disappointed officer with the cursing, stomping, red-faced neo-madman of twenty minutes earlier.

"Aye, aye, Captain" was all there was to say.

I didn't have to kick any fannies. I called my bo'sun's mates together before liberty that same evening: Holloway, the first class and leading petty officer of the deck force; Pete Kish, the fatherly second class who had already established an almost parental relationship with the young sailors in his division; Fred Manger, the wiry, feisty little second class whom I had known from previous duty; and "Pop" Deatherage, the gentle but rugged forty-five-year-old cox'n who, like Kish, was a father figure to his seamen. Each of those petty officers was to be responsible for the training and performance of each of his men, and would assure through individual instruction and observation that every seaman at every line and fender knew his job and the orders related to it. Each was authorized to use as much time each day after regular working hours as he considered necessary to conduct his training, which would not be limited to docking and undocking, anchoring and unanchoring, but would include towing and being towed, fueling and provisioning while under way, and launch and recovery of the whaleboat. The first training session was held that evening before liberty was called away.

The following morning early, I took the ship's docking plans to the Todd office, and by 0800 keel blocks and cradles were in place in the huge, empty dry dock, and water was roaring in through two big pipes near the gates at the harbor end. By 1000 the water in the dock was at the same level as the harbor, the massive steel gates swung open, and *Abercrombie* nosed in across the sill at 1034. It took about twenty minutes and much shouting back and forth between ship and dock and much adjusting of lines before she was positioned directly over the blocks and cradles. High-capacity pumps began to suck the water out of the dock, and by 1130 the ship was resting solidly on the blocks, her mossy, scummy bottom contrasting violently with the gleaming topside paint.

Abercrombie was five days in dry dock while her bottom was power-washed, sandblasted down to the bare steel, painted with primer, then sprayed with multiple coats of antifouling hot plastic. They were not happy days for the crew. Since the ship's heads and showers were not usable, all but necessary watch standers were moved to an adjacent barracks, and *Abercrombie* became a ship in suspended animation, her engines and generators shut down, receiving a minimum of electrical power and fire main pressure from the dock. The yard workers swarmed back aboard with their lines, hoses, clutter and dirt to perform a myriad of last-minute installations and alterations. It was Orange before commissioning all over again, but without flushing or cooling water. The only good things about those days were port and starboard liberty. Half the crew went ashore each evening. Those of us with families in the area were permitted to live on shore except when we had the duty. Galveston Beach and the bars, restaurants, night spots and casinos of the city saw a lot of *Abercrombie* people.

For some of the bars, *Abercrombie*'s business, and that of the other DEs in port, was a thoroughly mixed blessing. The young sailors, most away from home and parental supervision for the first time and suddenly released from the confinement and discipline of shipboard life, tended to act out the legendary roles of roistering, riotous sailors on shore leave—forgetting that those legends were based on the actions of a minority of seasoned, hardened seamen ashore after months or years at sea under the harshest conditions of danger, oppression and discomfort.

In one bar, a honky-tonk called the Congo Club, a dozen *Abercrombie* sailors gathered on the seventeenth of May to celebrate the twentieth birthday of one of their shipmates, a curly-haired quartermaster striker from Norfolk named Paul McMillan. After a few drinks each, they decided that good fellows, gathered together on such an auspicious occasion, should all be drinking the same thing. Not being able to achieve a consensus on what the common drink should be, one of them had an inspired thought. A galvanized washtub was procured from a back room, placed on the table, and into it all the good fellows poured whatever they had been drinking—beer, wine, gin, rum, brandy, whiskey—with vestiges of ginger ale, Coca-Cola and soda water. Then this lethal concoction was stirred, and each of the good fellows dipped his glass full of the mixture and drank it off in raucous toasts to good old Mac's natal day. Other sailors in the bar thought this was such a magnificent idea that they contributed to the washtub too, and dipped out their rations of liquid dynamite. The spirit of camaraderie had never waxed so full.

Then someone lost his balance, fell backward into a chair and smashed it into kindling, coming to rest in a sort of surprised seated sprawl among the pieces. This was so riotously funny that someone decided two smashed chairs were funnier than one, and broke his over the table. In seconds, chairs, pieces of chairs, glasses, bottles and table legs were flying across the bar. A sailor attempted, Tarzanlike, to swing across the room on a chandelier, which pulled out by its roots, sparking and showering plaster down on the disappointed but undiscouraged apeman. Women screamed and ran for the street. The barkeep ducked behind his bar and called the Shore Patrol.

The birthday party was at its lustiest and loudest when the SP van screeched around the corner, opened its rear doors and backed up solidly against the Congo Club's front door. If there were a back door, no one knew where it was. But there were exits other than doors, and as the SPs charged in with their white leggings, blue and gold brassards and swinging nightsticks, the *Abercrombie* sailors went out the windows, open or not, to scatter down the back streets of Galveston and eventually find their way back to the ship. The few cuts, scratches and contusions they brought back were apparently little enough to pay for a birthday celebration that would be relished and cherished down the years.

As a kind of positive side effect of all this carousing, *Abercrombie's* men began to evidence a mutual identity. Ashore they were no longer just sailors on liberty, they were *Abercrombie* sailors on liberty. They stuck together and they took care of each other.

Docking was completed on the afternoon of 15 May, and *Abercrombie* came alive again. The crew held field day, sweeping, swabbing, scrubbing and polishing away the soil of those dry five days.

On the fifteenth also *Abercrombie*'s evaporator plant was worked out for the first time in salt water. In twenty-four hours it distilled over 9,600 gallons of fresh water to feed the boilers, with a final salinity of less than five hundredths of a gram per gallon. Gus Adams explained that that was considerably purer than most drinking water, and that if the evaporators ever produced fresh water of insufficient purity for his boilers, he intended to pump it into the crew's drinking water supply. The human alimentary canal, it seems, could tolerate a much higher proportion of salt and other minerals than the clusters of long steel tubes in Gus's boilers.

In the three days left at Galveston, more stores and spare parts were carried aboard, but a check at the end of the third day showed that scores of items which had been ordered were still not aboard. Arrangements were made to pick them up in Boston after shakedown.

In those days also, *Abercrombie*'s people became physically aware for the first time, although the paper work had long been general knowledge, of the other ships in the division to which DE343 was assigned. While *Abercrombie* and her sisters had been building at Orange, another yard, Brown Shipbuilding in Houston, had been turning out DEs at the same prodigious rate. The new Escort Division 69 was composed of three ships from each yard: *Suesens* (DE342), *Abercrombie* and *Oberrender* (DE344) from Orange; and *Stafford* (DE411), *Wann* (DE412) and *Roberts* (DE413) from Houston. All six ships had been commissioned in the three weeks between 19 April and 11 May. *Walter C. Wann* (DE412) was commissioned the day after *Abercrombie*. *Richard W. Suesens* (named for a Devastator pilot of Torpedo Three from the *Yorktown*, also lost at Midway) was the flagship, with the Division Commander aboard.

The day before *Abercrombie* was scheduled to sail from Galveston, I was on the fo'c'sle supervising the marking of the anchor chain when a sailor in dress whites approached, saluted and then, when I returned the salute, stuck out his hand with an engaging grin. His grip was solid, his eyes clear and level. He looked like a good man.

"Mr. Stafford," he said, "Mr. Hicks said I should report to you. I'm Ted Gruhn, carpenter's mate first class. I'll be in your C and R gang."

"Gruhn," I replied, "I'm glad to have you aboard. And you'll be *in charge* of the C and R gang. You been in DEs before?"

"No, sir, DDs. *Farenholt* (DD491), nineteen months in the Solomons."

I had heard of the *Farenholt.* She had made a name for herself by smashing up enemy troop barges coming down the Slot at night to reinforce Guadalcanal. This kid was going to be a jewel.

"Then you won't have any problems with *Abercrombie*," I told him, "or with me as long as C and R is run right and gets the job done. Think you can find the carpenter shop? Stephens should be back there. You'll like him. He'll show you your bunk and locker."

I took my black notebook out of my back pocket and checked my section lists.

"You'll be in the first watch section."

I expected Gruhn to head on back aft, but he didn't.

"Sir," he asked, "which section has liberty tonight?"

"The first."

"Where can I pick up my liberty card, sir?"

"Jesus, Gruhn, you've been aboard five minutes and you want to go on liberty?"

Maybe this guy isn't as great as he seems, I thought.

But I got the open grin again as he explained that his new wife had traveled with him from Norfolk and that he had reported directly aboard without even finding a place to stay ashore. I told him Chief Larkin in the ship's office would fix him up with a liberty card and that I would see him the next morning.

Abercrombie was scheduled to depart Galveston at 0900 on 19 May in company with the *Walter C. Wann* (DE412), but early that morning water was discovered in the *Wann's* fuel and her tanks had to be pumped dry and refilled. Therefore, it was at 1900 that day when DE343 took in her last line, backed away from the dock, turned and followed *Wann* along the Galveston waterfront and out past Fort Bolivar to sea. Once clear, the two ships rang up their standard speed of fifteen knots and with *Abercrombie* one thousand yards astern of *Wann,* stood southeast across the Gulf for the Straits of Florida. As both ships settled down for their first night at sea, a confidential naval message, originating from the radio shack of DE343, was received by the Commander-in-Chief, U.S. Fleet, Commander-in-Chief, U.S. Atlantic Fleet, and Commander, Training Command, Atlantic:

USS *Abercrombie* (DE343) reports for duty. Departing Galveston for Bermuda in company senior ship USS *Walter C. Wann* (DE412) 19 May.

3. Bermuda

I HAD THE MIDWATCH that first night. The sea and sky were dark, with the darker shadow of the *Wann* waving her slim mast gently at the narrow end of her wake. The last time I had stood on the moving bridge of a man-of-war at night had been seven months ago and five thousand miles away on a wooden subchaser off the coast of Sicily. I remembered how close the wash of the sea down her sides and the muttering of her diesels had been. I remembered the quickness of her motion and the constant wetness of her decks. Now, some thirty feet above the waves, as this shining, brand-new ship of steel and heavy guns with her crew of hundreds sliced smoothly through the swells, I felt that I was hardly at sea at all. It seemed rather that I was in temporary control of a formidable seagoing machine, out of real touch with the sea itself as I had known it. Yet it felt good to be free of the clamor and clutter of the yard, to feel the rise and roll of the deck under my feet and the fifteen-knot flow of cool night air across the bridge. And it was good to feel the latent power of the new ship, to hear her breath in the rumble of the blowers forcing air below, and to hear the long, repeated pings of her sonar. It was good to feel, too, the alertness of the crew around me, although many were young and feeling queasy even with this gentle motion. The talker stood behind me on the open bridge, a firecontrolman from Roanoke named R. R. Rice, his earphones clamped to his head and the mouthpiece sprouting from his chest. On both wings of the bridge a sailor with phones stood lookout watch. Just inside the pilothouse ahead were helmsman, engine order man, quartermaster and bo'sun's mate. On the after end of the bridge a signalman and his striker were perched on the flag bags talking in low voices. The gyro repeater showing the ship's course glowed with a dim red light in the center of the open bridge, and through the open door to the pilothouse, similar red glows were visible from the steering gyro and engine order telegraph.

There was not a lot to do. Radar sent up periodic ranges and bearings to the *Wann;* speed changes of a few rpm sufficed to maintain the interval between ships at or about a thousand yards. The security watch checked the darkened ship for light leaks every thirty minutes. Occasionally the voices of the gun crew on the number one forty-millimeter drifted up from forward of the pilothouse. It was a pattern of activity, an ordered arrangement of sights and sounds, orders and acknowledgments which I knew would become as familiar as similar patterns on the wooden subchaser, already being crowded out of memory. But on this first watch, on this first night, in the intervals between required actions, there was time to think, and the thoughts came quickly and with unexpected clarity, prompted perhaps by a review I had made of the service records of the men assigned to deck force and damage control.

What an assortment of young men had been integrated into the crew now manning this sleek and deadly warship and feeling the night sea for the first time! In the deck force there were gutsy little Buckets Bowers from Bowersville, Georgia; Jack Dempsey Blackwell from Spartanburg, South Carolina, born in the year of the Manassa Mauler's greatest triumphs; pudgy, good-natured little Glenn Beach from Gastonia, North Carolina; tall, thin, easy-going Curtis Foley of Roanoke, Virginia; stocky, handsome Vernon Millsaps from Maryville, Tennessee; Clarence Krause of Oshkosh, Wisconsin; Jack Green of Riverdale, Georgia; Leroy Walker from Arab, Alabama; Sloan Duncan of Travellers Rest, South Carolina; chunky, good-natured John Boudreaux of New Iberia, Louisiana; dapper little George Ferroni of La Salle, Illinois; red-headed Joe Henderson from Ware Shoals, South Carolina; and a couple of dozen other green kids in their late teens. Most had left their hometowns for the first time to go to boot camp and had joined *Abercrombie's* crew in Norfolk before reporting to Orange in the big draft of 21 April. They were the raw material of the deck force in the process of being molded into the finished product by the experienced petty officers who shared their every waking hour. And I knew that the same process was under way in gunnery and engineering, and to a lesser extent in communications and supply. But the astonishing thing was that one short month ago, three quarters of her crew had never seen the *Abercrombie,* and the ship herself, now knifing southeast across the Gulf, had been an uncompleted hull up a muddy river, far from the sea.

It had of course been the same for the *Walter C. Wann,* half a mile ahead in the darkness, and for the *Richard W. Suesens,* the *Oberrender,* the *Samuel B. Roberts* and the *Stafford.* Now all were or would shortly be at sea, and after some concentrated training and necessary maintenance and adjustments to machinery and weapons, they would all steam out across the oceans to join the war. It occurred to me that all six new ships were, in effect, tiny, pointed fragments of the United States of America, ejected at some sacrifice from the mother continent and dispatched against the enemy to help assure the survival of the nation. I wondered how many other new ships were at sea that night, steaming out of other bays and rivers toward the war, each with its crew of Blackwells and Beaches, Foleys and Ferronis, Hickses, Hellmans and DeCosters.

All that mid-May weekend *Abercrombie* and *Wann* drew their long white wakes across the Gulf at fifteen knots, every minute another five hundred yards, every four minutes another mile. And on both DEs, the daily routine was the same. At 0330 the morning watch was called to relieve the midnight-to-four. At 0345 sleepy sailors, clutching mugs of the hot caffeine syrup left over from the coffee brewed for the previous watch, appeared at their duty stations topside and below, listened to quick reports of the situation, took over headsets or throttles, or a wheel or a radar scope, or a pair of binoculars, or the sights of a five-incher or a forty-millimeter, and settled in to await the dawn. An hour before sunrise Chief Marmon called Hicks, and half an hour later, when the stars were still out but the horizon was visible so that their altitudes could be measured, the two men were on the bridge, Hicks with the sextant and Marmon with stopwatch and notebook. Marmon would point out the morning navigational stars—"That's Aldebaran," or "That's Beetlejuice," or "That's Sirius," and Hicks would observe the star's altitude, giving Marmon a "mark" at the exact instant when the point of light in the sextant's mirror precisely brushed the line of the horizon. Marmon would mark the time to the second and record the altitude that Hicks read from the sextant. With five stars in Marmon's notebook, they would disappear into the charthouse to work out the sights for the 0800 position report to the Captain.

At 0545 the unwelcome screeching of the bo'sun's pipe and his grating voice were heard. "Now reveille! Reveille! Up all hands! Mess cooks, lay down to the galley!," roused the off-watch crew. Half an hour later in fair weather came the ancient order: "Sweepers, man your brooms! Clean sweep down fore and aft!" In dungarees and white hats, the young sailors swept decks and passageways clean of the stack soot and litter of the night and hosed down the main deck with salt water.

At 0700 the men of the forenoon watch went down to breakfast, passing along the chow line with their shining, compartmented metal trays while the mess cooks forked or ladled onto them scrambled eggs, hot cereal, sliced ham and toast. At 0730 the word was passed: "Now on deck the second [or first, or third] section. Relieve the watch. First [or third or second] section, lay down to the mess hall for breakfast."

At 0800 exactly, Hicks presented Katschinski with the eight o'clock position report, a small white printed slip with the latitude and longitude of the ship's position. All morning there were drills, General Quarters, fire, engineering casualties, steering casualties, abandon ship, man overboard. At 1145 the watch was relieved again, and shortly afterward, the Captain received the noon position report, updated by a morning sun line and an observation of the sun for latitude at Local Apparent Noon, and noting as well the number of miles steamed since leaving port, miles remaining to destination, fuel used during the previous twenty-four hours and percentage of fuel remaining. Also at precisely 1200, a messenger reported to the Captain, saluted and uttered the time-honored formula, "Sir, the Officer of the Deck reports twelve o'clock and the chronometers have been wound and compared."

In the afternoon there were more drills, often signal drills between *Abercrombie* and *Wann*, with strings of the new brightly colored alphabet and numeral flags and pennants soaring up the halyards, pausing three quarters of the way up ("at the dip"), shooting to the yardarm ("two-blocked") and then plunging back to the signal bridge on the "execute" of the ordered maneuver. There were also frequent tactical drills, with *Abercrombie* taking station on *Wann*'s beam, or 45 degrees on her bow or stern at a designated distance, and with the two ships turning together to form columns or lines of bearing or echelons.

Between drills the ship's work went on, with knife-edges to be sanded, gaskets to be cleaned, reports and other paper work to be prepared, and all watch bills, ship's orders and the ship's organization book finished and made ready for the grueling month of shakedown at Bermuda.

At 1545 the first dogwatch took over and was relieved by the next section two hours later, thus "dogging" or rotating the watch so that the same section would not have the same time slot each day. Ship's work was knocked off at 1630, and sweepers piped once more. Evening meal was served at 1715 so that the men on the second dogwatch could eat before going on deck and those with the first dogwatch could relieve them in the chow line. Breakfast, lunch and dinner were served in wardroom and chiefs' quarters in the same way, timed so that both ongoing and offgoing watch standers could eat.

Half an hour after sunset, Hicks and Marmon repeated their navigational ritual on the bridge, shooting the evening stars now that once again both horizon and stars were visible.

At 2000 the speakers ordered, "On deck all the eight o'clock reports," and each department head—Stafford, Parlon, Adams, Wheeling and Hellman—having first checked with his respective petty officer, reported to Hicks in the wardroom that each department was all secure, with no major problems or deficiencies.

"Taps. Lights out. Maintain silence about the decks" was heard at 2200, but by then fully half of *Abercrombie*'s men were in their bunks.

All that weekend, throughout the routine of work and changing watches, a good half of *Abercrombie*'s men were miserable with seasickness. Many followed Bowers's example, and buckets were in great demand. Others made periodic dashes to the lee lifelines or the heads. In the stifling sonar shack high up in the pilothouse, where the rolling and dipping of the ship was the worst, a green-faced sonarman sardonically announced to the man relieving him that normal search procedure had been changed from "ping, train, listen" to "ping, puke, listen." Even Butch, the black-and-white puppy which had instantly become the ship's mascot, staggered around glassy-eyed and spent most of the time asleep in his assigned billet by the scuttlebutt in the aft berthing compartment.

One of the ones who were not seasick was carpenter's mate first class Ted Gruhn, and he had been doing his homework. He knocked at my door on Sunday morning right after quarters, and I invited him in.

"Mr. Stafford," he said, very professional and all business, "there's a discrepancy in the custody of equipment between C and R and engineering that I think we ought to straighten out."

"Okay, Chips, what's the discrepancy?" Equipment custody between departments was not my primary interest; I found the subject dull and time-consuming.

"There's a welding machine aboard, Mr. Stafford. Welding machines belong to C and R, since we're responsible for hull repair and most metal work. It belongs back in the carpenter shop. But on here, the engineers have it. It's in the machine shop."

I got down my copy of the *Ship's Organization Book*. Gruhn was right.

"All right, Chips," I told him. "I'll take it up with Mr. Adams."

I found Gus in the wardroom later that day when I got off watch. He was not cooperative, maintaining, even after being shown the relevant text in print, that the welding machine should and did belong to him and must remain where it was.

So I went to Hicks. Who called in Adams. In due course a compromise was reached. The welding machine would belong to and be operated by the C and R department as provided in the regulations. But it would remain in the machine shop.

Gus was scowlingly unhappy with the compromise and it was apparent that his bitterness was directed toward me, where it was frustrated by my seniority in rank, and toward the blower of the whistle, where it was not. The incident left me with the uncomfortable conviction that I had let Gus, with his twenty-odd years in the Navy, take advantage of my relative inexperience in shipboard empire building. I resolved to be alert for similar tactics in the future.

One evening on the way across the Gulf, half a dozen men who were not seasick, or only a little queasy, assembled in after steering for a game of dealer's choice poker. They were well into the game, with a sizable pot of cash on the deck, when Gus Adams entered the compartment. The sailors jumped to their feet and stood at attention, or as near to it as they could get given the motion of the ship, while Gus quoted the chapter and verse of Navy Regulations which prohibit gambling in any form, and then proceeded to chew them out, individually and collectively, for violating that prohibition. Then, while the men looked at each other helplessly, he scooped up the pot, ordered one of them to count it, jotted the amount down in his little green government-issue notebook and announced that it would be donated to the ship's Welfare and Recreation Fund.

When Gus left, Don Wood, a fireman who was my talker at Repair II, had an idea. Wood was in charge of engineering stores, which, among a myriad of other items, contained large quantities of steel washers. From now on, he suggested, they would play with washers, which he would gladly supply, and only the players would know that each washer was worth five cents. And that was the way poker was played on DE343 from that moment on.

All the way across the Gulf, up along the coast of Florida and out into the Atlantic, three Officers of the Deck, Stafford, Parlon and DeCoster, followed each other around the clock, four hours on watch and eight hours off. On a given day, one of us would have the midwatch (midnight to 4:00 A.M., or 0000 to 0400), the afternoon watch (noon to 4:00 P.M., or 1200 to 1600) and the first watch (8:00 P.M. to midnight, or 2000 to 2400). The following day the same officer would stand the forenoon watch (8:00 A.M. to noon, or 0800 to 1200), and the second dogwatch (6:00 P.M. to 8:00 P.M., or 1800 to 2000). On the third day he would have the morning watch (4:00 A.M. to 8:00 A.M., or 0400 to 0800), and the first dogwatch (4:00 P.M. to 6:00 P.M., or 1600 to 1800). On the fourth day he would begin again with the midwatch. Tom Parlon always relieved me, Cy DeCoster relieved him and I relieved Cy in a cycle that ended only with the setting of Special Sea Details at the end of a passage or an operation. Every meal in the crew's mess was shared by an officer with orders to report to the Captain if it was in any way unsatisfactory.

One sunny morning on the way to Bermuda, right after the watch had been relieved and Tom Parlon had the deck, the offgoing starboard lookout came up to me before I could leave the bridge for breakfast. He was a very young seaman, small, almost beardless. His record said he was eighteen, but I suspected he was at least a year younger. His name was "J C" Clinedinst (there were two "J C"s in the deck force), but I knew his shipmates called him "Chicken," not for lack of courage but for lack of years. Clinedinst was very serious. "Mr. Stafford," he said, looking up at me like the kid he was, "when we get to Bermuda, could you please arrange for me to have my eyes examined?"

"I think we could do that, Clinedinst," I told him. "There'll be a Medical Officer on the tender and if he can't handle it, there'll be facilities ashore. What's the trouble? Your eyes hurt? You're not seeing well?" I looked at his eyes and they seemed clear enough.

"No, sir," he said. "They don't hurt and I can see all right—except that this morning—well, sir, I could have sworn I saw a fish jump right up out of the water and fly away!"

That same morning as I was finishing my breakfast coffee in the wardroom, there was a knock and Ted Gruhn entered, white hat in hand. One of Gruhn's duties was to check every compartment on the ship each time he was on watch.

"Sir," he said, "we've got about a foot of water in the double bottoms back aft, and I can't figure out where it's coming from. Can you come back and take a look?"

"Sure, Chips," I told him. "Let me get my flashlight."

On the way after along the weather deck, I asked him what kind of water it was—fresh? salt? clean? dirty?

"Well," he said, "it seems like fresh water and kind of dirty, smells like soap."

We rattled down a couple of ladders to the lowest deck in the ship, and Gruhn showed me the sounding tube through which he had taken a reading on the tape he carried. We lowered the tape again. It still showed a foot of water, and when I put a drop on my tongue, it did taste like soap.

"Can we get down in there, Chips?" I asked.

"Yes, sir, there's an access plate forward here. I'll get a wrench."

We wriggled through the access hatch and crawled aft under the deck, squirming through oval holes in the lateral steel plates which separated the double-bottom compartments. The only light came from our flashlights. When we got to the one we were looking for, the flashlight beams showed a little lake of scummy water sloshing back and forth to the rolling of the ship and leaving a shiny film whenever it receded. The odor of soap and stale water was unmistakable. We shone the lights up and down the sides of the little compartment, but they were smooth, painted metal. Then we checked the overhead. Gruhn saw it first. A pipe about two inches in diameter protruded slightly from the forward bulkhead right under the deck. It was dripping slowly and its end was threaded. We turned the lights aft. Another pipe at the same level protruded from the after bulkhead. It was dry and new-looking.

"Where does that pipe come from, Chips?" I asked Gruhn.

He was grinning and shaking his head. "They sure must have been in one hell of a hurry to build this ship," he said. "The one forward is the drain from the after officers' shower, sir. It's supposed to run through this compartment and overboard on the starboard side. One of those yard plumbers just forgot a length of pipe."

Gruhn and his gang capped the drain line, pumped out the compartment with a handy-billy, closed the officers' shower aft, and added a job order to the list of things to be accomplished in Boston after shakedown.

The next day Gruhn discovered that a carefully polished brass shower drain in the crew's head, like a Hollywood prop, led nowhere; it merely rested in a steel cup and *looked* like a drain. Another job was added to the list for Boston.

When the sun rose on the morning of Thursday the twenty-fifth, there was a hazy lump far out on the horizon dead ahead. It was Gibb's Hill, the southernmost height of land in the Bermuda Islands. All day the two ships stood in toward the islands, swinging wide to avoid the encircling reefs, while the cycle of drills continued. That last day before shakedown began, battle stations were manned in four minutes and ten seconds. At 1635 when *Abercrombie*, flying the red and white "H" flag to denote a pilot aboard, had just entered the narrow MacDonald Channel between the island and its offshore reefs, the wheel suddenly went slack and loose in the hands of the helmsman, Howard Amos. Quickly he spun it to port and then to starboard, but it clunked into the stops on both sides with no effect on the rudders. As he had done in scores of drills, but louder, Amos reported, "Lost steering control, sir!," and punched a button on the aft bulkhead of the pilothouse that set a siren wailing back in after steering. There an electrician threw a switch which engaged a wheel identical to the now useless one on the bridge, and a quartermaster wearing sound-powered phones took over, maintaining the heading shown on the gyro repeater over his head, alert for course changes sent down by phone. It was just three minutes before the difficulty was located and steering control shifted back to the bridge. The only remnants of the problem were a few fast pulses as *Abercrombie* continued her cautious passage between the reefs.

For ninety minutes at ten knots, a British pilot took *Abercrombie* down the narrow channel with the green island and its white roofs to port and the white water creaming on the reefs to starboard. It was 1835 when she nestled in against the port side of the *Wann,* shackled to a mooring buoy in Great Sound, in her first foreign port with her first ocean passage completed.

Abercrombie stayed twenty-eight days in Bermuda, but that idyllic island, the inspiration for Shakespeare's *The Tempest,* except for its gentle climate, could as well have been an outpost of Siberia or the Sahara as far as her crew was concerned. Those days and weeks went by in a whirl of work and a fog of fatigue while the raw material of new ship and green crew was forged and hammered into a usable weapon for warfare at sea. On all but a few of those days, *Abercrombie* was under way at first light, threading her way out the long channel to open water. Once clear of the outlying reefs, the drills began and continued until late afternoon when it was time to run the ninety-minute channel back to Great Sound. Evenings were spent reviewing the results of the day's drills, correcting the discrepancies and preparing for the next day's exercises. Most officers and leading petty officers averaged four to five hours of sleep a night. Occasionally the ship remained at sea for night formation steaming and night gunnery practice. The aim of this shakedown training was to provide *Abercrombie* with at least a basic ability to perform any task which could conceivably be assigned to her. To that end she fired at targets towed on sleds by seagoing tugs, and at target sleeves dragged overhead by low-flying planes. She maneuvered endlessly in tactical and formation exercises with other DEs, most often *Wann, McCoy Reynolds* (DE440) and *Carter* (DE112). She fired practice torpedoes at her sister DEs, set deep to pass safely well below their keels and float, nose up, at the end of their runs for retrieval. She served as target for other deep-set torpedoes. She towed one of the other DEs and was towed in turn. She pulled alongside a tanker in the open sea, got over her lines, hauled fuel hoses across and received a few barrels of Navy Special fuel oil while token bags and crates of provisions were transferred from the tanker by high line. Then, the fueling and provisioning over, she dashed out ahead to screen the tanker from submarine attack. She played deadly games of hide-and-seek with a "tame" submarine, learning to search, locate and attack, substituting a prearranged sonar signal for the launching of weapons. But at other times and with no sub around, she rolled depth charges over her stern, lofted them out abeam with her K-guns, and rippled her hedgehogs over the bow to make a circle of splashes far out ahead. She ran speed trials and found that at flank speed, with her propellers turning at 380 rpm, she made exactly 21 knots, but that in an emergency she could sustain almost 23.

Abercrombie's men were so busy and so continually tired that the great news of the Allied landings in Normandy on the sixth of June and the establishment and reenforcement of beachheads in occupied Europe passed through their senses but did not register its true importance.

The day after D Day, *Abercrombie* remained in port while a party of fifty men was loaded into open motor launches and then into trucks for a day of gunnery practice and recognition training ashore, where hundreds of rounds of five-inch, forty-millimeter and twenty-millimeter were fired from guns lined up along the coast at target sleeves pulled back and forth offshore by Martin Marauder B-26s. It was not until long afterward that the men realized that while they had been practicing, other sailors in other DEs had been firing similar guns in deadly earnest at winged targets over the English Channel, targets that dropped live bombs and shot back.

While most of the *Abercrombie* shore party were on the firing range, a smaller group of men, whose battle stations were at gun directors and lookout posts, were undergoing recognition training. In a darkened room, photographs and silhouettes of enemy ships and planes were flashed on a screen for fractions of a second to be identified. Then the identifications were scored, errors discussed and explained, the pictures left up on the screen for examination and the instantaneous projections repeated, with resultant better scores. The men returned to the ship with packs of flash cards to help sharpen their ability, and knowing that action was not far off, those with topside battle stations soon had the cards as dog-eared as a poker deck.

One piece of news did filter through to *Abercrombie*'s crew during those work-wracked weeks at Bermuda, and it gained their full attention because of its high degree of relevance. This was the antisub saga of DE635, the USS *England*.

On the day that *Abercrombie* and *Wann* had sailed from Galveston for Bermuda, *England* intercepted and sank with her hedgehogs a big Japanese submarine that was attempting to supply a bypassed enemy garrison on Bougainville in the Solomons.

Three days later, while *Abercrombie* was northbound between Florida and the Bahamas, *England* located and destroyed a second submarine, one of a scouting line of subs strung out across a corner of the southwest Pacific to determine the target of the next American assault.

The next day her unerring hedgehogs penetrated the hull of another sub in that scouting line, sending diesel oil and deck planking to the surface.

And the following day *England* repeated the deadly ritual of search, attack and kill, and a fourth submarine went down.

On the day after *Abercrombie's* arrival in Bermuda, with shakedown just beginning, *England* did it again; and four days later, after a quick trip into port for more hedgehogs and fuel, she returned and with incredibly consistent accuracy, sank still another submarine with a single hedgehog pattern.

Six submarines destroyed in twelve days! Five out of the six subs in the scouting line sunk (a patrol plane got the sixth).

England's accomplishment was unheard of, unprecedented in the annals of any navy. She was awarded the Presidential Unit Citation and her name was written large in the long, long history of war at sea.

To the men of *Abercrombie,* caught in the dawn-to-dusk pressures of shakedown, the *England's* triumphs meant just one thing—their weapons worked. *England* was an older ship, even though by only five months, and an earlier model. If she could destroy six subs with such apparent ease, with the same sensors and weapons, and without a glove being laid on her, they could expect success against the subs they would encounter. All they had to do was sharpen their skills. They went back to work with new confidence and vigor.

But everything did not go smoothly during *Abercrombie's* shakedown. The day after the gunnery practice ashore, she went back to sea for another fueling exercise with the big fleet oiler *Chicopee.* The seas off Bermuda were running higher than usual, which did not affect the deeply laden 520-foot tanker, but caused *Abercrombie's* starboard bow to make momentary contact with the *Chicopee's* port quarter. Damage was limited to bent lifeline stanchions on the DE and minor scratches on the tanker, but the accident demonstrated a need for much greater proficiency. It was apparent to all hands that *Abercrombie* would have to fuel and provision at sea under much worse conditions, and she had better be able to do it with no collisions, however minor.

Abercrombie's brush with the oiler showed her skipper to be a warmer and less arrogant man than he had seemed to many. When the exercise was over and the ship on her way back to port, seaman first Howard Amos, who had been at the helm during the refueling drill, was seated on the deck in a corner of the pilothouse, his head in his hands, deeply depressed and heavy with guilt about the incident. Amos, a quartermaster striker, at twenty-seven was more mature than most of *Abercrombie*'s men; he was a naturally serious and conscientious married man with a young son. Amos had been helmsman at Special Sea Details and General Quarters since taking over from signalman Paul Fry at the mouth of the Sabine on the ship's first day at sea, and he was acknowledged as her best man at the wheel. From his station in the pilothouse, he had observed at first hand his Captain's terrible temper each time it was displayed. Now he waited for the blow to fall, fully expecting a Deck or a Summary Court Martial.

But Katschinski ducked down from the open bridge to the pilothouse and put a fatherly hand on Amos's shoulder.

"Don't feel bad, old man," he said. "It wasn't your fault. I just brought her in too close."

Later that same week Amos's newfound affection for his Captain was inadvertently reinforced. The ship was at sea, and Amos as Quartermaster of the Watch, was reporting to the captain's cabin to pick up the Night Orders. Katschinski had not quite completed them and asked Amos to wait. On the desk, face-up, lay a half-written letter from the skipper to his wife, Nancy. The handwriting was bold and clear, and although Amos had no wish to violate his Captain's privacy, a glance took in several lines. They described the writer's agitation with his subordinates, his difficulty with his temper, and expressed the belief that he was learning to control it.

However, the next day there was a crisis when Katschinski gave the order to fire hedgehogs, and nothing happened. The Captain's face took on its familiar sunset hue and the bridge echoed with his "what-the-hells" and "goddamns." Nor was he mollified when his talker reported that Mr. Parlon had countermanded the order. Tom appeared on the bridge, slightly flushed himself but not in the least intimidated, and firmly explained that he had countermanded the order for the safety of the hedgehog crew, one of whom was slightly out of position and could have been hurt. He had no intention, he told Katschinski, of having his men injured in practice; although in combat it might be necessary to accept the risk. The Captain, while still not happy, could not argue with that reasoning. Tom was sent back to his station and the incident was closed, with an improved understanding between the skipper and his Gunnery Officer.

Another incident with dangerous potential also involved Tom Parlon. An ensign from the training command ashore came aboard to inspect the gunnery department. His lack of experience was evident from his youth and his untarnished braid and buttons. He stopped at the small-arms locker forward of the wardroom, asked to have it opened and removed a .45-caliber automatic pistol. Before Tom could stop him, he operated the slide and pulled the trigger, sending the big slug crashing deafeningly into the steel overhead and ricocheting around the passageway. He was still protesting that there should not have been a clip in the .45 when Tom ordered him off the ship.

A beneficent side effect of all the hours at General Quarters and Special Sea Details at Bermuda was the knowledge that *Abercrombie's* crew gained of each other. On fo'c'sle and fantail especially, for three hours each day leaving and entering, and crowded into the passageways and mess halls where repair parties were stationed at General Quarters, officers and men drifted into conversation and friendships began to form that built on and transcended the mere accident of assignment to the same ship.

In a wonderfully revealing conversation on the fo'c'sle early in shake-down, I learned more about bo'sun's mate first class Holloway.

"Where are you from, Boats?" I asked.

"The Tri-Cities, sir."

"The what?"

"The *Tri-Cities*, sir." Apparently he thought I had not heard.

I searched my geographical memory for several seconds and could not come up with any tri-cities.

"What the hell are the Tri-Cities?" I asked irreverently.

Holloway looked at me, aghast. It was as though I had admitted ignorance of bow or stern, or port or starboard. "You don't know the *Tri-Cities*, sir?" He could not believe such ignorance existed. Disappointment in his Division Officer and department head was evident in his voice.

"I'm afraid I don't, Boats," I admitted lamely. *Maybe I should know the Tri-Cities*, I thought.

"Moline," he said firmly, looking straight into my face for the instant recognition he expected, "East Moline and Rock Island!"

"Oh," I said. "Of course."

It was several weeks before I could bring myself to admit to Holloway that I had never heard of any of the three.

Another bo'sun's mate, Jim Allen, held the younger sailors spellbound with his tales of action in the Mediterranean. His most dramatic concerned the landings at Gela, Sicily, on 10 July 1943. Allen had been a seaman in the destroyer *Murphy*. In the early morning hours of the tenth, the *Murphy* and a sister destroyer, the *Maddox*, were steaming slowly back and forth offshore, guarding against submarines and torpedo boats, while the attack transports were putting their troops ashore in wave after wave of landing craft. Allen could see a broken line of fires along the coast set by U.S. air attacks designed to soften up the invasion beaches and disrupt the defending forces. It had been a rough and windy night, but by 0500 the wind and sea had smoothed out and it was beginning to be light. Light enough for enemy aircraft to get into action for the first time.

Murphy and *Maddox* were less than a mile apart. High overhead came the loudening drone of an airplane engine. *Murphy*'s gun crews searched the sky, but it was still too dark to see the plane. Then suddenly in the gloom ahead, there was first a towering splash close alongside *Maddox*, then two bright, crashing explosions that lighted the sky. *Maddox* vanished in a swirl of flame and black smoke. *Murphy* rang up flank speed and dashed in to help. She reached the scene in two minutes, but where *Maddox* had been there was only a spreading patch of black oil and a scattering of oil-covered sailors holding on to pieces of debris. Allen learned later that two big bombs had ripped *Maddox* wide open, flooding her instantly and driving her to the bottom with 210 of her 284 men.

I could vouch for Allen's story because at the instant of the *Maddox* loss, my subchaser had been lying off Gela after delivering a wave of landing craft to the beach, and I had seen the bright yellow flash and mushroom of thick orange smoke astern.

The moral of the story, Allen was careful to tell his listeners, was the need for constant, unrelenting vigilance on the part of lookouts, gun crews and every man topside every minute a ship is within range of the enemy.

The same lesson was drawn by Cox'n Harry Whitworth, a young-old salt who had been riding destroyers in the North Atlantic since the Neutrality Patrol of 1940. It was hard for the young sailors to believe that although their country was not at war in those days, U.S. warships were escorting convoys of war materials to Britain and the Soviet Union. Whitworth's most chilling sea story was of a convoy of 102 ships that sailed around the North Cape to Murmansk and arrived after weeks of nonstop assault by submarines, destroyers and aircraft with thirty-eight ships left.

Water tender first class Charles A. Bailey had had the same sort of duty and pointed the same moral. *Abercrombie* was the third destroyer type he had helped place in commission, going through the same process and training as with *Abercrombie* at Orange. In the first destroyer, the *Gwinn* (DD433), he had served in the "short of war" Neutrality Patrol of the North Atlantic. In the second destroyer, *Chevalier* (DD451), he had sailed from the builder's yard out to the South Pacific, where DE343 also was headed, and there the new destroyer had been sunk off the Solomons in the battle of Vella Lavella only seven months ago. Bailey hoped he would have better luck this time and his listeners fervently agreed.

By the last weeks of June, *Abercrombie*'s crew could man their battle stations in three and a half minutes. On 21 June, the sun reached the limit of its apparent incursion into the Northern Hemisphere and started south again. Meanwhile, in the southwest Pacific the greatest carrier battle of the war was just over. Three to four times the number of ships and planes that had fought at Midway were involved. The enemy had lost 480 planes and three carriers against U.S. losses of 130 aircraft, most of which went down from fuel exhaustion at the end of a long-range strike. The Japanese carrier task groups, which had swept the seas from Pearl Harbor to Ceylon, had been decimated for a third and final time. They would never again be effective fighting forces.

But for *Abercrombie*'s men, that longest day of the year meant only that there was more time for the incessant practices and drills and training sessions of shakedown. Yet the end was in sight. Two days after the summer solstice the Captain commanding the training group at Bermuda (Commander Task Group 23.1) conducted a final inspection. In the ancient tradition of the sea he was piped aboard between two pairs of side boys, and his staff followed, saluting quarterdeck and colors. Officers and men in khakis and whites were lined up at quarters, the First Division on the fo'c'sle, the "O" and "C" Divisions on the boat deck, the Second and Engineering Divisions on the fantail, and were reviewed by the training group Captain with Katschinski and Hicks at his heels. Then the men were dismissed to stand by their cleaning stations, and the inspecting party dispersed to tour the ship, checking every compartment from bridge to bilge and chain locker to after steering.

By 1400 it was over. The inspecting party was piped ashore, the men went below to change to working uniform, and at 1425 came the welcome call "Now go to your stations all the Special Sea Details!" So proficient had the crew become, so many times had they manned those stations, and so glad were they to be clear of the grind of shakedown, that the last line snaked aboard at 1435 and *Abercrombie* was under way. With *Wann* again a thousand yards ahead, she stood out the long, familiar channel for the last time and swung northwest for Boston.

Every man in *Abercrombie* would remember that June in Bermuda. It had not been without its goofs and fumbles. DE343 rammed a tanker, missed a surface target so widely as to threaten the towing tug, fired an erratic, porpoising torpedo, lost steering control in a reef-bordered channel, failed to fire hedgehogs on her Captain's order, nearly dumped her whaleboat crew in the sea when the forward fall was disengaged first after lowering, fired a twenty-millimeter barrel over the side when a loader failed to lock it in place, and suffered the indignity of a .45-caliber slug ricocheting around her officers' quarters. But for a warship only a month past commissioning, with most of her crew fresh from boot camp, such embarrassments were the norm, and at the end of shakedown she had risen above them. The alacrity with which her Special Sea Details had been manned was indicative of the progress that had been made in fusing a new ship and a raw crew into a man-of-war. Ship and men now were a unit, an entity, as *Abercrombie* steamed past the Bermuda reefs bound for Boston. In conversations among her crew, two words were heard far more often than before—"we" and "us." These words included both the men and the metal which now formed a new entrant in the war at sea, one worthy of worry by her country's enemies.

4. Boston, Aruba
and Panama

Abercrombie AND *Wann* took only forty-seven hours to cover the seven-hundred-odd miles between Bermuda and Boston, and those hours included two on 24 June, during which both ships slowed, circled, S-turned and searched in pursuit of a sonar contact first picked up by the *Wann* at 1906. At first the echoes sounded crisp and hard, and sonar plot showed a definite course and speed. But before an attack could be made, the echoes would get mushy and contact could never be held long enough to fire hedgehogs or drop charges. Finally the contact was reclassified as nonsub, probably a school of fish. Not at all reluctantly the two DEs left whatever the contact was astern, and cranked on twenty knots for Boston.

Abercrombie seemed to come alive at twenty knots—"Ahead full" on the engine order telegraph. At "Ahead one third," five knots, she seemed barely to be moving. At "Ahead two thirds," ten knots, she was moving all right but slowly, tediously. At "Ahead standard," fifteen knots, she was businesslike and efficient; this was her normal speed under way, the routine speed the OODs were used to working with, a nautical mile every four minutes, five hundred yards in one minute. But at twenty knots things were different; there was a lift and a surge that felt easy and natural, not strained and shaking as at "Ahead flank" when the ship tried for the last possible knot. At twenty knots the sea tore away from her bow and slid astern, and the deck trembled just slightly underfoot. Her wake streamed straight out, churning white, with parallel borders of foam. The whole effect was of speed, power, grace and competence.

All day and late into both of those nights between Bermuda and Boston, the green baize of the wardroom table was covered with handwritten notes, coffee cups and stacks of printed forms as each department head struggled with the scores of job orders which had to be ready for the Navy Yard on arrival. As far as any of us knew, this would be the last opportunity before action to make the repairs, alterations and improvements revealed by the shakedown process, and no one begrudged the hours of midnight oil required as long as the jobs would get done.

On the evening of the twenty-fourth, in the middle of the first watch, it suddenly turned cold, men topside shivered and sought what shelter they could find; those below pulled on sweaters or pulled up another blanket. When the watch was relieved at midnight, the oncoming watch standers wore foul-weather jackets freshly broken out of storage. At day-light the reason for the sudden drop in temperature became apparent; the sea was no longer clear and blue but a cold and murky gray. *Abercrombie* had left the Gulf Stream and was crossing the continental shelf two hundred miles east of Cape Cod.

DE343 was in the approaches to Boston Harbor in the late morning of Sunday, the twenty-fifth of June. All of Massachusetts Bay was under a blanket of heavy fog. Visibility was less than the ship's own length. Katschinski slowed her to ten knots, and at Special Sea Details, radar and fathometer pulsing, the whistle sounding its required prolonged blast every minute, DE343 slipped between the outer islands and headed for the Navy Yard. Before radar, that short voyage would have been a sailor's nightmare of figuring tides and currents and listening for bells and whis-tles and the sound of surf on half-submerged ledges and rocky islands along the way. But that foggy Sunday morning it was a simple matter of reading radar ranges and bearings from Boston Light, the oldest light-house in North America, on its little pile of rocks between the reaching fingers of Deer Island and Long Island, and plotting them every two minutes. On the harbor chart, a line of penciled dots a third of a mile apart showed *Abercrombie*'s progress. A straight-edge, laid from the last dot to the next navigational aid and slid over to the compass rose, showed the proper course to steer. One by one the channel buoys passed down the sides in the predicted order and at the predicted times, and at 1345, with the fog still beading the men's eyebrows and dripping from the lifelines, *Abercrombie* materialized at her assigned berth at pier one and got over her lines.

That same afternoon a large leave party left the ship. *Abecrombie* was scheduled to be ten days in port, so leave was granted on a port and starboard basis, five days for half the crew, and when those men returned, five days for the other half. In the first leave party was Howard Amos, the helmsman, who went straight to South Station and boarded the first train for Baltimore and his wife and son. Men whose homes were too far away to visit stayed aboard and enjoyed liberty in Boston. The lucky ones came from Boston itself or from Quincy, Fall River, Swampscott or Lowell: they could take their leave and then visit again on liberty. Butch was one of those fortunates—Harry Miles took him home to New Bedford, and in view of the forthcoming period of prolonged shipboard celibacy and despite Butch's early adolescence, solicitously searched the city for a ready female.

Of the men in my watch section, Red Shiel, the tall, freckled and curly-haired signalman, spent his leave with his family in Providence, Rhode Island; Fran Wall, the young quartermaster, rode out to his parents' spacious home in Swampscott; and two sonarmen, Tim Ferris and Frank Grout, traveled downstate to Springfield, where Grout's father was Superintendent of Streets and Engineering. Don Wood left his big talker's helmet in the gear locker at Repair II and rode the train up to Greenfield to spend five days with his wife, Rachel.

I, too, passed through Greenfield, driving home with my wife to visit her family and our year-old son in Bennington, Vermont. As we went through Greenfield, the radio news reported the collision of a DE and a minesweeper in Buzzards Bay, and I wondered if it was any DE I knew. But I soon forgot about it in the blessed relaxation of a normal life in the familiar tranquillity of the little Vermont town with its ring of emerald mountains. For those four days it was as though the war had gone away. After the long passage to Bermuda and the grueling weeks of shakedown, Bennington was another world, a world in which love and tenderness, comfort and continuity played their normal roles. I felt at first as I had felt after returning less than a year before from what now seemed another war. I remembered then stepping out into the autumn sunshine on some errand or other, whistling a current song as I walked, and being suddenly struck by the realization that I had whistled the same tune before, light years and eons away in a world of gray ships and scarred brown hills, salt spray, black smoke, cordite, casualties and killing. It had been a shock to realize that the whistler had been same man in both worlds. That had been only eight months ago, but I felt much older now, old enough to appreciate this oasis of normality between the wars and to drink deep of its restorative magic before it was time to return to sea.

On 26 June the Boston Receiving Station sent a draft of men to join the DE343's company. The officer making up the draft was apparently working from the bottom of his list: the men were S. S. Zanca, J. F. Zarenski, L. D. Zaza, L. Zeccardi and R. R. Zenger.

In Boston itself, *Abercrombie*'s men conducted themselves with considerably more restraint and decorum than they had in Galveston. Perhaps the younger ones were learning their capacity or had discovered that the rowdy, roistering seamen of legend too often paid too high a price for a few hours of drunkenness and violence. An exception to this improvement in conduct occurred late one night in Scollay Square, when Dick Marston, a muscular machinist's mate from California, flung open the door of a bar to discover the place was filled with British sailors.

"What the hell is this?" he bellowed, "a goddamn Limehouse?" And the free-for-all was on.

While in Boston, married men whose wives were nearby were allowed overnight liberty and were required only to be aboard for "Turn-to" at 0730. Single men had to return by 0100. This apparent but eminently reasonable discrimination brought bo'sun's mate first class Holloway to the door of my stateroom the first day in port. He knocked a little more loudly than necessary and filled the entire entrance as he stepped through. "Sir," he rasped, his face flushed and scowling, "have you seen the Plan of the Day, the part about liberty hours?"

"Sure, Boats, I've seen it. What about it?"

"It isn't fair, Mr. Stafford, giving the married men overnight and ordering single men back by 0100! What about us shackmasters?"

I explained as best I could that "shackmaster" was not an officially accredited designation and thus could not be considered when promulgating liberty policy, however unrealistic and inconvenient that might be.

Holloway retreated, respectful as always, but unconvinced and shaking his head in incredulous indignation.

Those who stayed aboard had to suffer through another period of dry-docking. When *Abercrombie*'s bottom was routinely checked after shakedown, bubbles and wrinkles were discovered in the hot plastic that had been applied in Galveston. Apparently this had occurred because in the rush of getting the ship ready for sea, insufficient drying time had been allowed between coats. So the whole job had to be done again, sandblasting down to bare metal, spraying with a 10 percent solution of phosphoric acid, priming and repainting.

While that work was going on down in the dock, more crates and boxes were coming aboard topside—all the hundreds of missing items on *Abercrombie*'s allowance lists which had been ordered from Galveston: socket and monkey wrenches; padlocks, pressure gauges, piston rings and pipe plugs; bolts, breathing apparatus, ball bearings and bore-sighting gear; graphite grease and gaskets; light bulbs and three-conductor cable.

The five weeks at sea since Galveston—and especially the arduous month at Bermuda—had turned up, as intended, hundreds of changes and additions, some essential, others merely desirable, but all aimed at increasing directly or indirectly the fighting efficiency of the ship. The Boston Navy Yard tackled them all with impressive energy and skill. A spray shield was welded onto the forward part of the number one forty-millimeter mount. Fire-retardant canvas bloomers were fitted around the bases of both five-inch guns where they protruded from the mounts. Canvas covers were fitted over the spindles on which the hedgehog projectiles were mounted, and over the entire hedgehog mount itself. Another canvas cover was made for the master range finder on the open bridge. Seals were installed around the telescopes in the five-inch gun mounts. Mount Captains' open sights were installed on both mounts so that the guns could be aimed and fired independently, in local control if necessary. Case deflectors and additional ready-ammunition boxes were added to both forty-millimeter mounts.

Portholes were cut into the wardroom, the captain's cabin and the ship's office and fitted with steel battle covers. A new smoke generator was welded and bolted to the fantail. The hydraulic system by which depth charges could be released by activating levers on the bridge, was rerigged and improved. A vegetable locker was installed on the boat deck. Shelving was fitted into a score of storerooms and working spaces around the ship. A locker for navigational and quartermaster supplies and instruments was located under the chart table. A bridge chair was welded into place on each side of the pilothouse for the Captain's use. Watertight first-aid boxes were located in the vicinity of the five-inch and forty-millimeter mounts. Additional insulation was installed between all officers' bunks and the skin of the ship. A watertight pyrotechnic locker was provided on the bridge. Magazines aft were modified to provide stowage for 79 additional depth charges, 143 of the cylindrical pistols which activate and fire the charges and 26 additional arbors, which hold depth charges in the K-guns.

Operating stands for the signalmen were installed at the port and starboard twelve-inch signal searchlights and along the length of both flag bags. All sights and fire-control equipment were aligned and calibrated with the ship motionless in dry dock. A canopy was made and fitted to the whaleboat. Everything on the ship was tested and checked, from dishwasher and laundry equipment to the degaussing system and blackout effectiveness. There was even a thermos-bottle holder for the captain's cabin.

Abercrombie also acquired a Coca-Cola machine in Boston. It took concentrated Coca-Cola syrup, pressurized cylinders of carbon dioxide, and fresh water, mixed those ingredients appropriately, and for a nickel, dispensed a cup of the mixture. The machine was paid for by the ship's Welfare and Recreation Fund, and any profits were to be returned to that fund. It turned out to be such a successful moneymaker that the profits swiftly exceeded those allowed to the welfare fund, even when the machine was adjusted to dispense two cups for a nickel. This problem was eventually solved by supplying free Cokes every other week. But in Boston the installation of the machine gave rise to another problem—the first outright confrontation between *Abercrombie*'s First Lieutenant and her Chief Engineer.

The Coke machine had been Gus Adams's idea, and was now his pet project. He had arranged to have it brought aboard and set up in its permanent location in a main-deck passageway, aft on the port side, at about 1615 in the middle of the week. Liberty was scheduled to begin at 1630, and the liberty party was mustering on the quarterdeck in dress blues. Included in the group was carpenter's mate first class Ted Gruhn, head of the C and R gang which was charged with whatever cutting, welding or brazing needed to be done on the ship. Gruhn's home was in Eureka, California; and his wife, Lillian, had made the long trek to Boston and was waiting for him ashore.

I was in my stateroom getting ready to go ashore myself when there was a knock and Charles Stephens, seaman first and Gruhn's assistant, stuck his broad shoulders and dark, curly head around the corner. Stephens always reminded me of George Eliot's Adam Bede—a big, quiet man with the natural, unassuming dignity of one who works with his hands and knows exactly what he is doing. It was always a pleasure to watch Stephens on the job, unerringly selecting precisely the right tool and using it with unhurried expertise.

"Mr. Stafford," he said gravely, "Gruhn's got a problem with Mr. Adams. Could you come aft for a minute?"

The liberty party was filing across the brow as Stephens and I walked along the main deck toward the stern. But I found Gruhn in dungarees, face flushed and jaw set tight, hooking up oxygen and acetylene lines and preparing to light his torch. Gus Adams, in rumpled, sweat-stained khakis and patchy five-o'clock shadow, was showing him where he wanted holes cut and the fresh water line run to the Coke machine. Clearly Gus had pulled Gruhn out of the liberty party to install his beloved machine, and without bothering to consult Gruhn's boss who he knew would not have consented. I looked at Gruhn's tense face again and could see that naval discipline was holding—but just barely.

"What's going on, Chips?" I asked him. "I thought you rated liberty today."

"I do, sir," he said between clenched teeth, "but Mr. Adams wants this thing installed tonight."

I looked over at Gus, who was wearing his impatient I-suppose-I-have-to-tolerate-this-goddamn-reserve expression.

"Gus," I said, "can I see you for a minute?"

I walked over to the port lifelines, out of earshot of Gruhn and Stephens, and Gus followed reluctantly.

"What," I asked him, "is so important about getting that thing hooked up tonight that you have to pull a first class out of the liberty party to get it done? A first class, with his wife waiting for him ashore, who doesn't even work for you?"

"Morale," he said with a patronizing little smile, as though I couldn't be expected to understand so professional a term. "The whole crew's waiting to use that machine. What's the matter, your boy have his feelings hurt?"

"He's obviously bitter, and I don't blame him; anyone would be," I told him. "And I doubt that here in Boston with liberty every other night the crew really cares whether they get a machine Coke or not. They sure as hell don't care whether they get one tonight or tomorrow. How long a job has Gruhn got anyway?"

"Three or four hours if he's on the ball and doesn't cry too much."

That did it. My wife was expecting me, too, *Abercrombie* would be sailing in a few days, and I knew how I would feel if I had been ordered suddenly and arbitrarily to stay aboard to complete a dirty job that could just as well be done the next day.

"Gus," I said, "Gruhn is not an engineer. He doesn't work for you. He works for me. You have no authority to assign him *any* job without my approval, and this one doesn't have it. If you think the job is so urgent, get one of your own guys to do it. I'm sending Gruhn ashore."

Adams's face turned red and he turned formal.

"Mr. Stafford," he grated, "you can't do that. I've given the man his orders."

I guess by then my face was red, too. I walked back over to Gruhn and told him to put away his gear and get ashore. When he was clear of the ship, I followed. We were both about thirty minutes late, but no one seemed to mind.

The big job in Boston was the creation of a newly developed concept called a Combat Information Center, or CIC. Combat experience had shown that with information coming in from radar, sonar, radio and visually, a clearinghouse was needed in which incoming data could be assembled, displayed, evaluated and delivered where they could best be used. CIC would answer that need and at the same time maintain a continuously updated picture of the ship's situation with regard to both friendly and hostile forces.

To create the new CIC, radar and radio consoles were removed from their old locations and reinstalled in the chart house with all the required rerouting of wires, cables and phone circuits. A large tablelike structure was constructed in the middle of the new CIC. At one end there was a circular area to display the situation in the air, including the bearing, distance, course, speed and altitude of enemy aircraft, and at the other end, a rectangular area for plotting friendly and hostile surface and subsurface units. Elsewhere in the room were the control consoles for air and surface radars, and on the bulkheads were status boards to show the names, radio call signs and other data on the ships and aircraft with which the *Abercrombie* would be operating. The overhead was covered with an array of voice radios on a variety of frequencies, voice tubes and a "squawk box" for internal communications. The idea was that all the information necessary to fight the ship would be acquired and displayed in this space, where it could be quickly evaluated and made available to the Captain. CIC was to be the battle station of the Executive Officer, who would be known there as the Evaluator, and it would be manned continually under way by five men under the leadership of a CIC Officer with the same cycle of watches as the Officer of the Deck.

By Thursday, 6 July, the new CIC had been finished, the ship's bottom repainted, all the smaller jobs completed, all hands were back from leave and liberty, and it was time to put aside the things of the shore and turn once more to the things of the sea, time for *Abercrombie* to be back on her way to the war.

When the Special Sea Details were manned that morning, there were four new chief petty officers aboard. Albert Lee Murphy Holloway of the Tri-Cities was one, his glistening new chief's cap jauntily on one side, and he presided over the fo'c'sle as though he had been a chief for a dozen years. In the control engine room, Don Puddy was similarly attired, as were Charles Holston in sick bay and Roy Glidewell in the galley. And on the bridge, Paul Fry, the leading signalman who, as the only qualified helmsman aboard at the time, had steered *Abercrombie* from Orange down the Sabine to the sea, was now signalman first class. Harry Miles, friend of Butch the mascot, was electrician's mate first class; and in the ship's office, Bob Strike wore the three chevrons and quill of yeoman first class. In addition, Art Hellman, Cy DeCoster and Gus Adams were each now wearing the double silver bars of a full lieutenant, having been promoted effective 1 July.

Abercrombie was under way at 0840 that Thursday, and stood out of Boston Harbor as she had stood in thirteen days before—in heavy fog. But by early afternoon the fog had burned off and blown away, and the green coast was in sight to starboard as *Abercrombie* and *Wann* ran southeastward past Cohasset and the Scituates, Plymouth and the Duxburys, to the Cape Cod Canal. Two vertical lift drawbridges rose ponderously, like huge open elevators, for the two DEs as they transited the waterway in their bold Pacific camouflage. At the south end of the canal, white summer cottages sprawled at the tops of long lawns, and motor yachts gleaming with varnish and white paint lay tranquil at private piers. Out on the fo'c'sle at Special Sea Details, we wondered what the people in those cottages were thinking as we swept past with our war colors and our guns. Were we unpleasant reminders of the distant, ugly war? Were we welcome evidence of a Navy that would keep them from harm? Or did the sight bring renewed anxiety for sons or husbands already at sea in hostile waters?

In the late afternoon, the two new warships slanted down through Buzzards Bay and Rhode Island Sound, and when darkness came to the summer sea, Montauk Point was abeam to starboard and the ships' bows were pointed southwestward for the Virginia Capes. All night they steamed along the coast, down the beaches of Long Island, across the sea approaches to New York, and southward off the Jersey shore. The night was as dark as only a night at sea can be with no moon and a low, thick overcast. But the sweeping strobe of the surface-search radar outlined the coast and showed other ships as little blobs of light on the dark disk of the scope. Down in the new CIC, those blobs were plotted and courses and speeds determined. When it appeared that a ship would pass uncomfortably close, the voice radios crackled tersely and the two ships swung temporarily to a course that would keep them clear.

Late on Friday afternoon, *Abercrombie* and *Wann* rounded Cape Charles and made their way up the long Thimble Shoals Channel toward Norfolk with radars still showing the way in the persistent low overcast and fog. Buoy after buoy in increasing numerical order appeared ahead, slid down the side and disappeared astern, their bells clanging irregularly to starboard, and whistles, hoarse and mournful to port. At 1700 the ships left Fort Wool to port, Fortress Monroe and the red-brick block of the Chamberlain Hotel to starboard, and entered Hampton Roads. Thirty minutes later *Abercrombie* was moored to her berth at the Norfolk Naval Operating Base, and stores and ammunition were already coming aboard.

Half the crew had liberty in Norfolk, and a few men, whose families lived in the area but who were not in the authorized liberty section, including Paul McMillan of the immortal Galveston birthday party, were granted special liberty to spend this one night at home. For those who stayed aboard, there was a chance to walk up to the head of the pier and use the telephone. The telephone facility had been built since I had sailed on my first war cruise from that same pier fifteen months before. To make a call you stood in line and worked your way up to a square counter in the center of the room manned by two or three operators. After giving one of them the number, you waited to hear your name and the number of the booth along the wall in which you could take the call. Afterward you returned to the counter to pay. A lot of money went across that counter this Friday evening, which, for all the men of *Abercrombie* knew, would be the last one they would make in the United States for a very long time.

Some of that money was my own. A persistent rumor in *Abercrombie's* little wardroom said there was a good chance the ship would make a West Coast port before heading out into the Pacific, and I wanted to cover all bets. I called my wife in Bennington and told her that I would send a scenic postcard from Panama; a happy card would mean a West Coast visit, a sad card none. If we did get to California, I did not know where it would be—maybe Los Angeles. Nor did I know how long we would be there. She would have to decide whether to chance the long trip on that kind of sketchy data.

DE343 stayed in Norfolk for exactly thirteen hours that summer Friday; on the dock the lights stayed on and the work went on all night. In the early hours, Holloway and Pete Kish were able to draw enough manila line to replace the hated springlay mooring lines at both bow and stern, leaving only the waist lines still made of springlay.

At 1040 on Saturday, 8 July, *Abercrombie* took in her lines, backed out into the current with one long blast of her whistle and three shorts, and followed the line of buoys back between the forts, out of the Roads and into the channel for the Capes. For her crew there was a different feel about this departure. Not only was it in all probability their final leavetaking from their homeland, but now for the first time there was a serious operational job to do. The two brand-new DEs, fresh out of shakedown, had been entrusted with the protection of two big fleet oilers (AOs), *Salamonie* and *Chepachet,* and two smaller gasoline tankers (AOGs), bound from Norfolk to the refineries of Aruba in the Dutch West Indies and then to Panama and the Pacific.

The four tankers followed the DEs in single file out Thimble Shoals Channel. Off the Virginia Capes they formed into a tight little convoy with the two big oilers in line abreast one thousand yards apart and an AOG seven hundred yards astern of each. *Abercrombie* took station four thousand yards on the port bow of the convoy, and *Wann* took the starboard bow.

While the convoy was forming, there was an opportunity to get a good look at the tankers. The two AOs were impressive. *Salamonie* was 550 feet long with a beam of 75 feet and a top speed of 18 knots. With a full load she displaced 23,000 tons and drew just under 30 feet of water. She carried four 5-inch guns like ours but in open mounts. *Chepachet* was thirty feet shorter, two feet narrower, three-and-a-half knots slower and armed with six 3-inchers. Both ships bristled with forties and twenties, and both wore the same bold, deceptive patterns of white, gray and black as the DEs. The AOGs were similar, but they looked squat and stubby by comparison, being shorter than the DEs at 220 feet, with beams of 37 feet.

The tankers picked up a base course of due east, zigzagging at fourteen knots, the best speed of the AOGs, while *Abercrombie* and *Wann* at sixteen knots swept back and forth on either bow, sonars probing ahead, ready guns manned and lookouts alert for a glimpse of a periscope. After dark the ships stopped zigzagging, and at midnight they turned south for Aruba.

For four days the little convoy of dazzle-painted ships stood southeastward through the summer sea, the big tankers stolid and steady in heavy ballast and the small ones laboring in their wakes. Out on the bows to port and starboard, the slim DEs sliced back and forth, their sonar beams reverberating steadily but with no hint of returning echoes. Flying fish skittered upwind away from *Abercrombie*'s sides, their wings translucent in the sun, and their long tails digging in for one more push and a few more yards above the surface. Frigate birds appeared from nowhere and followed high above the wake, hoping for a handout before sliding off on motionless wings toward better hunting grounds. Under clear skies and star-filled nights the ships' bells sounded and the watches changed in their age-old order, and each day the noon position was 340 miles farther along the track.

Late on the evening of the fourth day, the six darkened ships slipped through the Windward Passage, with Hispaniola to port and the high, dark bulk of Cape Maisí on Cuba's eastern tip to starboard.

In the Caribbean it was suddenly and unexpectedly rough and windy. *Abercrombie* rolled heavily and pitched green water across her fo'c'sle. Rattles of spray bedeviled bridge watch and lookouts, and the crew of the forward forty made good use of the new spray shield installed in Boston. One day out of Aruba the sonar went silent, having burned out a scarce and critical component far down in the bows above the transducer head.

On the afternoon of 13 July, Aruba came in sight ahead. The first time most of *Abercrombie*'s crew had heard of Aruba was when a U-boat had surfaced and shelled it back in 1942. The mental picture most of us had was of a flat island with clusters of large oil storage tanks. Surprisingly, although the island was not quite flat, the first sighting showed the expected storage tanks.

The tankers went in first, running along the coast to the harbor of St. Nicholas on the south end. The light was fading as *Abercrombie* followed them, the land low and dark green to starboard, and ahead over the harbor there was a huge yellowish cloud of haze. It was full dark by the time she picked up a pilot, dashed in through the gate in the antisub nets, and moored to the starboard side of the *Chepachet*. There the nature of the yellowish haze became apparent. It was oil. Not one of *Abercrombie*'s men would ever again envision Aruba without thinking of oil. Oil was in the air. Oil coated the waters of the harbor full of ships. The fresh water we took aboard tasted of oil. Even the water from Gus's evaporators by some obscure chemical process acquired an oily taste. The way between the dock and naval headquarters led between towering oil storage tanks and through great fields of pipes twisted into convoluted shapes and punctuated with valves and vents in a variety of shapes and sizes.

But there was an Officers' Club close by, and at least one airy and spacious restaurant on the main street, and after a few hours you began to get used to the smell. Katschinski, Hicks, Cy DeCoster, Otto Braunsdorf, Red Bond and I went over to check out the club, and spent what was left of the evening with a similar delegation from the *Wann*, including John Stedman, the skipper, and my friend Bill Rogers, the First Lieutenant. Scotch, difficult to get in the States, was plentiful, excellent, cheap and thoroughly enjoyable. There was a common feeling of relaxation now that all the arduous preparations had been completed, the ties to home broken, and we were on our way to the war. In a sense we had accepted the ship as home and our shipmates as our families, not out of preference but out of clearly recognized necessity. And most of us were young enough, despite some combat experience here and there, to have still that subconscious conviction of personal immortality which, foolishly or not, helps mask the face of war with that of high adventure, making it possible to look on without flinching.

We returned shortly after midnight from this convivial evening to find that *Chepachet* had been pumping out her ballast while we were enjoying ourselves and without anyone in *Abercrombie* having been notified. As a result, the tanker's decks had risen about fifteen feet since we had moored to her, parting one of our new manila lines and jamming the others so they were impossible to ease. When I roused out the *Chepachet*'s First Lieutenant and told him of our plight, he quickly pumped water and gasoline to starboard until we could clear our lines and make them fast again. A special watch was then assigned to tend them as the tanker first pumped herself empty, then began to take on fuel. By 0200 the problem was solved.

Orders received in Norfolk specified that the six-ship task force was to remain in Aruba only long enough for the tankers to take on full loads. That meant a departure sometime during the afternoon or evening of 14 July. The exact time was indefinite, being governed by pumping rates and tanker capacities. Such vagaries do not fit well with naval operations or the running of a ship. *Abercrombie*'s men went ashore in two parties, one morning and one afternoon, the last one to be back aboard at 1600. Several of the officers came back with high-quality Swiss watches purchased at about 20 percent of stateside prices, along with alligator shoes and purses, silk stockings and souvenirs to send home. But some men also bought and consumed large quantities of the local spirits, and far too many were logged aboard "D and D" (drunk and dirty). Special Sea Details were stationed at 1615 to be ready for immediate sailing, but no sailing orders came. Sea Details were secured at 2200, restationed at 2300, secured at 0200, restationed at 0500. Finally the ship was under way at 0954 on the fifteenth after further confusion in arranging for pilots and tugs for the tankers. It was a classic demonstration of how not to run a departure, resulting in mass frustration, lack of sleep and lowering of morale. (If Navy leadership were this indecisive and inefficient in the relatively peaceful Caribbean, how could it be relied on in action against the enemy?)

This time as the six ships pointed their bows west for Panama, *Abercrombie*, with her inoperative sonar, was part of the convoy, taking station 1,500 yards on the port beam of *Salamonie*, while *Wann* patrolled in wide sweeps ahead, her sonar pinging away. The sky was clear except for puffs of cumulus scudding along before the stiff northeasterly trades. To compensate for the debacle of the previous day, Katschinski decreed holiday routine for the afternoon, and Gus Adams organized the showing of a movie in the mess hall. Grumbling tapered off as sack time increased, and the movie provided something else to think and talk about. By taps that night, like the young men of which she was a seagoing composite, *Abercrombie* was her normal, happy self once more.

On the first watch that evening, with nothing to do but maintain course, speed and station, I learned from my fellow watchstanders about a part of Aruba I had missed. Apparently there was a bawdyhouse at one end of the main street in St. Nicholas, but it was out of bounds to U.S. military personnel. The proprietors, however, with the cooperation of the halcyon Caribbean weather, had long ago circumvented that technicality. Prospective patrons had only to hail a cab at a nearby stand and ask to be driven to the beach. En route, the cab would stop at the bawdyhouse and pick up one of the girls and her rolled-up grass mat, known variously to *Abercrombie*'s sailors as a magic carpet or a flying carpet. Once at the beach, the driver would wander away discreetly for a cigarette or two. After sounding his horn he would return and take his passengers back to town. Total cost to the patron, including round-trip cab fare, eleven guilders, or about six dollars during daylight, ten guilders at night when it was not necessary to drive so far.

Ted Gruhn, still slightly pale and pink of eye, explained to me how he had acquired those typical signs of a big liberty. He had gone ashore with one of *Abercrombie*'s most unusual characters, a forty-year-old former real estate salesman from Chicago named Hibbert C. Eckroad, now a seaman second class and the ship's barber. Eckroad was a man with an astonishing variety of talents. He could play almost any musical instrument he was handed, do a stand-up comedy routine, sing with professional style, dance a creditable buck-and-wing, and dash off perceptive, incisive cartoons at a moment's notice. Although advancement would have been easy for a man of his talents and intelligence, he had made an early decision to remain a seaman second for the duration. It made for a simple, relaxing life, he said, and with no responsibility there was nothing he could be blamed for and a minimum of trouble. His obvious intelligence, however, earned him the critical job of Captain's talker at General Quarters, an assignment he was unable to avoid. Ashore with Gruhn in Aruba, he visited half a dozen of the joints along the main street, enjoying the people-watching and drinking a rum cola in each place. Toward the end of the evening the two sailors ran critically short of cash. Gruhn emptied his pockets into Eckroad's hands, who counted the change and found there was enough for one more drink apiece. They entered another bar and ordered the drinks, but when the bartender came for his money, Eckroad drew on still another of his talents. He reached across the bar and pulled one coin from the man's ear and another from his empty shirt pocket. When the incredulous barman demanded to know how he could do such a thing, Eckroad played his trump card. "Bring my buddy and me a drink and I'll show ya." The fascinated barkeep bought so many drinks, while Eckroad explained his tricks in suddenly halting and difficult English, that the two men were barely able to navigate the few blocks back to *Abercrombie*.

All the following day the little convoy zigzagged to the westward, with the trades blowing briskly from astern. Every few hours a Catalina or Mariner seaplane appeared from the direction of Panama and circled protectively while the unloaded guns of the DEs followed them across the sky for training. The Captain spent all morning in the wardroom with his department heads, revising certain battle stations and duties because of an action report received from another DE.

Early in May one of the first of the DEs, the *Buckley* (DE51), was vectored in on a surfaced U-boat by a carrier plane with radar contact. Apparently the sub's batteries were so low she was afraid to dive, and her skipper elected to fight it out on the surface with the *Buckley*. The U-boat turned away, firing, and the DE, also firing, increased speed to ram. For a minute or so, the two ships ran parallel, only twenty yards apart, so close that *Buckley*'s three-inch guns could not depress enough to bear. It was like a Nelsonian battle in which each Captain sought to "lay his ship alongside that of the enemy." But *Buckley* pulled away, then put her helm hard over, and rammed the sub at twenty knots. The DE's bow rode up over the rounded pressure hull of the sub forward of her conning tower and hung there. None of the guns on either ship could bear on the other, but the angry Germans swarmed out of their conning tower and opened up with rifles and machine pistols. The DE sailors dodged back behind their bulkheads and rushed to break out their own small arms. Before they could arm themselves the sub crew began to scramble up over *Buckley*'s bow, and the old cry of the fighting frigates rang from the DE's loudspeakers, "All hands repel boarders!" Up on the crazily canted bow, the DE sailors fought the Germans with empty shell cases, clasp knives, hurled coffee mugs and bare fists until rifles, pistols and grenades began to arrive. The enemy submariners fell, jumped or were driven back to their ship just as the DE's bow slid back down, and the two ships again lay parallel, rolling against each other. Now the DE, higher up and with many more men, had the advantage over the damaged U-boat. While small-arms fire swept her decks, grenades exploded in her deck hatches and in the open conning tower, sending up flashes of flame and smoke. Still moving slowly ahead, the sub went down, her charred conning tower and deck hatches still open. *Buckley* was ordered into New York to get her bent bow straightened.

Six weeks later in the bright Caribbean sunlight, *Abercrombie* distributed small arms and grenades to the repair parties and assigned the best-qualified men to use them if the need arose.

At the end of the evening meal in the wardroom on that sixteenth of July, John Bailey, the duty steward, set before me a yellow cake iced in white and painstakingly inscribed in yellow: "HAPPY BIRTHDAY 1ST LT." I was twenty-six, but I had no idea anyone knew it was my birthday. I was surprised and deeply touched, a seemingly unmanly emotion in that company, successfully concealed by the banter which ensued when I dribbled the rather crumbly cake across the tablecloth in serving it.

At nightfall *Abercrombie* changed station, ranging well out ahead three miles on the starboard bow of the *Wann* to act as a radar picket and warn of approaching ships or surfaced subs. After a night of warm, drenching showers and weirdly flickering horizontal lightning, she rejoined the convoy, and at 1100 the low, jungled coast of Panama was in sight.

At noon, with lunch on the wardroom table, the unpredictable Katschinski burst in, red of face and loud of voice. "Get out there, every one of you!" he yelled. "Break out your people and get this ship cleaned up. She's a goddamn mess!" Fo'c'sle, fantail and boat deck looked okay to me; they had been washed and swept down as usual that morning, but we did it again, and heard no more from the Captain.

It was calm, hot and humid as *Abercrombie* nosed in through the breakwater and tied up near the two oilers in Cristobal, Canal Zone, in midafternoon. But in Cristóbal there were pay, ice cream and technicians to repair the sonar. And, surprisingly, there was mail, although *Abercrombie* was only eleven days out of Boston. The eager way officers and sailors responded to mail call, the way the ones who got letters treasured them and retreated into their private worlds to read them greedily, and the hurt that darkened the faces of the men who received none were evidence of the vital importance of mail to the morale of crewmen on a man-of-war. It is a naval axiom that morale depends on "pay, liberty and chow." Mail from home should be added to that list and given equal stature.

That night all the parts, stores and supplies we asked for were promptly delivered. There was also a series of rapidly changing orders and rumors of orders. First, *Abercrombie* would transit the Canal in the morning and proceed to San Diego for exercises with the amphibious forces there. A few hours later, word came that the trip to San Diego would be delayed for four or five, may be ten days. Then it was learned that the ship would be temporarily assigned to the Panama Sea Frontier for whatever odd jobs they might have, and after that probably San Diego.

I weighed all the factors, took a calculated risk and sent off a happy postcard to Vermont.

All rumors dissolved at 1730 the following afternoon when *Abercrombie*, *Wann* and *McCoy Reynolds* (DE440) got underway in rain squalls and gusty winds on a scheduled ten-day antisub sweep of the tanker route to Aruba.

The three DEs formed a line abreast, with *McCoy Reynolds* in the center, *Wann* three thousand yards on her starboard beam, and *Abercrombie* the same distance to port. In rough seas and high winds, they plunged, lunged, rolled and lurched back toward Aruba at ten knots, sonars doggedly searching, solid water running off their decks, and heavy spray soaking everything and everyone topside. Every man with a weather deck watch station, including those on the bridge, was soaked after the first half hour, with salt smarting in his eyes and stiffening in his hair. Binoculars had to be wiped dry each time they were used. Under the continuous seawater bath, a rash of rust broke out from waterline to truck. Down below, eating and sleeping were both difficult. A man grew tired simply from the constant necessity to hold on to something.

To add to the general misery, the Officer in Tactical Command (OTC) in the *Reynolds* conceived of a way to keep the ready gun crews alert. Without warning, *Reynolds* would put up a five-inch AA burst, and the OTC would see how long it took for the other ships to open fire on it. On the very first such exercise, *Abercrombie* was quick to get her own burst right up beside the first one, but not without cost. At the sudden roar of the forward five-inch gun just over their heads, the chiefs came running out of their quarters, and chief quartermaster Zeke Marmon, a tall man, ran too high, laid his head open on the knife-edge at the top of the hatch and knocked himself cold.

On the morning of Thursday, 20 July, I was sound asleep in my snug stateroom forward of the wardroom on *Abercrombie*'s port side when the loud, insistent, electric clanging of the general alarm sent me scrambling into my clothes and dashing aft along the deck to Repair II. Katschinski had wisely ordered at the beginning of shakedown that the general alarm would be used only for actual General Quarters; for drills the word would be passed by voice to "Man your battle stations." So this was no drill. I could see the difference in the faces of the men I passed, hear it in their quickened steps and feel the tension throughout the ship. The narrow fore-and-aft passageway outside the damage control locker quickly filled with the ten men of the repair party, still buttoning their shirts, tying their shoes and settling their helmets. Don Wood was already there with phones on under his big gray helmet; and every eye in the passageway was on him, waiting for news.

I looked at my watch: it was 0620. Repair I and Repair III checked in ready. I took a head count, and Wood reported to the bridge: "All repair parties manned and ready." He listened for a minute and then reported: "They've got a strange ship out there; trying to get her to identify herself." We could feel the motion of the ship as she circled, and overhead the whir of the aft forty training around to stay on target. Inside the passageway it was dark except for the red battle lanterns, warm and stuffy, and it smelled of many bodies jammed close together. I was not used to having an airless closet as a battle station, and I could see that some of the sailors were not either. But we were stuck with it. It was something we would *have* to get used to. I ordered an inventory and checkout of the gear in the locker to keep us busy, but it had barely begun when the word was passed: "Away the visit and search party, muster on the torpedo deck!"

Delighted with the opportunity to break out of the close quarters of Repair II, and with my heart thumping at the prospect of an actual visit and search, I strapped on my .45 and headed for the whaleboat. Cy was already there, and in about three minutes our six musclemen, armed to the teeth and grinning at the prospect of some action, were lined up with their gear, ready to go. Off to port about five hundred yards we could see a small tanker hove to, her light flashing rapidly. The crew was in the whaleboat with Jim Allen at the tiller, and we were ready to lower away when from the topside speakers came the order "Secure the visit and search party. Secure from General Quarters. Set Condition Three, Section One has the watch." With *Abercrombie*'s guns trained on her, armed men assembling on deck, and two more DEs hull down to the eastward, the tanker had finally identified herself as the SS *Mechanicsville*, a U.S. ship.

Later, at breakfast in the wardroom, Hicks announced that in this, *Abercrombie*'s first actual General Quarters, battle stations had been manned in just under three minutes.

Early on the twenty-first, *Abercrombie*'s cranky sonar died once more. By afternoon it was pinging again but only when pointed dead ahead, and DE343 was ordered back to Cristóbal for repairs—to the regret of not a single member of her crew.

But by noon on the twenty-fourth, *Abercrombie* was back on patrol with a functioning sonar and in calmer seas. This time it was a solo patrol. While *Abercrombie* was in Cristóbal, *Reynolds* and *Wann* had made a speed run two hundred miles to the northward to rescue forty people down at sea in a Martin Mariner PBM flying boat.

That very afternoon it was *Abercrombie*'s turn. Coded orders came by radio to rendezvous with a tanker convoy in the Windward Passage and escort it to Aruba. The same radio message warned of storms and high seas in the area of the rendezvous.

Abercrombie headed north at eighteen and a half knots, with her crew busy securing all loose gear topside and below and battening down for heavy weather. It took two days of slicing into head seas and throwing white water to reach the rendezvous. Chief Bailey and Doc Bour were kept busy in sick bay tending to bruises, bumps, scrapes, cuts and contusions resulting from the constant violent motion of the ship. But the 343 rounded Cape Maisí, at the eastern tip of Cuba, at the end of a black, rough midwatch, picked up the convoy on radar, and assumed her screening station at 0600 on the twenty-seventh with a final, savage 49-degree roll that hurled men from their bunks and made disaster areas out of mess halls and washrooms. It was a small convoy: the big oiler *Nantahala* with the AOG *Nemascet* astern, and screening ahead, *Abercrombie*'s sister ship from Orange, *Oberrender* (DE344).

Once again *Abercrombie* swept a path across the Caribbean with radar and sonar. All the way across, Gus's evaporators built a surplus of fresh water so that when the four ships arrived back in Aruba on the morning of 28 July, the crew had clean and not oily water to drink.

On the twenty-ninth it took the tankers all day to fill up, and early on the thirtieth, DE 343 took her second departure from oil-soaked St. Nicholas, and for the second time set course for Cristóbal.

In Cristóbal this time there was no opportunity for either rumors or recreation. *Abercrombie* anchored briefly off the old coal dock; then at 1030 on the first of August she entered the Panama Canal, astern of *Nantahala* and ahead of *Oberrender*. For the men on the fo'c'sle and other topside Special Sea Details stations, it was a daylong sightseeing tour. The Canal was narrow at first, winding between steep green banks until the first set of the concrete Gatun Locks towered up above the jungle. In the locks, to get the heaving lines over, the Panamanian line handlers used a tricky little double windup and behind-the-back flip which fascinated *Abercrombie*'s deckhands. The water rose in the locks at an astonishingly rapid rate, and the ship was lifted as though on a huge, aquatic elevator. When the electric mules took up the strain and the towlines made an angle of almost 45 degrees with the axis of the Canal, it was hard to see what kept them on their tracks.

For an hour and a half in the early afternoon, *Abercrombie* anchored in Gatun Lake, pumped the fresh lake water through her fire main system to kill marine growth, and held "swimming call" for the crew. After the tropic heat of the past weeks and the oil and dust of St. Nicholas and Cristóbal, the cool fresh water of the lake was a glorious treat to DE343's young crewmen. They dived from every vantage point on the ship, even going up to the bridge level thirty feet high, splashed and gamboled and surface-dived like a school of young porpoises. But there was a surprisingly strong current in the lake and two men got in trouble. Paul McMillan tied a line around himself and swam out astern to retrieve a trash can that had been knocked overboard. He fastened the line to the can, and it was hauled back aboard. But when it came time for McMillan to return to the ship, the current was so strong that a buoyed line had to be thrown out to him or he could not have made it back. Young radarman Bill Watkins, who prided himself on his ability in the water, swam out so far from the ship that he was caught in the wake current of a passing freighter and would have drowned if Jim Allen, patrolling in the whaleboat, had not seen him in difficulty and picked him up.

Leaving the lake at 1500, *Abercrombie* followed the winding channel between scores of tiny, lush green islands, then through cuts in the jungle so close to the trees you could almost grab a branch. Occasionally small detachments of soldiers in fatigues appeared along the banks, and the barrels of antiaircraft guns glistened through the trees. Looking at them from the fo'c'sle, we thought that probably was the worst way to spend a war, waiting in the jungle for enemy planes that would never come: no danger, but no adventure, no feeling of accomplishment or contribution, no ribbons, no home, little liberty—nothing but the Canal, the passing ships and the empty sky. Red Shiel, semaphoring unofficially from the aft end of the bridge, drew from an Army signalman at one antiaircraft emplacement the wistful admission that he would love to swap duty with Shiel, join us in the western Pacific and "get a piece of the action."

In the late afternoon *Abercrombie* and *Oberrender* were lowered through the Pedro Miguel Locks and crossed Miraflores Lake to the last set of locks. It was 2115 and dark when DE343 tied up to *Oberrender*'s port side in Balboa, with the waters of the Pacific lapping along her hull for the first time. Some crewmen had to be shown the chart before they could be convinced that although they had steamed from the Atlantic to the Pacific, they were twenty-seven miles farther east then when they had entered the Canal that morning.

Half of *Abercrombie*'s crew went ashore in Balboa on the evening of 2 August. It was something of a celebration because that morning Katschinski had picked up *Abercrombie*'s orders at the office of the Port Director. They read: "Proceed independently to San Diego, California...." *Oberrender* was not so lucky: she was ordered to sail directly to Pearl Harbor as escort for *Nantahala*. The orders meant that many of us would see our families once more before joining the war. For the men who lived in the western states, including Katschinski and Hicks, it meant going home for the first time in many months. It felt like a reprieve.

5. San Diego, Hawaii and the Admiralties

Abercrombie, Oberrender AND *Nantahala* WERE under way from Balboa at noon on 3 August. At the mouth of the Gulf of Panama the little force divided, the tanker and the 344 turning westward for Hawaii while the lucky 343 headed northwest for ten more days in the States.

Abercrombie's passage from Balboa to San Diego was as nearly idyllic as is possible for a warship in wartime. For an hour in the morning and again at evening twilight, times when a periscope is difficult to see but a ship is not, battle stations were manned and the guns were test-fired. The remainder of each day was spent on fire- and damage-control drills, routine ship's work and in preparing job orders for the yard in San Diego. The sea was uniformly calm, and after the first three days of high overcast, the sun was bright and warm. The men on watch topside removed their shirts, improved their tans and munched on small, sweet bananas from Balboa. Flying fish skittered away from the ship's sides as she bore steadily north-westward at fifteen knots. Porpoises occasionally played tag around her bow. Whole watches passed without an order to helm or engines. The mood of the men was one of contentment and anticipation. And on that peaceful pleasure cruise came the final resolution of what had become known aboard as "the great accordion caper."

On *Abercrombie's* first visit to Cristóbal, men going and returning from liberty had to pass through a long, open warehouse on the dock filled with crates, trunks and boxes of what were apparently personal belongings. Several crates and trunks lay open, either from rough handling or otherwise, with their contents temptingly available. One such trunk contained among other things, several bottles of Canadian whiskey and an accordion. Two sailors on their way ashore, Tom Rutters and Bill Watkins, took special note of the accordion and resolved that if it were still there when they returned they would bring it aboard: it would, they rationalized, provide many hours of relaxing entertainment out in the forward areas where any sort of entertainment would be in short supply and doubly welcome. And anyway if they didn't take it, someone else, no doubt less deserving, would.

The accordion was still there when they returned, so Rutters brought it aboard. The repercussions were not long in coming. *Abercrombie* was at sea on the antisub sweep of the tanker route to Aruba when a message came in from the Port Director at Cristóbal demanding the immediate return of the accordion. Katschinski himself got on the public address system and announced that the accordion was known to be aboard and must be turned in immediately. Then he told Hicks that he had better find it, "Or else!"

Rutters and Watkins held a hurried conference. Watkins suggested they give the accordion "the deep six," thus eliminating the evidence, but Rutters decided to hide it instead.

Hicks called in chief bo'sun's mate Holloway, who was also the ship's Chief Master-at-Arms, and ordered a search of the ship. However, Rutters had hidden the accordian so well that the search turned up nothing. In the course of the interrogations incident to the search, the two culprits were identified by the Petty Officer of the Watch, who had seen them bring aboard something about the size of an accordion.

Hicks sent for Rutters and told him that it was known now who had stolen the accordion, but that in view of the pressure being brought by the Port Director, no disciplinary action would be taken if it were turned in. "Nothing will happen," Hicks told him. "All we're interested in is getting it back to the Port Director."

Several days passed. Just before the ship returned to Cristóbal for repairs to her sonar, Hicks called Rutters in again and reiterated his assurances that all would be well if the accordion was simply turned in so that it could be given back. The pressure was too great and the two sailors yielded, figuring that this was their best way out of a bad situation. Rutters, a signalman striker, dug the accordion out of the bottom of the starboard flag bag and delivered it to Hicks. With the instrument in his hands, the Executive Officer's conciliatory manner changed.

"Rutters," he announced sternly, "you will get not less than a Summary Court Martial out of this, and you'll probably end up in Portsmouth." Portsmouth, New Hampshire, is the location of the U.S. Naval Prison, reserved for the more serious offenders against naval discipline.

Later that day, Rutters and Watkins, bitter and incredulous, watched from *Abercrombie*'s deck as Katschinski climbed down into the whaleboat and motored off across the harbor to the Port Director's office, personally returning the accordion. Soon after they had watched him return empty-handed, the PA system blared: "Now Rutters, seaman second class and Watkins, seaman second class, lay up to the captain's cabin."

The two men, their white hats at their sides, stood at attention in the middle of the little cabin. Katschinski sat at his desk against the aft bulkhead and turned to face them.

"I am very disappointed in you two men," he told them. "You have given the ship a bad name when she is new and just beginning to build the reputation that will follow her wherever she goes. In stealing you have committed an offense which cannot be tolerated at sea where men must live in close quarters and trust each other. You are young and thoughtless and inexperienced, and I hate to see you in such serious trouble, but I don't see how I can keep you out of Portsmouth in this case."

Rutters explained respectfully their reasons for bringing the accordion aboard and pointed out that if it were stealing, they had stolen for and not from their shipmates. "And Captain, sir," he finished, "that wasn't the only thing taken from that trunk. There was lots of other stuff, including whiskey, and I saw officers taking it. If we're going to Portsmouth, sir, they're going with us."

Katschinski restricted the two men to the ship indefinitely, awaiting disciplinary action, and when their shipmates went ashore again in Cristóbal and later in Balboa, Rutters and Watkins were far down below, cleaning bilges.

One day out of Balboa, bound for San Diego, Rutters and Watkins were called back to the captain's cabin. Again Katschinski was at his desk facing the two young seamen. His manner was mild, almost paternal.

"I'm glad to tell you," he said, "that Panama Sea Frontier has left disciplinary action in your cases up to me. I've given it a lot of thought. You two are really just kids, although you are doing men's work. If you were *my* kids, I would hate to see you get in serious trouble over this incident, especially since your motives were certainly not criminal or those of the ordinary thief. So I am going to consider the loss of liberty you have already suffered as sufficient punishment. There will be no entry in your records. . . ." Katschinski paused, looked into the faces of the two men and waggled a finger at them. "But I don't ever want to see you up before me again! Now go."

Thus was the great accordion caper wiped from the record. But what was not wiped away was the hatred that Tom Rutters had acquired for his Executive Officer. After sticking it out for two and a half months, Rutters requested transfer from the signal gang to the deck force because he could not trust himself on the same bridge with Hicks.

Early one sun-and-sea–filled afternoon, dipping gently northward through a smooth and easy swell 150 miles west of Baja California, *Abercrombie* had a visitor. A magnificent man-o'-war bird, black with shadings of chocolate on his seven-foot spread of wings, slanted swiftly down from dead astern to perch on the bedspringlike antenna of the air-search radar, the highest point on the ship. He had a scarlet patch at his throat, a long, deeply forked tail, and a beak curved like a scimitar. It was easy to see how he had come to be named back in the age of sail, this master of the air on motionless wings and fierce despoiler of fatter, slower breeds. But the proud aerial pirate had a problem. His feet and legs, shortened and weakened by evolution over eons in the air, provided an uncertain grip and balance—and the radar antenna was rotating. First, he would be heading forward and into the wind in a natural and normal way; then as the antenna turned, he would find his tail pointing upwind and his feathers would ruffle backward in a most undignified and abnormal fashion. With a fancy little cross-over footwork, he would face forward again, only to have the process repeated. Although it was evident he was not getting the rest he had come for, he was not discouraged and stayed with the ship for several hours, reversing direction with every turn of the antenna.

Every man topside on the afternoon watch observed the regular rotations of the great bird high above the ship, and called their buddies up from below to see. Cooks came out of the galley and mess cooks from the mess hall. Machinist's mates, water tenders and firemen on watch took a minute to blink up out of engine-room and fireroom hatches. The quartermaster and electrician in after steering poked their heads out of the scuttle on the fantail to watch. Stewards came from the pantry and officers let their coffee cool on the wardroom table. To most the sudden visit of the man-o'-war of the air to their man-of-war of the sea's surface, and his persistence in remaining aboard, seemed in a vague way omens of good luck, as though some primal incarnation of air-sea warfare had paused to confer a blessing. When finally the long wings spread and the forked tail pivoted, rudderlike, to bear the bird away, a touch of sadness, like the passing shadow of a cloud, seemed momentarily to brush across the ship.

It was a bright, clear, calm morning, Friday the eleventh of August, when signalman first class Paul Fry raised the San Diego Harbor Entrance Control Post (HECP) atop Point Loma. *Abercrombie* was still so far at sea that he had to use the big thirty-six-inch searchlight with its blue-white carbon arc. The heavy shutters clattered on the light as Fry identified the ship and began a routine message requesting berth assignment, fuel and a representative from the Naval Repair Base to meet us on arrival. But he had sent only the first few words when HECP broke in with a steady flashing of the distant light. Fry stopped sending and made a dash, a dot, and a dash—"K"—"Go ahead with your transmission."

From my Special Sea Details station on the fo'c'sle, I had seen HECP break in on *Abercrombie*'s message and wondered what was up. As the new message began to come in, slowly because of the distance and the clumsier big light, I spelled it out to myself with increasingly mixed feelings.

"M-S-G," it flashed, "F-O-R   L-T   S-T-A-F-F-O-R-D . . ." Then there was a procedural sign meaning a break or pause while I swallowed and tried to imagine what was coming next. "M-R-S   S-T-A-F-F-O-R-D" —the dots and dashes continued implacably—"I-S   A-T   T-H-E   U-S   G-R-A-N-T   H-O-T-E-L   A-R [end of message]."

I calculated mentally how long it would take Fry to walk forward on the bridge to show Katschinski the pad on which the message had been copied. About thirty seconds, I figured. And in just about thirty seconds the fo'c'sle talker pushed down the button on the mouthpiece strapped to his chest, said, "Aye, aye," and turned to me. "Mr. Stafford, the Captain would like to see you on the bridge."

I found Katschinski, wearing his reddest face, and Hicks, glowering at his side.

"Jesus Christ, Ed!" Katschinski exploded, trying unsuccessfully to keep his voice low enough that it would not be heard by the bridge full of fascinated sailors. "Don't you know there's a goddamn war on and ships' movements are supposed to be secret? This is the goddamnedest breach of security I've ever seen! I've a damned good mind to put you in hack while we're in San Diego! How the hell did she know we would be arriving here today?"

I had been wondering the same thing. All I had told her was that there was a good chance we would make a West Coast port. I had expected to spend a day or two and lots of money on long-distance calls trying to find out first, if she had come to California and second, if so, where she was. All I could do was explain the happy-card, sad-card message, knowing that no breach of security had actually taken place; and as I did so, Katschinski's color faded slowly to normal and I was permitted to return to my station on the fo'c'sle. I knew the Captain was still not happy, but I heard no more about spending the San Diego visit in my stateroom.

That evening in the cocktail lounge of the U.S. Grant Hotel, I learned the circumstances behind that startling message. On receipt of the happy postcard, my wife had taken the first train for Los Angeles. It was a five-day trip, and being alone, twenty-four years old, and quite attractive, she had no dearth of attention from the other, predominately male passengers. One group of three invited her to be a fourth at bridge, and she spent many hours with them as the train made its way across the continent. Among the bridge players was a Navy captain wearing the twin dolphins of a submariner. Inevitably in the course of converation, it came out that my wife's destination was Los Angeles, where she hoped to meet her husband who was arriving on a Navy ship.

What kind of a ship? the Captain wanted to know.

A destroyer escort.

When was she due in?

The lady was not sure.

Well, the Captain allowed, DEs don't come into Los Angeles, they go to San Diego.

Oh.

It was obvious that the lady needed assistance.

When the train arrived in Los Angeles, the Captain took my wife to his mother's home while he did some telephoning. He learned when and where the ship was due, made reservations for her at the U.S. Grant, and put her back on the train for San Diego. Then, not a man to leave a job half done, he telephoned the Officer-in-Charge of the HECP at Point Loma and dictated the message that had incurred the wrath of *Abercrombie*'s Captain.

When, just before noon, *Abercrombie* tied up to the starboard side of the destroyer *McFarland* at pier four of the Naval Repair Base, *Wann* was in sight at an adjacent pier. She had already been in San Diego for five days and was scheduled to stay for nearly a month while the yard installed a new high-pressure steam turbine. A couple of nights later, I ran into Bill Rogers, *Wann*'s First Lieutenant and my opposite number; and in his soft South Carolinean drawl, he related the midnight rescue of forty male and female passengers from the downed PBM in the Caribbean.

Wann and *McCoy Reynolds,* making twenty-two knots in line abreast, picked up the crippled seaplane on radar at 2130 on 21 July; and at 2145 they saw red distress flares from a Very pistol pop into sight on the horizon ahead and drift slowly down. At 2224 the bright amber flashes of an Aldis signal lamp appeared dead ahead, and eleven minutes later the big, twin-engine Mariner was in sight. With lots of sail area and hardly any draft, it was tossing around badly in the heavy seas and blowing rapidly downwind. The starboard wing float was missing, apparently lost in the violent open-sea forced landing, and three or four men were clinging to the top of each wing, well out toward the tip, in what appeared to be an attempt to improve the plane's lateral stability and keep it from capsizing.

McCoy Reynolds launched her boat immediately, and in the *Wann,*

Captain John Stedman asked for volunteers to man the whale boat under what were obviously risky conditions. *Wann*'s boat was away at 2315 with Bill Rogers in charge. The night was dark and moonless with forty knots of wind kicking up seas of ten feet or better. Fighting wind and sea and dodging the plane's flailing wings and tail, *Wann*'s cox'n brought the boat gingerly alongside the barn-door-size waist hatch on the plane's lee side, and nine passengers were able to jump aboard, timing their leaps as boat and hatch came level momentarily. But as the last man came aboard, he cast off the whaleboat's long painter, which had secured it to the plane, and dropped it in the sea, where it promptly trailed aft, wound up in the propeller and stalled the engine. The engineer threw the engine into neutral and restarted it, but each time the gears were engaged, it stalled. There was only one thing to do. Over the side went Bill Rogers into the tossing black water. With his survival knife and hanging on to the shaft three feet below the surface, being banged and slammed against rudder and hull, he managed to cut away the line and free the prop.

While Rogers was taking care of the casualty to the whale boat and the *Reynolds* was taking off the PBM's remaining passengers, the *Wann* herself had a casualty: a rotary clamp on the starboard engine carried away and the engine had to be shut down for repairs.

It was twenty-seven minutes after midnight when Rogers brought his nine survivors back to *Wann* and the whale boat was finally hoisted out.

Since the plane was still intact, *Wann* stood by, circling at eight knots on one engine, while *Reynolds* prepared to take it in tow. But before the hookup could be made, a subchaser arrived on the scene to do the job. The two DEs left the scene of the rescue at 0400 with *Wann*'s starboard engine back on the line, and the next evening they disembarked their passengers in Kingston, Jamaica.

When I saw him in San Diego three weeks later, Bill Rogers was still nursing a badly bruised shoulder and shopping to replace a smashed wristwatch.

Abercrombie spent eleven days in San Diego while the Naval Repair Base worked over the ship, and the crew made the most of their last days in the States for no one knew how long. Liberty policy was generous. All chief petty officers, all first class seamen, and all men with wives in the San Diego area (except those in the engineering department—Gus wasn't going to be *that* easy) were permitted liberty all night every night. Men with relatives in the area were off from 1615 on Saturday to 0745 Monday. In many cases three-day leaves were granted.

Meanwhile aboard the ship, the myraid big and little jobs required to keep a warship in working order went on. Shower valves, mess tables and the potato peeler were repaired. The wardroom, adjacent passageways and the ship's office were repainted. Legs were attached to the movie screen, cleats welded to the davits to secure the whaleboat better, and pad eyes added to the steering arms in after steering to facilitate steering by chain falls in an emergency. Shelves were installed in after steering for stowing radar and radio vacuum tubes. A new barometer was installed on the bridge and a punching bag put up on the fantail. Throughout the ship, CO_2 fire extinguishers were checked and recharged where required, dogs (devices which secure doors and hatches) were greased, heaters in the ventilation system were cleaned and stuck ventilators were freed up. In CIC, holdback hooks were added to the doors. Even the two bicycles were overhauled and their stowage improved. A working party went to the salvage yard and returned with a desk and a bookshelf for the ordinance office, another bookshelf for the coding room, six chairs for the chiefs' quarters, and four aluminum wind scoops for the portholes that had been installed in Boston. The repair parties spent a day at the rifle range becoming familiar with the rifles, carbines, shotguns and pistols provided them as a result of the *Buckley's* U-boat encounter. Seven seamen second class took and passed the requisite exams and were promoted to seamen first.

Abercrombie's men enjoyed San Diego. There were visits to Tijuana, afternoons on the broad beaches of Coronado, and evenings at a restaurant and nightclub officially named Paul's Inn but referred to locally as the Passion Pit. Tom Rutters made use of his first liberty since Aruba to have a heart with a scroll bearing his wife's name, Gerry, tattooed on his upper right arm, having decided that the vaccination scar on his left arm might mar the artistic effect. In a kind of moral reenforcement, radioman Sal "Sparks" Martrildonno went with Rutters to the tattoo parlor and acquired a magnificent red rose in the same place. Both men returned with massive ugly scars, and it was not for several weeks that the full splendor of the tattooist's art became apparent.

Early on the afternoon of Tuesday, the twenty-second of August, the San Diego interlude was over. At 1405 the last line was lifted off its bollard, splashed briefly and was hauled aboard; the jack at the bow and the ensign at the stern came down as the steaming colors soared to the truck; the whistle sounded its long blast, the oily harbor water churned below the broad transom with that long name spelled out across it, and *Abercrombie* turned and pointed her sharp bow westward toward the war.

While *Abercrombie* had been refitting and resupplying in San Diego, the tempo of the war had increased. On 15 August the U.S. Navy, with important assistance from British and French naval units, put three U.S. Army divisions ashore on the Mediterranean coast of France, which immediately began a drive northward to link up with their comrades-in-arms who had landed the hard way over the Normandy beaches in early June. In the Pacific, the mightly amphibious assault on the Marianas had swept them clear of the enemy, and Guam, Tinian and Saipan were now in American hands.

The pattern of the Pacific war was evident as *Abercrombie* left the high, rounded cape of Point Loma to starboard and began breasting the Pacific swell. It was a pattern of successive hammerblows, battering back and compressing the periphery of Japanese control, wresting away the enemy naval and air bases on which that control depended, bypassing and cutting off the less important bases and leaving them to wither into impotence, slashing always closer to the home islands and the seat of enemy power. As the might of American industry began to peak and as more and more weapons came into the hands of the troops, the interval between those hammerblows grew shorter and their force increased. But while the assault increased in intensity, the enemy defense stiffened. Although Japan had been wounded and weakened, she was still strong. The closer the attackers came to the sacred soil of the home islands, the more determined were the defenders. In the just-completed occupation of Saipan, some 24,000 Japanese were killed and less than 1,800 captured, more than half of whom were Koreans. Even Japanese civilians on the island had committed suicide, leaping off the northern cliffs by the hundreds. It was apparent that the fighting ahead would be prolonged and vicious. And it was also apparent that when the next blow was struck, *Abercrombie* would be among the strikers. All across the great hemispheric sweep of the Pacific, the collective surge of gray warships was westward. Now another ship had joined that surge, one more bow was pointing west, a bow on which the small white numerals read "343."

On the first day out of San Diego, that bow plunged with disconcerting determination into the relatively mild head sea, digging deep and throwing solid water in an unaccustomed way. On the bridge the helmsman sensed a different feel in the way the ship answered her helm; she seemed less crisp and responsive. It was not long before the reason was discovered. Gus Adams, always conservative, had taken aboard an extra twenty tons of fresh water in the peak tanks far up in the bow. As the boilers consumed their feed water and the extra supply was pumped aft, the ship regained her buoyant motion and the helm felt right again.

The first two days out of San Diego were not happy ones for *Abercrombie*'s men. Added to the fresh ache of separation for many of them was the physical agony of seasickness. Sea legs had been lost during the eleven days in port, and stomachs abused by last-night-ashore indulgences reacted violently to the lift and drop of the laden bow and the wallowing roll that went with it. But on the third day, the sun began to bless the little ship with a gentle warmth, the sea flattened to a silver-blue mirror for the drifting cumulus, and at night the moon with its timeless magic made the thought of war obscene.

But obscene or not, the war was there. On the morning of the twenty-ninth, with Oahu's cloud-topped Koolau range clear and green on the starboard bow, a radio message directed antiaircraft gunnery practice, and a few minutes later a twin-engine Martin Marauder came droning out, dragging a target sleeve. *Abercrombie* manned her battle stations, and the forties and twenties slammed their tracer streams up into the tropic sky, searching out the cloth tube as the plane made repeated passes parallel to the ship, up one side and down the other. At the end of thirty minutes, many hundreds of rounds had been expended, the sleeve was thoroughly riddled, and the sky on both sides was peppered with the small gray puffs of the two-pound forty-millimeter projectiles detonating at the end of their effective range.

Every man who did not have a watch station below at Special Sea Details was topside as *Abercrombie* steamed in past Diamond Head, Waikiki and Honolulu and approached the Pearl Harbor entrance. The morning sun, breaking through the cumulus on the mountaintops, flooded down the valleys of Palolo, Manoa and Nuuanu and backlighted the hotels on Waikiki with the famous pink palace of the Royal Hawaiian at their center. Most of *Abercrombie*'s young crewmen gaped unashamedly. Only a few busy months ago they had been immersed in their accustomed daily routines in Sevierville, Bowersville, Centerville, Lynchville and Maryville; in Bartow, Beatrice and Beaver Dam; Wilmington, Torrington, Oshkosh and Travellers Rest; New Iberia, New Philadelphia, New Carlisle, Tempe and Ware Shoals. For most Hawaii had been a picture of Diamond Head on a postcard and headlines about December 7 at Pearl Harbor. Now, in the uniform of their country, they stood on the deck of a man-of-war looking out across a blue sea ruffled by the trades, and there it all was— a moment to preserve in memory.

On the fo'c'sle I gaped with the others, and even Ted Gruhn, who had sailed to war from here before, stood by the anchor windlass, silent and staring at the lush and living beauty of the place.

At Special Sea Details and with her men at quarters in whites, *Abercrombie* picked her way through twenty to thirty other warships—destroyers, DEs, minesweepers, net tenders, little yard tugs and big salvage tugs, patrol craft and subchasers—found the sea buoy, and stood down the channel between pairs of red and black buoys. An assortment of aircraft now buzzed back and forth overhead—Army planes from Hickam Field off the starboard bow, Navy planes from Ford Island still out of sight ahead, and Marine planes from Ewa a few miles down the coast to port. Steadily the land grew closer until the channel narrowed between Hickam and Hammer Point, where the banks were bright with hibiscus and the smell of the flowers and the hot, dry earth was in the air. Then suddenly Hospital Point was close aboard to starboard, and on the long balconies of the hospital itself and on the lawn before it, a few convalescing patients in blue robes and nurses in starched white watched the little DE go by. I remembered that it was here that a reserve lietuenant commander had grounded the old *Nevada* on December 7 after enemy planes had thwarted her attempt to get to sea and she was in danger of sinking in midchannel, blocking the harbor entrance.

Beyond Hospital Point *Abercrombie* angled off to port across the end of the Ford Island runway and the cavernous hangars, rebuilt since that infamous Sunday morning; and at exactly 1047 she moored portside to the *Oberrender* at mooring buoy number four in the sheltered cove of Middle Loch.

Pearl Harbor turned out to be far more than a refueling and reprovisioning stop on the way to war. Instead, it was an intense, accelerated, twenty-day postgraduate curriculum to the Bermuda shakedown. *Abercrombie* spent a lot of time at sea. With the *Stafford* (DE411), the *Roberts* (DE413) and the *Le Ray Wilson* (DE414), she practiced screening and plane-guarding an escort, or jeep carrier, the *Manila Bay* (CVE61). First, the DEs would form a cresent-shaped antisub screen ahead of the stubby little carrier, maneuvering when necessary to stay in the same relative positions as she changed course this way and that. Then, when she turned into the wind and increased speed to launch or recover her planes, one of the escorts would drop back and take position 1,500 yards astern, with her rescue detail and their gear ready on the fo'c'sle to pick up any aviators who for one reason or another might end up in the water. Given the short, rolling and pitching carrier deck, it was easy to see how that could happen. With the carrier heading upwind during flight operations and the DE dead astern, the astringent and distinctive odor of aviation gasoline and the roar of airplane engines at high power became familiar aspects of plane-guard duty.

As an adjunct to operations with the carrier, *Abercrombie* had an opportunity to practice the specialized but urgent art of evading air-dropped torpedoes. Three TBF Avenger torpedo planes (so named after the decimation of the old Devastators at Midway) would roar in, low on the water about 45 degrees on the bow, flying in line abreast, torpedo bays open. Thirty seconds or a minute later, another three would attack in an identical way on the other bow. It appeared inevitable, had the torpedoes been set shallow and fitted with warheads, that *Abercrombie* would be blasted to the bottom. But, surprisingly, with her tight turning circle, she was able to evade all six "fish" every time. Her tactic was to turn toward the first three torpedoes as soon as they were in the water, presenting only her narrow bow as a target and combing the wakes on an exactly reciprocal course. Then, with the first three torpedoes safely clear, she would continue the turn to present her stern to the second set of three torpedoes, taking their same heading and watching their wakes pass up her sides. Had they been the real thing, she would of course at the same time have been blasting away at the attackers with every gun aboard. It was highly realistic and exciting training, from which the crew gained a new confidence in the fighting ability of their little ship.

That new confidence became evident at the almost daily antiaircraft practices. With increasing regularity *Abercrombie* riddled the target sleeve; and on two successive days the twenties severed the towline, sending the cloth tube into the sea like a dropped sock, to the lusty cheers of the crew.

Abercrombie's big guns were worked out as well, firing special red-dyed ammunition at tall canvas targets rigged on sledges towed by a fleet tug. There were night shoots, with star shells breaking over the target and drifting down while the splashes of armor-piercing projectiles bracketed and straddled. And there were daylight shore bombardment exercises, with *Abercrombie* running parallel to the shore of the target island of Kahoolawe while both five-inchers methodically sought out target after target on the barren coastal hills and gunsmoke and cordite briefly enveloped the ship.

Red Bond, DE343's Assistant Gunnery Officer, took up temporary residence ashore to attend an intensive thirty-day gunnery school under the auspices of Commander, Destroyers, Pacific Fleet.

Since *Abercrombie*'s primary task was to defend against submarines, she spent a day at sea playing hide-and-seek with a Pearl Harbor-based U.S. submarine, a training session that also helped the sub, which was scheduled for a war patrol in enemy waters.

At the end of each period of underway exercises, *Abercrombie* returned to one of the big concrete mooring buoys in Middle Loch which she shared at various times with *Roberts, Stafford, Oberrender* and *Le Ray Wilson*.

In port, the training still went on. Gun crews spent hours on the gunnery range, working out with the same weapons as aboard ship; lookouts, director operators and bridge watch standers spent more hours before the fast-flashing screens of recognition training; five radarmen attended a special CIC school; repair parties went to a fire-fighting school at the Naval Base, attacking and extinguishing very real, flaring and smoking oil fires with fog and foam, and building their confidence as a result; men assigned to rescue details went over to Ford Island to learn how to locate and operate cockpit enclosure releases and escape hatches on the TBF Avenger torpedo plane, the FM-2 Wildcat, the F6F Hellcat fighter, and the SB2C Helldiver divebomber.

Although most of these sessions went smoothly, there was an occasional foul-up. On Repair II's day at fire-fighting school, the whaleboat became overscheduled and never arrived to return the nine men to the ship at the end of the day. But the school staff was more than equal to the challenge. They provided *Abercrombie's* smoke-smelling and soot-smeared sailors with hot showers and a hot meal, broke out a keg of homemade pineapple wine (the pineapple trains ran past the school area), and finally dragged out clean mattresses and bedded the fire fighters down in a cool and spacious recreation room. Don Wood reported it was the best training duty he had yet experienced.

Somehow, along with the heavy training curriculum there was some time for liberty in Hawaii. Every man had an opportunity for a bus tour of Oahu. One man from each division—selected by cutting cards, drawing straws, or drawing numbers from a white hat—spent three days at the Royal Hawaiian Hotel in Waikiki. Signalman Tom Skoko drew the ace of hearts and represented the bridge gang at the Royal. He shared a single room with five other sailors, was locked into the hotel from sunset to sunrise and could not go swimming from the famous beach because of the rolls of barbed wire at the water's edge, but he enjoyed the luxury of the legendary Royal and the bars, shops and sights of Waikiki and Honolulu nevertheless.

For the men who did not rate liberty in town, there was plenty of softball competition on the dozen or so well-laid-out diamonds of the Naval Base. After one such game, played despite an afternoon squall that turned the ball field into a mudhole, *Abercrombie's* team had to be washed down with a firehouse before returning aboard.

On 16 September two new members were added to *Abercrombie's* little wardroom. Ensign James F. Russell reported aboard as Supply and Disbursing Officer, and Ensign E. Merton Olson came on as Assistant First Lieutenant. Jim Russell was a likable Irishman from Newtonville,

Massachusetts, and Boston College who knew his own job and was eager to learn more outside of it. No one was more delighted to have him aboard than Art Hellman, who as Stores Officer had been doing the "supply" side of Jim's job since the ship's commissioning and without having had any formal training. And no one was happier to see Mert Olson (the E. was for Elmer) than the First Lieutenant. Mert was five years my senior, a slim, quiet, steady, thorough midwesterner from Hartington, Nebraska, who fitted into the ship's organization, his new job and the wardroom mess as though he had been working toward that goal all his life. He turned out to be the kind of assistant one dreams of but seldom sees. Mert would understand a problem at once and take appropriate corrective action without waiting for orders. When given instructions, he followed them with such reliability that soon I was secure in the happy knowledge that I could tell him once that a job needed doing and then forget about it because it was certain to be done and done well. Mert went into immediate training as Officer of the Deck, standing his watches under instruction with me.

On Tuesday, 19 September, postgraduate school was over. The last souvenir gifts from Hawaii were mailed, and the last letters censored and sent home. At precisely 1619 *Abercrombie* was under way on the final lap of her long westward journey to the war. Her destination: Manus in the Admiralty Islands, only recently wrested from the enemy. Her mission: escort and screen the tanker transport *General Hase*. Her departure instructions: rendezvous with *General Hase* with Barber's Point bearing 292½ degrees true, and the Royal Hawaiian bearing 063.

For eleven days the big gray ship and the small one in dazzle camouflage slanted southwestestward across the broad blue curve of the South Pacific, passing between the clustered atolls of the Gilbert and Marshall Islands, crossing on successive days into east longitude and south latitude as first the international date line and then the equator fell astern. Many crewmen scratched their heads and tried to figure out how it was that aboard the *Abercrombie* they had no Saturday the twenty-third of September but skipped directly from Friday to Sunday. The old salts explained that it really had not been done right; Navy tradition called for crossing the date line east to west early on Sunday morning so that there would be no day off, and west to east on Friday morning in order to have two Friday field days for cleaning ship.

A few hours before the ship was scheduled to cross the equator, chief machinist's mate Schoeneman as King Neptune convened his court, and ordered into effect the first phase of the ceremonies that were required to transform "lowly pollywogs" who had never sailed into south latitude into "trusty shellbacks" who had. The second phase would have to await the ship's arrival in port when it would not detract from her vigilance or readiness.

The first phase of the ceremonies concentrated primarily on Assistant Engineer Otto Braunsdorf, known to the crew as "Junior," who was made to don an asbestos suit and stand in the eyes of the ship with a so-called telescope fashioned from a three-foot length of fire hose to "locate the line," and a grapnel and a coil for picking it up as it was crossed.

For the entire eleven days the sea was calm, the sky clear, the sun hot and the horizon uniformly empty. The two ships drawing their seventeen-and-a-half-knot wakes down the curve of the globe might have been the only ones on the planet. Watch followed watch in the now-accustomed routine. There were flag-hoist drills between the ships, the bright flags soaring in careful sequence out of the bags and up the halyards to the dip, pausing to be understood, shooting to the yardarm, then plummeting back down to be bagged again.

On the morning of Sunday the twenty-fourth, *Abercrombie* went alongside *Hase* for her first actual underway refueling. *Hase* slowed to twelve knots and Katschinski eased the ship up parallel on the tanker's starboard side, fifty to seventy-five feet away, until her bridge was opposite the "Sugar" flag draped across a guntub on the larger ship, then slowed to maintain position. A line-throwing gun cracked from *Abercrombie's* fo'c'sle, and a long brass pin trailing a light line arched over and draped itself across the transport. It was quickly picked up and a heavier "messenger" line was secured to it. On *Abercrombie's* deck the shot line and messenger were hauled back in, bringing over an eight-inch manila towing hawser. With the hawser secured well forward on the *Hase* and tending aft at a sharp angle to the big towing bitts just under *Abercrombie's* bridge, other messenger lines went over fore and aft and were hauled back aboard, bringing with them two heavy black, four-inch fuel hoses, which were thrust down into *Abercrombie's* fueling trunks and secured with light line to pad eyes so they could not pull out. A heaving line from the transport brought over a phone cable rigged bridge-to-bridge, and a distance line, marked off by red, yellow, blue, white and green flags every twenty feet, was secured on the transport and kept taut by the DE sailors for a constant check on the width of the twelve-knot river of blue Pacific water rushing between the ships. Then after a go-ahead by phone, the *Hase* started pumping, and the black Navy Special fuel oil gushed into *Abercrombie's* tanks at a rate of fifteen thousand gallons an hour from each hose. Down below, Joe McGrath, the "Oil King," and his assistants watched their gauges and turned their valves to guide the torrent of oil evenly into service and storage tanks so that the ship would maintain her trim. In an hour and forty minutes the tanks were full, the hoses were capped and swung back across to the transport, distance and phone lines were returned, and last of all, the big towing hawser was sent back. Then, while the *Hase* maintained her twelve knots, the DE angled away, her stern settling as she increased speed with a chuff of brown smoke from her stack, and dashed back out to her screening position three thousand yards ahead.

The only things to see on that long and peaceful voyage were the afternoon rain showers which, suspended from the bases of their parent clouds, swept like watery curtains across the face of the sea, and an occasional waterspout, looking exactly like the seagoing tornado it was, a dark tube reaching down from a black cloud, joining a matching but shorter protuberance from the surface, together forming a spiraling snake of water between cloud and sea. The waterspouts moved rapidly across the surface—*Abercrombie*'s radar tracked one at fourteen knots—and as in a tornado, the low atmospheric pressures and high wind velocities in and around those water columns were potentially destructive, but none came close enough to be a threat. They appeared easy enough to evade, given *Abercrombie*'s speed and maneuverability.

On the long run down to Manus, in the same corner of the world where it had happened, I persuaded Tom Parlon to tell the story of the night torpedoing of the merchantman to which he had been assigned as Armed Guard officer.

The vessel was the S.S. *William K. Vanderbilt* out of San Francisco, a new seven thousand-ton liberty ship, steaming alone and empty from Efate in the New Hebrides to Suva, Fiji. She was equipped with a three-inch gun at the stern, a forty-millimeter on the bow and a twenty-millimeter on either side of the bridge structure amidships. To man the guns and help with flashing light, semaphore and flag-hoist communications, Tom had a crew of fifteen U.S. Navy sailors. The sailors slept aft in a compartment directly under the three-inch gun. Tom, the merchant Master and the First Mate had staterooms below the bridge amidships.

At 0220 on 17 May 1943, two hundred miles west of Suva, with the ship making seven to eight knots in bright moonlight, not zigzagging, Tom was awakened by the jolt and blast of a torpedo hitting the ship well aft on the port side. The roar of the explosion was followed immediately by the sound of the ship's steam engines racing out of control, then stopping. It was apparent that the torpedo had blown off the propeller or shaft and propellor both. Tom and his crew had been sleeping fully dressed except for their shoes, according to his standing order, and they immediately manned their guns. But there was nothing visible on the calm, moonlit sea to shoot at, and the only round fired was one from the three-incher, which went off accidentally the moment it was loaded because of a short in the firing circuit caused by the torpedo hit.

While the sailors were manning their guns, the ship was already settling at the stern, and the merchant crew rapidly abandoned ship, launching all four lifeboats and all the rafts except one, which was jammed in place. With the sea rising around the stern gun platform, Tom ordered his crew to assemble amidships and went back to his stateroom to get the weighted, perforated metal box containing his classified codes and documents. On the way out the door, box in hand, Tom was deafened and slammed back across the room by a second torpedo, which hit directly below him at 0245, bulging up the deck under his feet, searing the room with flame and then plunging it into darkness. Choking on the cordite fumes from the warhead, he groped his way out, staying close to the bulkheads for fear of falling through the blown-up decks, and joined his men at the one remaining raft. Only then did he give the order to abandon ship. The time was 0255.

The sailors were able to cut away the jammed raft and get it overboard, where it was held alongside the ship by a long painter run to the deck. One after the other, the men jumped feet first, crossed arms holding down their life jackets, and climbed onto the raft. One young sailor refused to go. "Sir, I'd rather stay here than jump in that water!" he said. Tom picked him up and threw him overboard. When he finally jumped himself, there was no one left aboard, he was the last man off the *Vanderbilt*.

With all sixteen men on the raft, Tom ordered the painter cast off, the raft's two paddles manned, and slowly the survivors moved away from the sinking ship, while fighting the flow of the sea into the gaping holes in her side, and picked up two merchant seamen on the way. They were about fifty yards away when the *Vanderbilt* went down, stern first, in a series of hissing explosions at 0306.

At 0307 the long, low black shape of a submarine surfaced just forward of where the liberty ship had sunk. The sub was heading from port to starboard across the now-vanished bow of her victim. Tom and his men could hear the splash and sputter as her diesels fired up, and watched while searchlights on her bridge came to life and began to sweep the seas around her. Tom ordered his men off the raft into the water on the side away from the sub, keeping the eighteen-inch-high steel pontoons of the raft always between them and the enemy.

The sub made a leisurely starboard turn at four or five knots, passing between the Navy raft and the swirl of flotsam marking the spot where the ship had gone down. A searchlight briefly illuminated the empty raft, but the sub continued in a wide circle to starboard. A few minutes after she passed the raft, the sub swung by one of the lifeboats, and Tom's men heard with horror the rattle of machine-gun fire. Apprehension increased in the little group of sodden sailors clinging to the offside of the raft as the sub continued her starboard turn in a sweeping loop and headed back, straight for them. It looked to Tom Parlon as though the enemy skipper had decided to ram the raft and chop up its occupants in his screws. Tom ordered his men to slip out of their life jackets, but keep them handy and stay as low in the water as they could and still breathe. There were some desperate minutes as the sub's bow bore down on the men cowering behind the frail protection of two pontoons with a wood platform between, so desperate that several of the men broke under the strain and in hoarse whispers urged Tom to surrender rather than be ground up or drowned. "Hell, no!" he told them. "You heard that machine gun. That's what we'll get if they see us. We're going to sweat it out right here." He was right. At the last minute the submarine turned a little to starboard to clear the raft. But then it stopped about ten yards away. The Americans could hear voices speaking Japanese, apparently giving orders and responding. A searchlight came on and flooded the empty raft. The survivors held their breaths. Several men took gulps of air and submerged completely. Then the machine gun began to rattle, sounding loud and vicious at such close range. It fired a short burst of half a dozen rounds, paused, fired another burst, paused, fired again, for a total of four bursts —about twenty to twenty-five rounds. Deep in the water behind the raft, the survivors could not tell where the bullets were hitting. Then, blessedly, there were more orders and replies in Japanese, the firing stopped, the light went out, and the sub, diesels muttering, moved off across the moonlit sea, passed slowly through the spreading patch of debris left by the sunken ship, and submerged with a clanging of hatches and a roar of escaping air.

As the sky began to lighten, the men looked at each other and found they were black and slimy with fuel oil, which explained their semiblindness and the painful smarting of their eyes. At dawn the *Vanderbilt's* motor lifeboat, commanded by her Second Mate, chugged up to the raft, towing a second lifeboat, and took the Navy crew and the two merchant sailors aboard. As the water casks and emergency supplies were being transferred from raft to boat, the men found out where the machine-gun rounds had gone; a cask and a sealed metal container of emergency rations had several bullet holes apiece and were abandoned with the raft. By midmorning all four of the merchantmen's lifeboats were assembled and lashed together. *Vanderbilt's* radio operator had been able to send an SOS giving the ship's position, and the message had been acknowledged. The survivors settled down to wait.

At noon they heard the loudening drone of aircraft engines, and squinting up with reddened eyes into the blazing tropic sky, they saw a Mariner patrol plane fly low overhead and settle into easy circles. A signal light blinked from an open hatch abaft the wing. Tom's signalman read it and waved a spread-armed "Roger." "P-C C-O-M-I-N-G F-R S-U-V-A," it flashed. "E-T-A 3–6 H-R-S." A PC, Tom knew, was a 170-foot steel subchaser capable of nearly twenty knots. This happy news was even more welcome in view of the four or five twelve-foot sharks which had arrived at sunup and had circled hungrily around the clustered boats all morning.

The PC arrived at dusk the following day, rigged a cargo net down her side, and *Vanderbilt's* oil-soaked and thoroughly sunburned survivors scrambled aboard to safety. At the Army hospital in Suva, when the clinging oil was finally removed, Tom discovered that he was missing eyebrows, eyelashes and front hair—singed off by the explosion of the second torpedo.

One result of that experience was that Tom, having very logically concluded that "submarines held all the cards," promptly applied for sub training and duty. His presence as *Abercrombie's* Gunnery Officer was the result of the denial of that application because of age. He was thirty-two. Another result was his determination to do everything possible to train both himself and his men in the use and care of weapons and equipment, to inspire and motivate those in his charge, in order to avoid ever again being placed *in extremis* on the ragged, crumbling edge of bare survival.

Abercrombie followed *Hase* in past the outlying reefs and low, sandy islands of Manus early on the morning of Saturday, the last day of September. She was sent immediately to fuel from a small yard oiler, and then assigned an anchorage at the east end of the miles-long Seeadler Harbor just inside the entrance. As soon as the anchor chain had rumbled out and the black anchor ball run up her forestay, the second and more comprehensive phase of initiation ceremonies began for all the lowly "pollywogs" who had become "shellbacks" on crossing the equator and then "golden dragons" on crossing the date line.

Chief machinist's mate Schoeneman as King Neptune, suitably attired and wielding a gilded trident symbolic of his office, held court on the fantail and decreed various ordeals for the pollywogs, who had been ordered to appear before him wearing only white regulation, boxer-type skivvy shorts. (Little George Ferroni, *Abercrombie's* laundryman, arriving on deck in polka-dot shorts, was forced to remove them and be initiated in the raw.) All pollywogs were made to crawl through a long canvas tube about three feet in diameter into which had been thrown assorted slippery and evil-smelling refuse from the galley, while a double row of shellbacks wielded canvas straps against their vulnerable sterns. At the destination end of the tube a fire hose at full pressure materially slowed their progress and added to their already considerable discomfort.

Then one by one they were forced to kiss the "Royal Baby"—the hairy protruding belly of shellback Dave Allen, smeared with grease and an evil-smelling cheese—and then had the same substance liberally applied to their faces and hair. Ted Gruhn, as the "Royal Barber", supervised a team of grinning sadists armed with scissors and clippers who did weird and wonderful things to the tonsures of the persecuted pollywogs. One of the officers came in for special treatment. *Abercrombie's* Engineering Officer, "Gloomy Gus" to his men, was fitted out with an old enlisted-man's jumper on which was sewn a handmade rating badge with the conventional three chevrons and eagle of a first class petty officer, but in the space between, denoting his specialty, was a graphically drawn horizontal phallus, designating him a "first class prick."

Gus also came in for special attention by Ted Gruhn, the Royal Barber, who although relatively gentle with the other commissioned pollywogs, left his old nemesis with only a Mohawklike tuft on the front and center of his scalp. Gus, who had apparently resigned himself in advance, tolerated his ordeal with unexpected good humor.

All these shenanigans were also enjoyed by the crews of *Elden* (DE264) and *Gendreau* (DE639), which had tied up to *Abercrombie's* starboard and port sides, respectively, shortly after her anchor went down.

Manus was filled with gray ships and with rumors of a huge forthcoming amphibious operation. Only a degree and a half south of the equator, it was humidly hot, the heat somewhat relieved several times a day by lukewarm, drenching showers.

Abercrombie's priority project at Manus, especially in view of the approaching operation (the rumors had to be right or what were all these ships doing there?), was to make her main battery fully functional. The two 5-inch guns worked well for a dozen or so rounds, but in the sustained practice firing at Pearl Harbor, the breech blocks and the operating shafts which worked them had heated up and jammed after twenty to twenty-five firings, giving Red Bond the risky chore of freeing up the hot gun mechanism with its projectile and load of propellant powder still in the breech.

Obviously this was no way to go to war. The ship had sailed from Pearl before Tom could have shore-based ordnance experts come aboard to analyze the problem, but on the way to Manus he had attempted in *Abercrombie*'s little machine shop to lathe down the operating shafts where they showed gripe marks from the jamming, and to hand lap the breech blocks with emery cloth. The day after the initiations, Red arrived in Manus from the school at Pearl, and he and Tom drew a new operating shaft from one of the destroyer tenders and installed it. But when *Abercrombie* went outside the harbor for test firings, both guns jammed again. The only thing to do was to get the tender to lathe a few thousandths of an inch off the shafts where they were binding. The gunnery warrant officer on the tender refused to do that, citing Bureau of Ordnance regulations against it. After a conference with Parlon and Katschinski, Bond volunteered to do the lathing personally, regulations or not. He took one shaft down .007 inches and reinstalled it. *Abercrombie* got under way and test-fired the gun. No jamming. Red removed and lathed down the second shaft. Back at sea the shaft also passed the test. *Abercrombie* had no further problems with her main battery.

At the unbelievably sweaty and crowded Fleet Officers' Club at Manus, I ran into my friend and fellow First Lieutenant, Larry Flynn of the *Suesens* (DE342), our division flagship. I learned from him that it was his ship that had been involved in the Buzzards Bay collision I had heard reported on the radio news when passing through Greenfield, Massachusetts, in late June. Larry had, in fact, been the Officer of the Deck at the time and he told me the story.

Suesens had been about a week in advance of *Abercrombie* all along, commissioned a week earlier and following the same Orange-Galveston-Bermuda-Boston itinerary a week ahead. She sailed from Boston on 29 June at 1455, ran just offshore to the Cape Cod Canal, and by 2030 had dropped the canal pilot, and was headed southwest down Buzzards Bay at fifteen knots as night fell. At 2106 she increased speed to twenty knots in the smooth, sheltered waters of the bay and had unlimited visibility. At 2135 her lookouts picked up the red port running light and white mast lights of another ship just slightly on the port bow (bearing 355 degrees relative). Radar reported a range of five miles. Larry could see three vertical white lights above the port running light and identified the other vessel as a tug with a tow. As the range rapidly decreased, *Suesens* maneuvered to hug the starboard side of the buoyed channel so that the two ships could pass port to port on opposite headings as required by Inland Rules of the Road. When the range closed to eight hundred yards, she sounded a single short blast indicating her intention to pass port to port. There was no sound from the approaching ship. Several seconds elapsed, with the yards of dark water rapidly shrinking between the two ships. *Suesens* sounded another short blast, and when there was still no response, Larry ordered, "Right standard rudder," electing to leave the marked channel in the hope of avoiding collision. With the DE swinging to starboard, he sounded a third short blast, but now it was too late. The rudder was spun to right full, both engines were stopped, the collision alarm howled throughout the ship, and the crew set to slamming and dogging down all watertight doors and hatches.

At 2147, just twelve minutes after the stranger had first been sighted, there was a rending crash at *Suesens*'s bow, followed by the shriek and snap of splintering wood and a confusion of urgent shouting in which the only intelligible words were: "Abandon ship! Abandon ship!" At the same instance, *Suesens*'s fo'c'sle crew was startled by the sudden arrival of an additional man. A badly frightened but agile sailor had leaped from the bridge of the other vessel onto the DE's bow at the instant of impact.

A minute after impact, *Suesens* backed clear of the splintered wreckage under her bow. Shouts came up from the water alongside, and the dark heads of swimming men appeared. Number one life raft, forward on the starboard side, was released and splashed down among the swimmers. Three minutes after the collision, *Suesens*'s motor whaleboat was in the water pulling in survivors. One officer and seven men were brought aboard and treated for shock, immersion and exposure. They were crewmen of the USS *Valor* (AMC108) a ninety-seven-foot, wooden coastal minesweeper.

At 2206 *Suesens* anchored, turned on her searchlights, and for the next four hours combed the night sea for more survivors. There were none. Five men were missing and presumed dead.

The following morning DE342 got under way, dropped off the survivors at Newport and continued down Long Island Sound through Hell Gate to the Brooklyn Navy Yard, where a court of inquiry was convened and where divers reported no damage to her hull below the waterline. At 0855 on the Fourth of July she steamed out of the East River, left the Statue of Liberty half a mile abeam to starboard, and resumed her passage to the Pacific. At Pearl Harbor *Suesens* got a new skipper.

At Manus I encountered another good friend, one we seemed destined to follow all up the Pacific. His name was Owen B. Murphy, and he was skipper of a beat-up old destroyer transport, the *Humphreys* (APD12), converted from a World War I flush-deck, four-stack destroyer. His primary mission was the relatively hairy one of transporting Underwater Demolition Teams (UDTs) of frogmen to selected invasion beaches *before* the invasion, to reconnoiter and remove underwater obstacles. This was ironic in a way because "Murph" was a former Merchant Marine officer, a seaman who loved ships but hated guns. In the first months of the war we had been instructors together at the Naval Reserve Midshipmen's School in New York, and had lived in the same apartment building up in Riverdale. Murph was about ten years my senior, a lieutenant when the rest of us were ensigns, and he and his wife Alice became kind of an *ex officio* uncle and aunt to the group of young instructors and their brides who worked and lived together in close proximity. He was a warm, likable, salty Irishman and a true friend. He had been at Pearl while *Abercrombie* was there, but there had been little time to visit. At Manus there was.

For two long, hot weeks, Seeadler Harbor filled with warships—blocky little escort or jeep carriers; long, low LSTs looking like small tankers with their flat decks and aft superstructures; real tankers, big AOs, and smaller AOGs and diesel tankers; bulky troop transports, their sides lined with landing craft in davits; scores of square-built LCIs with submarinelike conning towers and extendable ramps to port and starboard on their foredecks; dozens of the new LSMs that looked like very small carriers because of the island structure far over to starboard, which left their cavernous well decks unobstructed; dozens more destroyer types, lithe and lethal-looking *Fletcher*s with their five 5-inch guns all on the center line; fast transports converted from World War I four-stackers; DEs like *Abercrombie* and her sisters, and older ones with higher bridges and three-inch guns; and an assortment of the smaller ships so familiar to me from the Mediterranean—wooden subchasers and minesweepers, longer steel PCs, and still larger, beamier PCEs.

As the harbor filled with ships, it also filled with rumors. It was apparent to the dullest man at Manus that a mighty force was gathering. The question of utmost import to every man in that force was "What is its objective?" One had only to glance at a map of the Pacific to come up with any number of possibilities. The recapture of Singapore? The seizure of the Dutch East Indies with their oil and rubber? The liberation of the Philippines? An assault up the long ladder of volcanic islands that stretched southward from the Marianas to Japan? The reconquest of Hong Kong and a linkup with Chiang Kai-shek? All of those conjectures and a dozen others had their advocates, but no one actually knew. Certainly no one in *Abercrombie* did.

Then on Tuesday 10 October an officer-messenger wearing a sidearm came aboard with a heavy, tightly wrapped document that he would deliver only to the ship's Custodian of Registered Publications. Keith Wheeling came out to the quarterdeck, signed for it, logged it in and delivered it to the Captain. Now someone in *Abercrombie* knew.

On the tenth, ships began to leave Manus. They were mostly mine-sweepers—converted destroyers, old and new; stubby, square-bowed, 220-foot AMs; and even stubbier 136-foot wooden YMSs, with their high bows and high bridges giving the impression they would roll to a ripple; and a salting of destroyers as escorts. On the eleventh the LSTs reeled in their big stern anchors and turned their blunt bow doors toward the harbor entrance, their decks dark with troops. On the twelfth a dozen escort carriers (CVEs) filed past *Abercrombie*'s anchorage and disappeared to seaward with their escorts of destroyers and DEs. Among the DEs, slicing purposefully down the long, hot harbor toward the narrow exit channel were *Wann*, *Oberrender* and *Roberts* of *Abercrombie*'s own Escort Division 69; old friend *Le Ray Wilson* (DE414); and *John C. Butler* (DE339) and *Raymond* (DE341) from that distant building yard at Orange on the Sabine in what already seemed another world and age. One of the little carriers was also familiar—*Manila Bay* (CVE61), her short deck jammed with Wildcats and Avengers, wings folded, crowded aft. *Abercrombie* had worked out with her, screening and plane-guarding during the postgrad workouts at Pearl.

For three days on all sides of *Abercrombie*, anchor chains clanked up or were unshackled from mooring buoys, jacks and stern colors dropped and steaming ensigns soared to gaffs, engine order telegraphs jingled, and warships moved toward the harbor entrance, fell into single file and steamed out.

Why was everyone leaving while *Abercrombie* still swung around her hook in the steamy swelter of the Admiralties? Was she part of a reserve force to be thrown into the breach if things went badly? Was she scheduled to bring up reenforcements later? Or was she just going to sit this one out after the long voyage from the States and all the workouts and work-ups she had undergone? Only Katschinski knew and he was saying nothing.

In what might have been but assuredly was not a concession to superstition, no ships left Manus on Friday the thirteenth of October.

But the next day it was *Abercrombie*'s turn.

BOOK · II

1. Samar

SHORTLY AFTER 1600 on the fourteenth of October, two DEs and two jeep carriers stood out past the sandy, tree-lined islands at the entrance to Seeadler Harbor and turned due west. They were *Abercrombie, Suesens, Kadashan Bay* (CVE76) and *Omaney Bay* (CVE79). Behind them Manus was virtually empty of ships; but ahead, ordered columns of landing craft and troop transports spread across some 30 degrees of horizon, ploughing westward behind a curving screen of destroyers and DEs and flanked by smaller escorts.

As soon as the two carriers had settled down on course astern of the convoy with the DEs screening ahead, Katschinski pulled down the mouthpiece of the public address system and depressed all three selector switches to send his voice to every manned compartment of the ship.

"Now hear this," he said, as serious as I had ever seen him, "this is the Captain speaking. Now that we are at sea, I am permitted to tell you the objective of the force which we are now escorting." He paused, and there were only the coarse hum of the blowers and the steady pinging of the sonar. "Our objective is the island of Leyte. We are on our way to liberate the Philippine Islands. *Abercrombie* and *Suesens* will screen *Omaney Bay* and *Kadashan Bay* while they provide air cover for this force on the approach to Leyte. In the objective area we will join other CVEs and their escorts to cover the landings and support the troops. Determined enemy opposition is to be expected." Katschinski paused then went on less formally. "This is what we have been training for. We are ready. I expect every man to do his job to the very best of his ability. Good luck."

The silence that had descended on the ship held for several moments after the Captain finished speaking. Men looked at each other wordlessly, each thinking his own thoughts.

Then the talk began.

Liberate the Philippines! It had been apparent since Panama that another big move was coming and that when it came *Abercrombie* would

111

play her part. But what a ring that phrase had! History was in it. A turning of the Japanese tide of invasion and conquest. A fulfillment of Douglas MacArthur's often-quoted promise, "I shall return." There was a confident boldness to the very concept. With the Philippines in U.S. hands, the enemy would be cut off from all the resources to the south that, risking national survival, they had gone to war to get. To let that happen would be to accept the inevitability of eventual defeat. The Japanese would have to oppose it with everything they had. And when they did, *Abercrombie's* men knew that they would no longer be comfortably remote, reading about the event in the paper or hearing of it on the radio. They would be there, at their battle stations, doing whatever job was assigned to counter whatever form of opposition took place.

Hardly anyone in *Abercrombie* had heard of the Philippine island of Leyte, but when they checked the chart spread out in the pilothouse, Katschinski's announcement became even more dramatic. The attack on the Philippines would not be a conservative slogging northward through the islands from Mindanao, but a daring assault on the central portion of the chain, nearly halfway to Manila.

Reaction to the Captain's announcement was as diverse as *Abercrombie's* crew. There was no cheering but there was a lot of excited talk. The young sailors, who were in the majority, reacted with real or feigned bravado. To them the mass of troop-laden fighting ships ahead with their steel ring of escorts and the dozens of armed aircraft snarling off and back on the carrier decks were obviously invincible. For the last four days at Manus they had watched other armed and loaded warships steaming seaward, and they knew that they were assigned the same mission somewhere up ahead. And if by some remote and implausible chance this force were to get into trouble, there was always the fabled Admiral Halsey, with the attack carriers and new, fast battleships of Task Force 38 (even then smashing up enemy planes and bases on Formosa), who would come riding to the rescue like the cavalry of the silver screen, assuring the eventual victory of the good guys.

The older hands who had been shot at—Harry Whitworth, Jimmie Allen, Kella Turner, Ted Gruhn, Paul Fry, Harry Miles, Jim Triplett— tended to be quieter and more thoughtful, remembering the random and unpredictable nature of action once joined, the long shots which so often beat the odds, and the sure things which suddenly are not so sure.

In *Abercrombie's* little wardroom there was a sober sense of history in the making, a feeling of relief now that the nature of the operation was known, and a welcoming of movement after two weeks of sweltering stagnation at Manus. Some of that sense of history came from knowledge of the scale and scope of the assault as listed in the Operation Order—as many ships en route from Hollandia, New Guinea, as from Manus, the Army Rangers in fast transports seizing the approaches to Leyte, the old battlewagons lumbering westward to batter the beaches with their heavy guns, the Army Air Corps and Marine squadrons massing for the attack, the fast carriers flattening air opposition throughout the area. My own private journal of those days records that "I was happy to leave on our first operation—my first, after all those months of preparation—against the Japs." And under the heading of Monday, 16 October, "As I write this I am again very much aware of the pages of tomorrow's history books that will be born out of this moment, this day, this week."

Perhaps the best term for the mood in DE343 as she tended her carriers and turned her bow toward the enemy for the first time was restrained exhilaration. And the exhilaration was restrained by more than just a natural anxiety about hostile action off the beaches of Leyte. The bulky Operation Order delivered to Katschinski in Manus included a specific warning that enemy submarines could be expected to oppose the invasion forces converging on the attack area. Further, up to eight German subs were reported to be operating with their Japanese allies—which meant not only a more experienced and skillful enemy, but the added threat of the new German acoustic torpedo designed to home on the propeller noises of a target ship. And this warning against subs was no *pro forma* verbiage of a staff officer attempting to cover all contingencies. On 3 October *Shelton* (DE407), operating with two jeep carriers off Morotai, had been torpedoed and sunk by a submarine, with thirteen killed and twenty-two wounded. *Shelton*, like *Stafford*, *Wann* and *Roberts*, was a product of Brown Shipbuilding in Houston, commissioned less than a month before *Abercrombie*.

In view of the submarine threat, the eight-knot speed of advance of the convoy seemed excruciatingly deliberate. There was not a man in *Abercrombie* who was not grateful to be operating with the carriers, which ran up their flag hoists half a dozen times a day and sheered out of formation into the wind to launch or recover while DEs 342 and 343 screened ahead or plane-guarded astern.

Flight operations began just before dawn and ended well after sunset with at least four launches and recoveries between. The first and last patrols were TBM Avengers on antisub sweeps whose mission was to drive down any submarines shadowing or approaching the convoy before they could reach attack position. Between dawn and dusk a Combat Air Patrol (CAP) of four FM-2 Wildcats was maintained overhead as a precaution against air attack.

Out of the whole broad spectrum of chores to which *Abercrombie* was assigned during her short and violent active life, carrier operations were by far her crew's favorites. There was an inherent drama in the burst of bright bunting at the signal halyards; in the sharp, fast turnaway from the crawling convoy and the welcome breeze over bridge and deck as speed built up; and in the roar of aircraft engines on the carriers' stubby decks that rose to sustained successive snarls as the blue-winged planes made their short runs and took the air, the agile Wildcats leaping skyward, the heavier Avengers lumbering level with the deck or sinking slightly as they picked up speed. As the Wildcats climbed out, their landing gear folding, they bobbed gently as the pilots' right hands, holding the stick, absorbed some of the motion of their left hands, which were cranking up the wheels.

With the outgoing patrol launched, the returning planes swept in low over the carriers, from stern to bow, to land. They roared overhead in pairs or fours stepped back in right echelons. At the carrier bow the lead plane flipped into a steep left bank, slammed down wheels and hook, and leveled out downwind, abeam of the ship on an opposite heading. Three seconds later the next plane in echelon duplicated the maneuver; and three seconds later the next and the next until all four were in the landing pattern. Then one at a time they banked and came snarling up the carrier wake, flaps full down, wheels and hooks dangling, seeming to hang on their whirling props, wings dipping slightly, noses high, responding to the precisely moving paddles of the Landing Signal Officer on his little platform at the port quarter of the deck. As the LSO chopped his right paddle down across his body to the left, the pilot cut throttle, the roar of the engine changed to a popping sputter, and the plane banged down on the deck, bounced slightly then jerked to a stop as the tail hook caught the cross-deck wire of the arresting gear. If *Abercrombie* was astern of the carrier in plane-guard position, the watch on her bridge could occasionally see a crewman dive under the tail of the plane to disengage the hook, hear the renewed roar of its engine as it blasted clear of the landing area, and watch the next plane thump down in the same spot seconds later.

With flight operations temporarily completed, *Omaney Bay, Kadashan Bay, Suesens* and *Abercrombie* dashed back toward the now-distant convoy, the carriers making their maximum speed of eighteen knots and the DEs patrolling ahead at twenty. Back in formation, the carriers took position directly astern of the huge, slow-moving rectangle of ships, and the DEs moved out 60 degrees and three thousand yards to port and starboard, becoming in effect part of the convoy screen but still in position to join up with the CVEs for the next cycle of launch and recovery.

The first few days out of Manus, as the ships steamed at a shallow angle almost parallel to the equator, the daytime heat was like a physical weight pressing down on the men topside and slithering down through the forced-draft blowers to roast the watch below. A slight breeze ruffled the South Pacific, but it came from astern at about the same velocity as the convoy speed, thus producing a relative wind of zero. Relief came only with flight operations, and at nightfall when many men dragged up their mattresses and slept topside. Then *Abercrombie* slipped along through the tepid sea at barely nine knots, patrolling gently back and forth in her assigned sector, sonar pinging and radar spinning. Her surface radar scope showed the geometrically arranged columns of white blobs ahead and the two larger blobs of the carriers back on the quarter while the whole massive array moved inexorably up over the waist of the earth toward Leyte.

The sweep of history was evident as the bristling U.S. task forces converged for the liberation of the Philippines, but the components of that history were individual warships with crews made up of individual Americans performing specific, routine, unglamorous, sometimes demanding seafaring chores. In the USS *Abercrombie* those chores began with General Quarters (GQ) thirty minutes before sunrise. Since the time of day decreed for the task force differed from that which was normal for those longitudes, sunrise occurred around 0420 and GQ came very early indeed. The daily chores ceased with another General Quarters half an hour before the sun set, again at a similarly unnaturally early 1710. Evening GQ was actually pleasant—at least for men with topside battle stations—because of the spreading, flaming, glorious South Pacific sunsets, which covered half the sky and colored the calm sea with shades from scarlet to violet that were so vivid and yet so delicate that they would cause a man to catch his breath. And when under that impossible panoply of colors the Wildcats and Avengers, beautiful and deadly, came roaring up the wakes to roost, it was actually possible to enjoy the war for fifteen or twenty minutes.

Between sunrise and sunset there were watches to stand, logs to write, meals to be prepared, consumed and cleaned-up after; weapons and machinery to be adjusted and maintained, inspections to be made; paint to be chipped, scraped, primed and repainted in the ceaseless struggle against rust; signals by flag hoist, semaphore, flashing light and voice radio to be sent and received; position reports and fuel status reports to be made; laundry to be done, hair to be cut, bunks to be made up and encased in flameproof covers; knife-edges to be sanded and gaskets to be cleaned; charts to be corrected; radio messages to be copied, decoded, logged, distributed and initialed. And all the while, night and day, whatever else was being done, the primary, eternal chore of keeping an alert watch for the enemy—in the air, on the surface, and especially below the sea—increased in urgency with every slow mile of progress toward the enemy waters and enemy bases ahead.

On the second day out of Manus, 16 October, the men topside at morning GQ could see the high, irregular dark mass of New Guinea broad on the port bow. Radar range was twelve miles. Land was still visible at evening GQ, but faded into the twilight sky back on the quarter. That same day *Abercrombie* picked up official mail from *Kadashan Bay* and *Suesens*, sliding up alongside the other ships, slowing to match speeds, passing lines and hauling the mail bags across, with a seamanlike efficiency that drew a rare "Well done" by flag hoist from the Division Commander in *Suesens*.

Then for three days nothing broke the normal routine except an occasional brief and violent shower which, for one reason or another, the Officer of the Deck had been unable to evade. Those showers were visible for miles, hanging like gray curtains under their parent clouds and moving slowly across the sea on courses and speeds plotted by radar in CIC. Evading them and yet remaining within the limits of assigned station became a kind of game for the OODs.

On the fourth day the at-sea routine was broken by an accident and a serious injury. A young fireman was lubricating the ram and gear teeth on the steering engine, scooping up the heavy grease and applying it by hand to the shining horizontal athwartships shaft which controlled the rudders through a straight set of gear teeth that turned the gear wheels atop the rudder posts. Topside, the OOD was chasing the carriers and a zigzag plan was in effect. The rudder was busy. The fireman was daubing grease onto the straight gear on the shaft, close to where it meshed with the geared rudder post. As the wheel on the bridge was turned, the shaft moved across the gear wheel away from the fireman, turning the rudders to port. Then the helm was reversed as the ship came to a new course in the zigzag plan. The straight gear moved quickly back across the wheel, taking the young sailor's hand with it. In an instant his hand and then his forearm were ground into the merciless steel gearing, blood spurting, and the bones were crushed like cardboard. Cox'n Jimmie Allen, on watch as emergency helmsman in after steering, saw what was happening and instantly pulled the pin which disconnected the steering engine from bridge control. He spun the wheel that directly controlled the steering engine until the gears reversed and released the fireman's mangled arm, then reengaged bridge control.

On *Abercrombie*'s bridge the helmsman had suddenly lost control in the middle of a turn and in an ocean full of other ships. Before the OOD had a chance to demand where the hell he was going, he sang out, "Lost steering control, sir!" A siren sounded in after steering, bells jingled and the buzzer from the bridge sounded insistently. It was all over in less than a minute, but for an OOD a minute is a long time to have no control of three hundred feet of ship steaming in formation at fifteen knots. On the phone Cox'n Allen explained what had happened, and Doc Bour and his chief arrived from sick bay to care for the fireman, now slumped ashen-faced and blood-spattered on the deck and cradling his mangled arm. As they were helping him away, Gus Adams appeared in the compartment and demanded a personal explanation. When he had heard it, his response was one Allen was never to forget. "Damnit, Cox'n, you risked the safety of the ship. We've got lots of sailors, but only one ship!"

That same day, the young fireman was transferred in a wire stretcher by high line to one of the CVEs for treatment. Amazingly he was back in about a month, proudly showing his shipmates the marks of the gear teeth on hand and arm.

As the invasion forces converged on the Philippines, planes from the fast carriers of Task Force 38 continued to slash and batter at enemy airfields and bases from which opposition to the assault might be launched on Formosa, and the China coast, and in the Philippines themselves. Two reports of those operations came out of *Abercrombie*'s radio shack within two hours—one from Tokyo and one from San Francisco.

From Tokyo:

> Throughout the Empire there is dancing in the streets. The American Navy has suffered its greatest defeat since Pearl Harbor: in aerial attacks on U.S. task forces, Task Force 38 has been scattered to the four winds; 500,000 tons of ships have been sunk, including 15 aircraft carriers, 2 battleships, 4 cruisers and 6 destroyers. Services are being held for 25,000 American dead in this great Japanese victory.

From San Francisco:

> Strikes against the Philippines, Formosa and the China coast continue. No substantial damage has been suffered by any of our battleships and carriers; two medium-sized U.S. ships have been damaged by aerial torpedoes and are returning from the area; during one night and one day 191 Jap aircraft attacked one of our task

forces; 95 were shot down by our fighters, 32 by our AA. We lost 5 planes.

On the same day came this terse comment from Canberra, Australia:

There are four U.S. task forces operating in the western Pacific, any one of which is capable, alone, of defeating the entire Jap fleet.

On the afternoon of the nineteenth, *Abercrombie* was ordered alongside *Omaney Bay* for fuel. It was *Abercrombie*'s first fueling from a carrier. From the fo'c'sle the difference was definite and worrisome. Instead of the smooth vertical sides of a tanker, reassuringly hung with heavy fenders, we looked up at the carrier's island structure projecting some twenty feet out from her side at a level just slightly above *Abercrombie*'s bridge. Forward and aft of the overhanging island, gun sponsons protruded from her side. It was only too apparent that any collision with a carrier would not be the kind of embarrassing but minor brush which *Abercrombie* had experienced with *Chicopee* off Bermuda. But the Captain brought her smartly alongside and held her there while the lines went over and the fuel hoses came back and were secured in their trunks. And then he (with Howard Amos at the wheel) held her there for the hour and a half it took *Omaney Bay*'s pumps, lacking the capacity of those in a tanker, to deliver 41,000 gallons of black oil. Except for some delays in getting the fuel hoses over—attributable as much to the carrier as to the DE—it was a well-executed operation that provided *Abercrombie* with full fuel tanks and increased confidence on the eve of action.

The next day, 20 October, was "A Day," attack or assault day, at Leyte. *Abercrombie*'s task force was approaching the southernmost Philippine island of Mindanao. The sea was relatively calm. Visibility was good. The force continued at its leisurely nine-knot pace. Almost nothing happened. A small escort reported a sub contact, which turned out to be false. A fighter was added to the evening Avenger antisub patrol as a precaution against snoopers. A patrolling Catalina out of Morotai startled the lookouts by breaking a bright green recognition grenade over the force that night. The next morning a Wildcat ran out of gas and made a crash landing near the *Suesens*, which quickly recovered the pilot alive and intact.

Reports from the beachhead told of good progress against light opposition and the attack going as planned. One twin-engine enemy plane was said to have attacked the landing forces, but when taken under fire, it jettisoned its bombs into the sea and crashed in flames.

Then on the twenty-first, *Abercrombie's* men learned that they had been sunk. The news came direct from Radio Tokyo:

> The task force of two carriers, forty transports [fifty-six ships in all] and their escorts approaching Leyte from the New Guinea area, has been annihilated, all ships either sunk or scattered to the four winds.

The only evidence of enemy presence that day was a report from *Omaney Bay* that her Combat Air Patrol was chasing a couple of "bogies" (unidentified aircraft) over Mindanao.

Beneath the jibes at Radio Tokyo and the elation at the lack of opposition at sea and ashore, there was a feeling of unease in *Abercrombie.* It was not like the Japanese to offer such limited and ineffective resistance to a major assault on one of their most vaunted and valuable conquests. They had to be doing *something,* readying some counterblow. And given the size and power of the invading force, it would be a beauty when it came.

At dusk on 21 October, when the last patrol had been recovered off the approaches to Leyte Gulf, the two carriers and two DEs were detached from the force of transports and landing craft, cranked on seventeen knots and turned northeastward to join four other carriers and their escorts, one of three similar groups providing air cover for the landing force. By midnight *Abercrombie's* radar showed the ships she was looking for, and speakers on the bridge and in CIC buzzed and scratched with the staccato chatter of their tactical maneuvering. The voice call of the task unit commander ordering the various course and disposition changes was easy to remember: it was "Taffy 2." At first light on the twenty-second, *Abercrombie, Suesens* and the two carriers joined up with Taffy 2.

The arrangement and employment of jeep carriers and their escorts off Leyte Gulf in those late October days was classic in its symmetry and order. On a clear day an observer from near-Earth space would have seen three pairs of moving concentric circles spaced thirty to fifty miles apart along a north-south axis well offshore across the mouth of the gulf. The northernmost concentric circles (Taffy 3) were off the south end of Samar, the southernmost (Taffy 1) off northern Mindanao, and the middle circles (Taffy 2) directly opposite the entrance. In each pair of circles, the inner one, with a radius of 2,500 yards, was formed by six escort carriers, and the outer one with a radius of 6,000 yards was made up of three destroyers and four or five DEs. Each morning the three circles drew in closer to land and launched their Wildcats and Avengers to strike against enemy bases, to intercept attacking enemy planes, to run antisub patrols over the gulf and its approaches, and to form Combat Air Patrols over the vulnerable amphibious forces along the beaches and anchored off them. Each evening the circular task units pulled back offshore, erecting a barrier of darkness and distance against the hostile land.

When *Abercrombie* and *Suesens* joined the screen of Taffy 2, it was a reunion of old friends. Already present on that six thousand-yard circle around the carriers were *Wann, Oberrender* and *Le Ray Wilson.* The three destroyers, all fast, deadly-looking 2,100-ton *Fletchers,* were *Haggard, Franks* and *Hailey,* none of which *Abercrombie* had encountered before. But one of the CVEs, the *Manila Bay,* was familiar from four days of training operations out of Pearl.

That first morning with Taffy 2, Paul Fry, Red Shiel, Tom Skoko and others in *Abercrombie's* signal gang were kept busy with a stream of flashing-light messages from the screen commander in the *Haggard:* when to make fuel status reports, how to adjust position when an escort left the screen, surface- and air-search responsibilities, fueling schedules, procedures for rescuing downed pilots, special lights to be shown during night air operations, orders to "Expedite!," changing stations. The OODs were as busy as the signalmen. With seven escorts on the screening circle, each had a responsibility for more than 50 degrees of that circle, and each was required not only to remain at all times within that 50-degree area, but to be at different points within it, depending on the maneuvers in progress, and to change position with maximum speed and precision.

Daytime cruising disposition differed from night cruising, and disposition for air operations differed from both daytime and nightime cruising. There were column movements with ships turning in sequence, then plain turns made simultaneously by all ships. During daylight zigzag plans were followed and the escorts alternated plane-guarding for each launch and recovery. CIC was as busy as the OODs and the signalmen, as it sent and acknowledged voice radio transmissions; computed and relayed courses to steer, time to reach stations and closest points of approach to other ships for each change of course or disposition; maintained a continuous and accurate plot, not only of the other ships—especially the flagship, the screen commander, and those in adjacent screening stations—but on the unoccupied center of the formation as well.

Busy it was. Demanding it was. And even with the manufactured breeze of ship's speed, it was hot topside and below. But rewarding it also was. There was a solid feeling of contribution and accomplishment. Half a dozen times a day from first light to no light, the TBMs and FM-2s roared off loaded and droned back with ammo expended or patrols completed. The stubby carriers swung into and back out of the wind, the concentric circles contracted and expanded, the CAP swung in wide circles in the tropic sky, the antisub Avengers prowled the distant horizon —radars rotated, watching—sonars swept the upper levels of an ocean almost five miles deep—and the job got done. The operation, the liberation of the Philippines, was going forward, and *Abercrombie*, although she had not yet seen an enemy, was part of it, doing what she was designed and equipped and her men trained to do; and the feeling was good.

It was a far different kind of invasion from those I had known at Sicily and Salerno with coastal batteries and hostile planes to worry about. So far, off Leyte Gulf my most serious problem was station-keeping during the hectic eight hours out of each twenty-four when I had the deck.

Some of the younger sailors began to believe that this was what war was like and to anticipate the rewards of participation. "What a way to earn a battle star!" one of them said. "No pain, no strain." But the older hands frowned and cut them off. "Stow it!" they told them. "It ain't over yet. Those Japs are tough and tricky. You could still get your ass blown off."

Early on the morning of the twenty-third, the reality of war touched *Abercrombie* for the first time. It was a light touch but sufficient to arrest the trend toward unhealthy complacency.

It was 0540 and the ship was at morning GQ when the word was passed; "Man plane crash stations." We had rehearsed this evolution scores of times, and when I arrived on the fo'c'sle from Repair II, one of the rubber boats was already inflated, the two swimmers were buckling on their harnesses and their inflatable life belts. Vic Bour, the pharmacist's mate, was there with his medical kit, a rigid, wire-built Stokes stretcher was ready on deck and line handlers were standing by. I had checked over the men and their equipment and was reviewing with them the way to bring an injured man aboard, when the PA system blared again: "Plane in the water to starboard." The rubber boat's long painter was led well forward outboard of the lifelines on the starboard side, and the starboard rescue net was cut loose so that it hung down the side of the ship just under the bridge. The ship slowed and turned, passed downwind of an iridescent slick on the sea's surface. The morning breeze carried the strong distinctive odor of aviation gasoline. The whole ship seemed to be holding its breath, watching and listening while the carriers and the other escorts drew away, continuing the dawn launch. Nothing was visible on the surface except that shiny patch of spreading fuel. *Abercrombie* circled once slowly, with all hands straining their eyes and ears, and came back upwind to the gas slick like a hunting hound. Still nothing. Then suddenly there was a voice yelling off to starboard, a strong voice but weakened and diluted by the immensity of the sea. It was a minute or two before we saw him, and then it was only a glimpse as he was lifted to a crest, a tiny dark head, a hint of a yellow Mae West collar, an arm raised when he shouted. He was only a couple of hundred yards away, but he was only a speck, a nearly invisible dust mote in all that waste of water.

When the pilot was sighted, he was abeam to starboard at a distance just about equal to the radius of *Abercrombie*'s turning circle so that simply turning toward him brought the ship no closer to him. In a moment the order came down from the bridge to get the boat over. It flopped in quickly and towed even with the bottom of the rescue net. I scrambled down the net followed by Jim Triplett, a husky machinist's mate from Repair I who had learned to row in a johnboat on the Kentucky River, and "Doc" Bour with his medical kit. Trip and I broke out the boat's two pairs of light aluminum oars, the painter was cast off and we started rowing in the general direction of the downed pilot. From our position, almost precisely at sea level, all we could see was Pacific, but far above us on *Abercrombie*'s bridge a man pointed and that was the way we went. The little boat was light and easy to move but hard to keep on course. A strong, light line trailed from the boat's stern back to the fo'c'sle where it was tended and paid out. In a few minutes Doc Bour, the only man facing forward, had the pilot in sight, and Trip and I followed his directions.

Neither his crash landing, his immersion in that shark-infested sea, nor the chancy nature of his rescue had dampened this pilot's sense of humor. "Good morning, Captain," he said cheerily as we bobbed up to him. "Permission to come aboard?"

"We're damned glad to have you aboard," I told him, and Bour and I unceremoniously hauled him in.

It was not necessary to row back to the ship. A raised-arm signal put the line handlers on the fo'c'sle in motion, and the little boat came home stern first as though motor driven. Two men were at the bottom of the rescue net and two more at the top when we came alongside. As the ship rolled down to starboard, the pilot grabbed the net, the two men at the bottom grabbed him and with the help of the men at the top, pulled him quickly aboard. On successive rolls Trip, Bour and I went up, the boat was hauled aboard, and *Abercrombie* cranked on twenty knots to rejoin the force.

Despite his high spirits, the pilot, who turned out to be a Lieutenant Gerald Lee Bridge, USNR, looked a lot worse under examination in sick bay than he had out there in the water. A gash in the back of his head required two stitches. His back and shoulders were livid with heavy bruises. His face looked as though he had gone several rounds way above his weight class, an effect heightened by two monumental black eyes. He reported that on his predawn takeoff, the deck had tilted at exactly the wrong instant, causing the right wing of his FM-2 Wildcat to catch a twenty-millimeter gun and dumping him into the sea a few hundred yards off the bow.

Chief Bailey sewed him up, treated his bruises and put him to bed in my bunk. There he rested comfortably all morning and later informed me with a battered grin that he had thoroughly enjoyed the pictures of my wife. Shortly after 1300 that day, *Abercrombie* nosed up alongside the starboard quarter of *Marcus Island,* rigged a bo'sun's chair, and Lieutenant Bridge went swinging home.

Exactly a day after the safe return of Lieutenant Bridge to his carrier, it looked as though there would be a repeat of that little operation. At 1315 on the twenty-fourth, *Abercrombie's* men manned their battle stations and spent a couple of hours searching the sea for the three-man crew of an Avenger reported to have crashed in the vicinity of Taffy 2. There were faint ribbons of fuel on the surface but no dark heads above Mae Wests, no raised arms, no shouts. As *Abercrombie* reluctantly returned to her place in the screen, *Oberrender* pulled out and with *Edmonds* (DE406) and two CVEs, *Saginaw Bay* and *Chenango,* from Taffy 3 to the northward, she headed south for Morotai to pick up replacement planes.

Late that afternoon, not quite five days after the initial landings on Leyte, the word that the old-timers had been worried about began to come in. The Japanese, as they had predicted, were not sitting this one out. By radio and flashing light came reports of very heavy enemy task forces converging on the Leyte area. *Abercrombie's* little CIC was no Situation Room, and there was no wall map of the Philippines on which to plot friendly and enemy forces. From dispatches on which she was a legitimate "information addressee," and from occasional intercepts of others out of the flood of voice and Morse code traffic which laced the sky over Leyte Gulf that afternoon and night, the men on DE343 acquired a fragmentary, confusing and exciting picture. At least one and possibly two task forces of battleships, heavy and light cruisers, and destroyers appeared to be approaching from the west, with a third, of unknown composition, heading south from Formosa and northern Luzon. There was a report that one of our submarines had put four torpedoes into an enemy battlewagon in the Sulu Sea. Another said that strong U.S. forces, including several old battleships recently raised from the Pearl Harbor mud and a couple of squadrons of PT boats, were positioned to waylay the enemy in the narrow southwestern approaches to Leyte Gulf. One intercepted voice message ordered some task unit (identity garbled) "plus *Alabama,* plus *Massachusetts,* plus DesDiv [Destroyer Division] One Hundred" to intercept someone (identity also garbled). It appeared that whoever that garbled someone was, he was in trouble; two fast new battleships and half a dozen destroyers were on his tail. The impression of close and imminent action was strong enough to cause speculation as to whether the flashes of major-caliber guns would be visible from Taffy 2's position at the mouth of the gulf. Just before I went off watch at midnight, CIC reported that our PTs in Surigao Strait had made their attacks, and that the old battleships at the top of the strait were engaging the enemy. After Tom relieved me, I spent several minutes searching the night sky to the westward for gun flashes, but none were visible.

As I went below shortly after midnight I remembered that this was the day we were scheduled to fuel.

The feeling aboard the *Abercrombie* as I turned in (fully clothed) that night was excitement with only a tinge of anxiety. After all, sixteen escort carriers with their attendant destroyers and DEs were patrolling east of Leyte; the old battleships, which might be slow but packed lethal punches in an ambush situation, would certainly clobber any enemy attempting to force the strait; *Alabama, Massachusetts* and DesDiv 100 were out there intercepting; and somewhere, presumably close by, was the awesome and patently invincible power of Halsey's Task Force 38 with attack carriers and fast battleships. It looked from *Abercrombie* as though there would probably be one hell of a fight, for which DE343 and her sisters would have a ringside seat but be in little danger.

Then came the morning of 25 October 1944.

In predawn darkness the three pairs of concentric circles had closed the land as usual, and a full hour before sunrise the carriers began launching routine CAP and antisub patrols both for their own task units and for the ships in Leyte Gulf. All launches by all ships were completed by 0600, except for *Omaney Bay,* which sent a special ten-plane search to the northward that had suddenly been ordered by the task force commander at 0155. The last plane of that search left *Omaney Bay*'s deck at 0658, and air operations were over until the next launch and recovery around noon. Taffy 2 secured from General Quarters, and the crews went down to breakfast. In *Abercrombie* breakfast was French toast and syrup with bacon, which I shared with gusto, it being my turn to sample the General Mess. I was back in the wardroom enjoying a cup of coffee before heading for the bridge to relieve Cy DeCoster at 0745 when the general alarm began its loud, insistent clanging, and over the wardroom speaker came the startling announcement, "Man your battle stations! Attack is imminent!" As I slammed out of the wardroom for Repair II, I glanced at the clock. It was 0727.

In the crowded passageway and gear locker that was our battle station, Don Wood reported enemy battleships and heavy cruisers within twenty-five miles and closing. Taffy 3 to the north was already under fire. On the bridge they were hearing orders to arm all Avengers with torpedoes, and the announcement by at least one of the carriers that "we are under attack." The three destroyers of Taffy 2, *Franks, Hailey* and *Haggard* under the screen commander, had been ordered to form a line between the enemy and our carriers, the DEs under ComCortDiv69 to provide a carrier antisub screen ahead.

As soon as the repair parties had reported manned and ready and the ship was fully buttoned up, I climbed up through the hatch above Repair II to the torpedo deck to see what was going on. We were running east through a calm sea with long swells and under an overcast sky at eighteen knots, the top speed of our six carriers which were still in their circular formation. Four identical DEs, *Abercrombie, Suesens, Wann* and *Wilson* formed a shallow crescent ahead of them. Back on the port quarter, three identical *Fletcher*-class destroyers, *Haggard, Hailey* and *Franks*, were silhouetted against the low, dark clouds to the northward. They were in an evenly spaced column and on the opposite course of the carriers and DEs, throwing curves of white water from their bows as they headed back toward the enemy at what looked like thirty knots.

As I watched, there was a sudden mushroom of thick white smoke on the cloudy horizon beyond the three destroyers. A minute or two later, four huge yellow splashes rose from the sea very close to them, towering well above their masts. The destroyers doubled the distance between them and reversed course, forming a protective line between the running carriers and whatever was out there over the horizon. They had hardly settled on the new course before four more yellow splashes bloomed among them, so close and so high that the three slim ships were momentarily buried and hidden by the yellow water.

Astern, although the twelve-knot breeze was on the port beam, several of the carriers were catapulting planes, which quickly joined up in pairs and threes and roared off to the northward. Down in Repair II, Don Wood reported that as the planes headed out, a voice message warned, "You'd better stop them this time!"

The sight of the towering yellow splashes was the first hard evidence that most of the men of *Abercrombie* had that this was a surface action.

So confident were they that no enemy ship could approach across a sea dominated by their own attack carriers and fast battleships, and so certain that the only real threat would be an occasional enemy plane that managed to elude the CAP, that even after they had seen the splashes, most gun crews were still searching the skies for the planes which must have caused them. There were enemy planes in the air that morning, and they gave a very bad time to Taffy 1 fifty miles to the south, but what Abercrombie's men were seeing, and hearing about on voice radio, was a general attack by thirty-knot battleships and heavy and light cruisers with eighteen-, sixteen-, fourteen-, eight-, and six-inch guns on the four 18-knot CVEs of Taffy 3 with one 5-inch gun apiece, and the four DEs and three destroyers of their screen. All four DEs were identical to Abercrombie. Dennis (DE405) had been built at Houston in the same series as half of Escort Division 69. The John C. Butler (DE339) was the first ship of the class, the one most nearly completed when I had first reported at Orange in the early spring. Raymond (DE341) had been third in line at that Orange dock that day. And Samuel B. Roberts (DE413) was a division mate and an old friend from Bermuda, Pearl and Manus, commissioned at Houston three days before Abercrombie.

At 0754, Taffy 2 turned northeast into the wind (and toward the enemy), and all six carriers launched everything that was ready, the planes snarling down their decks and clawing for altitude right on each other's tails, tucking up their wheels and heading north. As Abercrombie slashed out ahead of the turning CVEs at her best speed of twenty-three knots, her men sensed the desperate urgency aboard the carriers. These were not routine air operations. These were carriers in action fighting for their lives. They slammed up into the wind with full rudder. The first planes were moving down the decks before the launch course had been reached, and as the last planes began their takeoff runs, the carriers were already turning southward. Nor did the airborne planes circle overhead as usual to rendezvous. Instead, they formed their Vs and echelons as best they could at low altitude and full throttle, boring straight in against the enemy.

For about a half hour Taffy 2 resumed a southeast course, but at 0833 the ships turned back to windward and launched a sixteen-Avenger strike, covered by eight Wildcats. The launching course took Taffy 2 back toward the enemy, and by the time the last plane left, fourteen-inch splashes began to appear astern.

At 0910 CIC intercepted a voice message from a Kitkun Bay Avenger that two of the enemy battleships were headed straight for Taffy 2 at an estimated twenty-seven knots.

Shortly thereafter Abercrombie's own lookouts reported battlewagon masts rising from the northern horizon, and *Haggard*, *Franks* and *Hailey* were ordered to "prepare for torpedo attack on enemy BBs." A second message, action to *Abercrombie*, read "Dog Easys prepare torpedoes and stand by."

While Garland and Whitelock, *Abercrombie's* two rated torpedomen and their strikers, Heineman and Strawa, worked over the long fish in their triple mount amidships, topping off alcohol, setting running depth, speed and gyros, and checking rudder throw and air pressure for launch, that last message went through the ship at the speed of light. The prospect of a twenty-three-knot daylight torpedo attack against enemy battleships was, to say the least, sobering. A few men paled and sickened, a few blustered and cursed, but most grew quiet and went quietly about their work. There was a feeling akin to fatalism—"what is to be will be"—but heavily laced with a silent, healthy determination. My own mouth was dry at the prospect, but what I did was visit all three repair parties, checking the readiness of the men and their gear.

Neither the destroyers nor the DEs of Taffy 2 made torpedo attacks that day, although planes from our carriers took a decisive part in the action. But just over the horizon to the northward, the DDs and DEs of Taffy 3 did exactly that, and more.

While *Abercrombie*, *Wann*, *Suesens* and *Wilson* were running south-eastward that morning, screening their carriers as they launched, recovered, rearmed and relaunched the planes which finally turned the tide of battle, *Dennis*, *Butler*, *Raymond* and *Roberts*, with destroyers *Hoel*, *Heerman* and *Johnston*, were engaged in a desperate attempt to defend their own CVEs with close-range gun and torpedo attacks against columns of onrushing Japanese battleships and cruisers. The white mushroom of smoke I had seen earlier from *Abercrombie's* torpedo deck was a hit by a major-caliber enemy salvo on CVE *Kalinin Bay*, and much of the darkness low over the water to the north was funnel smoke laid down by the carriers and their escorts to spoil enemy aim.

For *Abercrombie* and her sisters of Taffy 2, the morning of 25 October 1944 meant dashing across a smoothly rolling sea under heavy clouds to maintain station ahead of the busy carriers. It meant tight stomachs and dry mouths. It meant a sky constantly full of aircraft coming and going from all directions and at all altitudes, returning aircraft smoking and unsteady, outbound aircraft heavy and noisy with full power, and carriers that looked from a distance like square honeycombs being worked by bees. It meant a never-to-be-forgotten respect for the men who manned those planes, men, we learned later, who continued time after time to attack the enemy even when all bombs and ammunition had been expended, driving gunners to cover, distracting fire control, forcing evasive maneuvers—and reducing the threat to the carriers.

But to the hundreds of destroyer and DE crewmen of Taffy 3, that late October morning meant bloody wounds, the flaming loss of gallant ships, and death by blast, bleeding, fire, drowning and shark bite.

Although it was a long time before *Abercrombie's* men got the story, this is how it went for the escorts of Taffy 3 just beyond the horizon that terrible morning off Samar.

At 0650, while I was enjoying French toast and bacon with *Abercrombie's* sailors thirty miles to the south, lookouts on bridges identical to ours reported black puffs of AA to the northwest. Two minutes later, while Evaluators in half a dozen CICs were puzzling over who was shooting at whom in that location, an Avenger pilot from Taffy 2's *Kadashan Bay* ended their puzzlement in a most unwelcome way. Out of speakers in the pilothouses and CICs of Taffy 3 came his unbelievable message:

> Enemy surface force of four battleships, seven cruisers and eleven destroyers twenty miles north of your task group and closing at thirty knots.

Any lingering wishful thoughts that *Kadashan Bay's* aviator might have misidentified a friendly task force were cruelly crushed when lookouts reported the unmistakably pagodalike top-hampers of Japanese warships coming up over the horizon. Eleven minutes after the Avenger's initial sighting, bright flashes began to appear at the bases of the pagodas, and at 0659, tall, gaudy purple, yellow and red splashes fountained the sea just outside Taffy 3's ring of escorts.

It was as desperate a situation as any naval commander had ever faced: slow, thin-skinned, poorly armed ships with an escort intended primarily for defense against submarines, under attack by fast, heavily armed and armored first-line warships screened by two squadrons of destroyers (which alone were sufficient to annihilate Taffy 3). But Taffy 3 was commanded by tough and salty Rear Admiral Clifton "Ziggy" Sprague, a combat-tested attack-carrier C.O. and a veteran of December 7 at Pearl Harbor, where his ship had been first to open fire on the attackers. And Ziggy Sprague did all the right things right away. He ordered his carriers to maximum speed. He launched every plane he had against the enemy. He ordered every ship in Taffy 3 to make all the smoke they could from smoke generators and stacks. In plain language he screamed for help from anyone who could give it. And at 0716, with the lethal colored splashes of fourteen-inch salvos straddling his carriers and with the volume and accuracy of enemy fire increasing, Admiral Sprague ordered his escorts to counterattack with torpedoes.

The first to respond was destroyer *Johnston*. Her position in the screen was closest to the rapidly approaching enemy, and she had already been in action for six minutes, laying smoke and slamming her five-gun salvos at the nearest heavy cruiser, the *Kumano*. Now she cranked on twenty-five knots, heeling as she whipped around, and headed straight into the teeth of a column of four heavy cruisers. With all four heavies firing at her and her own guns blazing back and hitting, she tore in through the shell splashes to ten thousand yards and got off ten torpedoes from her two quintuple mounts aimed straight at the lead cruiser. After a fast port turn into the protection of her smoke, *Johnston*'s men heard three booming underwater explosions at the instant the torpedoes were scheduled to hit, and when she nosed back out of the smoke, the stern of the target cruiser was enveloped in flame. The cruiser was the *Kumano*. Holed by *Johnston*'s torpedoes and smashed up by the destroyer's five-inch guns, she slowed to fight her fires and patch her holes, and took no further part in the action.

But at 0730 *Johnston*'s luck ran out. In less than a minute she was clobbered by a three-shell, fourteen-inch battleship salvo and three 6-inch shells from a light cruiser. The after fireroom and engine room were knocked out and the men there killed. The steering engine and the three after five-inch guns lost power. The heavy "bedspring" of her air-search radar was blown off the masthead and smashed down on the bridge, killing three officers. The skipper, Commander Ernest E. Evans, had his shirt and undershirt blown off and lost two fingers from his left hand. However, *Johnston* was able to duck into a providential rain squall that shielded her temporarily while her crew turned to to repair the damage. This they did so well that at 0750 when the squall had blown by, the destroyer was making seventeen knots on her one remaining engine and all guns could fire, although some were in partial or fully local control. As *Johnston* emerged from the squall, *Hoel, Heerman* and *Roberts* in a fighting column were slashing in for their own torpedo attacks, and Commander Evans, burned and bleeding, swung his wounded ship around and followed them in, although his torpedoes were all gone, to "provide gunfire support." Less than a minute later, *Johnston* opened up on a battleship only seven thousand yards away, hammering out thirty 5-inch rounds in forty seconds and making at least a dozen hits. The battlewagon, the *Kongo*, swung her ponderous fourteen-inchers around and blasted a few salvos at *Johnston*, but all missed, and the destroyer ducked back through the smoke to look for other targets.

There were plenty around. *Johnston* was banging away at a heavy cruiser pumping eight-inch shells into the CVE *Gambier Bay* when a light cruiser and four destroyers were sighted boring in for what was obviously a torpedo attack on the carriers. Without a moment's hesitation the badly damaged *Johnston* took on all five ships, plunging out of her smoke screen and opening up on the light cruiser leading the column. As the range closed, the destroyer took several more hits, but her men saw at least twelve 5-inch bursts aboard the cruiser before she suddenly turned hard to starboard and pulled away. Instantly the determined *Johnston* shifted fire to the lead destroyer, hit her several times, then attempted to cross ahead of the oncoming enemy column. Before she could do so, all four Japanese destroyers duplicated the cruiser's maneuver, turned 90 degrees to starboard and opened the range. Although *Johnston*'s battle-blasted warriors did not know it, those hard right turns were not evasive maneuvers but done to launch torpedoes against the carriers. Thanks to *Johnston*'s hell-for-leather assault, the destroyers launched too soon, at too long a range, and not one of those excellent Japanese torpedoes found a target.

But *Johnston* paid heavily for that daring defense. With their torpedoes away, the four enemy destroyers turned back and concentrated their fire on her. For a brutal half hour the crippled *Johnston* was caught between the enemy destroyers to starboard and a column of cruisers to port, gamely blasting away at first one group and then the other to prevent them from closing on the carriers. All the while she herself was absorbing hit after hit. One forward gun was knocked out and the other damaged. Fires started amidships. The mast came crashing down and dangled over the side. A forty-millimeter ready-ammunition box caught fire and the exploding shells raked the topside. Fire forced the Captain from the bridge, and he ran aft to conn his ship by yelling helm orders down the hatch to after steering, where men with chain falls moved the rudder by hand.

But when a salvo wiped out her remaining engine, there was no longer any point in moving the rudder. With only one gun working in local control, no power, no internal communications, and the enemy destroyers smashing at her from a circle of which *Johnston* was the center, the Captain ordered depth charges set on safe, and at 0945 gave the word to abandon ship. At 1010 *Johnston* rolled over and sank. One of her sailors laboring in the oily sea looked up to see a Japanese destroyer skipper saluting from his bridge as she went down. Of *Johnston*'s 327 officers and men, only 141 survived, and her Captain was not among them.

When destroyer *Hoel* received Admiral Sprague's order to attack with torpedoes, she immediately began a run on the nearest enemy battlewagon, the *Kongo*, then eighteen thousand yards to the northward. Both attacker and attacked opened fire when the range had closed to fourteen thousand yards, and at 0725, a *Kongo* shell smashed through *Hoel's* bridge, wiping out her voice radios. At nine thousand yards, under heavy fire, *Hoel* launched five of her torpedoes and turned away to the southeast. But *Kongo* was not about to let her get away that easily. She had hardly settled on the new course before the battlewagon's big shells wrecked her port engine and her three after guns, and jammed her rudder full right. By the time she regained steering control she was headed straight back for the battleship, her two forward 5-inch guns barking defiantly at *Kongo's* nine 14-inchers.

Disdainfully the enemy battlewagon evaded the torpedoes by turning sharply to port and continued her pursuit of the carriers. *Hoel*, with one engine, two guns, no fire-control radar, and steering from the stern, turned to attack the nearest enemy, a heavy cruiser column led by *Haguro*. With power and communications cut off to the remaining quintuple mount, sweating sailors trained the torpedoes around manually, the Torpedo Officer mentally solved the geometrical problem from atop the mount, and at about 0750 the five fish flashed out toward *Haguro*, then showing her starboard bow at a range of five thousand yards. At the time the torpedoes should have hit, large columns of water spouted at the cruiser's side.

Again *Hoel* turned southeast to rejoin Taffy 3, but that was the way the Japanese were going, too, and *Hoel's* one remaining engine provided just enough speed to make her a *de facto* addition to the enemy formation. *Kongo* on her port beam and the heavy cruisers on her starboard quarter held her in a murderous cross fire while she snaked back and forth, dodging most salvos and hammering resolutely away with her two forward guns at whichever enemy came closest. In that final hour of her life, *Hoel* took as bloody a beating as any warship ever had to suffer. Some forty enemy hits ripped through her and littered her decks with dead and dying young men, yet she managed to get off over five hundred well-aimed rounds in response. By 0830 her remaining engine had been shot out, a forward magazine was burning, and she was dead in the water, listing to port and settling by the stern. Two thirds of her crew were dead and there was hardly a man aboard who was not wounded. Although the numbers and the century are different, Alfred Tennyson's lines on the last fight of HMS *Revenge* could well have been written about USS *Hoel:*

... we had not fought them in vain,
But in perilous plight were we,
Seeing forty of our poor hundred were slain,
And half of the rest of us maimed for life
In the crash of the cannonades and the desperate strife.

At 0835 when her skipper finally gave the word to abandon ship, he had to send a messenger to order the crews from the forward guns, which continued to bang away stubbornly in local and full manual control. At 0855 with enemy shells still smashing into her, *Hoel* rolled over slowly and went down. With her on that long, sad settle to the bottom of the planet's deepest sea went 253 destroyermen. Fifteen more, mortally wounded, died on the rafts and flotation nets that day.

Taffy 3's third destroyer, *Heermann*, positioned in the screen on the side away from the approaching enemy, was later than *Johnston* and *Hoel* in joining the action—and luckier. Shortly before 0800 she sliced right through the fleeing formation of CVEs, one of which, *Kalinin Bay*, was already smoking from the impact of an eight-inch hit by a heavy cruiser. At 0749 after a hairy series of near collisions in the rain and smoke that spread in patches across the sea, *Heermann* formed a column astern of *Hoel*, with *Roberts* following and the badly damaged *Johnston* bringing up the rear to provide gunfire support, and joined in the second torpedo attack of that busy morning. So close were the pursuing enemy ships that five minutes later, *Heermann* launched seven of her ten torpedoes at the heavy cruiser *Haguro* only nine thousand yards away. *Haguro* deftly turned to parallel the torpedo wakes, and as the fish passed harmlessly down her sides, she blasted away at *Heermann* with fifteen salvos, tearing up the sea around her but making no hits.

With the enemy heavies making twenty-five knots to the southeast and the destroyer slashing northward at the same speed, *Heerman* suddenly found herself with four heavy cruisers and four battleships in sight. Big yellow fountains from the battlewagon's fourteen-inchers joined the shorter splashes from *Haguro*'s eight-inch battery around *Heermann*. With cool logic, the destroyer skipper selected the most threatening enemy, the battleship *Haruna*, and with his guns hammering at her bridge and superstructure, he dashed in through a sea full of fountaining explosives and unloaded his remaining torpedoes at the practically point-blank range of 4,400 yards—about the normal distance between the carriers and their screening ships in Taffy 3. As *Heermann* turned away, her lookouts reported a torpedo hit just below *Haruna*'s bridge. But hit or not, the battlewagon's big guns continued to fire and the yellow splashes continued to blossom in uncomfortable proximity to *Heermann* as she laid down a cloud of smoke, ducked into it and zigzagged back to the carriers, still miraculously untouched.

Long after this action, which became known as the Battle off Samar, when *Abercrombie's* people learned what had happened to the escorts of Taffy 3, they were deeply impressed by the fearless, aggressive and effective counterattacks by the three destroyers, and were genuinely saddened by the terrible losses in killed and wounded. Still, there was a feeling, unspoken but accepted, that such actions were to be expected of destroyers. To the men of the DEs in the Pacific in those grim years, destroyers were rather like big brothers. They had five 5-inch guns to the DEs two, and those guns were equipped with radar fire control, enabling them to fire effectively on unseen surface or air targets at night or in fog or smoke. They carried ten torpedoes to the DEs' three. They were ten knots faster and carried a hundred more men. Nearly all their captains, most of their officers and a high proportion of their chiefs and sailors were regular Navy professionals. In *Abercrombie's* little wardroom, Gus Adams was the only "USN," all the rest were "USNR." Of roughly two hundred *Abercrombie* enlisted men, only thirty were USN. Destroyers ran with the attack carriers and fast battleships, they were the "A Squad," the varsity. DEs were definitely "B Squad," the "poor man's destroyers." A destroyer could do everything a DE could do, usually better, and other things a DE could not do at all. The fact that DEs had been designed and built specifically to fill that B-Squad role, relieving the DDs to do what they could do better, was understood but irrelevant to the big brother image of destroyers in the eyes of DE sailors. Thus destroyers were somehow *expected* to perform the way *Johnston*, *Hoel* and *Heermann* had off Samar. But the feeling was different when it came to *Abercrombie's* DE sisters in Taffy 3—*Dennis*, *Raymond*, *Butler* and *Roberts*. They were not big brothers but identical twins with whom *Abercrombie* had variously shared building, fitting out, shakedown, Boston overhaul, Caribbean convoys, Pearl Harbor workouts, and anchorages and moorings from Bermuda to Manus. And with whose men friendships had been formed over a half year of joint training in damage control, gunnery, recognition, refrigeration, administration, radar, sonar and a dozen related fields. Chance alone had assigned *Abercrombie* to Taffy 2 and relative safety, the other four to Taffy 3 and mortal danger. There was not a man in DE343 who did not wonder how his ship would behave in battle. The closest each could come to finding out was to learn how her identical sisters had behaved that morning off Samar. Eventually they found out.

Dennis was the senior DE in Taffy 3, where the voice radio code word for destroyers was "wolves," and for DEs "little wolves." When Admiral Sprague ordered another torpedo attack at 0742, the screen commander, on his way to do so in *Hoel*, ordered, "Little wolves form up for second attack." In the confusion of running carriers, smoke, rain, shell splashes, racing destroyers and the charging enemy, forming up was hard to do. *John C. Butler* tried to locate *Dennis* and form up on her; but *Dennis*, having seen the hit on *Kalinin Bay* and the mortal danger to the carriers, had headed straight for the enemy at twenty-two knots as soon as she heard the order, and was firing whenever she had an enemy in sight. Within two minutes she came under eight-inch fire from the four heavy cruisers which had already tangled with *Johnston* and *Hoel*. But *Dennis* weaved like a boxer, evaded the salvos, combed through a wicked spread of torpedoes and launched her own three at 0759 at a range of eight thousand yards. With no hits observed, she turned back southwest and opened fire on a pursuing cruiser with her number two five-inch. For seven minutes the DE and the cruiser swapped fire, and then at 0809 *Dennis*, still untouched, ducked back through the smoke to join temporarily with *Heermann*, *Johnston* and *Roberts* heading in the same direction.

By 0826 two enemy heavy cruisers were rapidly closing in on the carrier formation, charging up on Taffy 3's port quarter to cut them off from seaward; *Kalinin Bay*, *White Plains*, *Gambier Bay* and Admiral Sprague's flagship *Fanshaw Bay* had all been hit, some several times; and at that point, the Admiral ordered the DEs on his starboard quarter to take position between the attacking cruisers and his carriers. *Dennis* and *Butler* were on the flagship's starboard quarter, and they immediately cut across the carrier formation, pouring out smoke on the way, and opened fire on the leading cruiser. *Butler* still had her torpedoes aboard, but with the faster cruiser on a roughly parallel course abeam, she could not get into firing position. For thirty minutes the two little DEs slugged it out with two enemy heavy cruisers which fortunately for the DEs were concentrating their eight-inch fire on the carriers.

Then *Dennis* began to get hit. At 0850 an armor-piercing shell punched an eight-inch hole cleanly through her, entering her deck to port and leaving through the starboard side just above the waterline. It fatally wounded a sailor in Repair I, wrecked the chiefs' quarters where the repair party was stationed, and broke pipes and scattered shrapnel, flooding the forward five-inch magazine. At 0900 *Dennis* took three more shells in rapid succession. The first smashed the base of the after forty-millimeter director and was deflected down through the fore-and-aft passageway into the big after berthing compartment, killing three of the men in the director and one below. The second shell or a large piece of shrapnel from a near-miss tore a one-foot by one-and-a-half-foot hole in her port side aft, wrecking the gas-ejection and compressed-air systems and severing electrical cables. The last hit was a glancing blow to Mount 51 that did no damage to the gun, but wounded and shook up most of the crew.

At this point *Dennis* found herself with three big holes and both five-inch guns silenced; Mount 51 had a flooded magazine and a wounded crew; and Mount 52 had a broken part in the breech mechanism. Temporarily ineffective in defense of the carriers and still under heavy fire, she turned to starboard into *Butler's* smoke to make repairs. While her repair parties worked on the other damage, the gunnery department started to get the main battery back in commission. What resulted was a marvel of logical thinking under pressure. The intact crew of Mount 52 ran forward to man the still operable Mount 51. A working party was organized to carry ammunition from 52's dry magazines forward to 51. And while gunner's mates were working to repair the breech in 52, the crew of 51 was being reorganized with replacements where necessary.

At 0907 the situation was sufficiently grim to cause the Captain to order the jettisoning of classified publications in their weighted bags. But a few minutes later, Mount 51 was ready to fire, and at 0920 the repaired Mount 52 got its crew back, while the reorganized crew took over in Mount 51. *Dennis* was ready for action again. But at 0930 the enemy turned away and the surface part of the battle off Samar was over.

Like *Dennis*, *Raymond* (DE341) went straight for the enemy's throat the instant the form-up order crackled from her bridge speaker. From 0743 until 0756, *Raymond* charged due north to meet the heavy cruiser column led by *Haguro*. It was a long thirteen minutes. Torpedo wakes were reported close aboard and no less than fifteen 8-inch salvos ripped up the sea around her. *Raymond* concentrated her fire on the relatively vulnerable enemy superstructure and had the satisfaction of seeing the smoke and sparkle of several hits. At the end of that time the range to *Haguro* was only six thousand yards, so DE341 launched her three torpedoes and sensibly turned away, still under heavy eight-inch fire and still blasting back. *Haguro*, already turning to dodge Avenger torpedoes, managed to evade *Raymond's* fish at the same time, although two of them passed close astern. As *Raymond* was spinning on her heel to retire, her men caught sight of *Roberts* abeam to starboard almost lost in a maelstrom of shell splashes, her five-inch guns flashing back repeatedly under the storm of enemy fire.

Having delivered her torpedoes as ordered, *Raymond* resumed her assigned station in the screen of Taffy 3. But that station was on the port, engaged side of the task unit, so at 0814 she found herself in another

David-Goliath duel with a heavy cruiser, probably *Chikuma.* After four-teen minutes of that extremely hazardous engagement, she was joined by *Dennis* and *Butler* from the other side of the screen, and together the three DEs did their best to interpose between the Japanese cruisers and Admiral Sprague's CVEs. However, when at 0902 *Dennis* pulled away with both guns out of action, and at 0918 *Butler* ran out of five-inch ammunition and was ordered ahead to cover the carriers with smoke, *Raymond* continued to steam boldly between the hostile cruisers and the battered friendly carriers, firing as fast as her guns could be loaded and miraculously suffering not a single hit.

The *Samuel B. Roberts* (DE413) of *Abercrombie's* own Escort Division 69 could have used a similar miracle.

The "Sammy B" had been commissioned at the Brown Shipbuilding yard in Houston on 28 April, three days before *Abercrombie,* and had followed roughly the same itinerary—Bermuda, Boston, Panama, Pearl and Manus—arriving in Manus just in time for the Leyte operation. She had sailed from Manus early with the initial invasion force, taken a twenty-four-hour mauling by a typhoon, and had been on station with Taffy 3 since 18 October.

On the midwatch of the twenty-fifth, *Roberts's* Captain, Executive Officer and the watch in CIC listened with great interest to the short-range, tactical TBS circuit and other radio transmissions between U.S. battleships, cruisers and destroyers engaging the enemy in Surigao Strait. Some of the messages were broken up or garbled by distance and the intervening islands, but enough came through to provide an exciting and fairly accurate picture of the action. By morning it was clear that the Japanese force had been routed and its remnants were withdrawing.

At 0650 that morning *Roberts* had secured from dawn General Quarters, and her skipper, Lieutenant Commander Robert W. Copeland, USNR, was on his way down to the wardroom for coffee when the contact report by *Kadashan Bay's* Avenger pilot came in. At the same moment, his lookouts reported AA fire to the northwest, and a minute later reported, "Object on the horizon. Looks like the mast of a ship." Lieutenant Bill Burton, DE413's Gunnery Officer, thoroughly trained in recognition, at once identified the "mast of the ship" as the pagoda-shaped fighting top of a Japanese heavy cruiser. After having spent most of the night listening to a blow-by-blow account of the defeat and dispersal of enemy forces at Leyte, it was logical for *Roberts's* officers to assume that what they were seeing were the defeated Japanese in retreat. Lieutenant Bob Roberts, the Executive Officer, pulled down the mouthpiece of the PA system on the bridge and passed the word: "Now hear this! All hands desiring to see the fleeing remnants of the Jap fleet, lay up topside." Sailors in dungarees, some still chewing their breakfasts, some with shaving lather on their faces, appeared on deck fore and aft, pointing and staring at the smudge on the northern horizon which was the enemy. But at 0655, with the carriers increasing speed and launching planes, DE413's sailors ran back to the battle stations they had just left. Three minutes later, the first enemy rounds came in, big green and purple splashes erupting at the center of a triangle formed by *Roberts*, *Johnston* and *Fanshaw Bay*, the rear carrier. Bo'sun's mate first Red Harrington, Mount Captain on the forward forty, watched in awe as the colored splashes appeared off the starboard bow, and voiced the feeling of most of the crew when he muttered, "Fleeing my ass!"

DE413's skipper flipped down all three switches on the PA system and spoke into the mike. "Men, this is the Captain speaking. A large Japanese fleet has been contacted. They are fifteen miles away and headed in our direction. They are believed to have four battleships, eight cruisers and a number of destroyers. It is our duty to protect the carriers in our task unit." That was all. The click of the PA as it shut off was loud in the momentary silence throughout the ship.

By 0700 CIC had a radar plot that showed the leading enemy cruisers making thirty-three knots on a southeasterly course to intercept. With the first colored splashes, the order came to "make smoke. Make protective smoke." DE413 lighted off the smoke generators on her fantail, and clouds of white FS (phosphorused sulfur) smoke began boiling out astern, forming a solid barrier to visibility. At the same time *Roberts*'s men could see heavy, black fuel oil smoke begin to pour from the funnels of *Johnston* and *Hoel*. The black smoke seemed to lie on top of the white, and there was not enough breeze to blow either away. The effect on the enemy was immediate. The big splashes came less frequently and not as close. To reenforce this highly desirable effect, *Roberts*'s largest burners were plugged into the DE's boiler fireboxes, and soon she was adding her own black funnel smoke to the screen around the carriers. At 0706 *Roberts* entered the most welcome rain squall in the history of war at sea, and enemy fire fell away to almost nothing. She was still there at 0716 when Admiral Sprague ordered his destroyers to attack with torpedoes. Since it was not clear to Captain Bob Copeland whether the order included the DEs as well as the DDs, he called the screen commander in *Hoel* on TBS. "Do you desire little wolves to attack with wolves?" "Negative," the reply came back. "Little wolves form up for second attack."

Roberts was on the engaged flank of the carriers, and when the rain squall had passed over, enemy fire increased in volume and accuracy.

Copeland and the others on the bridge were soaked by falling water from the near-misses of heavy shells. DE413's Captain kept them misses instead of hits by "chasing salvos," steering straight for the splash of the nearest salvo, figuring that since it had been a miss, the enemy would not hit there again but would correct up or down. From *Roberts*'s bridge they saw *Hoel, Heermann* and *Johnston* peel off for their attack. There were no other DEs in sight on which to form up. The enemy cruisers were coming up fast, and DE413, on the enemy's starboard bow, was in good position. At 0840 Bob Copeland gave the order that committed his ship to the attack—"Left standard rudder. All ahead full." As the bow came around toward the enemy and the deck vibrated with the rising whine of the turbines, he estimated the proper course by seaman's eye and steadied on it. CIC came up on the bridge squawk box with the calculated course —a difference of only 6 degrees. Seconds later *Roberts*'s Executive Officer and CIC Evaluator also provided the relative bearing on which the torpedoes should be fired, based on a high-speed (forty-five-knot) torpedo setting, launched from five thousand yards, 60 degrees on the starboard bow of the target cruiser.

Then, as they headed straight for firing position through bands of smoke and rain, Copeland called his Chief Engineer on the phone. "We are going in on a torpedo attack, at twenty knots," he told him, "but as soon as we fire our fish I'm going to ring up emergency flank, and I want you to hook on everything you've got. Don't worry about your reduction gears or boilers or anything because all hell is being thrown at us and we're lucky we haven't been hit already."

The big enemy cruiser was now within range for *Roberts*'s forward five-inch gun which was loaded and leveled at the enemy, but Copeland refused permission to open fire. No salvos were falling close to his ship now. DE413 was in and out of black and white smoke and curtains of rain. With every minute she was about 1,500 yards or three quarters of a mile closer to firing position. There was a good chance that the little DE with her low silhouette and her black, gray and white camouflage had not yet been spotted. Even the ship's five-inch armor-piercing rounds were not going to stop or even slow that armored ten-thousand-ton cruiser, and Copeland wasn't going to attract her attention unnecessarily.

As *Roberts* approached her torpedo release point, she passed *Johnston* retiring after her own attack, still under heavy enemy fire. Back on the DE's triple torpedo mount, the chief torpedoman was using a special wrench to change speed settings from the normal intermediate to high. An enemy shell, intended for *Johnston*, flashed across *Roberts* and severed a radio antenna mast. The broken mast fell across the torpedo tubes, smashed the chief's hand and knocked the wrench overboard. There was no time left to get the spare wrench from the torpedo shack. The torpedoes would have to be launched at intermediate speed (thirty-five knots). But that required reworking the torpedo launch geometry and there was no time for that either. The Evaluator made a seaman's-eye adjustment in his head, sent the data to the tubes, and the three big torpedoes leaped out into the sea just four thousand yards from the enemy hull.

The instant his torpedoes were away, Copeland ordered full left rudder, emergency flank, turned back into the smoke he had been making all the way in, and headed back for the carriers it was his mission to protect. Three or four minutes after the torpedoes had entered the water, running "hot, straight, and normal," Copeland heard someone yell, "We got her!," and glanced aft in time to see a tall column of steam and smoke blast upward from the cruiser's side parallel with her aftermast.

Down in *Roberts*'s firerooms, the safety valves were secured and steam pressure was allowed to rise to 670 pounds in boilers designed for a maximum of 440. In the engine rooms, the twin propeller shafts spun up to 477 rpm in a plant designed for no more than 420. And at the Captain's conning station on the open bridge, the pointer on the pitometer log, which indicates ship's speed through the water, moved steadily over to 28½ knots—for a ship with a designed maximum speed of 24 knots.

When *Roberts* rejoined Taffy 3, the enemy cruisers had moved well up on the beam of the carrier formation and were steadily closing the range. But a different cruiser was now leading the column. DE413's torpedo target had slowed and dropped back.

At 0805 Copeland released his guns and they opened up at a range of 10,500 yards on the *Tone*-class heavy cruiser now in the lead. *Roberts* was back in her position on the port flank of the careening carriers between them and the enemy heavies converging from her port beam. The DE's target was awesomely beautiful, with a gracefully flaired bow, a long fo'c'sle and four 2-gun turrets forward—one low, one high, one low and one high, in that order, from forward aft. And all four of these big turrets were busy. Two were firing at the *Gambier Bay* ahead and to starboard of the *Roberts*. The other two were devoting themselves to DE413. By 0815 the range had closed to 8,500 yards, and for the next twenty minutes it varied between 6,000 and 7,000 yards. The cruiser was so close that her guns, designed to fire at much longer ranges, apparently could not be loaded at the low angle of depression required to engage the little DE. From *Roberts*'s bridge her men could see the big guns elevate and train forward to be loaded, then swing aft and down until their eight-inch muzzles looked like round holes in the face of the turret. Then a twin flash emerged from those muzzles, and seconds later there were a simultaneous thud of concussion and a tearing sound as the projectiles passed close overhead.

After a solid hour and a half under fire, Copeland was still skillfully chasing salvos, and except for the broken antenna mast, his ship was still untouched. Furthermore, she was hitting back. Forward and aft her five-inch guns never paused in their steady, rapid firing. Mount 52 with a crack, well-drilled, well-led crew was putting out a round about every ten seconds, and Mount 51 was doing nearly as well. The action was so desperate and the odds so long that the niceties of selecting any particular type of rounds in any particular order were forgotten. The sailors in the handling rooms below the mounts sent up whatever was at hand and the gun crews loaded and fired what they got. As a result, the enemy was belabored with armor-piercing, common antiaircraft, proximity fuses, star shells, and even blind-loaded and plugged target projectiles. And belabored she really was. The DE gunners concentrated on the cruiser's guns and on her bridge and superstructure, more lightly constructed than her armored vitals; and by 0845 her number three turret had been silenced, her bridge was holed and burning, and several small fires were visible in her superstructure. But she never faltered in her relentless pressing forward to close the range, and the deliberate, methodical blasting of her remaining big guns never stopped.

Standing in the center of the open bridge, in gray helmet and life jacket, binoculars slung around his neck and resting on the front of his kapok jacket, Bob Copeland concentrated on evading the determined, close-range fire of the cruiser's eight-inch turrets while the ship shook with the repeated slamming of the five-inchers fore and aft. Brass shell casings rattled across the deck, and the acid smell of cordite was heavy on the wind. At 0845 his ship swept past *Hoel*, dead in the water, holed, burning, listing heavily to port, her fantail awash and her men scrambling to launch life rafts and floater nets. All of Copeland's instincts as a seaman demanded that he heave to and assist *Hoel*. But his duty to keep his own ship afloat and fighting in defense of the carriers drove the thought from his head, although he could not suppress the lump that formed in his throat as the dying destroyer fell astern.

Just six minutes after passing *Hoel*, *Roberts* was in trouble. Copeland's concentration on the cruiser was broken by an excited cry from a lookout, "Captain, there's fourteen-inch splashes coming up astern." He turned and looked aft just as a salvo landed half a ship's length back in the DE's wake and threw thick columns of water high above the mast. A circular patch of disturbed water showed that the previous salvo had hit an equal distance farther astern. The next one would be right on. There was nothing to do but ignore the cruiser for a moment and try to counter this more immediate threat. Without even a "Stop" bell, Copeland ordered, "All back full!" The whine of the turbines died then rose again, the ship shuddered violently as the backing screws dug in, the stern settled so deeply that the ship's own wake wave nearly came aboard, the pitometer log's white pointer began to fall toward zero—and in the next instant there was a close, tearing sound, a heavy, vicious slap, and two white columns erupted one hundred yards dead ahead. Instantly Copeland rang up "All ahead flank!" At 0851 the ship was just beginning to gather way again, but still dead slow, when the cruiser hit her. Three 8-inch armor-piercing shells ripped into her port side forward. One simply drilled a neat, round eight-inch hole from just above the waterline on one side to just below the waterline on the other, flooding the lower handling room for Mount 51, but slowly enough to permit the sailors to move what ammunition was left up one level and move up themselves. The other two did much more damage. One flooded the IC room—the ship's interior communications center, which also housed the master gyro—drowning the two electricians there and shorting out all electrical power and internal communications except for the sound-powered phones. This meant there was no power to train the guns or operate the ammunition hoists, no radars and no radios. The final shell ruptured the main steam line in the forward fireroom, killing three of the five-man crew instantly and scalding the other two, one fatally. The only man left in the fireroom capable of action was an eighteen-year-old named Jackson McKaskill who had been a fireman for only two weeks. But he had the presence of mind of a veteran. Moving fast in the blinding, scalding steam, he pulled the fires under the boiler, shut off the air and fuel oil. Then he took the phones from a dead shipmate, reported the damage and casualties, asked for the escape hatch to be opened to release the live steam, and only then made his way below to the relatively low temperatures in the bilges. He paid for his heroism with the loss of all the flesh from the bottoms of both feet.

The loss of steam from one of the ship's two boilers reduced her speed from twenty-eight and one half knots to seventeen. Which was fatal. With most of her agility lost, she was unable to dodge the incoming salvos as she had done successfully for nearly two hours. The enemy cruiser closed the range to four thousand yards, and at 0900 two of her twin eight-inch turrets made hits. The four big shells ripped into the DE well abaft the bridge. One encountered the heavy steel supporting structure for the after forty and exploded, instantly obliterating the gun with its mount and shield, its adjacent director and the thirteen men who had been manning them. Bob Copeland heard the crack of the detonation and looked aft to see bodies hurtling out of a patch of white smoke where the gun and director had been. Other shells demolished the number one control engine room, killing the Chief Engineer and all but one of the men on duty there. The starboard shaft and propeller stopped, and the DE's speed was reduced to about thirteen knots, permitting more enemy ships to bring their guns to bear. A destroyer shell hit between the two 20-millimeters just abaft the bridge, killing four of the six men there, fatally wounding a fifth, and spraying the signal bridge and the open bridge itself with shrapnel, which wounded more officers and men.

Like *Abercrombie, Roberts* had a mascot, a small black puppy picked up as a stray on the dock at Norfolk and named Sammy. When Copeland looked aft to survey the damage to the two 20-millimeters, he saw Sammy down on the main deck. The gentle little dog had gone berserk, racing here and there, howling and showing his teeth, his puppy brain unable to handle the long slamming of the guns, the crashing explosions, and the sight and smell of men he had loved lying dead and broken in their gore.

Shortly after 0900, *Roberts* received her mortal wound. Her Captain was standing on the short steps between pilothouse and open bridge helping a scared young helmsman with the unfamiliar task of steering by magnetic compass. Her First Lieutenant, former chief quartermaster Lloyd Gurnett, was on his way aft along the port side of the main deck to supervise a fire-fighting party. In the next instant, the Captain was catapulted across the pilothouse to the forward, starboard corner, bringing up violently against the chart table. His Executive Officer, Lieutenant Bob Roberts, and the helmsman he had been helping landed on top of him. Blood ran from the helmsman's mouth where a front tooth had broken off. Lieutenant Gurnett was swallowed up in a searing blast and concussion that hurled him to the deck on his back, covered him with pulverized asbestos lagging from the engine room, and so shell-shocked him that it was years before he fully recovered. The entire crew of Mount 51, except for the pointer and trainer in their seats, were hurled into a pile at the back of the mount. Every man in the *Roberts* who was not seated or did not have a firm grip on something was thrown to the deck.

DE413 had been smashed by a two- or three-round salvo of high-explosive fourteen-inch shells from an enemy battleship. The shells had blasted a hole in her port side aft at the waterline, thirty to forty feet long and seven to ten feet high, wrecked her remaining engine room, ruptured her after fuel oil tanks, and started fires on her fantail. The ship went dead in the water, listed to port and settled by the stern as the sea cascaded through the gaping hole.

Bob Copeland was forced now to consider saving the remainder of his crew by abandoning ship, but he was not going to give the order as long as she had any fight left in her. Now that all internal communications were out, he sent one officer forward and another aft to determine the condition of the five-inch guns, silent for the first time in thirty-five minutes. As Copeland waited for their report, his heart sank at the sight of a torpedo wake arrowing straight in at the DE's starboard beam. Grabbing for support with both hands, he yelled a warning, "Stand by for torpedo explosion!" He closed his eyes against the blast and waited. But there was no explosion, and the narrow, lethal wake reappeared to port. The torpedo had passed under *Roberts*'s keel.

Copeland's pulse had barely returned to something approaching normal when out of the bands of smoke to starboard the *Johnston* appeared, her bridge an unrecognizable jumble of charred metal, her mast broken and bent double, her air-search radar antenna dangling and swinging with every roll of the ship. One of her two quintuple torpedo mounts and her entire number three five-inch mount were missing and her searchlights were smashed. But she was still stubbornly under way. She passed within one hundred feet of *Roberts*, and back on her fantail Copeland could see her Captain, Commander Ernest E. Evans, a man he knew. Evans was stripped to the waist and covered with blood, his left hand wrapped in a handkerchief. He was yelling conning orders down the scuttle into after steering. As *Johnston* slipped past, Evans looked up and waved.

Shortly after *Johnston* had limped away into the smoke, Copeland's two officers reported back. Mount 51 had no power and had been jammed so that it could not be trained by hand. It was useless. The officer who had been sent to check on Mount 52 could not get there because of fires and ruptured decks and bulkheads, but from the closest point he could see that the back of the mount had been blown out, the barrel was cherry red along its entire length, and there was no sign of life in the vicinity. Obviously Mount 52 was also inoperative.

But before it was wrecked, Mount 52 had given as good an account of itself as any piece of ordnance in naval history. In thirty-five minutes of action, under the inspired leadership of gunner's mate third Paul Henry Carr, that gun crew had fired 324 well-aimed rounds—and each round had had to come up on the hoist from the handling room in two pieces, case and projectile, and be placed by hand in the loading tray, rammed, and fired. When the power went out, the gun crew handed up the fifty-four-pound projectiles and the twenty-eight-pound cases, and trained and elevated the gun by hand. When the battlewagon salvo turned *Roberts* into an inert mass of steel plates and machinery, there were only seven rounds left. There was no compressed air to clear barrel and chamber of hot powder grains and wadding and cool the hot metal. But the gun crew fired six rounds anyway, knowing the danger. The seventh and last round cooked off in the hot chamber before the breech could be closed. The resulting explosion killed or fatally wounded all but one of the ten-man crew, shredded the breech of the gun and blew the mount apart. A metalsmith from Repair III was the first man to enter the blasted mount after the explosion. He found Carr, the Gun Captain, split open from neck to crotch and eviscerated. But Carr was not only conscious, he was leaning against the battered mount and holding up the last fifty-four-pound projectile, which he begged the metalsmith to load and fire. The man took the projectile from Carr and dragged an unconscious sailor from the mount. But when he returned, Carr was once more holding up the heavy shell and begging to have it loaded and fired. Carr was then carried from his beloved gun and died on the deck beside it.

With his main battery out of commission, a quarter of his crew dead or wounded and his ship sinking, Copeland sadly gave the order to abandon. But even that was not easy. There was more to do than launch life rafts and jump aboard. Navy Regulations called for destroying classified documents and equipment, and the broken ship was littered with prostrate men, some dead, some dying, but also many merely wounded. A determination had to be made and the wounded helped to the rafts. Although the depth charges had been wired on "safe" before the action, they had to be checked before abandoning because a single exploding charge could kill or maim men in the water over a wide area. The wires on three charges had been broken in the battle, and those charges were reset and rewired. Copeland set men to smashing up the radars and other classified gear. He saw to it that the Communications Officer loaded his Secret and Confidential publications into a weighted bag for jettisoning, ordered his Executive Officer into the water to be responsible for the men in the rafts and nets, detailed other men to get the wounded onto rafts, and with Lieutenant Gurnett took a final turn around the ship to be sure all who could be were saved. Walking aft on the port side of the main deck under the dangling, splintered whaleboat, Copeland slipped in a pool of blood and fell heavily while more blood spattered down on him. Looking up, he saw a headless man doubled over what was left of his twenty-millimeter gun station. Shaken, Copeland continued aft and stopped just short of plunging through the broken deck into the flooded but still burning engine room. It was about 0940—less than three hours since the first colored splashes had bloomed in the midst of Taffy 3—when Copeland and Lloyd Gurnett went over the side from the DE's still intact but steeply listing fo'c'sle. They were followed by the chief pharmacist's mate, who received a wounded man being lowered on a rope. Then the man who had done the lowering jumped, the last off the *Roberts*.

One of the first men off had been Ensign Jack Moore, DE413's Supply and Disbursing Officer, who reported later that when the order to abandon ship was given, he had heard only the first word before jumping. In his hip pocket, carefully tied in a condom, was the pay list of *Roberts*'s officers and men. Tucked in his belt was a heavy-duty rubberized and waterproof flashlight. When Moore checked his safe, anticipating the order to abandon, he had made a choice between a bundle of hundred-dollar bills, amounting to ten thousand dollars, and the flashlight, which could well mean rescue and survival.

One group of a dozen sailors narrowly averted death by fire after abandoning. The portside raft they were manning was caught by a torrent of seawater pouring through the shell hole into the after engine room. As the men grasped the jagged edges of the hole and paddled furiously against the current, they could feel the heat and see the red flare of fuel oil burning in the flooded hull.

Most of the survivors were only a few yards from the ship when fire reached the forty- and twenty-millimeter ready ammunition, and the detonating rounds tore into the sea around them.

They had been in the water only a few minutes when an enemy light cruiser and two destroyers steamed past at about twelve knots. Copeland ordered the men off the rafts and into the water for fear they would be machine-gunned, but the enemy ships, although they pumped half a dozen rounds into the listing hull of DE413 and passed within a few hundred feet of her crew, leveled no weapons at the men in the water. One enemy sailor thumbed his nose. Another took long and careful motion pictures. Another took off his cap and waved. Then they were gone, leaving only the sinking ship and the empty sea and sky.

Half an hour after the last man had left, the *Samuel B. Roberts* lay over on her beam ends to port, her mast parallel to the water; then her stern went down and down, and she twisted to starboard until her bow rose straight up out of the sea and her mast was parallel again to the surface. Holding on to a floater net two hundred yards away, bo'sun's mate Red Harrington saw that the port anchor was missing and the port bow was stained with green dye from a heavy-caliber near-miss. Slowly, very slowly, as if reluctant to leave the daylight, *Roberts* sank out of sight, the waves closed over her bullnose—and she was gone.

Thus died the first of the DEs of Escort Division 69. She had been a commissioned warship of the United States for three days less than six months. In the last two hours, two hundred 2- and 3-gun salvos had been fired at her, and her fragile sides and superstructure had taken twenty direct hits. Clinging to a life raft a quarter mile away, Lloyd Gurnett, who as her First Lieutenant had known her most intimately and loved her best, wept uncontrollably and unashamedly, like a small boy with a broken heart.

When the men had been in the water about five hours, an Avenger from one of the Taffy carriers droned overhead, dropped down to fifty feet, circled and gave a cheery thumbs up. To the bloodied, shell-shocked men it seemed as if rescue would be prompt. But the pilot's navigation was faulty. The position he gave was over twenty miles in error. It was two days and two nights, fifty hours, before rescue came, and during that terrible time, 116 men from *Roberts, Hoel* and *Johnston* died of their wounds in the water or were torn apart by sharks. Sammy, the black puppy, died with his drifting shipmates.

In his Action Report later, *Roberts*'s Captain wrote that the reason his ship was not sunk long before it was and that his casualties were relatively low (three officers and eighty-six men, many of whom died of wounds on the rafts), was because her low silhouette provided enemy fire control with "no real point of aim and is defensively one of the best silhouettes of all the navies of the world." There were no tall, obvious bridge and superstructure to catch the enemy eye and draw fire to that heavily populated section of the ship, and thus DE413 suffered no hits in that area.

As the survivors of the *Samuel B. Roberts* were exchanging the ordeal of battle for the far more prolonged ordeal of survival in the oil-covered, shark-patrolled waters of the Pacific, Taffy 2 was continuing to launch every available plane against the enemy's heavy ships. Before 0930 it became apparent that the Japanese were disengaging. Incredibly, the vastly superior enemy force, which should have been able to annihilate all three Taffy task units and then demolish the Leyte beachhead, was turning north and opening the range, still under angry attack by the Avengers and Wildcats of the CVEs it had attempted to destroy. One CVE, *Gambier Bay,* had been sunk along with *Johnston, Hoel* and *Roberts,* but the Japanese had lost two heavy cruisers and another would not last the day; their surviving ships were scattered in a welter of smoke and rain, the airwaves buzzed and crackled with messages in plain, emphatic American which left little doubt that powerful forces were rushing to the rescue; and always the blue planes with their white stars attacked and reattacked with torpedoes, bombs, machine guns and even depth charges.

All that day, while the enemy Admiral reformed his battered, scattered fleet, circled indecisively and finally headed home, Taffy 2, ringed by DEs and DDs, stayed at General Quarters in nearly continuous air operations, ploughing upwind to launch, racing downwind out of enemy gun range to prepare for the next recovery, the next launch. For all the men of Taffy 2, 25 October 1944 was a day marked forever by admiration for the pilots and aircrews who took off cross-wind as often as not, delivered any ordnance they could get right down the throats of the enemy, landed back on heaving postage-stamp decks in their damaged planes to reload and relaunch—and save the day.

Twenty-five October had been scheduled as fueling day for the escorts before the Japanese rewrote the schedule, and after a day of high-speed maneuvering, the DEs were dangerously low. In *Abercrombie* Gus Adams's habitual scowl grew even darker. He made frequent trips into the foreign territory of the bridge with the folded white slip of the fuel status report in his hand, only to climb back down, ominously shaking his head.

All that night, *Abercrombie* ran with her task unit, black oil sloshing in the bottoms of her tanks, all the next morning while the blue planes pursued the retreating Japanese, and all that afternoon. Then, finally the fueling orders came. Just before five o'clock she nosed up along the starboard side of the *Manila Bay*, the heavy towing hawser was rigged, distance and phone lines stretched between the ships, the two long loops of hose supported by their saddles dangled across, and their discharge ends were jammed down, fore and aft, into *Abercrombie*'s thirsty fueling trunks and lashed in place. At 1705 the hoses stiffened, the Navy Special fuel oil began to flow, and down in the control engineroom, Gus's worried scowl began to fade.

But topside things were going wrong. The late afternoon of 26 October off Leyte Gulf was mild and pleasant. There was very little wind, and except for a moderate swell, the sea was calm. The fueling of *Abercrombie* by *Manila Bay* should have been easy and routine. Instead, it was difficult, unusual and downright dangerous. The ordered fueling course brought the Pacific swell in from the starboard quarter of the two ships, which tended to pick up their sterns and push them off course. *Abercrombie*, being by far the lighter and since she was to starboard of the carrier, the first to feel the wave action, was most affected. Despite Katschinski's increasingly impatient orders to the helm, the DE veered away repeatedly from *Manila Bay*, then, correcting, she turned and angled back in until a collision seemed inevitable, only to recover a few scant yards from the carrier's side and attempt to go off on her own once more. The team of Katschinski at the conn and Howard Amos at the wheel which had been so successful thus far appeared to have lost its competence. As the violent maneuvers continued, Katschinski's face became redder and redder, his voice louder and higher. On the wheel Amos spun and sweated and cursed under his breath, his stomach in painful knots with tension, until after some twenty minutes the Captain exploded. "Get that son of a bitch off the wheel." Signalman first Paul Fry was ordered to the helm from his signal bridge, but he could do no better; and after another twenty minutes of wild gyrations, he was relieved by chief quartermaster Marmon himself.

When *Abercrombie* had been more or less alongside *Manila Bay* for almost an hour, the frantic fueling fiasco came to a climax. The DE took a final wide swing away until the two fuel hoses were pulled nearly horizontal, the other, smaller lines stretched to their breaking points and the towing hawser dragged to a 60-degree angle from the fueling course. Then out there in that ridiculous and unseamanlike position, frazzled and embarrassed and feeling the need for drastic corrective action, Katschinski yelled an order he never should have given: "LEFT FULL RUDDER!" In the pilothouse Zeke Marmon spun the brass disk of his wheel to port, the white pointer of the rudder angle indicator swung around to 30 degrees left, *Abercrombie*'s twin rudders bit into the sea, and around she came in a sharp-bowed rush for the side of the carrier.

On the fo'c'sle we could hear the CVE's winches chattering as they raced to take up the slack in the fuel lines, hoisting the looped hose saddles higher and higher above the surface. With a mere fifty feet of roiling water between carrier and DE, Katschinski ordered opposite rudder, but it was too late. With collision inevitable, I ordered everyone within yelling distance to the starboard side and ran aft and starboard myself. *Abercrombie* hit with a tearing, rending crash, jammed in under *Manila Bay*'s overhanging island, and scraped painfully aft along her side. On the open bridge, those forward, including the Captain and his talker, dived for the protection of the pilothouse; the signal gang, aft, leaped or scrambled down onto the torpedo deck; the port lookout yanked off his phones as the carrier loomed over him and dashed across the bridge to the starboard lookout tub, which already held two men caught in the middle of the bridge. On the torpedo deck, Bob Zuzanek, an engineer, saw the carrier coming and jumped down onto the main deck, bruising both his feet. The massive overhanging structure of the carrier's island crunched down on the open bridge, grinding and smashing the tall, T-shaped Mark 51 optical range finder, and snapped both portside shrouds supporting the mast before the starboard rudder took effect and *Abercrombie* began to veer off once more.

Down on the main deck, I ran through the athwartship passageway to cut away the fuel-hose lashings and found CPO Holloway already there, but it was no use. The forward hose had been pinched between the ships and severed, spewing black oil across the deck and down the side. Aft the men were able to release the hose and ease it back to *Manila Bay*. All that had to be done was to cut the towing hawser, but the part around *Abercrombie*'s bitts was made of heavy-gauge wire, impervious to anything except an acetylene torch. However, in seconds the carrier crew had axed through the ten-inch manila end, the DE crew had hauled it aboard, and the two ships, finally free of each other, pulled apart to clean up and assess their damage.

The most serious damage to *Abercrombie* was the destruction of the range finder and the parting of the two shrouds, which seriously weakened the mast, which, in turn, supported nearly all her radar and communications antennas. While the rest of the deck force turned to with swabs, wiping rags and fire hoses to clean up the gooey, sweet-smelling black oil, bo'sun's mate Pete Kish tackled the job of repairing the severed shrouds and keeping *Abercrombie*'s mast where it belonged.

Pete had been in the Navy ten years when he reported to DE343 in Orange, and he had served all ten years in one battlewagon, the USS *West Virginia*. On that fine old warship his training had been thorough. He was not only a good all-around bo'sun's mate, he was also proficient in such seafaring specialties as fancy rope work—Turk's heads, sinnets, the intricate, salty snow-white decorations found on captains' gigs, admirals' barges and on the bridges and flag quarters of capital ships—and, far more relevant at the moment, at working and splicing heavy wire. The collision had provided him with the materials he needed to do the job. Still looped around *Abercrombie*'s port towing bitts because it had been impossible to cut, was the heavy wire pendant sent over by *Manila Bay*. Pete collared two cox'ns (bo'sun's mates third class), Pop Deatherage, the oldest man aboard, and "Pappy" McAleer, and the three men went to work. With Pete making the first splice in each case and the other two finishing up, they spliced *Manila Bay*'s wire into what was left of the two shrouds, spliced in turnbuckles at deck level to adjust the tension, and Pete himself went up the wobbly mast to ensure that the new rig was firmly attached. By the end of the day *Abercrombie*'s mast was so firmly in place that Pete's quick fix, which was intended as temporary, became permanent and remained with the ship to the end of her days.

But there was other damage. On the port side of the fo'c'sle, half a dozen of the stanchions supporting the lifelines were bent and twisted at odd angles. The number two life-raft support structure was all bent out of shape. The outboard bulkhead of the twenty-millimeter clipping room at the port gangway was deeply dished-in but still watertight. Amidships one of the heavy chocks at the deck edge was bent inboard, deeply denting the deck. There was no damage that could not be repaired by *Abercrombie*'s own crew except that of the range finder. Since this instrument was useful only against surface targets during daylight, and since after 25 October no more such opportunities could reasonably be expected, it was not a crippling loss. Best of all, not one man had been injured, and the twenty thousand gallons of oil she had received would keep DE343 at sea for several more days.

The following morning *Abercrombie* was an information addressee on the longest flashing-light message of her career. It was from the Commanding Officer of the *Manila Bay* to the task group commander, and in it he pulled no punches:

> During fueling under excellent conditions yesterday, *Abercrombie* steered very erratically throughout with excessive rudder, finally colliding and then sheering off radically, breaking all lines and connections. I consider accident attributable almost wholly to conning by eye by inexperienced officer instead of by method recommended in paragraph 622, Appendix four, USF 10A.

The message went on to spell out damage to the carrier which included a hole in her side ("already repaired"), a wrecked fueling winch, a boat boom carried away, and the loss of four lengths of fueling hose and a ten-inch towing hawser.

The caustic message made no noticeable impression on Katschinski, but Howard Amos found it grossly unfair. "No reason to send a message like that," he said, bristling. "With that quartering sea, the Captain did the best he could, the collision wasn't his fault." This from the "son of a bitch" who had been ordered off the helm. There was at least one Christian gentleman in *Abercrombie*'s crew's quarters that eventful October of 1944.

Early on the morning of the twenty-eighth, Taffy 2's escorts were replaced by an impressively beefed-up screen consisting of the heavy cruiser *Louisville*, the light cruiser *Boise* and four destroyers. By 0730 *Abercrombie*, *Suesens*, *Wilson* and *Wann* were steaming at eighteen knots for Leyte Gulf, in line abreast, five hundred yards between ships. Orders received by flashing light directed the four DEs under ComCort-

Div 69 to report to SOPA (Senior Officer Present Afloat), Leyte Gulf, for "orders and logistics."

It was a beautiful, clear day and land was in sight before noon, high and dark green off the port bow. As the little formation approached the entrance to the gulf, the ships swung smartly into column with *Suesens*, the flagship, leading and *Abercrombie* bringing up the rear. A similar column of minesweepers was departing as the DEs entered, and five or six miles off to port three Avengers were bombing a low, wooded hill, circling and taking turns making their runs.

Leyte Gulf was loaded with more ships than *Abercrombie*'s men had ever seen at one time, including Pearl Harbor and Manus. There were warships of every description, from bristling old battlewagons with their bulging torpedo blisters, which had so recently and so effectively barred Surigao Strait to the enemy, down to little wooden subchasers (SCs) and minesweepers (YMSs). A long row of LSTs lined the beach with their bows up on the sand. Just offshore were anchored dozens of big attack transports (APAs) and attack cargo ships (AKAs). Farther off a dozen long, low tankers were also anchored, and beyond them dozens more of merchant freighters. Beyond the freighters were the warships—the battlewagons, heavy and light cruisers and destroyers—which were not anchored but patrolling slowly back and forth at barely steerage way, their AA guns manned and their radars spinning. As soon as the four DEs drew close, they found out why. A voice message over TBS warned, "Stay alert. This area under frequent enemy air attack."

With half her guns manned, *Abercrombie* went alongside an anchored tanker for fuel, but the tanker pulled up her hook and got under way, like a nursing bitch bothered by her puppy, before the DE's tanks were full. As the sun was setting, the four DEs re-formed their column and headed back to sea at General Quarters. Astern the enemy planes were coming in with the darkness; the aircraft warning net reported them at forty-five, thirty-two, twenty-two and sixteen miles. We were well at sea before the planes were over the gulf, but we learned later that this time they had hit the beachhead itself and not the ships offshore.

Early the next morning the DEs rejoined Taffy 2. Shortly after noon a huge logistics force of fleet tankers with an escort of destroyers came up over the eastern horizon, and all of Taffy 2, the carriers and the two cruisers included, snuggled up to them for fuel. This time *Abercrombie*'s fueling was done with seamanlike proficiency, and at last Gus's tanks were filled, but not without attempted interference by the enemy. Half a dozen Japanese planes were shot down by the CAP within twenty miles of the force; and once the watch on *Abercrombie*'s bridge was startled by a sudden exultant shout on the fighter director circuit, "Splash one Nell!"

As soon as fueling was completed, the cruisers *Louisville* and *Boise* and their attendant destroyers pulled out of the screen, formed up and disappeared over the horizon to the northeast.

For two more days, Taffy 2 plied the seas off Leyte Gulf while its aircraft performed the routine chores of CAP, antisub patrol and troop support exactly as they had been doing before the temporary interruption of 25 October. Then on the morning of the thirtieth, just ten days after the first landings at Leyte, with Army aircraft now operating out of captured fields ashore, the Taffy task units were dissolved and pulled out. Early that morning *Abercrombie* found herself in a screen of twenty destroyers and DEs escorting two old battlewagons, five cruisers and ten jeep carriers back to Manus. It looked at first like easy duty. There were enough escorts to form a tight, full circle around the heavy ships. The DDs and DEs were no more than two thousand yards apart around the circumference, so that it was not necessary to dash around madly changing stations when formation course was changed. Speed was a comfortable fourteen knots, and the zigzag plan simple and straightforward. But there were air operations and there was some after-action tidying up to do.

Each day two carriers and five escorts were detached to provide air cover, and the days when *Abercrombie* drew that duty were busy ones, especially since the air was calm and the carriers were forced to their full speed to get sufficient wind over their decks for safe flight operations.

On the second day of the voyage south, *Abercrombie*'s big task group overtook and passed a smaller force of landing craft escorted by large and small minesweepers and a large steel subchaser. *Abercrombie*'s screening station was on the side toward the landing craft, and as the two forces came abreast, a TBS message ordered her to go alongside an LST in the other group and take off several men. That sounded as if it would be fairly routine but it wasn't. Large ships such as carriers and tankers, accustomed to transferring people at sea, have breeches buoys and their attendant lines and tackles standing by and they know how to rig and use them. Small ships like landing craft and minesweepers, unless they are exceptionally smart and salty, don't know how. So while Katschinski was determining which LST was his target and making his approach, *Abercrombie*'s deck force was busy rigging a breeches buoy of their own from a bo'sun's chair, a ring, a shackle, a snatch block, a high line from which the chair would be suspended, and a couple of hauling lines to pull it back and forth. A dozen men came swinging across between LST and DE that afternoon, all survivors of the action off Samar on the twenty-fifth. Then one more man had to be taken from one of the big minesweepers (AM) in the screen. The equatorial dusk was settling across the sea as *Abercrombie* drew alongside the AM to make the transfer, and her crew seemed to be in no hurry. They took our shot line all the way aft, then deliberately moved it forward, outboard of everything, to the bridge, then up into the superstructure before hauling over messenger and high line so the chair could go over. Meanwhile, the two ships rolled and pitched within a few feet of each other—a collision just waiting to happen—while helmsmen and conning officers sweated and grew gray hair. It was nearly dark when the operation was finally completed and *Abercrombie* could head south at flank speed to rejoin her own force.

DE343's new passengers ranged from a commander, the former Executive Officer of the carrier *St. Lo* (hit by cruiser gunfire and finally sunk by the first suicide air attack of the war), to a fireman from the same ship. Most were pilots who had ditched for one reason or another. *Abercrombie*'s tight little officers' quarters were solidly full that night, but with the use of the wardroom transom, an overflow into the chiefs' quarters, and the "hot bunk" system, everyone had a place to sleep.

At 1100 the next morning, *Abercrombie* began delivering people, mostly the aviators and air crewmen, back to their own ships. That task was easier because the carriers had their own rigs and were proficient in their use. It was also a happy task because the airmen, who had been reported missing, their fates unknown, were returning to their squadron mates and flying buddies. As each one dangled across to his home carrier (*Manila Bay, Marcus Island* or *Sangamon*), the ship's sides and sponsors were lined with grinning faces and the air was filled with gleeful, raucous shouts.

On the fo'c'sle, where the breeches buoy was rigged and handled, we noticed that often when he spotted his friends on the carrier, the pilot being transferred would point vigorously to his mouth and grin, a gesture we did not understand. Finally we were informed that the pilot was showing that he still had his front teeth, usually knocked out when ditching.

There was even an element of humor. One of the rescued pilots was a husky, ebullient young man with a handlebar moustache and cowboy boots who was known to us only as "the Greek." When his turn came to be transferred, the carrier sailors tending the high line had let a little slack develop so that this pilot did not leave *Abercrombie*'s deck with steady progress, but instead swooped sickeningly down toward the foaming twelve-knot river between the ships in a rush that would have left another man pale with fright. But not the Greek. As though it were an amusement park roller-coaster ride, he took one hand from the triangle of line supporting the chair, shook a big fist high over his head, and yelled a gleeful "Yaaahooo!," following that with vigorous pseudoswimming motions his free hand as though to assist his progress across. By 1400 all the transfers had been completed except for one pilot from *Kadashan Bay*, which was far astern conducting flight operations. He stayed aboard and was transferred by whaleboat in Manus.

Lieutenant (later Lieutenant Commander) Bernard H. Katchinski, *Abercrombie*'s Captain from commissioning through the worst of the Okinawa Operation.

Abercrombie on patrol in the Bungo Suido, October 1945.

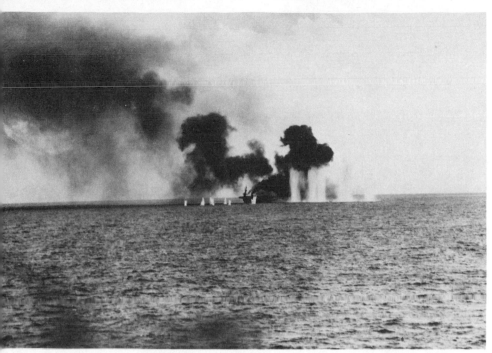

▲ A Japanese heavy cruiser finds the range of one of the escort carriers of Taffy 3 on 25 October 1944 off Samar. The carrier is trying to hide behind her own smoke.

▼ When salvos from battleships and heavy cruisers began falling around his slow and thin-skinned carriers, Admiral Sprague "ordered every ship in Taffy 3 to make all the smoke they could from smoke generators and stacks." Here *Dennis* (DE405) is doing exactly that.

A daylight kamikaze attack off Okinawa. The psychology of the suicider was foreign and incomprehensible to U.S. seamen, but the rugged planes and determined pilots were hard to stop.

Abercrombie's identical twin and division mate *Stafford* (DE411) showing the armament and deck layout of her class.

The destroyer *Hazelwood* after a bomb-laden kamikaze smashed into her bridge off Okinawa, killing forty-six men, including her Captain and Exec, and wounding twenty-six others.

▲ Four thousand tons of explosives in the ammunition ship *Mount Hood* go up in smoke in Seeadler Harbor, Manus, killing 372 men and wounding 371 more. In the right foreground is *Abercrombie's* sister ship, *Oberrender* (DE344), which was badly damaged.

▼ "Then suddenly, perhaps 500 yards away [the Val] banked violently left, nosed down and headed straight for the *Columbia*."

Ensign William Warner Abercrombie, Torpedo Squadron Eight, USS *Hornet* (CV8).

Ship's mascot and "Morale Officer" Butch, with his friend, electrician's mate first class Harry Miles.

2. Lingayen

Abercrombie ARRIVED OFF THE familiar entrance to Seeadler Harbor, Manus, Admiralty Islands, early on the morning of 3 November. However, it was noon before she entered, having spent the forenoon patrolling offshore with her sister DEs while the battleships, cruisers and carriers filed in. Then there was an hour's wait for space alongside an anchored tanker, another hour for fueling, and a long ride to an anchorage at the far western end of the harbor. It was 1500 when Holloway knocked the pelican hook open and the starboard anchor rattled down into ten fathoms of water to end twenty continuous days under way. Just at the end of the short, tropical evening twilight, *Suesens* came ghosting down the harbor, made a sharp turn to port and moored to *Abercrombie*'s starboard side. Thus the two DEs from Orange, Texas, began a reluctant three-and-a-half-week sojourn at Manus in the Admiralties, while staff officers at Pearl Harbor, on flagships off the Philippines, and at General MacArthur's headquarters on Leyte planned the next assault against the enemy and the special roles 342 and 343 would be assigned.

Life at Manus quickly settled into a routine that was pleasant enough the first week after the hectic days at sea; tolerable the second week while all the ship's work that had been difficult or impossible to accomplish under way was done; but increasingly irritating, boring and frustrating thereafter because all hands knew that only action, whatever the risks, would end the war and get them home.

It was at Manus that *Abercrombie*'s men learned what had happened to the DEs of Taffy 3 off Samar—the loss of their division mate *Samuel B. Roberts,* the exploits of *Raymond* and her unbelievable luck to have come through untouched, the damage to *Butler* that had sent her back to Pearl for repairs. And especially they heard of the stubborn bravery of the escort carrier crews, in their vulnerable, thin-skinned ships packed with bombs, torpedoes and aviation gasoline, miraculously quenching fires and patching holes while their single five-inch guns snapped back at heavy cruisers and made effective hits.

It began to dawn on the men of *Abercrombie* that they had been very lucky participants in a really major naval engagement. They could not know that one day it would be described in *The Oxford History of the American People* as "the most gallant naval action in our history and the most bloody—1,130 killed, 913 wounded."

It was at Manus in November also that they first heard about the suiciders.

Sailors from the escort carriers in Taffy 3 and Taffy 1 told of fanatical enemy pilots who deliberately crashed their bomb-laden planes on the carrier decks, blowing huge holes and starting searing gasoline fires. *St. Lo* in Taffy 3 had been set afire from stem to stern, and had sunk with heavy casualties after having survived attacks by enemy cruisers all morning. She had thus earned the undesirable distinction of being the first U.S. ship to be sunk by a suicider. *Kitkun Bay* had been hit a glancing blow, *White Plains* had had a near-miss, and *Kalinin Bay* took a suicider on her flight deck but was able to patch the hole and put out the fires. In Taffy 1 to the south, sixteen men were killed on *Santee* when an enemy suicide pilot blew a hole fifteen by thirty feet in her deck and started fires below. More lives were lost when a plane dived through *Suwannee*'s flight deck and a bomb punched another big hole in her hangar deck.

Abercrombie's young sailors, and her officers as well, were first incredulous, then horrified at this evidence of the enemy's fanaticism. The psychology of the suicider was foreign and incomprehensible to them. All would have agreed with General George Patton that a man's personal aim in warfare should be not to die for his country, but "to make some other bastard die for his." They would have liked to write off the experiences of the CVEs as isolated, spur-of-the-moment decisions by a few psychopathic superpatriots. But the attacks had obviously been carefully planned and coordinated, the planes coming in flat on the sea below radar detection, then zooming up to five or six thousand feet and diving on their targets. The entire concept was eerie and strangely unsettling.

The experiences of the DEs and the carriers provided humbling, thought-provoking information that helped many men temper their objections to the peaceful inactivity of life at Manus.

Those objections were tempered further by several pleasant aspects of living in an equatorial harbor. First, and most important, was the regular arrival of mail from home—conventional mail, photocopied and reduced V-mail, and even packages which became more frequent as December approached. After each mail call there was an easily detectable surge in the spirits and morale of *Abercrombie's* crew, and a renewed burst of letter writing with a resultant increase in the workload of the reluctant censors in the wardroom. Next in importance was the regular serving of fresh food in both General Mess and wardroom. This was especially evident on Thanksgiving Day when a creatively prepared menu, carrying an improbable cross between an anchor and a turkey on the cover, a sailor dozing in a digestive coma on the back, and a seahorse and a DE inside, listed the following:

Cream of Tomato Soup
Soda Crackers

Roast Tom Turkey   *Baked Spiced Ham*

Corn Bread Dressing
Cranberry Sauce   *Giblet Gravy*
Snowflake Potatoes   *Buttered Peas*
Apple, Carrot and Raisin Salad

Sliced Pickles   *Ripe Olives*

Raisin Bread

Mincemeat Pie   *Ice Cream*
Sugar Cookies   *Doughnuts*

Lemonade

Cigars   *Candy*

After that incredible meal, served so far from the origin of the tradition and from the sources of supply, regular Navy bo'sun's mate Fred Manger, after his third trip down the chow line, made the point to his reservist buddies (he had been making it since Orange): "You guys must be nuts to want to get out of the Navy! Where else can you get chow like this? Three squares a day and all you can eat? You *gotta* be nuts!"

Finally there was "liberty" and the movies. "Liberty" is in quotation marks because it wasn't liberty in the usual sense of visiting a town or city with people, bars and entertainment. Every day at 1400, the LCI 1020 came alongside the two-ship nest of *Abercrombie* and *Suesens* and took aboard one third of their crews, each with an officer in charge and a petty officer to assist him. The LCI took the men to a so-called recreation island with sand and palm trees where they were issued up to six cans of beer each, and where for three hours they could swim or play softball or cards, or just sun themselves and talk and drink their beer.

Each Sunday morning the whaleboat shuttled church parties dressed in sparkling whites to Protestant and Catholic services on the destroyer tender *Sierra* anchored nearby.

When they were off duty but still aboard, the men found dozens of ways to entertain themselves, pass the dragging hours and preserve their sanity, ways which in many cases were to stand them in good stead when the war heated up. Since most still possessed the hearty appetites of the young, there was much interest in food and drink. Ted Gruhn's carpenter shop was a veritable snack bar and delicatessen for the C and R gang and their friends. And Gruhn's boys were very careful indeed to cultivate the men who worked in the galley, especially Harry Heinl, the baker, and Dave Allen, the big cook. They also maintained close relations with the officers' stewards whose supply room for the wardroom mess was between after steering and the laundry. As a supplement they or their agents routinely infiltrated working parties engaged in loading provisions and beer for use in the recreational areas ashore, and they diverted the flow of those commodities sufficiently to maintain a comfortable inventory.

The carpenter shop had such a secure hiding place for the beer that no search or inspection ever found it. Below the deck of the shop there was a shallow space which in a pinch could hold several cases of beer. The only access to it was through an oval-shaped plate secured by twenty-seven bolts. No search party ever had the patience to remove all those bolts, and it was presumed that neither would the C and R gang. The presumption was in error. On a hot night at anchor a can of beer, instantly cooled by a blast from a CO_2 fire extinguisher, was more than enough reward for the removal of a few bolts.

Steve Stephens, the big, quiet carpenter's mate, contributed in a different way. He made a big coffeepot. Three powder cans for the five-inch ammunition were appropriately cut and fitted together for the pot itself. Some fire brick from the boiler room and a length of tungsten wire from the radio shack made up the heating element; some copper tubing from the engine room carried the boiling water up to the coffee; a little drilling and turning was done in the machine shop; a spigot, and a bail to open and close the top. The coffeepot was a work of art.

George Ferroni learned to use the steam iron in the laundry as a toaster, and Gruhn had a hot plate. As a result a man could get sandwiches, coffee, canned fruit, bacon, and even a cold beer at almost any hour, if he knew the right people back aft.

In the engine room Don Wood and his friends rigged up an ice-cream maker, and arranged the acquisition of the necessary ingredients in the same way as the carpenter shop. Coffee was made there, too, but more directly—by dipping a clean white sock filled with grounds into a pot of boiling water.

Of the nongastronomic activities, card games were the most popular, followed by Fred Manger's boxing matches on the fantail, where "Dago" Paiva and George Ferroni were frequent antagonists. Weight lifting also had its devotees, principally engineers Rudy Amelio, Joe McGrath, Dick Marston and radarman Bill Watkins.

The weights themselves were examples of the kind of improvisation of which American sailors are capable when the need is there. They were five-gallon paint cans cut in half and filled with concrete to levels which produced sets weighing 50, 80 and 120 pounds, attached to the ends of ¾-inch iron bars.

For the officers at Manus there was a pleasant little club on nearby Kuruniat Island, a modified, opened-up and expanded Quonset hut on a sandy point close to the surf where the sea breeze rustled a couple of palms, the beer was cold and there were peanuts to munch on. In the heat of Manus it was a place to meet with friends from other ships, swap experiences, speculate on the date and location of the "next operation" and the degree of enemy resistance to be expected, and to escape for an hour or two every third day from the Spartan painted steel of a man-of-war.

Each evening movies were shown on the fantail. Since two ships were nested together, each with its own projector and movies, the movies were usually double features, shown without the usual interruption to change reels, because the ships alternated reels, one taking even numbers and one odd, projecting them on a screen rigged between ships with a leg on each. If the movie was unacceptably bad or one you had seen before, you could always read. Some considerate publisher had designed wartime editions of good books so that they fitted neatly into a hip pocket, readily available at spare moments. While in *Abercrombie* I read twenty-six books that way, not an unusual number. In the three weeks at Manus I was able to lose myself for hours at a time in *Random Harvest, The Razor's Edge* and *The Robe*.

After the movies and frequently when the quantity demanded instead, there was mail to be censored in the wardroom, a chore no one relished but which security required. Outgoing mail from the crew, unsealed and written on one side only of each page, was piled on the wardroom table where each letter was read by an officer with a pair of scissors handy. It felt like an ordered prying into the men's most personal lives (which it was); and despite the continuous posting of censorship regulations specifying what could not be written, many letters went back into their envelopes in lacy tatters.

Each envelope, after being sealed, was stamped with a small circle in which was inscribed "Passed by Naval Censor," then it was initialed by the censoring officer. The officers stamped and initialed each other's mail unread, on the principle that those who were charged with enforcing the regulations would neither violate them nor jeopardize a fellow officer whose initials attested to his confidence in one's own integrity. That may well have been a violation of the rules, but that was the way it was. There was room, also, even in wartime, for exceptions based on judgment, trust, responsibility and integrity. The same courtesy the officers extended to each other was extended in special cases to solid, responsible individuals in the crew. After a thorough explanation of what could and could not be said, I certified, unread, the personal correspondence of Gruhn, Stephens and Don Wood. Other officers did the same for men they knew could be trusted, and whose privacy they felt it unnecessary to violate.

Working days at Manus were taken up with routine maintenance, drills and training. All the guns had to be overhauled, checked and lubricated and the sensitive fire-control devices—sights, directors, motor drives, selsyns—kept in perfect operational condition. All the primary and auxiliary machinery under Gus's charge had to be checked and maintained. All the electronics in CIC—radars, transmitters, receivers, direction finders, identification gear—had to be continually checked, tuned and tested. There were daily sessions for sonarmen and conning officers on the attack teacher in the destroyer tender *Sierra*. For the deck force there was the continuing battle of knife-edges and gaskets, and the ongoing contest with rust, a fact of life for all steel ships in salt water. In the case of *Abercrombie* and her sisters, the rust had had an initial headstart due to a disagreeable phenomenon called mill scale resulting from the necessary haste of the DEs' construction. When their steel plates were extruded from the rollers of the mill, adhering to their surfaces was a thin, tenacious scaly substance composed of impurities in the metal that had been forced to the surface as the metal cooled. In normal times most of the scale would have been removed by a chemical bath known as "pickling." In the abnormal years of the 1940s, there was no time for such luxuries, and the steel was shipped to the fabricating yards, mill scale and all. At sea, salty moisture penetrated the paint that covered the scale, rusted and lifted off both scale and paint in a pox of ugly blisters. The omission of the pickling process simply passed along the problem to the crews of the ships built with that scaly steel. And instead of a few hours of pickling, the problem had to be solved by thousands of man-hours with chippers, scrapers and wire brushes.

Aboard the *Abercrombie*, Pete Kish, the leading petty officer of the Second (Deck) Division, was the number one enemy of mill scale. The Second Division was responsible for the aft half of the ship, including the broad, relatively uncluttered area of the fantail. Pete was determined that as soon as it was humanly possible, every spot of mill scale would be banished from his area. All day, every day, every Second Division sailor not otherwise occupied plied chipping hammer and wire brush to the fantail. By the end of the twenty-five-day respite in Manus, Pete had achieved his goal. Every square inch of *Abercrombie*'s broad stern had been chipped and scraped to the bright, bare metal, primed with several coats of zinc chromate and finished off with two coats of deck blue.

For the officers, being nested with the division flagship was a mixed blessing. On orders from the Commodore there was a one-hour class for all officers in the wardroom each afternoon in which the finer points of navigation, gunnery, damage control, communications, seamanship and tactical maneuvering were reviewed and discussed. Each officer was required to complete a nineteen-assignment correspondence course issued by Commander, Destroyers Pacific Fleet (ComDesPac), at a minimum rate of one per week. *Suesens* and *Abercrombie* were required to inspect each other's deck, C and R and ordnance departments daily and report any discrepancies to the appropriate skipper. On 11 November the Division Commander staged a full-dress matériel and personnel inspection of both ships, which had been freshly cleaned and painted inside and out, and in which the crews were lined up dressed in whites with neckerchiefs, and the officers in khakis or grays with neckties.

As the days and weeks at anchor wore on, the strain began to tell in minor ways. The Captain increasingly isolated himself from the other officers, speaking to them only in the course of necessary business, and associating almost exclusively with the skipper of the *Suesens* and with the Commodore. At the infrequent meals which he attended in *Abercrombie*'s wardroom, he was impatient and irascible. One evening at dinner when the main course of beef stew was placed before him, he crashed his fist down on the table and bellowed at the serving steward, "Take this shit away and bring me a steak!" Then he sat there at the head of the table of this mess of "officers and gentlemen" of which he was president, glaring at his watch and roaring at the pantry every five minutes, "Where the hell is my goddamn steak? How long does it *take* to grill a steak, for Chrissake?" And when the steak finally came, he carved and gulped it, still flushed and angry, and stomped up to his cabin while the others finished their stew in embarrassed silence.

On another occasion, when he was served Kadota figs for dessert, Katschinski called the leading steward into the wardroom, chewed him out for five minutes and threatened to have his stripes if he, Katschinski, ever saw another Kadota fig on his plate. After the meal when Gus Adams and I were on our way out on deck, Gus said the only funny thing I ever heard him utter. Passing the hatch down into the forward mess hall where a sailor was lustily polishing off his dessert, Gus said, "Look at that son of a bitch! He's eating the Old Man's figs!"

But my relations with Gus, never good, deteriorated further under the strain of inactivity, aggravated by his persistent resistance to recommending Ted Gruhn for a well-deserved promotion to chief carpenter's mate. Gus's animosity to Gruhn, born out of the issue of custody of the welding machine and reinforced by the Coke machine incident, my refusal to permit Ted to work for Gus in engineering spaces, and no doubt his Mohawk haircut at the line-crossing initiation, were translated into an absolute and thus far successful determination to prevent the promotion.

Gus could on occasion also be downright offensive. "Come on, Ed," he said in all seriousness one day. "Which would you really rather do, have a good piece of tail or scratch your spik itch?" "Spik itch," it turned out, was old Navy for athlete's foot.

Friction also increased among the crew. More men than usual grew ugly and abusive on a few beers ashore and carried their grudges back aboard. Bo'sun's mate second Fred Manger knew how to handle that problem. At the first sign of serious friction among his men, he ordered them back to the fantail, laced them into big sixteen-ounce boxing gloves and refereed as many three-minute rounds as it took to work off their hostility.

There were a few occasions, some good, some bad, which punctuated and enlivened the long stay in Manus. When *Abercrombie* arrived on 3 November, a new officer was waiting for her. Ensign George Quinn was a twenty-two-year-old graduate of the University of Washington, Seattle, and a native of Spokane, and was recently commissioned at the Reserve Midshipmen's School in Chicago. George looked his youth. He was bright, affable, eager to listen and learn, and he was assigned as Assistant Communications Officer under Keith Wheeling. At the end of her Manus siesta, *Abercrombie* received still another officer, Lieutenant (j. g.) Melvin

I. Rosenberg, a former payroll auditor for the state of New York, originally from Willimantic, Connecticut, married, and with a son born since DE343 returned to Manus. Rosie was a relatively mature twenty-seven with several naval schools behind him, including recognition training, but this was his first sea duty. He was also a very lucky man. His original orders had assigned him to the *Samuel B. Roberts*. He had missed her by just one day at Pearl Harbor and again by one day when she sailed to Leyte Gulf from Manus. Rosie became Assistant Gunnery Officer under Tom Parlon, and Recognition Officer. The former job was available because right after *Abercrombie*'s return from Leyte, she had lost the first of her original ten officers. Red Bond, who had cured the main-battery problems and who besides being Assistant Gunnery Officer had also been Mess Treasurer, CIC Officer and Second Division Officer, was ordered back to Pearl to be an instructor in the gunnery school he had attended earlier. With calm acceptance, displaying neither joy to be out of the war nor regret at leaving his friends and shipmates, hearty, cheerful, amiable as always, Red simply packed, climbed down into the whaleboat, waved and disappeared from our lives, leaving a noticeable vacuum.

Over a beer or two at the little Kuruniat "O" Club, *Abercrombie*'s officers did a lot of talking. One sunny afternoon Tom Parlon reminded me that after his account of being sunk on the *Vanderbilt*, I owed him a sea story. He had heard of an encounter I had had with enemy shore batteries off Sicily, and insisted that I give a full account. This is what I told him:

We were only five miles from the breakwater at Porto Empedocle, Sicily, inbound in late afternoon with two landing craft astern, when the first dirty brown column of water suddenly sprouted a couple of hundred yards to seaward. It was followed at intervals of a few seconds by several more, moving purposefully toward the pair of LCMs. The LCM cox'ns reacted instantly, by separating and heading offshore at full speed.

Our main battery, a forward single forty-millimeter, swung its muzzle toward the shore, searching for a target while the hull pounded with the feet of men scrambling to their battle stations.

As we reversed course, I searched the coast through my binoculars, looking for flashes or smoke that would give us a target. The little harbor of Empedocle looked empty and deserted. About two miles east a light haze of blue smoke hung over a hillside cemetery. The gun crew gleefully opened fire, thumping out some twenty rounds of armor-piercing projectiles. The morale of my twenty-nine-man crew soared. Yet the shell splashes still chased the LCMs.

In a few, very long minutes, we overtook the churning LCMs, and I yelled at them to head for shelter at Punta Blanca, a high cape we had passed while coming west from the five-day-old beachhead at Gela. The cape was either in friendly hands or unoccupied. Around that corner we would be out of sight from Empedocle. We resumed our maximum speed of fourteen knots, zigzagging violently but staying between the LCMs and the cemetery—now well out of our range.

As soon as the two landing craft turned eastward, the enemy gunners shifted targets from the LCMs to us, and a new battery opened up. Twice shrapnel buzzed through our rigging and lodged in our sides. I ordered the crews of the forty-millimeters and the three aft twenty-millimeters to abandon their useless guns and hit the deck. I began to "chase the splashes," an old trick, but I gambled that the enemy artilleryman didn't know it. When a splash was to seaward, I turned sharply in that direction, figuring the enemy gunner would correct by reducing his range; thus, the next round would fall short. When it did, I turned shoreward, and when he corrected by increasing range, the next round would be long. It is not a game to be played for long unless the enemy is slow-witted. Each time we turned, I prayed that he had not yet caught on.

For about five minutes we played this game, taking us about a mile closer to Punta Blanca. Then like a bolt of lightning, a pair of enemy projectiles shattered the water surface about fifty feet to port. We went back to a radical zigzag at full speed.

As we approached Punta Blanca, the enemy fire became slower and less accurate. At the end of the longest twenty-five minutes of all our lives, we rounded Punta Blanca behind the two LCMs and slowed to idle speed.

It was the day before my twenty-fifth birthday, but that afternoon I learned about the responsibility of command. I learned that it means seeing your shipmates flat on the deck with helmets pulled down and life jackets pulled up, and seeing those vicious splashes slamming up the wake. It means hearing only one voice on that ship—your own—and knowing that twenty-nine other lives depend on what that voice says, when it says it, and that that voice had better sound confident and assured—or all confidence and assurance will be lost.

Now it was decision time. Our orders were to deliver the LCMs to the skipper of a minesweeper at Porto Empedocle. We had approached close enough before coming under fire to see there was no minesweeper in that little breakwater harbor. Was the minesweeper scheduled to arrive shortly? Were there friendly ground forces at Porto Empedocle? If so, were we expected to fight our way in, perhaps under cover of darkness, to make the delivery as ordered?

I took out the order I had received that morning from a U.S. Navy captain off Gela. It said to deliver the two LCMs to a commander in the USS *Staff* (AM114) at Porto Empedocle. And it also listed two radio frequencies by which to communicate with the writer of the orders and one by which to contact the *Staff*.

As our radioman tried to make contact, we patrolled slowly back and forth in the lee of Punta Blanca, and the LCMs lay to, close inshore. After twenty minutes the radioman reported no luck on any of the three frequencies. We then sighted several warships offshore, approaching Punta Blanca from the west—a group of U.S. minesweepers, including two of the *Staff* class. As they drew closer, we were able to signal them by flashing light and thus determined that one was indeed the *Staff*.

Incredibly, as the shutter of our signal light was clattering out a message to the *Staff*, a huge geyser erupted alongside her. Her light went out, and she began to settle by the bow. We thought she had been hit by shore batteries, but in a few minutes her light began to blink again. She told us she had struck a mine and to return the two LCMs to Gela.

The landing-craft crews received the news with unrestrained elation. It was dusk as we headed back. While still in visual contact with the crippled but slowly moving *Staff*, we blinked, "Is Empedocle in enemy hands?" The reply came flashing back across the evening sea, "Yes, we believe it is."

The date was 15 July. A week later [in port] in Bizerte, we learned that Empedocle had been occupied by U.S. Army Rangers on the sixteenth. It was not a bad little operation out on the periphery of a war. The timing was just slightly off.

Nothing like that distant adventure happened at Manus.

But on 9 November, three of the single-engine planes which routinely flew in and out of the local airstrip turned out to be Japanese. They blew up a large tank of aviation gasoline, destroyed an Australian fighter on the ground, and wrecked the postal tent and the snack bar. Casualties were light and the raid was recognized as an isolated fluke. CAP over Manus was reenforced, and identification procedures tightened. All ships present were ordered to maintain Condition III (one third of the armament manned) during daylight and to be prepared to black out at once in the event of a night alert. It didn't happen again.

Then on 10 November in a single instant, 372 men were killed, 371 wounded, a large ship and 10 landing craft (LCMs) sunk, and 34 anchored ships damaged more or less seriously. I had the eight-to-twelve watch that morning and had just ducked down off the open bridge into the pilothouse to make an entry in the log when there was a heavy, jarring thud and a blast of concussion strong enough even inside the pilothouse to stagger me. I jumped back out to the bridge to see a full quarter of the sky astern obscured by a huge, mushrooming cloud of brown smoke out of which were arching scores of dark objects trailing cometlike tails of smoke. At the same moment a row of three big splashes suddenly sprouted at the harbor entrance. I passed the word for all hands to take cover and buzzed the Captain in his cabin. The harbor voice radio circuit announced then that the ammunition ship *Mount Hood* (AE11), loaded with four thousand tons of explosives, had blown up and disintegrated, taking with her the ten LCMs and their crews, which had been alongside loading, and seriously damaging several ships anchored nearby. All ships in the harbor were asked to send blood plasma and medical help for the survivors.

Tom Parlon, who had spent the previous afternoon at the Kuruniat Officers' Club with a party of *Mount Hood* officers, volunteered to take charge of *Abercrombie*'s whaleboat, and it shoved off at once with Tom, Chief Bailey, Doc Bour and Holloway for the four-mile run to the scene of the disaster. But in less than an hour they were back alongside. Where the twenty thousand-ton *Mount Hood* had been anchored, they found only scattered pieces of wooden staging and a dozen empty life jackets. With no survivors to help, they returned to the ship under skies still overcast with debris from the explosion.

Over the next few days whatever details were known filtered down to the *Abercrombie*.

Of *Mount Hood*'s complement of 296 men and 22 officers, there were only 18 survivors. One officer and eleven men had been ashore picking up mail and official publications, and keeping dental appointments. A two-man working party in an LCM had been delivering ammunition to the *Omaney Bay*. One man had been in the brig ashore. And a boat crew of three men had just put *Mount Hood*'s Supply Officer aboard the repair ship *Mindanao*—where he was killed by flying debris minutes later. There was a rumor that a signalman had been blown from the bridge and landed in the water a mile away with only a few scratches on his back, but it was never confirmed. There was another rumor that a plane without distinguishable markings had bombed the *Mount Hood*. Tokyo Rose was quick to claim that a midget submarine had torpedoed the ship. However, no one knew, nor would ever know, what had caused the *Mount Hood*'s ammunition to detonate. All we knew were the results—a crater three hundred feet by fifty feet and thirty to forty feet deep in the harbor bottom, a chunk of metal sixteen by ten, which was the largest piece of the ship ever found, and a ring of battered ships around what had been her anchorage.

Worst hit was the *Mindanao,* a liberty ship converted for the overhaul and repair of gasoline and diesel engines for aircraft and boats. Her thin merchant-ship hull and superstructure were badly holed and battered, seventy men on deck were killed, including the unlucky officer from *Mount Hood,* and casualties totaled two hundred. *Argonne,* another converted merchantman, equipped for heavy repair and salvage work, was smashed up topside. The big destroyer tender *Piedmont,* anchored a mile away, was hit by two 500-pound bombs that penetrated four decks, but not being armed fortunately failed to detonate.

Of more personal interest to *Abercrombie*'s crew was the damage to their sister ship, *Oberrender* (DE344), anchored only 1,500 yards from the doomed ammunition ship. A few days after the explosion, Abbot Gibney, an *Oberrender* quartermaster, told a group of *Abercrombie* sailors on the recreation island what it had been like.

Gibney had been correcting charts in CIC on that bright Tuesday morning when the ship began to roll inexplicably and to rise and fall with a peculiar, abnormal motion. At the same time, the metal door to CIC, which had been closed and latched, swung open in a puff of dust and fine debris, then slammed closed and blew open again. When the men in CIC ran out to investigate, they saw a large wave approaching the ship's stern, which was enveloped in white smoke, and above the wave a towering purple cloud was boiling upward.

General Quarters immediately rang through *Oberrender,* and as Gibney made his way to his battle station in after steering, he found the deck cluttered with .50-caliber machine-gun rounds (although the DE carried no such weapons) and great numbers of the larger, more familiar twenty-millimeter cartridges. A shipmate running aft with Gibney recoiled in horror from a mangled red lump on the deck. "Jesus!" he cried. "There's some poor bastard's guts!" A closer look showed it was only a chunk of Spam that had been blown out of its can three quarters of a mile away. Back on the fantail, several twenty-millimeter gun barrels had been blasted through the depth charges, and yellow Torpex explosive was scattered across the deck under the racks. With his phones on, Gibney stuck his head out of the after steering scuttle and watched *Oberrender*'s First Lieutenant and chief bo'sun's mate lug up five-inch projectiles from the engineering spaces and throw them overboard. Later he learned that an eight-inch shell had plunged down through the boat deck, killed a torpedoman working there, severed the arm of another man on the deck below, and finally smashed the main control panel in the after engine room. Forward, a huge hole had been ripped in *Oberrender's* starboard bow from deck to waterline by a hurtling, heavy but unidentified piece of structure or machinery that had also demolished the forward crew's shower. There was no trace of a sailor who had been over the starboard side forward scraping and repainting rust spots when the explosion occurred.

At the moment of disaster, Ensign John Murphy, *Oberrender's* Supply Officer, had just left the wardroom for the ship's office with a handful of newly censored mail. As he turned into the athwartships passageway just abaft the wardroom, he saw a mass of thick yellowish smoke at the starboard end of the passageway, and in the next instant was knocked flat, face down, the mail scattering across the deck. As he picked himself up along with the letters, he could hear the machine-gunlike hammering of debris from the explosion striking the ship and the simultaneous clanging of the general alarm. When he arrived at his battle station, he discovered he was bleeding from deep lacerations of both shins, acquired he knew not how.

Oberrender spent the remainder of November alongside repair ships and tenders being put back together and made ready for sea.

In *Abercrombie* one man was very lucky. Machinist's mate third Bob Zuzanek had spent all the previous day visiting a friend in *Mount Hood*.

At 0900 on the Sunday following the explosion, a memorial service was held at the military cemetery ashore, and all ships in the anchorage lowered their colors to half-mast from 0900 to 0930.

For an hour on the afternoon of 16 November, a band from destroyer tender *Sierra* visited the *Suesens-Abercrombie* nest and entertained all with a concert of popular and semiclassical music.

On the twentieth *Abercrombie's* Mark 51 range finder, smashed in the collision with *Manila Bay*, was replaced with a new one from the Naval Supply Depot at Manus.

In the second half of November, rumors about the next operation increased in frequency and creativity. Twice there were orders to get underway, which were cancelled at the last minute. Then, on the twenty-seventh, *Abercrombie* received orders designating her as a control vessel for the next landing. That same day an LCM pulled alongside with four large, wooden, olive-drab crates of special radio transmitters, receivers and antennas. Finally at 0900 on 28 November, *Abercrombie's* hook came up from its long rest on the bottom mud at Manus; all alone, she stood out of the harbor entrance and took the sea.

It was clear from the use of the term "control vessel" that in the next operation, wherever and whenever it would be, DE343 would not be maneuvering in relative safety thirty or forty miles offshore as she had done at Leyte Gulf. The function of a control vessel was implicit in the phrase, and several of us had seen the job being done. It called for anchoring at a very precise location on the line of departure close in to an assault beach to act as a navigational checkpoint for the landing craft which would form up around her and which would then leave for the shore in carefully scheduled waves at a signal from the control vessel. Since a control vessel's function was readily apparent from the shore, she usually came in for considerable enemy attention.

However, when *Abercrombie* sailed from Manus in late November, she was bound not for battle but to practice for battle. It took three calm days and two glorious, gentle, moon-filled nights steaming at fifteen knots to reach the anchorage at Cape Torokina, Empress Augusta Bay, on Bougainville, the largest of the Solomon Islands. Land was nearly always in sight or on radar, high, green, heavily wooded islands—New Guinea, New Britain, the Trobriands, and finally Bougainville itself. It was a relaxing, easy passage, running a zigzag plan in daylight, steaming straight ahead at night, no station to keep, no other ships to worry about, no screen commander quick with his "Posits" (take proper position) and "Expedites." It was interrupted by only two unscheduled General Quarters, one for a sonar contact, which went bad, and one on the approach to Cape Torokina when planes were seen making bombing runs ahead but turned out to be "friendlies" training. For me the passage was memorable because for the first time, I had a roommate. The last day in Manus the little stateroom was pungent and smoky from the cutting and welding required to install an upper bunk over mine, and that evening the Division Medical Officer moved in. Don Ervin was a warm and likable young doctor from upstate New York, newly married and enthusiastic about both his marriage and medicine. His specialty was in, of all fields, gynecology.

Bougainville is so high it could be seen from *Abercrombie*'s bridge at sixty miles. Inland from the anchorage at Cape Torokina the land is low and flat and tangled with jungle, but a few miles back there are steep, thickly wooded hills, and mountains beyond whose bare tops are so high they are often lost in the clouds. One mountain was an active volcano with smoke pouring from its crater and steaming ribbons of lava flowing down its sides. The anchorage was crowded with all the ships and small craft associated with an amphibious assault—big attack transports (APAs) and attack cargo ships (AKAs), LSTs by the dozens, LSMs and LCIs looking more like awkward seagoing machines than ships; and little LCVPs (Landing Craft, Vehicles and Personnel) and bigger LCMs, with toaster-grill bow ramps and armored boxes at their sterns, churning back and forth among the larger craft. Here and there among the landing craft and transports were the PCs, YMSs and the subchasers (SCs) familiar to me from the Med. A line of SCs patrolled patiently offshore.

Abercrombie was allowed one day to prepare; then on 2 November, four generals, a commodore and a Navy captain came aboard to observe the first rehearsal, bringing with them an ensign and five radiomen to set up and operate the new radios. The next day DE343 got under way, manned battle stations and reanchored 4,500 yards off a nearby beach while the radios crackled and scratched, the LCVPs, LCIs, LSMs and LSTs approached from seaward, lined up abeam and at the drop of a flag from *Abercrombie*'s yardarm moved off toward shore. It was essentially a navigation and communications exercise, with the ship required to position herself with great precision and to launch each assault wave exactly according to schedule.

There were three more rehearsals and two days of screening formations of LSMs and LSTs as they practiced formation steaming and tactical maneuvers. Between days under way there were opportunities to see what things were like ashore.

Bougainville was a sleepy tropical jungle island in the process of being transformed by war and temperate zone energy. A year before, U.S. Marines had landed, seized the harbor and the airstrip, and pushed what enemy forces were left after that action ten miles back into the hills. They were still there. At night sailors sleeping topside on the anchored ships could hear the clattering of machine guns and the thudding of mortars in the interior as an occasional enemy unit attempted to penetrate the U.S. perimeter, now manned by Army troops who had relieved the Marines and who were in the process of being relieved in turn by Australians to whom the island had originally belonged. Japanese forces on Bougainville had long since been cut off from reenforcement and supply (the DE *USS England* had sunk the last sub attempting to supply the garrison back in May), and were no longer a threat except for occasional attempted raids for food and ammunition.

The great French sailor and navigator for whom the island had been named 176 years earlier could not have recognized his namesake in December of 1944. The jungle plain between the bay and the mountains roared and bustled with activity. Straight macadam or coral roads ran along the shore and back to the airstrip. Quonset huts and olive-drab tent cities lined the roads; trucks, jeeps and staff cars buzzed back and forth from harbor to airfield and driving was to the left because the island was Australian. Field telephones and military radios provided an efficient communications net. A noisy row of huge, gleaming diesel generators provided power. A roofed but wall-less movie theater provided entertainment. The airfield was busy with the arrivals and departures of C-47s, Venturas, Liberators and squadrons of Aussie Corsairs, which zoomed and rolled above the anchored ships after each sortie against the withering enemy garrison. Out of their unspoken but chronic homesickness, the tough Seabees who built the base had provided each facility with its own carefully lettered sign. The row of generators was named "Torokina Power and Light Company," the movie theater was "Loew's Torokina," and the airport was "Torokina International." There was also an Officers' Club which needed no sign. It was a long, open building facing the beach, with a bar at one end selling only beer and Coke, a jukebox in the middle, and lots of chairs and tables. It was there that I met a fraternity brother from college, and a young officer whom I had trained during a tour as instructor early in the war and who was now a staff communications officer. My former trainee provided food for thought. He said he had read the Leyte Op-Order without turning a hair, but after reading the order for the next operation he couldn't sleep for two nights.

Abercrombie was exactly two weeks off Bougainville, which again was too much inactivity for over 200 young men in a 306- by 37-foot steel hull in the tropics. Morale was not improved by the fact that even the local recreation island was too distant from DE343's anchorage to be used, and by the additional fact that there was no mail. It was being held at Manus for the ship's return. So while the occasional land breeze brought odors of earth and hot foliage and decaying vegetation, and while white dust rose from the roads ashore, and the C-47s settled toward Torokina International and thundered off again, *Abercrombie's* men tried to keep constructively busy preparing for the action ahead. Art Hellman and Mel Rosenberg held hours of recognition classes. Gus Adams ran engineering casualty drills, Tom Parlon worked his gun crews hard on the loading machine, and I held a variety of fire drills, demonstrations and lectures on damage control. The C and R gang earned the gratitude of the crew by making extensive, innovative (and unauthorized) alterations to the forced-draft ventilation system that made the living compartments tolerable at night. And every evening there were movies on the fantail.

In those two weeks also, Gus's objections were finally overridden, and the necessary papers were signed and mailed recommending Ted Gruhn for chief.

On 15 December, *Abercrombie* was under way shepherding a group of about one hundred LSTs and LSMs bound for a full-dress landing rehearsal at Huon Gulf, New Guinea—a site rumored to have been chosen for its close similarity to the actual invasion location. It was a slow voyage over a calm, hot sea, with the awkward landing craft shoving their big bow waves ahead of them at only eight knots. They were formed into a gray block of seagoing machines, ten columns of ten ships each. Three thousand yards ahead *Abercrombie* and *Picking*, a *Fletcher-*class DD, led the way in line abreast. On both sides an assortment of the PCs, PCEs and YMSs which would guide the landing craft to the line of departure guarded the formation's flanks. With the high jungle back of Huon Gulf in sight, a nearly identical force joined up, this one led by *Abercrombie's* old companion *Walter C. Wann*. When the two hundred landing craft and their escorts arrived off the rehearsal beach, the faster transports and AKAs were already there along with their escorts, which included the other three remaining ships of Escort Division 69 and all the DEs from Taffys 1, 2 and 3. It was an impressive force which gathered off that peaceful, curving beach, and for two days the landing practice went forward, wave after wave of boats and ships lining up abeam of *Abercrombie*, then charging for the shore on signal while the big ships lay at anchor farther out, the DEs and DDs patrolled for snooping subs, and sections of Corsairs circled protectively overhead.

Very early on the morning of 20 December, the masses of ships at Huon Gulf got under way, sorted themselves out, somehow managed to form into orderly dispositions, and departed for the run back to Manus. For *Abercrombie*, *Wann* and their two hundred plodding charges, that run took three days. But shortly after DE343's hook went down in familiar Seeadler Harbor, an LCVP came alongside piled high with bulging gray sacks of mail, and the long, slow, hot passage was forgotten. Those dirty sacks contained Christmas. Sonarman Frank Grout, *Abercrombie's* official postal clerk, had more volunteers than he could efficiently use to sort the mail by divisions, but eventually the job got done, division mail petty officers lugged their bags down to their living compartments, and within minutes crumbled cookies, Christmas candy and dried-out fruitcakes abounded throughout the ship. Some of the packages arrived torn and battered and some of the edibles were spoiled, since most had been two months on the way from the other side of the earth, but it didn't make the slightest difference.

It would have been easy for a man to feel sorry for himself at Manus at Christmas. After all, he was very far from home and those he loved. He had just participated in a major battle and was about to fight another.

But hardly anybody felt that way. It helped that Manus with its tropic heat and warship-crowded harbor held no reminders of familiar Christmases to pluck the heartstrings. The mail and the packages helped more. But simple, youthful optimism helped the most. There was not a man in *Abercrombie* who did not believe in his heart that this, or barely possibly the next, would be his last Christmas at war. It was not difficult with that conviction to tolerate what had to be tolerated anyway. And every effort was made by those in command to make Christmas between battles away from home as pleasant as possible. On the bridges of the anchored ships, the shutters of signal searchlights up and down the harbor clattered with a myriad of seasonal messages. Church services for all denominations were held on a dozen larger ships and the base chapel on the twenty-fourth and twenty-fifth. Free refreshments were served for Army and Navy enlisted men at the Fleet Recreation Center on Christmas Day. The Chief Petty Officers' Club invited all Army Master Sergeants to an open house on Christmas afternoon. Cocktail parties were held at the Officers' Club. Fresh provisions, including Christmas turkeys, were issued to all ships and were delivered to the smaller ones which had no boats.

In *Abercrombie*, wardroom, mess hall and chiefs' quarters were decorated with wreaths, boughs, candles and bows from home, and on Christmas Day a dinner was served that equaled the Thanksgiving triumph. The menu, designed, drawn and colored by tough but talented bo'sun's mate Fred Manger, depicted on its cover a rotund Santa Claus, clad only in red boots, mittens and a grass skirt, his bag of gifts on his back, being towed on an aquaplane by three lovingly detailed mermaids (two blondes and a redhead) against a background of cumulus cloud and a coconut palm.

Forty-eight hours after that sumptuous holiday meal, *Abercrombie* was under way, headed into action in a hostile bay 2,500 miles to the northwest. On the morning of the twenty-seventh, Keith Wheeling picked up his final batch of classified officer messenger mail ashore, the ship fueled to capacity from an anchored tanker, and at noon she stood out between the antisub nets to seaward. Although it was officially top secret, everyone on board that noontime knew their destination—Lingayen Gulf on the western shore of the northernmost Philippine island of Luzon. The troops going ashore were to take Manila and complete the reconquest of the Philippines. The sea route to Lingayen lay through Leyte Gulf, then for eight hundred miles through the narrow, contested waters between the islands of the Philippines, and in the final stages of the voyage, off Manila itself with its complex of enemy-held airfields.

It took literally all day for the huge armada to sortie from Manus and form up—a massive block of ships in ten columns of ten ships each, with major escorts ahead, the smaller ones patrolling the flanks, and a big tanker bringing up the rear. At sunset, with Manus still in sight astern, all ships were finally in formation, and fleet speed was increased from six to eight knots.

The first two days of this voyage back to the war were like a leisurely pleasure cruise with calm seas, moonlit nights, clear radar scopes and no sonar echoes. Then on the third day a deceivingly gentle ground swell developed from the northeast which kept the slim DEs rolling uncomfortably all the way to Leyte.

On 2 January a nearly identical group of landing craft and their escorts, including *Abercrombie*'s old companion the *Walter C. Wann*, plodded up over the horizon and fell in astern. On 3 January four CVEs escorted by four destroyers pulled in ahead, and an impressive force of two heavy and two light cruisers in line abreast *(Louisville,* HMAS *Australia, Columbia* and *Montpelier)*, with a full division of *Fletcher*-class destroyers ranging ahead, came plowing up purposefully from astern, making twice our speed, and passed rapidly out of sight. The sight of those swift, heavily gunned gray ships, signal flags snapping at their yards, steering in precise formation for our common destination, was at once comforting and deflating. Tied to the lumbering mass of landing craft, wallowing along at an eight-knot crawl, *Abercrombie*'s second-line position in the hierarchy of warships was never more painfully apparent.

The same day DE343 went alongside the tanker *Chepachet* (which she had escorted from Norfolk to Panama in the spring) and fueled with a seamanlike alacrity that drew a "Well done" from the task force commander, who named her first among the escorts in efficient fueling—a considerable accomplishment, since the competition included the *Wann* and six destroyers. It was a welcome boost to morale after the stigma of the *Manila Bay* disaster.

Also something occurred which could be put under the heading of "small world, big war." One of *Chepachet*'s officers appeared on the high wing of his bridge during fueling, recognized me far below on *Abercrombie*'s fo'c'sle, and yelled down, "Hi, Ed! Last time I saw you was in Casablanca!"

On that same eventful third day of January, another large formation of landing craft, this one including several columns of attack transports, converged from the westward and took up position ten miles ahead and about twenty miles behind the cruiser group, which had slowed and was still clearly visible on radar. So it was a truly massive assault force of well-escorted, troop-laden ships that turned westward into the now-peaceful waters of Leyte Gulf on the following afternoon of 4 January. With the surface-search (SL) radar on long scale, this was the way it looked from *Abercrombie*'s bridge:

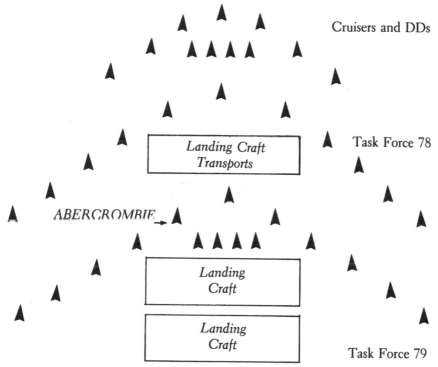

The mighty fleet passed through the now-historic Surigao Strait on the midwatch of 5 January. In *Abercrombie*, I had the deck. Of all the watches stood, four on and eight off, during three years at sea in wartime, that midwatch was the most memorable. It was punctuated by warm, drenching showers alternating with bright moonlight, and during the showers visibility was zero. In the moonlight the dark masses of steadily moving ships appeared on all sides, the high land bulking behind them. But at all times the SL scope on the bridge provided perfect visibility, the sweeping strobe painting the ships and land with light on each pass, leaving the narrow waters dark. The geometrical formations of bright blips on the scope turned in silent precision as the ships conformed to the channel in accordance with brief, crisp orders transmitted and acknowledged on TBS. Two decades before in peacetime, it would have been risky for a single ship to make the passage through the strait on such a night. Now, with the twin miracles of radar and radio, several hundred were doing so in wartime. Exactly seventy-one midwatches ago, while *Aber-*

crombie was screening her baby carriers just over the eastern horizon, those narrow seas had boomed and flashed with the final battleship-to-battleship engagement in all the long annals of naval history. Now the broken hulls and corpses of the enemy lay one hundred fathoms under *Abercrombie's* keel as the masses of U.S. ships steamed over them on their way to other actions.

At the south end of Surigao Strait, the invasion force entered the Mindanao Sea and all vestiges of a pleasure cruise disappeared. Bogies began showing up on radar at ranges of thirty to fifty miles, mostly over land, and a CAP of Wildcats from a covering group of four CVEs which had moved up astern was kept busy chasing them away. That afternoon a destroyer with a screening station on the starboard bow of the group ahead suddenly reported two torpedoes coming at her, then a midget sub, which broached momentarily at the other end of the torpedo wakes. A few minutes later *Abercrombie's* hull jarred repeatedly from the water hammers of a full ten-charge pattern of depth charges, and the destroyer announced that she had rammed, depth-charged and demolished the midget.

On 6 January as the force steamed slowly northward through the Sulu Sea, more and more bogies appeared on the scope, and disturbing reports began to filter in from ahead where minesweepers covered by old battleships and cruisers were already working in Lingayen Gulf. One highly relevant message warned that "convoys approaching Lingayen must expect sustained and heavy air attack from Mindoro northward. *Columbia*, *Australia*, *Colorado*, *O'Brien* hit and badly damaged by suicide bombers." Light cruiser *Columbia* and Aussie heavy cruiser *Australia* had just passed by on the approaches to Leyte. *Colorado* was a tough and famous old battlewagon, and *O'Brien*, a new, 2,200-ton *Sumner*-class destroyer.

And the news got worse. *Omaney Bay*—familiar to *Abercrombie* from Manus, the voyage to Leyte and Taffy 2—had been set afire and sunk by a suicider at the northern end of the Sulu Sea on the third. Heavy cruiser *Louisville*, which had swept by so proudly a few days earlier, had been crash-dived forward and heavily damaged on the fifth; and much closer to home, the *Stafford* (DE411), one of the five survivors of Escort Division 69, had been badly holed aft by another suicider also on 5 January, and had taken fourteen casualties. By the evening of the sixth, with three days to go before the landings at Lingayen, a total of sixteen ships had been reported hit; and a final gloomy dispatch said, "With the increasing damage to our ships, the possibility of action with enemy heavy surface forces becomes more likely, an action for which our forces are becoming progressively less and less prepared."

To many of *Abercrombie's* men it looked like Leyte all over again.

Where the hell was the invincible Task Force 38 this time? Could DE343 be so lucky twice?

The question about Task Force 38 was answered that same evening. Admiral Halsey, it appeared, was on station north of Luzon with his full force of big carriers and fast battleships, eager for a crack at any "enemy heavy surface forces" that might challenge the Lingayen operation. In the meantime, despite bad weather, his Hellcats, Helldivers and Avengers, were hammering at the home fields of the suiciders around Manila, attempting to stop their lethal raids before they started.

In the evening twilight of the sixth, standing helmeted and in life jackets at their battle stations in the soft, tropic evening, *Abercrombie's* worried sailors received a further measure of comfort when four of the Army's new P-61 Black Widow night fighters appeared overhead. They looked as deadly as their name with their long radar snouts and twin booms black against the darkening sky. They were to be night cover for the force and were most welcome as they swept protectively in tight formation across the moving ships.

Between General Quarters and taps that evening, there was a brief flashing and thudding of guns ahead, quick converging streams of red tracers, then on TBS came the clipped, laconic voice of the task group commander: "Bogey destroyed." Twice that night *Abercrombie's* men ran to their battle stations, each time for sonar contacts, which after several runs and careful evaluation turned out to be fish or currents or wake or thermal gradients, not submarines.

Very early the next morning, in the full darkness of the moonless, overcast night, DE343 made radar and voice contact with a group of tankers coming out from Mindoro. Once more, radar worked its miracle and the tankers slowed to formation speed and moved precisely into their assigned positions in the landing-craft formation, with no ship having seen the other until daylight showed each where it was supposed to be. At first light, *Abercrombie* fueled once more, this time from *Salamonie*. When DE343 pulled up to the big tanker's starboard side, DE412, the *Wann*, was already alongside to port. There was not much fuel to take and the rig was handled as smartly as before. But on the bridge, Katschinski was a yelling, cursing madman. Nothing was done well enough or quickly enough to satisfy him. Then, when *Abercrombie* had completed fueling, had cast off, and *Wann* was still alongside, the Captain was suddenly transformed into a calm, benignly smiling gentleman. He had beaten John, the skipper of the *Wann*, and that was all he had wanted. DE343 received another "Attaboy" for efficiency in fueling, but to the Captain's chagrin, so did the *Wann*.

All day on the seventh the invasion force moved northward with the high green ridges of Mindoro topped with long white clouds twenty to thirty miles to starboard. It was a beautiful Pacific day, flooded with sunshine and cooled by a light breeze, as gentle and peaceful as can be imagined. Yet here was where *Omaney Bay* had gone down in a storm of fires and explosions four days before. And that evening the first air attack came in.

It was dusk. There had been bogies on the fringes of the scope for an hour or more. *Abercrombie* was at General Quarters, waiting. Her screening station was on the port bow of the landing-craft formation. The Black Widows of the night patrol had been busy overhead, orbiting, then lining out first in one direction and then the other, according to the nearest threat. As usual, it was sweaty and stifling in the interior of the buttoned-up ship, and I climbed up to the torpedo deck through the little circular scuttle above Repair II to see if there was anything of interest to report to the men below. I arrived just in time. Two small, single-engine planes in loose formation were approaching high on the port beam. As I watched, they banked to their right, flew south for a moment in the opposite direction from the convoy course, then turned in toward it across *Abercrombie*'s stern. Despite all the hours of recognition training, I could not identify them, but something in my gut insisted, "They just don't look right." Art Hellman was up in the director for Mount 42, and I yelled at him and pointed. Just as he got his glasses on them they nosed over and began their dives—there were the red meatballs on their wings. They dived down together at 45-degree angles, rapidly gaining speed as they approached the convoy, which finally opened up with its forties then twenties. They were out of range of all *Abercrombie*'s guns except the aft five-incher, which couldn't be fired for fear of hitting the landing craft astern. Halfway down, the lead plane banked sharply and dived straight down at an LST in the second column. I was sure I was watching my first suicide attack, but at the very last instant, he suddenly pulled up and a small splash appeared alongside the LST. Then, with unbelievable stupidity, the enemy pilot leveled off at about three hundred feet and flew straight south down the side of the formation where every gun could bear. The whole port side of the convoy erupted with streams of twenty-millimeter tracers and small, dark puffs of the forty-millimeters detonating at four thousand yards, all converging on the lone low plane. In seconds it flashed into red flame and cartwheeled, blazing and smoking, into the sea.

The second plane was even less effective. He pulled out of his dive at about two thousand feet, as though he had changed his mind, then flew straight and level eastward across the front of the convoy, pursued by black sparkles of five-inch bursts, until he was out of range.

If this was the vaunted Japanese air attack, *Abercrombie's* men were not impressed. If this was the best the enemy could do, three years after the unscrupulous but bold and skillful attack on Pearl Harbor, they were relieved and comforted. I could not help comparing this first taste of action in the Pacific with German attacks in the Med, and I could not imagine a German pilot, with fat tankers, troop-laden transports and thin-skinned carriers in sight, dropping his single bomb on an LST, then committing suicide by flying at low altitude down the flank of a hostile formation where every gun could bear for minutes.

But as if to demonstrate that he would do better, the enemy gave DE343 a virtually sleepless night as the force steamed steadily northward past Manila Bay, Corregidor and Bataan.

At 2245, exactly an hour before I was scheduled to relieve Cy De-Coster for the midwatch, one of the destroyers ahead and to starboard picked up a "skunk" (unidentified surface target) on his radar. His challenge on TBS to the unknown ship rang crisp and clear on *Abercrombie's* bridge; he used the day's "shackle" code in which the letters of the alphabet represented the numbers zero through nine. "Unknown station," demanded the destroyer, "this is Voltaire. I have you bearing shackle Charlie Mike Xray unshackle, distance shackle Uncle Able William unshackle. Identify yourself. Over." There was no response, and "Voltaire" repeated the message. Silence. In a clipped, professional tone, the destroyer requested permission from the task group commander to open fire. The reply wasted no words: "Permission granted. Destroy all strangers." The sound of the last syllable had hardly died away when the darkness off to starboard was split wide open by the regular flashes of five-inch guns and in a moment was completely destroyed by the hanging white lights of star shells blossoming one after the other at equal intervals of perhaps ten or a dozen. Then the star shells ceased to appear, but the regular, relentless firing continued. The destroyer had sighted its target and was firing for hits. There were only two star shells left in the air, and darkness was closing down again when a great orange flash slammed the night back for several seconds, then died out with the dead star shells, leaving total blackness over all the steadily moving ships. The TBS crackled again: "This is Voltaire. Skunk destroyed."

That midwatch off Manila was a tense four hours. The scopes were never clear of bogies. The ships that were assigned radar warning duty reported closing ranges almost continually—twenty, ten, five and two miles. Often there were the sounds of engines low overhead. Occasionally off in the darkness were seen the white flash of an exploding bomb and the deliberate red flashes of a five-inch gun firing in full radar control.

Abercrombie ran totally blacked out, even the dim red instrument lights on the bridge were either turned out or shielded carefully from above. She no longer patrolled within the limits of her assigned station, but slowed to convoy speed and slipped quietly straight forward so as to leave as little wake as possible to guide the enemy. The ready guns trained quickly to each new danger bearing, muzzles pointing into the sky, waiting, loaded, cocked; tense hands were on their controls as their crews searching through the sights for the blacker shape in the black sky, the blue pinpoint of light from an exhaust flame, the first spit of strafing machine guns that would be the enemy. The only sounds were the hum of the forced-draft blowers ventilating the machinery spaces and berthing compartments below, the orders given and acknowledged in low voices, the hiss of the sea down the ship's sides, the periodic whir of electric motors elevating and training the guns, the whisper of the night breeze, and aircraft engines overhead, faint and loud, approaching, retreating.

Just before 0800 on the eighth, another attack came in and the men topside in *Abercrombie* witnessed their first suicide attacks. Again two single-engine planes had managed somehow to evade the CAP. They came in high from the west and dived nearly vertically on a formation of carriers that had taken position ahead. The impression given was of fast, reckless flying, but also of indecisiveness as to their targets. With the black bursts of five-inch blooming around it, the first plane reduced the steep angle of its dive at four or five thousand feet, slanted away to the northward, and flew straight into the superstructure of a transport in the starboard column of a group ahead of the carriers. All that could be seen from *Abercrombie* was a flash and a column of smoke. The second attacker continued his very steep dive to what looked like only a few feet from the water to starboard of the carriers, pulled out abruptly, and flew straight and very fast right into the side of the *Kadashan Bay* at her bow. There was a flash of red flame and a heavy puff of black smoke, which slid down the carrier's side, passed astern and died quickly to wisps of gray smoke in her wake. From *Abercrombie*'s bridge no damage to the carrier was visible, but in a few minutes it was evident that she was slightly down by the bow. Nevertheless, she continued on course and conducted flight operations all that day. The transport that had been hit quickly put out her fires, and she, too, maintained formation course and speed.

On 8 January *Abercrombie* was close enough to Lingayen Gulf to hear the radio traffic between the heavy ships that were shelling the shore and the light planes which were over the beach spotting for them. For example:

SHIP: Any more targets in that area?

SPOT: Well, you've hit all the important buildings; we *could* go back and level them if you want. Wait. Here's a shack in a field, might have a machine gun [technical spotting data]. Got it. Now let's walk up and down the road a little. Here come a couple of trucks [more spotting data].

SHIP: We are under air attack. Be with you in a minute.

By evening the number of ships hit by suiciders (now starting to be called kamikazes, which *Abercrombie*'s sailors somehow convoluted into kusi-kusies) was up to twenty, and a warning message came in by flashing light:

> Strong enemy suicide planes equipped to take phenomenal punishment. In one of yesterday's attacks a Frances advanced two thousand yards at two-five foot altitude against a most concentrated and accurate fire from all calibers of AA before crashing. Current practice is for fast planes to come in flying so low as to leave wake from propeller wash then by banking climb to collide with ships' superstructures. They generally come in from sun or from a land background suitable to their camouflage.

Those of us who stood watches on *Abercrombie*'s bridge took special note of that banking climb into the superstructure and were not comforted.

Although all hands were fully expecting one, there was no attack on the evening of the eighth. There was, in fact, a truly glorious sunset, with vivid reds and oranges blending in a clear, blue western sky. All appeared calm and peaceful when I came on watch for the 20–24. But at 2030 the bogies reappeared, and the next hours were an intensified repetition of the previous midwatch. Not only were the little blips of enemy planes constantly approaching from the periphery of the radar scope, and the sound of their engines droning overhead, but as the formation slowly turned to starboard and approached the relatively shallow and restricted waters of Lingayen Gulf, there were the added threats of mines and torpedo boats. Although the sweepers had cleared the minefields, there was always a danger of hitting a drifter they had cut loose and not destroyed. Floating mines were reported by several ships ahead. A special lookout with night-tinted binoculars and sound-powered phones was stationed at the jack staff in the eyes of the ship. He was relieved every thirty minutes, although it was doubtful that he could spot the dark bulk of a mine floating low in the night sea in time for the ship to be turned away.

Late in the midwatch, *Abercrombie* increased speed and pulled out ahead to be in position on the line of departure at daylight. Reveille was at 0415, steak and eggs were served in the mess hall at 0430, General Quarters was at 0500. It was 9 January 1944, S Day at Lingayen Gulf.

Her crew tense and expectant at their battle stations, *Abercrombie* ghosted in toward the hostile shore. It was a clear, starfilled night with a waning moon low in the west making a path on the still waters of the gulf and reflecting from the DE's dew-wet decks. Distant mountains rose against the stars to port and starboard but although it came in sharp and clear on radar, the low country ahead where the troops would go ashore could not be seen.

At 0600 the order was relayed through Don Wood to station the anchor detail. In preparation, that detail had been reduced to the minimum number. It consisted of *Abercrombie*'s First Lieutenant in charge, chief bo'sun's mate Holloway, carpenter's mate first Gruhn, and a seaman manning sound-powered phones. From the fo'c'sle, as the light increased and *Abercrombie* slipped silently forward, we could see only calm, empty sea ahead, but well astern and extending far out to port and starboard, loomed the dark shapes of hundreds of moving ships. Behind and above us in the center of the bridge we could see Katschinski's helmeted head as he stood on the raised platform behind the gyro repeater at the conn. Low voices came from the crew of the forward forty and the two 20-millimeters just below the bridge. Only a few feet aft of where we stood, Gun Captain Ed Schuh's head poked up out of the top of Mount 51, and the long barrel swung back and forth and up and down, though only a few degrees each way, and there was an intermittent whining of electric motors as the crew checked it out in train and elevation.

After a few minutes we could see the low, dark line of the beach ahead, and almost at once a ship astern and to port began firing. There was a yellow flash in the dusk, a red tracer arched across the sky, and seconds later we heard the muffled hammerblow of an explosion. As the light increased, more ships opened up until, as *Abercrombie* slowed and seemed to be groping for position, there was steady hammering from all sides. Loudest of all were the big guns of the *California*, which had moved up astern to about 1,500 yards and was lobbing her fourteen-inch shells right over our heads into the town of Lingayen, now visible behind the beach. Astern and to starboard at about the same distance, the light cruiser *Columbia* was delivering shattering six-inch broadsides.

Amid all this blasting of big guns, things were not going well on the bridge of DE343. It was vital to the entire operation that *Abercrombie* be precisely positioned off the beach, since the PCs, SCs and YMSs which would guide the troops to their assigned beaches would use her as a departure point. If she were out of place, then half the troops at Lingayen would be put ashore out of place as well which could lead at best to confusion and at worst to severe casualties. And Katschinski was not satisfied with his location as reported from CIC by Hicks, his Navigator. The Captain, his eye to the sighting vanes on the gyro repeater, kept shooting bearings of objects ashore and yelling down the voice tube at Hicks. One of his milder epithets was "Hicks, you son of a silly bitch!" Finally, with the ship dead in the water off the enemy beach and the masses of troop ships moving up astern, Katschinski dived into the pilot-house, down the steep ladder and around the corner into CIC, where he shoved Hicks aside, took a quick look at the chart, measured two distances with spread thumb and forefinger and ran back up to the bridge. On the fo'c'sle we felt the screws bite and the ship gather sternway. For what seemed a very long time, she backed along the beach, then the engines stopped and the order came down: "Let go the anchor." Holloway had been holding the light sledge in his right hand for twenty minutes. Now with one sweeping blow he knocked the pelican hook open, and the starboard anchor dropped with a jerk and a roar of chain through the hawse. Gruhn set up on the horizontal brass wheel of his brake and stopped the chain at thirty fathoms. Holloway set the stopper. It was 0700, exactly the moment at which according to the Op-Order *Abercrombie* was to be in position.

Out on the wing of the bridge, signalman Red Shiel lighted the arc on the big thirty-six-inch signal searchlight, pointed it seaward and began sending the dot-dash, dot-dash of the letter A for Attack Group "Able," the force which would capture the town and the airstrip at Lingayen. At the same instant, ten miles northeast along the beach, *Wann* began sending the dash-dot-dot-dot of the letter B for Attack Group "Baker," which would take San Fabian. The two DEs in effect were temporary floating lighthouses whose beacons would guide the invasion forces to their targets.

But on *Abercrombie*'s fo'c'sle, it was felt that her survival might well depend on her ability to abandon in a hurry the role of lighthouse for that of a fully maneuverable warship. To that end Gruhn and Holloway took apart the connecting link in the anchor chain at the thirty-fathom mark, greased it thoroughly and replaced it. Now, in a minute or less, the anchor and the 30 fathoms of chain that were in use could be separated from the remaining 170 fathoms in the chain locker and jettisoned if it became necessary to get underway in a hurry. In order to be able to recover the anchor and chain when the emergency was over, Holloway had prepared a buoy fashioned from a five-inch powder can (on which was tastefully painted in red "Here lies the anchor of the USS *Abercrombie*") and a thirty-fathom length of six-inch manila, the line to be secured on deck to the end of the section of chain in use. We were in the process of rigging line and buoy when the speaker at Mount 42 suddenly blared, "Clear the fo'c'sle! Stand by to commence firing!"

The thought of being on the fo'c'sle when the five-incher opened up was enough to get it cleared in record time. The little knot of four busy men vanished in three seconds. Holloway and I took no longer than that to make the shelter of the port side, Gruhn was even faster getting to starboard, and the talker, phones and all, dived down the open hatch abaft the anchor windlass, miraculously escaping serious injury. But it was a false alarm. There was no firing and we returned and completed the rig.

A few minutes after *Abercrombie*'s hook went down, the small craft of her control group appeared out of the masses of ships astern, homing on the flashing Morse "Able." As they had rehearsed it so many times, they positioned themselves along the line of departure that ran roughly east and west (077 and 257 degrees true) along the beach, with a YMS at five hundred yards and a PC at one thousand yards on either side of the DE.

It was now full daylight. On the bridge Hicks was checking the ship's position with bearings on charted objects ashore, reading the bearings to Zeke Marmon, who recorded them in a notebook for plotting. One bearing was on a charted church steeple in the town of Lingayen. Hicks sighted on it and gave the reading to Marmon. But in the thunder of gunfire the chief didn't hear and Hicks forgot the number. He swung the sight to check it again, straightened up frowning, put up his binoculars and shook his head. The steeple was gone.

By 0750 there had been no enemy opposition and it was getting uncomfortably hot in the airless passageway at Repair II. I requested and received permission for the repair parties to open one hatch at each station and step out for a brief breath of air. When we came out, blinking in the smoky sunlight, onto the main deck amidships starboard side, there were three planes circling in the distance, ahead and to starboard over land. Although the planes were too far away for positive identification, their appearance was unfamiliar, and we observed them with growing suspicion. As we watched, a black five-inch burst appeared among them, then another and another. As though triggered into action by the AA fire, all three planes turned and dived down toward the firing ships. I ordered the sailors of Repair II back inside the superstructure, but stayed at the hatch to watch. The lead plane was headed straight for *Abercrombie*. It grew rapidly in size as it slanted down, picking up speed. The ship shuddered as first the forward five inch and then Mount 41 began firing. The tracers of the forties were sailing up, clipping at the plane's wings. As the range closed, the forward starboard twenties opened up, pouring solid streams of tracers, which appeared to be converging on it. Then suddenly, perhaps five hundred yards away, the pilot banked left violently, nosed down and headed straight for the *Columbia* on *Abercrombie*'s starboard quarter. As he made the violent diving turn, his wing guns began to blink and the red tracers intersected at sharp angles with those coming up at him from the opposite direction. The cruiser was putting up a lashing torrent of AA, but the enemy plane was unstoppable. It looked as if the left wing just brushed the ship's forward main battery director high in her superstructure. Instantly there was no plane. Instead, there was a sudden streak of flame and smoke along the extension of the plane's flight path down to the water on *Columbia*'s port side. The flame vanished almost instantly. When the smoke blew away, the director was gone, the surrounding structure bent and blackened and emitting wisps of pale gray smoke.

I looked quickly for the second plane and saw it disappearing toward the horizon, surrounded by small black clouds of AA and pursued by streams of tracers.

The third enemy appeared to have reconsidered and was heading back overland in the direction from which he had come. He was out of effective AA range, and it looked as if he would make good his escape. Then suddenly he went into a steep dive, and from nowhere two dark Wildcats appeared on his tail. Light-colored smoke streamed back over the Wildcats' wings as they opened fire, and the Japanese plane began to make smoke of a darker shade as it plunged into a small cloud. The two fighters followed it in, and in a few seconds the enemy plane came spiraling out of the bottom of the cloud trailing heavy smoke and flame. The spiral continued straight into the ground, where first a puff and then a short pillar of smoke marked the end of the action.

For about twenty minutes after she was hit, *Columbia*'s six-inch battery was silent. When she opened up again, she seemed to be firing faster, as if to make up for the time lost. We learned later that in that instant of flame and explosion when the kamikaze's wing had seemed to brush the director, twenty-four of *Columbia*'s men had died and another sixty-eight had been wounded.

The second plane had gone on to cut off the mast of the *Hodges* (DE231), astern, but caused no casualties.

The nearest approximation to a casualty in *Abercrombie* occurred in the pilothouse. Helmsman Howard Amos, with no helm to tend while the ship was at anchor, was watching the progress of the attack from a starboard porthole when the heavy battle cover for the port, hinged at the top, was jarred free by the firing of Mount 51 and slammed down on the back of his neck, momentarily forcing his face out of the opened port, where it was liberally peppered with wadding and grains of cordite from the forties and twenties but suffered no lasting damage.

As 0900 approached, the sea astern of *Abercrombie* was filled with ships, amphibious vehicles and landing craft of every kind. Farthest offshore were the big troop transports, their LCVPs churning in precise circles alongside. Nearer shore were the long, flat LSTs with their bow doors open and long pontoon causeways secured to their sides. Still closer in was a line of LSMs with their thin, off-center islands. Closest to *Abercrombie* there was another line of LCI gunboats with racks of rocket launchers on their foredecks. For some time the LSTs and LSMs had been disgorging amphibious tanks and tracked landing vehicles (LVTs), which now came churning up to the line of departure, low in the water and noisy, looking as though one breaking wave would swamp them.

First to go, a few minutes before 0900, was a row of LCI gunboats; then at exactly nine o'clock, the red and yellow "One" flag, which had been flying from both yardarms, plummeted down, the roar of diesels increased, and the thirteen amphibious tanks of Wave One headed for the beach behind the LCIs. As the first wave of tanks approached the beach, the ships' firing slackened as they concentrated on the flanks and on targets well inland. Soon *Abercrombie*'s men could see the rippling flashes of the LCIs' rockets and clouds of dust and smoke rising from their impacts on the shore. Minutes later the amphibious tanks disappeared into the haze at the water's edge.

Waves Two, Three and Four were LVTs, the short, ugly barrels of .75-millimeter howitzers poking up forward, and rows of helmeted assault troops packed in aft. On *Abercrombie*'s bridge, they counted eighty-four LVTs. Then came LCVPs, faster, higher in the water, carrying twice as many soldiers, nine waves of them—165 boats. Then a dozen LCMs followed, each with a tank in its well; and finally came four big LSMs loaded with vehicles and troops. As the boats went by, some passing close down the DE's sides, her men looked down at the assault troops—soaked with spray, inhaling the diesel exhaust, packed in more tightly than the Seventh Avenue IRT subway at rush hour—and gave thanks for the relative comfort in which they lived, for their lockers, their clean, dry bunks and, as advertised by Fred Manger, their hearty three squares of hot food a day.

As wave after wave passed by and more and more troops dashed ashore, twin-engine Army A-20 light bombers appeared, bombing and strafing at low level over the land behind the beach amid occasional bursts of enemy AA. A couple of times they drew Tom Parlon's professional attention as they headed momentarily in *Abercrombie's* direction, looking, through the battle haze, a lot like Japanese Bettys.

By 1000, eight full waves were ashore, and as the empty LCVPs went by on their way back to the transports for another load, their crews were grinning. "Duck soup!" they yelled. "No opposition."

Around 1100 the last wave was ashore, and the big attack transports and AKAs began to leave the relative safety of the rear areas and move right in to the beach. They looked dignified and irresistible as they steamed slowly shoreward like sedate old hens or ducks, with swarms of landing craft in their wakes and cargo booms rigged out on both sides ready to begin unloading.

With all the troops ashore and the transports well inside the line of departure, *Abercrombie's* job as control vessel was over. General Quarters was secured, the ensign and five sailors who had been aboard as a Communications Control Team since Bougainville shoved off in an LCVP from one of the transports, the anchor came up, and the DE steamed slowly out to join a line of other DEs and DDs that were acting as an antisub and AA screen for the bigger ships.

At noon came a report on TBS that San Fabian and the Lingayen airstrip were in U.S. hands.

The afternoon was quiet and hot. *Abercrombie's* guns pointed constantly into the sky and trained around incessantly, watching. The great gulf was busy in deadly earnest with the complex business of unloading men and supplies for a major campaign over the surf-swept beaches. One by one the transports returned to the rendezvous area empty, their swarms of boats rigged in for sea, anchored and waited. By late afternoon they were all unloaded and ready, and the TBS began to crackle with orders to form a screen and a convoy and be off. At 1600 a message came in by flashing light from a small green ship in the distance. "Message for Lieutenant Stafford," it said. "About time you arrived here. Signed Murphy." He had been in the gulf for three days. By 1800, DE343 was under way again at twenty knots, following destroyers and DEs in a foaming column toward the open sea, and at General Quarters, was again under air attack.

The enemy planes came in from the south and west, flying high and seemingly not as determined as their dead brothers of the morning. The ships in the anchorage all made smoke, and the sky over them was heavy with several layers of clouds as *Abercrombie* steamed away. The gulf was a study in shades of gray, the clouds, the sea and the smoke all contributing their own variations, the whole picture repeatedly cut to pieces by red tracer streams shooting upward, converging toward the target, a single black plane, high and scared, dodging impossibly between the countless black puffs of flak and somehow escaping the red balls of forty-millimeters reaching up for it. One plane started to glide toward the heavy warships, but ran into such a blast of firing that he changed his mind, leveled off and flew entirely across the harbor before a five-inch burst came too close and he tumbled down harmlessly in flames.

The raid didn't last long and the dark came quickly. The convoy was formed invisibly but swiftly by radar and TBS in the face of a stiff breeze that blew out of the pitch-blackness of the night sea ahead—forty empty transports escorted by heavy cruiser *Australia*, light cruisers *Columbia* and *Denver*, seven destroyers, and four DEs. One of the latter was *Hodges*, looking strangely streamlined with no mast but doing her job nevertheless.

It was a rough, wet, uncomfortable night, but *Abercrombie*'s men, their combat mission accomplished competently, were relieved and content. They were also deeply impressed with what they had seen done on that busy ninth of January. Mert Olson commented that were he on the other side, he would be mightily discouraged. How could you hope to defeat a nation that was able to bring forty big transports full of men through hundreds of miles of hostile waters, unload the troops over an enemy-held beach at dawn and steam away again at dusk untouched?

But although the assault troops were safely ashore, the Lingayen operation was far from over. A message from the task group commander warned that "tonight enemy surface flank attacks from Manila Bay area and from west possible . . ." and ordered a destroyer to take picket position ten miles west of the formation, another ten miles in the direction of Manila Bay. "If enemy contacted," he instructed tersely, "interpose, engage, destroy."

There was no surface action that night, but at 0700 the next morning when Tom Parlon was Officer of the Deck, with no alert from the radar guard ships, a single plane appeared overhead. Since the CAP always flew in sections of two or in divisions of four, a single aircraft was immediately suspicious, and Tom quickly identified this one as a Zeke. *Abercrombie*'s station was on the port bow of the force as it headed south, and the Zeke was approaching from that side. Tom buzzed the Captain. There was no response. He gave the target to the ready guns, Mounts 51 and 42, and when they reported the plane in their sights, he ordered, "Commence firing!" As had happened the previous morning off Lingayen, when the first five-inch burst blossomed just below him, the enemy pilot rolled into a dive. As he did so, the other ships began firing. In an instant the whole sky in that direction was laced with tracers and AA bursts, and the enemy pilot, faced with a rising river of fire, leveled his wings, added power and retired rapidly toward the northeast. Apparently this plane had been one of three attackers because minutes later the CAP reported destroying two more.

The force of empty transports plunged and rolled southward at fourteen knots through the western fringes of a typhoon. Their escorts looked more like partially surfaced submarines than destroyers and DEs as they sliced through the breaking swells, throwing solid water mast high and rolling through 60 to 80 degrees. On *Abercrombie*'s bridge out on the port bow of the formation, the watch was drenched and nearly blinded by repeated deluges of salt water, binoculars soaked and useless because both hands were needed simply for holding on. But all day, typhoon or not, large task units of landing craft and freighters wallowed past in the opposite direction, bringing reenforcements to the beachhead at Lingayen.

The force passed through Mindoro Strait on the midwatch of the eleventh, and when it entered Surigao Strait on the morning of the twelfth, the typhoon had passed on to the northeast, and except for a residual ground swell and scattered violent rain squalls, the sea was moderate and the going comfortable once more. But the storm had left the narrow waters littered with debris—branches, whole trees, occasional boxes, barrels and timbers—which kept *Abercrombie*'s lookouts busy reporting and identifying.

Around 0800 their vigilance was rewarded. In the distance off to port they sighted what looked like a raft with several men aboard. When the sighting was reported to the screen commander, he ordered DE343 to "proceed independently, investigate and report." *Abercrombie* sheared out of formation and in a few minutes was circling the object. It turned out to be a capsized outrigger sailing canoe, with three ragged, brown-skinned young men perched uncomfortably on its keel. As the DE circled, her side lined with curious sailors, the castaways made their needs clear despite the language barrier by patting their concave stomachs, pointing down their open mouths, shaking their heads and rolling their eyes. After one full circle, the whaleboat was swung out, manned and lowered away. On Katschinski's orders I was in charge, armed with my .45 as a precaution against possible treachery.

By the time we arrived at the capsized outrigger, the boys (they looked fifteen to eighteen) had packed up what gear they had been able to salvage into a pair of straw baskets. As we pulled alongside, they left the bottom of the canoe and, balancing delicately, walked out to us along the outrigger. We searched the two baskets for weapons, then took them aboard and back to the ship, where Cy DeCoster, *Abercrombie*'s universal interpreter, questioned them in Spanish. Their names were Tarciano Patino, Pedro G. Clarin and Candido Pongeras. Their outrigger had capsized in the typhoon four days before, and three other passengers had drowned, including the sister of one of the survivors. The boys claimed to be anti-Japanese guerrillas, but since they came from the enemy-held island of Mindanao and were carrying over $100,000 in Philippine currency, the Captain ordered them placed under guard and isolated from the crew until they could be interrogated ashore. They were taken below for hot showers and a hot meal, fitted out with clean, dry clothes and issued mattresses, which were placed on the main deck in the shade of the superstructure where all three immediately fell asleep.

DE343 reentered Leyte Gulf in late afternoon. At 1730 she was released from the transport screen by signal and directed to "anchor in berth previously assigned." But it was two hours later and full dark before the starboard anchor finally rumbled down in San Pedro Bay far up in the northwest corner of the gulf. For the last hour under way, the bridge and CIC rang with profanity and verbal abuse directed at the Navigator by the Commanding Officer, some of it loud enough to be heard by the anchor detail on the fo'c'sle. Several times Katschinski made use of his favorite epithet, "You son of a silly bitch!" and twice *Abercrombie*'s Executive Officer was invited to confer with his Captain with a bellowed "Goddamnit, Hicks, get your ass up here on the bridge!" Sailors on watch in the pilothouse and on the bridge grinned in embarrassment as Hicks puffed up the ladder from CIC and ducked through the pilothouse to appear red-faced and sweating before his C.O.

With the starboard anchor down in eleven fathoms of water, and with sixty fathoms of chain out, Katschinski decided not to station the normal in-port watch of a gangway petty officer, OOD, and messenger and sentries fore and aft. There had been recent air attacks on ships in the gulf, so he maintained the "war cruising" setup of manned guns and control stations.

Daylight on the thirteenth showed an anchorage crowded with warships of every type and size, and a sky full of the roar and whistle of aircraft —sharp-nosed P-51 Mustangs, powerful-looking P-47 Thunderbolts, graceful, gull-winged F4U Corsairs, twin-engine B-26 Marauders and A-20 Hudsons—circling in and out of an airstrip extending for a couple of miles just behind the beach.

DE343 stayed at anchor with her guns manned all that day; then for two nights she joined the antisub patrol to seaward of the anchorage. It was not until the fifteenth that Keith Wheeling was able to lead a detail on a muddy all-day trek which finally delivered the three Filipino boys to naval authorities in the town of Tacloban—fifteen miles from *Abercrombie*'s anchorage.

Life in San Pedro Bay was like being at sea but without the breeze created by the ship's way. The guns were manned around the clock. There was no liberty or shore leave and an unsatisfactory trickle of mail. The tankers, tenders and supply ships were a two-hour whaleboat trip from where the DEs were anchored which could have used their services. The post office was two hours away by boat or fifteen miles of muddy hitchhiking.

At Leyte *Abercrombie*'s men heard for the first time about the bloody kamikaze attacks on *Suesens, Le Ray Wilson* and *Gilligan* (DE508). All three ships were on antisub patrol at the entrance to Lingayen and all came under attack in the low visibility of early morning. *Wilson* (DE414) was hit first. There was no warning. At 0710 the port lookout sighted a twin-engine aircraft racing in low on the water out of the semidarkness to the westward and already within half a mile of the ship. *Wilson*'s guns opened up immediately, and in seconds the plane's port wing and engine were blazing. But it would not go down and flew straight into the DE's superstructure at the aft end of the bridge. The fuselage and the engines demolished the whaleboat and the two amidships twenty-millimeters and their crews, crashed through between mast and stack, and tumbled flaming over the starboard side. The wings wiped out the port flag bag, perforated and distorted the stack, battered the torpedo tubes and spread burning gasoline over the superstructure deck. Six men were killed outright, two were fatally injured and five more wounded. But the *Le Ray Wilson* had her fires out in five minutes and continued her patrol.

Two days later *Gilligan* got it in much the same way, with the enemy again using exactly the tactics about which the invasion force had been warned as it approached Lingayen. Just before 0700 the DE's surface-search radar picked up a high-speed target eight miles out and closing rapidly from the west. Gunners and lookouts vainly searched the still-dark sea in that direction until they felt as though their eyeballs were well out among the prisms and mirrors of their binoculars. Then, only one thousand yards away and flying at an estimated two hundred miles an hour, a twin-engine Japanese Betty bomber broke out of the gloom, flat down on the morning sea, strafing viciously as it bored straight in on the DE's starboard beam. The instant the plane was seen, every *Gilligan* gunner opened up, firing fast and steadily, the tracers lining out horizontally to meet the hurtling enemy head on. But as advertised, the Betty could take terrible punishment and keep flying. Mount 42's twin barrels were level with the sea and pumping out their explosive rounds at the rate of one a second when the kamikaze flew right down their muzzles. The plane's bomb detonated on impact, its fuel tanks exploded, and in an instant flames one hundred feet high enveloped the DE from torpedo tubes to fantail. Repair parties ran aft with hoses, spray nozzles and chemical foam, and in a few minutes the fires were out. But Mount 42, its adjacent director and all the men who had manned it were gone. Only one man, the Assistant Gunnery Officer, survived. Badly wounded, he was pulled from the water by a rescue party from a nearby APD. *Gilligan* lost twelve men that morning, and thirteen more were wounded.

Suesens, two miles on *Gilligan*'s port beam, had witnessed the short, violent action and came alongside to assist with fire fighting and searching for survivors. But *Gilligan* had her fires out by 0716, and boats from the fast transport *Schley* (APD14) picked up all survivors. Which was just as well because at 0730 *Suesens* had her own troubles. Her air search picked up a single plane to the northeast, range five miles. A minute later it was in sight, a single-engine enemy Hamp fighter approaching at about four thousand feet from *Suesens*'s starboard quarter. Apparently plane and DE saw each other at the same moment. The plane nosed over in a diving left turn. The DE went to emergency flank speed with full right rudder to bring all her starboard guns to bear, and opened up with everything she had. And in this case that was literally everything because the plane was high enough so that even the portside twenty-millimeters had a shot. The Hamp came slanting down straight for *Suesens*, gaining speed at a terrifying rate through a fire storm of tracers and five-inch bursts. Somewhere short of the ship the pilot must have found the death he was seeking but the plane kept coming, pulled by gravity and its roaring engine. For a sickening instant it looked as though *Suesens* would be another *Gilligan* because the spinning prop seemed sighted directly on Mount 42. But in the final tenth of a second the relative movement of the racing ship and the plummeting plane combined to cause a miss. The Hamp hurtled across the mount and its director with less than five feet to spare, smashed into the sea and exploded so close to the DE's port side that her stern passed over the debris.

However, *Suesens* did not escape completely. Fragments of the plane and its bomb came whistling back aboard to bloody nine sailors with punctures and lacerations of faces, arms, thighs, backs and buttocks. My friend Larry Flynn, her First Lieutenant, was hit in the neck by a chunk of shrapnel, which mercifully lodged in the collar of his kapok life jacket and did him no harm.

Stafford (DE411) was also in Leyte, snugged up to a big repair ship, and with a jagged, gaping hole in her starboard side was awaiting dry-docking. On a visit to the repair ship for fire-control parts, *Abercrombie's* men learned what had happened.

Stafford was part of an antisub hunter-killer group composed of CVE *Tulagi* and four other DEs, steaming northward toward Lingayen on 5 January. By late afternoon the force was about one hundred miles south-west of Manila in company with several other task groups headed in the same direction. The sea was calm with light winds and good visibility. At 1745, DE411's radar picked up a group of planes approaching from due west. All guns were trained out in that direction, which was on the port beam, and in less than a minute, eight single-engine Zeke fighters came in sight, spread out in a ragged line low on the water. *Stafford's* five-inch guns opened up at a range of eight thousand yards, and almost immediately four of the Zekes peeled off to their right to pass well astern of the DE. The other four, their engines snarling at maximum power, continued straight ahead to pass just forward. Caught in the lash of forty-millimeter tracers and five-inch bursts, one of the Zekes flamed briefly, nosed over and tore into the sea about 1,500 yards off *Stafford's* port bow. A second one began trailing smoke and wobbling erratically but about five-hundred-yards dead ahead, it banked steeply around to the right and, like a wounded animal that turns on its tormentor, headed straight for the DE's bridge. Faltering and losing altitude in a hail of fire as the starboard twenties got the range, the Zeke stubbornly kept coming and slammed into *Stafford's* starboard side in a gout of flame and smoke just aft of amidships at the waterline. Two DE sailors died instantly, a dozen more were wounded, and *Stafford's* number two fire and engine rooms quickly flooded to the level of the throttle wheels. But her guns continued to fire, and seconds after the Zeke had ripped into her side, they flamed and splashed a third of the four planes off the starboard bow. The fourth plane flew on out of range, and lookouts saw it crash into the port side of HMAS *Australia* in the group ahead.

Stafford isolated and shored up the flooded compartments, jettisoned all heavy objects aft, including depth charges and K-guns, the loading machine, half a dozen spare forty-millimeter barrels, eight depth-charge trucks, and the torpedo truck. She stayed at sea under her own power for five more days, beating off daily enemy air attacks with her deadly gun-nery, and joined the first convoy returning from Lingayen to Leyte.

Abercrombie was in Leyte for almost six days. During that time she fueled, took on dry and frozen provisions and patrolled against subma-rines with *Wann* and destroyer *Wickes* off the transport anchorage.

One morning when she was at anchor, she received an urgent call to join two destroyers as a hunter-killer group to locate and destroy a submarine that had been located and depth-charged just inside the mouth of Leyte Gulf. She got under way at 0540, joined the two destroyers off the transport anchorage, and by 0705 the three ships, in line abreast, four-thousand-yards apart, swept over the point of the original contact and set up a "retiring search" plan in the form of an expanding box. At 0145 sonar picked up a solid echo, which Cy classified as "possible sub."

Abercrombie went to General Quarters and attacked at fifteen knots. The echo which answered the sonar's sharp "ping" of transmission came back hard and sharp as the range closed. Art Sanderson on the sonar stack turned the little crank that aimed the ultrasonic beam below the surface, watched the big dials before him, and sang out ranges and bearings. The horizontal tracers made by the ASW recorder were short, dark lines. At one thousand yards Sanderson shifted to short scale, and the pings and echoes came twice as fast. At the recorder Cy lined up the edges of the traces, which formed a diagonal descending from left to right, and at 1055 gave the order to fire hedgehogs. A full pattern of twenty-four rippled up, two at a time, a tenth of a second between pairs, arched high out over Mount 51, and plummeted into the sea in a circle of small splashes 200 feet in diameter 270 yards ahead. Then there was nothing to do but wait for the heavy, fast-sinking projectiles to hit or miss. A hit by even one would mean thirty pounds of TNT would detonate against the sub, more than enough to blow a hole in the pressure hull and kill her. Since the hedgehogs would detonate only on contact, no explosion would mean no hit.

There was no explosion.

Abercrombie circled, searching, trying to regain contact while the two destroyers stood by a couple of miles away, staying clear but alert to prevent the sub's escape. At 1125 the echo came banging in again, and with the Captain at the conn and DeCoster at his recorder recommending courses to steer, DE343 launched a second attack. At 1132 the hedgehogs streamed up over the bow again and formed their lethal circle in the sea. Cy punched a stopwatch and watched its dial as he listened for the explosion which would mean a hit. Since the projectiles sank at a known number of feet per second, he would be able to determine the depth of the sub and set his stern-dropped charges accordingly. But again there was only silence from below the surface. *Abercrombie* continued the search until 1255 when she was ordered back to screen the transport anchorage with *Wann* and *Wickes*. Her men would have liked to continue the search until the target was clearly identified as sub or nonsub and if it was a sub, until it was either killed or had obviously escaped. Many submarines, they knew, had been sunk by DEs on the fourth, fifth or sixth attack. It was an unsatisfactory and disappointing action.

On the afternoon of the seventeenth, *Abercrombie* and *Suesens* arranged a historic exchange of movies—*Suesens* got *Dracula*, *Abercrombie* got *Casablanca*. But DE343 was short-changed; only seven of *Casablanca*'s eleven reels were received. An urgent message flashed out across the anchorage, and the missing reels were delivered by movie time on the eighteenth.

As it grew dark and the wind picked up on the evening of 18 January, *Abercrombie* got under way with the destroyer *Waller* and DEs *Kimmel* (584), *Nickel* (587), *Wann* and *Oberrender* screening three columns of attack transports bound for Biak in the Schouten Islands to load troops and equipment. A check of the chart showed Biak was about 1,100 miles southeast of Leyte at the mouth of the great gulf that almost severs the island of New Guinea at its western end.

It stayed rough, and *Abercrombie* rolled and pitched uncomfortably the whole four days to Biak. There were dawn and dusk General Quarters, fire drills (DE343 was now routinely getting the first streams of water on a simulated fire in less than one minute), flag-hoist drills and damage-control drills. Every morning there was a fuel status report to the screen commander in the format "Able," "Baker," "Charlie." Able was the amount of usable fuel aboard in barrels. Baker was the percentage of usable fuel remaining. And Charlie was the amount of fuel used during the past twenty-four hours. Daily inspections were held of the ship's magazines and smokeless powder samples, with "condition normal" duly recorded in the log. Zigzag plans went into effect before first light and continued until full dark or moonset, whichever came later. And there were lots of instructions by flashing light from both the task group and the screen commanders—what stations to take in the event of air attack; who would have radar guard duty on which days; when and when not to patrol within the limits of screening stations; when to change from night to day stations and back again; what action to take if surface skunks were detected; when and on what radio frequency to check IFF (Information Friend or Foe) radar indications; and finally, precisely how to set up an antisub screen for the transports as they entered port at Biak. All in all, it was a busy four days; but for Parlon, DeCoster and Stafford, who had been standing four on and eight off as OODs since Galveston, it was almost a pleasure cruise. Art Hellman had qualified as Officer of the Deck under way, so now they had the luxury of four on and *twelve* off—one watch in four instead of one in three. That meant more time to get caught up on departmental administrative paper work and correspondence, to put in effect scores of small measures to improve the efficiency of the ship in action, measures which derived from *Abercrombie*'s first brief experience in combat and from the experiences of other DEs; and it also meant the downright sinful pleasure of a full night's sleep every third night, even under way.

The force of transports and their screen recrossed the equator at 0236 on the moonless, overcast morning of Monday, 22 January, and at dawn the Schouten Islands were in sight. At 0735 the transports began maneuvering to form a single column to enter port while the escorts took up their preassigned screening stations. The operation took all day. It was 1600 before *Abercrombie* slipped through the narrow opening in the antisub net, and 1618 before she moored to the port side of one of the transports, the *John Land* (AP167), for fueling. By 1745 she had received 43,000 gallons of Navy Special number two black oil. She shut down one boiler and remained cozily at the side of the big ship all night. The *John Land* was anchored only a couple of hundred yards offshore and beyond the beach *Abercrombie*'s men could see a bare, dusty plain covered with neat rows of square, khaki-colored tents, low shedlike temporary buildings, and a mile-long airstrip that buzzed and roared continually with the landings and takeoffs of fat-bellied twin-engine C-46 Army transports. The crew was not impressed with Biak.

However, early the following morning they had a change of scenery. At 0745, DE343 cast off, and at 0820 she joined the other DEs of the screen on an antisub patrol offshore. She patrolled back and forth in phase with the other ships all day and all night; but late on the morning of the twenty-fourth, she was released, and she steamed around a stubby cape and anchored in the green and pleasant little harbor of Mios Wowendi Lagoon.

Mios Wowendi, although only a few miles from the transport anchorage, was a different world. It was a base for seaplanes, submarines, and PT boats, and home to a division of Australian corvettes, which were roughly comparable to U.S. DEs. Ashore there were palm trees swaying gently in green, open glades, several softball fields, an Officers' Club, a movie theater, a hospital, a post office and a special little recreation island for swimming, sunning, shelling and, of course, drinking beer. The anchorage itself was calm and nicely sheltered with a cool breeze at night despite its close proximity to the equator. The people ashore were hospitable, competent and truly dedicated to the support of people afloat, characteristics unfortunately not always found at shore bases. There was also a native village nearby inhabited by diminutive, very black people whose teeth were stained red from the nearly continuous chewing of mildly narcotic betel nuts, and the whites of whose eyes had for some unknown physiological reason taken on the same color. But the villagers had learned fast, and as their canoes approached the anchored ships to trade shells for cigarettes, across the placid little harbor came the strains of "Lay that pistol down, babe,/ Lay that pistol down./ Pistol-packin' momma/ Lay that pistol down!" They made it clear to prospective customers which side they were on—"Japs no damn good. 'Mericans *gooood!*" They learned fast in other ways, too. At the beginning of *Abercrombie*'s stay, a big, beautiful shell could be had for a pack of cigarettes. Ten days later when she sailed, the same quality shell cost a carton.

The lagoon at Mios Wowendi was an oasis in the desert of the war. There were spirited softball games between the DEs, followed by a swim and a few cold beers on the recreation island. Along with movies ashore and afloat, there were pleasant evenings at the Officers' Club talking with friends from other ships.

But the war was still there, oasis or not. "Next operation" rumors were rife, the most credible being assault landings to recapture Corregidor and Bataan once the troops were loaded. Every other day two DEs went to sea for a twenty-four-hour stint on antisub patrol, and since there were only five DEs and considerable maintenance work keeping one or the other in port for more than a day, that meant alternate days at sea and in port. From the patrol line a few miles offshore the DE sailors could watch the big transports approaching the airstrip at Biak, some of them towing boxy-looking troop gliders which they cut loose to angle down and disappear behind the trees. There were always one or two submarines tied up alongside the big subtender *Griffin,* and they frequently slipped out to sea, submerged and disappeared into a "submarine sanctuary" area where they conducted training and checked out weapons and equipment.

About forty PT boats were also in Mios Wowendi. They were jungle green and mean-looking, bristling with weaponry. Most of the time the PTs stayed moored in a long row right along the beach, but one day one came alongside *Abercrombie* so that its crew could buy cigarettes and candy from our little ship's store. The PT sailors told us that Biak was the major staging point for squadrons of boats deploying north to the Philippines and east to the Marianas. We also had an opportunity to examine the PT boat at close range. A lot of improvements had taken place since I had been familiar with PT boat squadrons in Sicily and North Africa. The Mediterranean boats had been armed with two torpedoes in heavy launching tubes, two twin .50-caliber machine guns abreast of each other just forward of the cockpit, and a single twenty-millimeter aft on the center line. This PT boat had dispensed with the launching tubes, and the torpedoes were in light racks from which they could simply be rolled over the side. The twin fifties were staggered so that both could bear over either side. There was a single-barrel forty-millimeter aft in place of the twenty-millimeter. And a thirty-five-millimeter cannon and a small mortar had been added forward. With a crew of fourteen and a speed of forty knots or better, she looked as though she could take care of herself.

While in Biak, there was trouble with *Abercrombie*'s sonar, the first since Panama. After days of testing and poring over thick technical manuals, the sonar team and Yates, the country-casual but competent radio technician, found the trouble was in the massive projector forward in the lowest compartment just above the sonar head itself where it projected below the keel. It was not repairable aboard, but the always cooperative establishment ashore agreed to have a try at fixing it if it could be delivered to their underwater sound laboratory. In a major effort, two big bolted plates above it were removed, and the heavy but fragile projector was manhandled up from keelson to topside, carefully loaded in the whaleboat and gently ferried ashore. There some grounded coils were ungrounded, and the whole arduous process was successfully accomplished in reverse the following day.

Only one temporary tiff between ships marred the Mios Wowendi idyll. At 1145 on the morning of Monday, 29 January, this message was received by flashing light from Lieutenant Commander F. G. Storey, skipper of the *Kimmel* (DE584):

> Message to Captain. Don't know if you are trying to prove you are bigger gamblers or better ballplayers. So far it looks as if you are former and we are latter. It is my opinion that large betting takes away from and makes game too serious. We play for fun. If our bets not large enough recommend you seek games elsewhere. [Signed] Captain Storey.

It didn't take Katschinski long to respond. A few minutes after noon, *Abercrombie*'s twelve-inch light began clattering, and by 1215 the Captain of the *Kimmel* had his answer:

> Do not know what happened to cause your last dispatch but will investigate. Agree with you entirely and recommend all bets off. Sorry as hell if anything unpleasant occurred. [Signed] Ski.

Four minutes later the final message came: "Do nothing hasty. Will see you at 1330 Storey." The tempest in the teapot had blown itself out, but henceforth *Abercrombie's* gung-ho teams bet no more than six cans per man.

There was an underlying poignancy to those softball games in which all the unique ambience of the American ball park was temporarily re-created on a remote island in the South Pacific—the chatter of the team in the field, the heckling of the team at bat, the raucous arguments about rules, the howling at the umpire, the slides in the dust and the final triumph or dejection. Then in a few moments the field was returned to its tropical island and the players to the gray ships in the harbor soon to sail back to the war.

One of the principal social pleasures of Biak for *Abercrombie's* officers was associating with their opposite numbers on the Australian corvettes. It was the same quasi-symbiotic association that existed between U.S. and British warships around the world and still does. Each nation provides its men-of-war with amenities that the other lacks or has to a lesser degree. In this case the Aussie wardrooms were comfortable, whereas in the U.S. DEs they were Spartan, with carpets, wooden furniture (one even had a piano), lots of portholes, and decorated with no stinting of paint in warm creams and reds. The Aussies also had "wine messes," which really meant private bars, while nothing alcoholic was permitted to be consumed aboard a U.S. ship except for medicinal purposes. However, the quality of the Aussie food was not up to American standards, and they had no movies. Thus it has become a pleasant interallied custom for two ward-rooms to join forces for an evening; cocktails on the British ship, dinner and movies on the American, and back to the Britisher for highballs and entertainment. In Biak the U.S. DEs and the Aussie corvettes were anchored in such convenient proximity that it was possible, and even customary, to visit several corvettes in the course of an evening; and as the hour grew later, each welcome was more boisterous and convivial than the one before. In their warmly clublike wardrooms, Aussies and Ameri-cans would settle back with a highball or a beer, and talk and sing. Singing was the Aussie officers' forte. They knew literally dozens of songs, each with many verses which progressed from mild to moderate to outrageous but hilarious indecency, and these they sang with loud, lusty and utterly contagious enjoyment.

The evening before departure from Biak, with the movies over and the fantail swept down and squared away, the men were preparing to turn in. Many had developed the habit of sleeping topside in port, escaping the hot and crowded berthing compartments. One was tough and salty Harry

Miles, who had staked out a claim on a twenty-millimeter ready-ammunition box where he had slept every night in Biak. On this particular evening, Roe Combs, a third class machinist's mate from north central Oklahoma, had the bad judgment to spread his mattress on Miles's ammunition locker and, furthermore, refused to remove it when Miles rather firmly asserted his prior claim. Miles, always quick to anger, wasted no more words and belted Combs in the mouth, badly splitting his upper lip and nearly breaking his jaw. He was treated in sick bay, but he bled profusely all night and had to be taken to a Medical Officer on another ship the next day. Miles was placed on report for "striking another person in the naval service" and restricted to the ship pending the next Captain's Mast. Mast was held at 1515 the following afternoon, and Miles was awarded a Summary Court Martial.

On 2 February the transports completed loading troops and equipment, and the pleasant Biak interlude was over. *Abercrombie* was on antisub patrol off the harbor entrance when first the other escorts and then the tall troop carriers filed out through the nets in the bright moonlight and began to form their cruising columns. It was almost midnight when she took her assigned screening station on the port bow of the disposition and moved off at thirteen and a half knots. With a calm sea, a bright moon, a good speed of advance, a simple zigzag plan, no skunks, no bogies and no sonar contacts, it was only four days from Biak to Leyte. There *Abercrombie* fueled and the whaleboat was dispatched to the Fleet Post Office for the accumulated mail which reportedly had been held there during the long stay in Biak. The suspense and expectation aboard was nearly palpable, and every long glass and pair of binoculars aboard was in use to detect the first sign of the returning boat. However, when it clanged up alongside, only one small mailbag was flung up. Mailman Frank Grout brought the incredible and depressing news that there were three to four thousand bags in the warehouse which had yet to be sorted. It was an angry and disappointed crew that turned in that night in DE343.

But there was no time for brooding. At 2345 that evening *Abercrombie* relieved DE509 on the antisub patrol for the anchorage, and at 1028 next morning she was back in screening station as the force of transports set course for Mindoro, where they would deliver their troops. The course to Mindoro lay back through the Surigao Strait. Those narrow waters where so many men had recently died were idyllic in their peaceful beauty as if to compensate for that earlier night of blood and thunder. The sea was light blue and mirror calm, the azure sky clear except for a scattering of small white clouds. The force was so big that *Abercrombie*'s starboard flank station took her in close to the deeply carpeted green hills of southern Leyte. Brown fishermen's shacks lined the shore where there were cozy little coves with overhanging trees, and blue smoke rose from cook fires high up on the hillsides. Flying fish now and then broke the surface and skimmed along to splash back in awkwardly a hundred yards or so away. Had the air been still, it would have been too warm, but *Abercrombie*'s thirteen knots made a pleasant breeze. An occasional outrigger with a brown lateen sail ghosted slowly along on invisible zephyrs from the land, but here the ugliness of war intruded to mar the scene. The DDs and DEs of the screen were ordered to investigate each one; it was sadly ridiculous to see a long, heavily gunned destroyer burst into speed and bear down on a little canoe whose mast reached barely to the DD's main deck. There would have been no need for gunfire; the warship's passage would have swamped and capsized the outrigger. But the escorts were gentle and passed by slowly with only a close visual inspection and friendly shouts of "*Mabuhay!*", which seemed to be the universal Filipino greeting.

The group steamed into Mangarin Bay on the west coast of Mindoro on the morning of 9 February, and the big ships immediately anchored in a line just offshore and began disembarking troops. *Abercrombie* was assigned a merchant tanker, the SS *Kennesaw Mountain,* from which to fuel, but had to anchor for an hour and twenty minutes while the merchant seamen had lunch before she could go alongside. Then it was right back out on patrol, but with a difference. Although there was a destroyer squadron commander and a DE division commander present, and although nine escorts were involved, no one had organized the patrol. No stations or sectors were assigned, no reference points, no courses to steer. The ships simply milled around, trying to stay out of each other's way. This worked marginally well during daylight, but at night it was a dangerous mess, with OODs trying to read each other's minds and using the radar scope as a kind of crystal ball. As a result the ships were occasionally fairly well spread out, but more often they were bunched in ways that would have permitted half a dozen enemy subs to enter the anchorage in line abreast. Fortunately, the Japanese were not aware of this opportunity, and the transports, secure in their fool's paradise with nine escorts on patrol, survived intact to sortie for Leyte the following afternoon.

Mindoro was the busiest air base *Abercrombie*'s men had ever seen. All day and most of the night, scores of B-24s, B-25s and A-20s roared out over the harbor at masthead height from runways just behind the beach, circled up, formed in Vs and echelons, and droned off to unknown targets while other formations swung in over the field, broke into landing circles, approached and put down. An officer who came aboard with official mail said there were two thousand planes at Mindoro and that half could be airborne in a matter of minutes in the event of enemy attack. It looked to *Abercrombie*'s crew as if the mighty Mindoro base alone, only an hour's flight time from Manila, could assure the quick reconquest of the Philippines.

On the morning of the tenth, a group of battered green destroyer transports (APDs) filed out of the harbor and turned north for Corregidor and Bataan. So much for the rumored "next operation." It was disappointing in a way. There would have been a lot of satisfaction in helping to recapture those places with names made both famous and infamous just three years before.

But on that same day back at Pearl Harbor, although no one on *Abercrombie* knew it, the detailed plan was issued for the real next operation. Its code name was "Iceberg," and it would make another island as famous as Corregidor. The name was Okinawa.

3. Okinawa

WITH WIND AND SEA astern it was a fast run back to Leyte, and by 1630 on Monday the twelfth of February, *Abercrombie* and *Wann* were both moored to the starboard side of a yard oiler, the *Mobilube*, in San Pedro Bay, refilling their tanks with black oil.

In Leyte there were five bags of old mail, and rumors. The rumors were pleasant ones for a change. The transports were going back to Pearl, and *Abercrombie*, *Wann* and *Oberrender* were to escort them there. Someone (unidentified) had seen a dispatch certifying *Abercrombie*'s availability for the job. Lending credence to this rumor was the fact that improved fire control and other gear for Escort Division 69 was known to be in Pearl and could be installed only there. The rumor turned out to have at least one element of truth. *Abercrombie* was going east all right, but only one thousand miles, not five thousand, and to Ulithi Atoll in the Caroline Islands, not to Pearl Harbor in the Hawaiian Islands. Departure was scheduled for 15 February. In the meantime there was the Summary Court Martial in the case of Harry Miles, who had requested me as his defense counsel.

On the afternoon of Tuesday the thirteenth, with *Abercrombie* swinging to her anchor in berth 518 in San Pedro Bay's inner harbor at Leyte, the wardroom became a courtroom and the trial began. As originally appointed, the court consisted of Hicks as Senior Member with Adams and Doc Ervin as members. Keith Wheeling was Recorder, which means both secretary and prosecutor. The three members of the court, in unaccustomed neckties and looking appropriately solemn, sat along the long forward side of the green-baize-covered mess table, each with a lined pad and a sharpened pencil. Keith sat at the narrow port end, with his dark red volume of *Naval Courts and Boards* open before him. Miles and I sat across from the court. Miles was freshly showered and shaved, in sharply creased, immaculate whites, and looked the model of a regular Navy first class petty officer (which, apart from rare explosions of violence, he was).

The proceedings began at 1335. It was apparent from the start that this was to be one of those trials typified by the probably apocryphal remark of an anonymous court member, "Let's bring the guilty bastard in, give him a fair trail and hang him." All three officers on the court were at least tacitly if not admittedly convinced of Miles's guilt and considered the trial by Summary Court simply a means of awarding a more severe punishment than the Captain could impose at Mast. So the first act of the defense was to challenge the members of the court as prejudiced. It was easy to show prejudice on the part of Hicks and Adams, and the accused was allowed one peremptory challenge which required no proof of prejudice, and that took care of Doc Ervin. Thus by 1400 the original court had been dissolved, and after some frantic typing back in the ship's office, a new court was sworn in with Tom Parlon as Senior Member and Cy DeCoster and Art Hellman as members.

With the new court seated, Miles pleaded not guilty, and Keith presented his evidence, which consisted of a parade of witnesses who had seen Miles slug Combs. The defense attempted to show that although the "striking" undeniably occurred, it was not done, as the specification charged, "willfully, maliciously, and without justifiable cause." The trial lasted all afternoon, with much clearing of the court to consult relevant paragraphs of *Naval Courts and Boards* while the accused and his counsel stood by outside the closed wardroom door. After a recess for evening chow, the court reconvened and finally adjourned at 2045. Much of the defense evidence was declared irrelevant and not admitted, but some strong points were made which may have reduced the severity of the sentence. Miles was found guilty and heavily fined, but not reduced in rate to electrician's mate second class as he had feared, all subject to the approval of the Division Commander as Convening Authority.

The run east to Ulithi was made in the teeth of twenty to thirty knots of northeast trades all the way, but there was something happy about just steering a base course of 093 degrees true day after day. Each morning there were tactical maneuvers and flag-hoist drills, with the ships swinging around in simultaneous turns so that suddenly the whole formation of transports and escorts would be steaming 90 degrees from the original course or on a 45-degree diagonal, all lined up exactly as before but pointing in a different direction, the bright flags snapping straight out from their halyards in the brisk trades augmented by a thirteen-knot speed of advance. On the morning of the seventeenth, the transport force split into two parts, the faster ships pulling ahead to arrive early at Ulithi. *Abercrombie* and *Wann* were assigned as escorts, increased speed to fifteen knots, and by midafternoon the last mast of the slower group had dropped below the horizon astern. The following afternoon an Avenger from Ulithi appeared overhead towing a sleeve, and the forties and twenties got in their first practice in months while the repair parties exercised at fire and damage-control drills, and the boarding and salvage and fire and rescue parties mustered on the boat deck with their gear. At 1430 the transports began filing past the low islands and submarine nets into the huge anchorage while the two DEs covered them from seaward. By 1530 the big ships were safely inside, and *Wann* and *Abercrombie* turned west at twenty knots to rejoin the second section. It showed up ahead on radar at 1830, and the rendezvous was made in the full dark of the 20–24 watch. At 2030 *Abercrombie* slowed to twelve knots and eased into her assigned station on the starboard bow of the formation without ever having sighted another ship. Daylight on the nineteenth found the second half of the transport force ready to enter port, and at 0840 *Abercrombie* herself slipped through the nets into the anchorage. Before she could even find her berth, an LCI came alongside with several bags of mail, as fine a greeting as could be imagined, and at 0934, DE343 dropped her port anchor in 23 fathoms, veering out 120 fathoms of chain.

No one in *Abercrombie* had ever seen anything like Ulithi. It was all sea and sky, you had to look for the land. The lagoon inside the thin ring of reefs and low islands was so large (twenty miles by about eight miles) that ships at one end of the anchorage were invisible from the other. Except for the lack of ground swell it was like anchoring in midocean. And add to sea and sky the trade wind. This was a continuous fact of life, like night and day, steady, always from due northeast, endlessly sweeping atoll and anchorage, driving the white breakers booming against the reefs, and the white masses of cumulus clouds overhead casting purple shadows on the sea as they passed. On the tiny islands in February of the fourth year of the war, there was a short airstrip, a small hospital, a post office, and on flat, sandy little Mogmog at the northern end, a glorious recreation area. But the lagoon could comfortably hold seven hundred ships—destroyer tenders, submarine tenders, seaplane tenders, tankers, repair ships, ammo ships, supply ships, floating dry docks—so that Ulithi was in effect a secure base in midocean for the warships needing those services, and a rest area for battle-weary seamen who could sleep there all night with no GQs at dusk and dawn, get some mail, see movies, and have a beer and a steak and a swim on Mogmog.

It was also uniquely a temporary United States community in mid-Pacific, a community in which all the homes and stores, offices and warehouses, churches and theaters, filling stations and repair shops were gray ships; in which all the cars and trucks were boats; all the streets and highways, water; all the telephones were radios, flashing lights, flag hoists or semaphore; and all the people, young and male. There was even a comparable social stratification—big, impressive homes (carriers, battle-ships and cruisers), project housing (destroyer and DE types), low-rent apartments (LSTs, LCIs, YMSs, PCs, SCs and their ilk). This unique community was literally the crossroads of the western Pacific; 830 miles north of Manus, 900 east of Leyte, 1,200 (less than four days' steaming at fifteen knots) from Lingayen and Okinawa. Almost every officer and man who served aboard a ship in the Pacific in 1944 or 1945 spent at least a few days at anchor in Ulithi. It was a place to run into friends and get news of others—and to hear the newest rumor about the next operation.

In Ulithi I myself found two old friends, heard news of several others, and said good-bye to another. Owen B. Murphy's beat-up old green APD, the *Humphreys,* was in, tugging at her anchor in the trade-wind chop. He sent one of his many boats over for me, and we had lunch in his narrow but salty World War I wardroom. Murph was now a full commander and had been officially commended for his skill and courage in command of the destroyer transports at Leyte and Lingayen. This was the seaman who hated guns! He was as warmly gossipy as ever, with news of mutual friends. One young couple was expecting a second child. Two other officers were on duty in the Aleutians. Another, a fine officer from an old Philadelphia family, was dead, blown up on the fantail of the cruiser *Birmingham* where he had been in charge of a repair party. *Birmingham* had been alongside the light carrier *Princeton,* mortally wounded by a kamikaze off the Philippines during the battle for Leyte Gulf. She was helping to fight the carrier's raging fires when *Princeton's* torpedo stowage detonated, almost sinking the cruiser and decimating her topside crewmen.

Later Murph returned my visit with dinner in *Abercrombie's* ward-room and a seat of honor at the movies.

Two former roommates at the Naval Academy, now submariners, were also in port. One was in *Skipjack,* and the other in *Archerfish,* which only four months before had acquired immortality by putting down the biggest ship ever sunk by a submarine—the 59,000-ton Japanese carrier *Shinano,* destroyed with five torpedo hits on her maiden voyage after an all-night, all-out surface chase.

Abercrombie lost Art Hellman during her stay in Ulithi. The paint-salesman-turned-naval officer (and a fine one at that) was detached to attend a month-long gunnery school at Pearl, but his orders were appar-ently changed later because we never saw Art again. His consistent good humor had been an important element in the atmosphere of DE343's little wardroom from the day of commissioning, and had been a blessing to the busy precommissioning crew from the day of his arrival at the shed on the dock in Orange opposite the yellow hull which would one day be *Abercrombie*. Art's departure changed ever so slightly the developing character of the living ship. He was also missed in a more definitive way by Parlon, DeCoster and Stafford, who would now go back to the all-too-familiar routine of four on and eight off under way.

Abercrombie's unique personality underwent another change at Ulithi, one brought about, like Art Hellman's departure, by one of her officers. Mel Rosenberg, aboard only two months, had his turn one sun-and-wind-filled afternoon to be Officer in Charge of the liberty party on Mogmog. An essential part of his duty was personally to issue the four or five cans of beer allotted to each man, assuring an equitable distribution but using discretion and good judgment in so doing. Rosie, stripped to the waist, stood behind a barrels-and-plank bar, opening the cans and handing them out to the fifty-odd sailors ashore, one of whom kept track on the liberty list of how many each man was issued. The island was noisy, with liberty parties from other ships also ashore, men playing softball and touch football, yelling, singing, and always the dry thrashing of the palms in the trades and the rumble of the surf. Out of that broad, confused spectrum of sound came an occasional angry voice, and Rosie, alert to quench any trouble before it began, sought out the source. It was my erstwhile client, Harry Miles. Harry had consumed three of his four cans and was turning ugly, pushing and threatening. When Miles made his way to the bar for his final can, Rosie had a condition.

"Miles," he told the electrician's mate, "your shipmates are ashore to relax and enjoy themselves, not to fight or be threatened. Apparently you don't hold your beer very well. I'll issue you one more can if you will give me your word that you will ease off and cause no more trouble with your mates."

But Miles was morose and truculent. "I *rate* my four beers, and I don't have to make no promises to get 'em!" He stood glowering at Rosie, fists clenched, but the big jaygee just shrugged his shoulders and ignored him, methodically issuing beer to a continuous line of other sailors. It was chief machinist's mate Schoeneman who cooled the situation down. He knew Miles for the crack electrician and devoted family man he was, and he had a good idea of what was eating him.

"Mr. Rosenberg," he said, "I'll be responsible for Miles if you'll let him have that last beer. I'll see there's no trouble."

Without a word Rosie opened a can and handed it to Miles, who accepted it in matching silence and walked away with Schoeneman, muttering and shaking his head.

In the packed LCM returning to the ship, Miles was still vocally resentful. "Goddamn jaygee," Rosie heard him grouse, "he's just hiding behind that gold braid 'cause he knows I'd knock his block off!"

Rosie disembarked first and waited for Miles to come up the ladder to *Abercrombie*'s quarterdeck where he confronted him. "You seem to have a lot of resentment and some serious misunderstandings," he told Miles. "Want to put on the gloves and have a crack at me?" Rosie pointed to his bare and sweaty wrists and shoulders. "See? No gold braid."

"Yes, *sir!*" said Miles, and the two men, comparable in height, weight and age, headed aft for the open space on the fantail. Someone came up with the ship's sixteen-ounce gloves, and while they were being laced on, someone else found Fred Manger, the ship's perennial referee. The "ring" was a circle about fifteen feet in diameter with no ropes or posts, its circumference lined with several rows of fascinated sailors. Manger was serious and professional, with stopwatch and whistle. There would, he said, be three 3-minute rounds with two-minute rest periods between. The men would shake hands before and after the fight. There would be no decision.

They shook hands quickly, a token touching of the clumsy gloves. Manger blew his whistle and Miles charged. Harry had learned to fight on the playgrounds and waterfront streets of New Bedford, and in a hundred bars around the littoral of the Atlantic. He was quick and he hit hard, which made him dangerous (and a good man to have on your side) in a brawl. But the ring was not his element. The advantage of surprise was missing, and the heavy gloves got in his way. Nevertheless, this was his chance to get even, to hit an officer legally! He bored in, swinging, and the circle of sailors cheered as the officer backed away, ducking and blocking. In the first round Harry threw about fifty punches, roundhouse rights and lefts and wicked uppercuts. One hit Rosie high on the head, staggering him a little. An uppercut painfully grazed his nose, making it red and sore. The rest he ducked or blocked. Rosie was a boxer.

When Miles came out for the second round, he was running out of gas. He swung mightily and often, but much of his speed was gone. Rosie stopped backing off and stood his ground, blocking with forearms and shoulders, slowing Miles and keeping him off balance with a long left lead to the face.

The fight between the tough sailor-electrician and the former payroll auditor went the full distance. Thanks to the pillowlike gloves, no damage was done. There were some scrapes and red spots and lots of sweat, but the final handshake was a real one with solid contact of the eyes.

On the bridge a few days later, with *Abercrombie* bound westward from Ulithi, a signalman who bunked near Miles reported to Rosie that Harry Miles had been heard to say on more than one occasion, "That Rosenberg is the best goddamn officer on the ship!"

Harry Miles, the professional first class petty officer, missed his family with a chronic agony that his tough-guy self-image could neither admit nor share. Little Butch helped. It was okay for even a tough sailor to have and love a dog. But there had to be some release from the hurting loneliness, the awful awareness of wasted months—and Harry, groping, found it in belligerence and violence.

And Miles might well have been right about Rosie, if consideration for the crew was the criterion. In that respect, Rosenberg was the opposite of Gus with his "lots of sailors" philosophy. I don't think Rosie ever made a significant decision without first considering its effect on the welfare or morale of his men.

Abercrombie spent two weeks at Ulithi. Working on stages over the sides and in the superstructure, and bobbing on jury-rigged rafts alongside, the crew repainted the entire ship. She had entered dressed in the dazzle camouflage applied in Orange and left in a coat of solid, dark blue-gray. The men caught up on their mail. Everyone went over to Mogmog a couple of times or more. Movies were shown every night—some of them good, like *Random Harvest* and *Hail the Conquering Hero*—and the men learned to take their raingear with them, putting it on as quick showers blew over and the show continued.

One evening just at dusk, the war came back for a moment to Ulithi. The harbor radio net suddenly broadcast a "flash red" (attack imminent), and on all ships the crews ran to man their guns. From *Abercrombie* no plane was visible, and a "flash white" (all clear) came in only a minute or two. Later we learned that a single plane had come in high from the southwest, circled once over the other end of the lagoon and dived vertically on what the pilot had apparently picked as the biggest ship in sight. It was big all right, but it was an island, not a ship, and the single-engine fighter hardly made a dent in the sand and coral among the palms. It seems that the by-passed enemy garrison on Yap about once a month was able to put together a flyable plane out of the wreckage around their island, hide it in a cave, and at the appropriate time launch a suicide mission against Ulithi. This had been the mission for February.

Midway through the second week, *Abercrombie* received her orders. She was to proceed back to Leyte and report for duty to an amphibious group commander. That meant a landing somewhere, the next operation. Speculation was rife as to where it might be, but no one knew. Not yet.

DE343 left Ulithi early in the afternoon of 3 March with two old friends, *Wann* and *Oberrender* (now fully repaired after the *Mount Hood* explosion), screening three big, new, fast, well-armed tankers with the wonderfully resounding names of *Manatee*, *Monongahela* and *Cimarron*. *Wann* as senior ship and screen commander took station one, dead ahead, *Oberrender* station two to port, and *Abercrombie* station three to starboard. The tankers formed up in a wide triangle with the base forward, and for the three days it took to reach Leyte at fifteen and one-half knots, the little task group looked like this.

Wann
(412)

Oberrender
(344)   *Abercrombie*
                                                                                (343)

            Manatee   *Cimarron*

                        Monongahela

It was a hot westward run, with the trades astern at about the same velocity as our forward speed, giving us a relative wind of zero. The little task unit ran a continuous zigzag plan all the way. Aboard DE343 the deck force finished the whole-ship paint job by completing the decks, always the last parts to be done.

Except for one day of antiaircraft practice and a three-day training exercise with a group of attack transports and attack cargo ships, *Abercrombie* spent two weeks from 6 March to 21 March in the quiet anchorage at Leyte, sheltered by the dry, jungled hills, fueling, provisioning, making necessary repairs, taking on ammunition and receiving most of her back mail, figuratively charging her batteries for what lay ahead. And at Leyte, despite classification and security, the ominous Oriental place name where the next operation would take place inevitably leaked out and spread, like oil on the blue waters of the lagoon or like blood on a gray deck—Okinawa.

In *Abercrombie*'s pilothouse we broke out the charts and looked it up. Okinawa was astonishingly close to Japan itself. With spread dividers we

measured only 340 miles from the southernmost home island of Kyushu.
The same dividers picked off the same distance to enemy-held Formosa,
and only twenty miles farther to the Japanese-occupied coast of China.
Three hundred and sixty miles is less than two and a half hours even in
a slow bomber. How many airfields, how many planes, how many kamikazes, we wondered, were in range of Okinawa from Kyushu, Formosa and
the China coast, not to mention bases in other island groups even closer?
It seemed evident that each successive next operation was fated to be
hairier than the last, and that *Abercrombie* was equally fated to be part
and parcel of them all. No one permitted himself to envision what the
one after Okinawa would be like.

During the same two weeks, 1,500 miles to the northeast, U.S. Marines were blasting and burning the stubborn enemy out of the fortified
caves and tunnels of Iwo Jima; the fast carriers of Task Force 58 were
striking the airfields of Kyushu and getting clobbered in return by kamikazes; a Royal Navy task force of four carriers, two battleships and five
cruisers was moving up to Ulithi to join the war against Japan; in Europe,
American, British and Canadian Army groups were moving into position
to cross the Rhine and assault the heart of Germany, while to the east,
masses of Soviet armor, artillery and infantry were preparing a final assault
along a front extending from the Baltic in the north to Yugoslavia in the
south; and halfway around the globe in Burma, British and American
troops were occupying Mandalay and readying an assault on Rangoon.

But in the tiny world of the USS *Abercrombie*, waiting in now-tranquil
Leyte Gulf for the call to sail into action for the third time, small things
occupied men's minds. The Captain had a new daughter. The whaleboat
was staved in and abandoned. There were nurses at the DesPac Officers'
Club.

News of Katschinski's baby girl came in via a letter from his wife,
Nancy in the first load of mail on arrival at Leyte. She had been born 3
February, weighed six pounds even, and mother and daughter were flourishing. The news was almost as welcome to *Abercrombie*'s officers as to
the Captain himself. For the past month he had been withdrawn and
edgy, fretting at the lack of news, sweating out every mail delivery, terse,
abrupt and even less sociable than usual. Now he broke out the traditional
cigars, smiled, joked and went ashore with the other skippers and Commodore Phifer for what was apparently an entirely successful celebration.

Monday morning, the twelfth of March, broke cool and windy and the
seas in Leyte Gulf were short, steep, and five to eight feet from trough
to crest. But at 0610 *Abercrombie*'s whaleboat shoved off on its usual

routine of errands around the anchorage. Tall, dark, skinny Foch Costner was the cox'n, husky, blond Jack Green the bow hook, and Jim Bell the engineer. Costner had his orders straight from Hicks. He was to deliver some men to LCI751, anchored about a mile away, then drop an officer off at a small pier ashore, and return to the ship. The LCI was relatively easy, and by timing it right and jumping as a crest brought the whaleboat even with her deck, the working party was delivered as ordered. But making the pier was different. Unlike the LCI, which rose and fell with the whaleboat, it just sat there and let the seas break against it. And it had no give. The very first time that Costner attempted to come along-side, a sea picked up his bow and smashed it heavily against a piling. There was a splintering of wood, and water spurted through the broken side. Costner rang three bells and Bell jammed the diesel into reverse in an attempt to back clear. But before the boat could gather sternway, another wave threw it back against the pier, breaking off the rudder and nearly knocking Costner overboard with the resultant wrench of the tiller. With the engine running full throttle in reverse, the boat finally cleared the dock and backed out into the gulf. But it was in bad shape. It had taken a beating in the constant high chop of Ulithi with a dozen big ships a day to make, and now it was missing a rudder and taking on water. While Bell nursed his engine and Green bailed, Costner steered as best he could with one of the two emergency paddles. It was slow, risky work, and although all the men wore kapok life jackets as required by regulations, Costner could not swim.

After about an hour of this, with Green despite his best efforts losing ground to the incoming water and the waves that occasionally broke over the sides, a passing LCM threw over a line, took *Abercrombie*'s crippled boat in tow and brought her alongside an anchored attack cargo ship, the *Suffolk* (AKA69). There nonswimmer Costner hastily disembarked. With the help of some *Suffolk* sailors, a temporary patch was rigged, the boat bailed dry, and with Bell and Green aboard, the LCM began the tow back to *Abercrombie*.

But the day's adventures were not over.

Under the pounding of the seas, the temporary patch quickly failed, and even with Green and Bell both bailing furiously, the whaleboat began to fill. The LCM crew saw what was happening, slowed to bring the boat alongside, and the two men scrambled to safety. But when the towing resumed, the weight of the half-swamped boat was too much and the towline parted. Jack Green, not about to be charged with losing his ship's only boat, jumped back aboard, secured a new line—and was promptly knocked overboard by a cresting wave. Green was a strong swimmer. Since the LCM was closer but upwind and up sea, he elected to swim to an attack transport some fifty yards downwind and down sea. She was the *Henrico* (APA45). The LCM delivered the swamped boat and Bell to the same ship.

Aboard *Henrico* Green tried to have his boat hoisted out, but the OOD refused on the basis that the weight of the boat full of water would strain his gear. Then Green requested the LCM to tow the boat to the beach and let him and Bell off to take care of it. But the LCM cox'n had had enough and would not risk his boat in the surf along the beach to deliver either boat or men. With wind and sea setting strongly onshore, it was decided to cut the whaleboat loose and let her find her own way to the beach, where she could be salvaged later.

It was late in the afternoon when Green and Bell, soaked, chilled and exhausted, arrived back aboard DE343. Costner returned shortly afterward in a *Suffolk* LCVP. That same day a message was flashed to the destroyer tender *Cascade* requesting the manufacture of a replacement rudder and tiller.

The next morning *Abercrombie* got under way for three days of rehearsals for the Okinawa landings. This time she was not assigned as a control ship, but with the other escorts, she screened the transports en route to the landing beaches and patrolled offshore against subs and aircraft while they lowered their boats to practice the assault, then she joined up again to shield the theoretically empty ships as they withdrew.

Late in the evening of Thursday the fifteenth DE343 returned to her anchorage, and early the next morning began a three-day effort to locate and recover the ship's only boat. During that time *Abercrombie* shifted her berth three times in order to take on fuel, ammunition and provisions, but on the nineteenth, the boat was located and I took a salvage party, including Chief Holloway and engineer Jim Bell, ashore to recover it. It was a long trip. The *Wann*'s boat put us ashore at the town of Tacloban, and from there we hitchhiked south along the shore, past the old fort of Tolosa, now Navy headquarters ashore, through Dulog with its new U.S. Army cemetery, to the Army base at Tarraguna, a total distance of twenty-six miles.

Abercrombie's whaleboat looked like a derelict, canted over to starboard twenty yards from the water's edge, half filled with sand and with a splintery hole in her port bow. It took a couple of hours, while the tide was flooding, to dig the sand out of her and another hour to patch the hole with plywood. We flagged down a jeep on the coastal road which, as it roared away in four-wheel drive, tugged her down to the edge of the advancing sea. We had counted on the heavy boat traffic along the beach for help from there, and after about thirty minutes, with the first wavelets now smacking against the whaleboat's hull, the driver of a DUKW (pronounced "Duck") answered our arm-waving signals and came in to help. The big amphibious truck came lumbering up out of the sea like a monster from the deep, its diesel bellowing, until it stood towering over the whaleboat and its salvage crew. The DUKW's tires must have been six feet in diameter and its deck eight feet above the sand. With much roaring and rumbling it turned around and lined up ahead of the boat, pointed back out to sea. We secured a towline and ran alongside as the DUKW pulled the whaleboat through the shallow water like a toy. When she began to float, we clambered in. The patch held and in a few minutes we were several hundred yards offshore.

There the obliging DUKW driver cast us off to continue on his interrupted business, and we were on our own. The whaleboat's diesel was drowned out, its vital parts clogged with sand, and there was of course no rudder. But there were four paddles, and we plied them with a will, heading for the nearest ship where we hoped to get a tow back to the anchorage of San Pedro. The whaleboat had been solidly built by the Philadelphia Navy Yard and was reluctant to move under our puny paddles. And the onshore breeze was making up, adding to the effect of the still-flooding tide. Therefore, our progress was minimal and whenever we rested we were pushed back toward the surf on the beach.

After a couple of hours of this, the tropic dusk began to settle over the gulf, and what little boat traffic there had been in our vicinity dwindled to nothing. I stood up on the tillerless cox'n's platform in the stern and attempted to raise a ship, any ship, by semaphore. Nothing. We soaked a roll of canvas in diesel fuel and attempted to light it for use as a torch to attract attention. We should have known better. It takes more than a cigarette lighter to ignite diesel fuel in the open. I jumped back up in the gathering dusk to try semaphore again. At last an answering flashing light came from an LSM a couple of miles to seaward.

"F-R-O-M F-I-R-S-T L-T D-1-3-4-3 (*Abercrombie's* call sign)," I spelled out laboriously, not being the Navy's greatest signalman. "U-R-G-E-N-T-L-Y R-E-Q-U-E-S-T T-O-W T-O S-A-N P-E-D-R-O T-H-I-S O-U-R O-N-L-Y B-O-A-T." The unseen signalman provided a reassuring flash of his light at the end of each word and a satisfying dot-dash-dot "Roger" at the end. We waited rather nervously as the light faded and the surf line drew ever closer; but just before full dark an LCVP came charging downwind, pushing a big froth of white water ahead of its blunt ramp bow, and took us in tow. The cox'n said he had orders to bring us back to the LSM for the night. We were in no position to object and back we went.

Aboard the strange-looking craft, with its off-center cylindrical bridge structure that looked like a medieval battlement, I got a message off to *Abercrombie* reporting the situation and our location, saw that Holloway and his crew were provided for, had a welcome but really terrible supper which included not quite rehydrated dehydrated potatoes—and turned in.

The next morning, Tuesday the twentieth, Katschinski brought DE343 the twenty-six miles south from San Pedro to Tarraguna, and picked up his boat and his men. There was a final moment of excitement when the heaving line from the ship fell short, and Holloway, thoroughly fed up with the salvage operation, dived out of the drifting whaleboat and retrieved the monkey fist before it sank. When *Abercrombie* got under way again with boat and salvage party aboard, she was in such shallow water that the bottom mud swirled chocolate at her stern.

One of the creature comforts in Leyte Gulf was a truly delightful little Officers' Club on the southern shore of the island of Samar. It was known as the DesPac (for Destroyers Pacific) Café. Its membership card displayed graceful green palms, and one could buy books of twenty-five-cent chits for three dollars, good for a dozen drinks. In that benign climate, the little club had open sides and a peaked, thatched roof covering a large, square mahogany bar surrounded by tables. There was a regulation, stateside jukebox which filled the place with the tunes and songs of peace and home—Frank Sinatra, Bing Crosby, the Andrews Sisters, Benny Goodman, the Mills Brothers, both Dorseys, Glenn Miller, Ella Fitzgerald, Les Brown, Patti Page, Harry James. On any evening when *Abercrombie* happened to be moored within a reasonable distance, the whaleboat (before disaster befell it) would take two or three of her officers over for a couple of pleasant hours of relaxation and conversation.

On one such evening it was my turn, and I went over with Keith Wheeling. The DesPac Café was crowded with khaki uniforms. Japanese lanterns hung in the surrounding palms and lighted the short path up from the dock. The moon was bright. The music was full and mellow but not so loud that it interfered with conversation. We bought beers and sat down at one of the tables. Then we noticed that one of the khaki uniforms surrounded by a dozen others at the bar was shaped in a disturbingly different and disturbingly familiar way, and that it came with softly wavy brown hair and a young, animated, unutterably feminine face.

The sight of that attractive little nurse was an emotional, psychological and even physical shock that would seem exaggerated and incredible to a man leading a normal life. But at Leyte in the spring of 1944, no one was living a normal life. I was twenty-six years old. It had been seven months since I had been in the same room with a warm, living, flesh-and-blood woman. During that time, except for dreams, which I could not control, and the surges of longing released by my wife's occasional letters, a vital part of my life, as of any man's life, had been necessarily excised. In wartime in the western Pacific, the world contained only gray ships, green islands, blue sea, and men—there was effectively no such thing as a woman. The two-dimensional shadows a noisy projector caused to flicker across the movie screens of an evening were only tantalizing symbols from another world.

But over there at the bar, that was no symbol! I felt a little dazed, as though I had been solidly hit in a boxing match. My pulse quickened. In the cool of the tropic evening I felt flushed. My palms were damp. My mouth was dry. My attention span shrank toward zero. I drank my beer, got another and drank that too, and another. They were no help. I got up and moved across the room almost like a sleepwalker toward the semicircle of khaki backs. Somehow I penetrated the circle until I was close enough to sense her female fragrance and feel her warmth. I said something and she replied. The words are gone. Her eyes were clear and they looked directly into mine with—what? Interest. Perhaps tinged with compassion. My breathing actually became shallow and I had difficulty speaking. But there were too many other voices, other faces, other bodies. It was hopeless, without even a conscious realization of what it was that was hopeless. I went away, had another beer, tried to regain some measure of composure. Then, suddenly, the club was closing, people were moving out and down the lantern-lighted path to the dock—and the lovely little nurse was beside me, close, her small warm hand in mine, our bodies touching as we walked. She said something like "I just want to be with *you,*" and I said something lyrical like "Jesus Christ!" or "thank God!"

It was probably "thank God" because that was literally how I felt. I had received a gift, unasked for, undeserved, but straight from heaven. The obvious question—what was I going to do with such a gift?—never entered my mind. I was beyond logical or even coherent thought. I was going to take this warm, affectionate, compassionate little creature home and love her forever. Home? The *Abercrombie,* of course, there was no other. I put my arm around her and pulled her close. The whaleboat was waiting. I helped her aboard and forward under the canvas canopy. Keith must have followed, sitting across from us. I ordered the cox'n to shove off and make the ship. He jerked his lanyard, the bell clanged once, then four times rapidly, and we were off. I turned and kissed my gift from heaven. Her mouth was unbearably sweet and she clung to me. Keith, the boat crew, all in the same twenty-six feet, did not exist. We kissed again. Surprisingly, after the months of deprivation, I did not feel urgently lustful, rather hungry and tender and blissfully happy.

Leyte Gulf was calm and quiet in the moonlight, and the whaleboat churned purposefully out toward the low, dark silhouette of DE343, a couple of miles away. But about halfway out, the night was shattered by the roar of another engine close aboard, and a voice full of authority hailed us.

"Stop your engine and lie to! This is Captain Something of the hospital ship *Something*. You have one of my nurses aboard. She is to return to the ship!"

The whaleboat's bell clanged twice and the diesel died to idle. We drifted while the other boat came alongside. It was a thirty-knot "skimmer" of the type used by heavy ships to whisk their VIPs around an anchorage. In the stern stood a full captain, the moonlight glistening on his gold-braided visor and the silver eagles on his shirt. The little railroad tracks on my own collar had never looked so puny. Reality had returned. The gods were taking back their present.

The unwelcome transfer was duly accomplished with only the quick, strong squeeze of a small hand for good-bye, and the skimmer departed with an angry bellow of its big engine and a smother of spray.

That was it. A mini-romance. A love affair in twenty minutes. I never saw her again. I never even knew her name.

The next morning in the wardroom Keith said to me, "What the hell were you going to do with her when you got her aboard?"

"Mr. Wheeling," I told him, unashamedly pulling rank for the first and only time with Keith, "that's none of your goddamn business!"

Abercrombie sortied from Leyte in the late morning of 21 March, the vernal equinox, the first day of spring. It didn't feel like spring. It was cold and rough as the six destroyers, two DEs and three APDs of the screen patrolled outside the gulf while the transports filed out, and it got colder and rougher as the force moved north. Foul-weather jackets and parkas were issued to all hands, and the forced-draft blowers turned down to low speed. When the nineteen big APAs and AKAs were in cruising disposition, the screen spaced out around them and base course established, Keith broke out the Operation Order and the men of DE343 found out where they were going. It was Okinawa all right. But first, six days before the main assault, *Abercrombie*'s force, with others out of sight over the horizon (collectively labeled the Western Islands Attack Group), was to seize a group of islands ten miles off the southern tip to be used as a supply, repair and seaplane base during the expected long battle of conquest and occupation. The name of the island group was Kerama Retto. In the nineteen big ships astern were elements of the 77th Infantry Division of the U.S. Army, combat veterans from the battle for Leyte. The other DE in the screen was the *Stern* (DE187). The destroyers were *Picking, Sproston, William D. Porter, Isherwood, Kimberly* and *Charles G. Badger;* the APDs were *Kline, Bunch* and *Hopping.* In company but not in sight were three escort carriers to provide antisub patrols and CAP, minesweepers to clear the seas around the target islands, troop-laden LSTs, and another group of APDs of which Murphy's *Humpreys* was one, carrying Underwater Demolition Teams (UDTs) to recon the beaches and remove obstacles.

The Op-Order (even its black cover looked ominous) provided little comfort beyond what could be inferred from the massive strength of the assault and covering forces. It warned of the heavy air opposition to be expected, including the expanded use of kamikazes, and likened the anticipated opposition to that recently encountered at Iwo Jima, the bloodiest Pacific battle to date. One succinct paragraph laid it all out:

> All screening ships be prepared for action—against enemy aircraft, surface ships, submarines, midget submarines and PT boats; to prevent enemy barge movement along the coast; to prevent enemy movement between islands and between Okinawa and offshore islands, and against swimmers carrying limpet mines, human torpedoes, explosive motor boats.

Nor was there any comfort in the news that three of the fast carriers engaged in softening up Okinawa and adjacent islands had been hard hit by kamikazes, one, the *Franklin,* so badly that she became the most seriously damaged ship ever to survive and return to base. Even the legendary "Big E," the *Enterprise,* had been wounded and forced to curtail the operations of her night fighters.

On the morning of the twenty-second, the first of a stream of cautionary and warning messages was issued by the task unit commander. "All ships hold following daily," it read. "Instruction and drills in aircraft recognition, damage-control drills, fire-fighting drills, tracking and gun-pointing drills. Thorough and realistic drills may pay large dividends later."

A day later another admonition: "In the event of suicider or other direct attack on any ship of this group, it is confidently expected that all gun crews will stand to their guns and destroy the enemy attacker before he reaches his target. Keep alert."

On the twenty-fourth: "At 1625 the *Robert J. Keller* in CVE screen destroyed three mines, two of which gave heavy detonations. Keep a sharp lookout for floating mines and other objects. Lookouts must be on the alert."

On the twenty-fifth, as the force approached the target area, an even more graphic and ominous note: "Three hundred suicide boats; also beware swimmers carrying knife, gun and hand grenades."

Thus for four and a half days the force of transports and their screen steamed northward under low, squally skies with brisk northeasterly winds and frequent cold showers, drilling, watching, and making ready. Aboard the lead ship, the USS *Abercrombie,* in the screen's number one position, the only living creature unconcerned was Butch. He was warm and contented in a new navy-blue blanket emblazoned with the gridded globe of an electrician's mate, custom-made by his friend Harry Miles.

On the afternoon of the twenty-fifth came a final warning message: "Tractor group [LSTs and LCIs] ahead spotted by enemy planes at 1225. Be alert for visual contact." That evening a destroyer left the screen and moved well out ahead with orders to report "radar landfall with bearing and distance when identified." At 0330 the next morning *Abercrombie's* men went to General Quarters for their third assault landing in her six months in the western Pacific. It occurred to me as I ran to my battle station that there had only been one operation in the Pacific since she reported for duty in which DE343 had not taken part; that was Iwo Jima. Must have been a slip somewhere.

Nothing happened for about three hours, at least as far as could be determined from the tool-filled closet and red-lighted passageway of Repair II. Then at 0615 Don Wood aroused from his semidoze to report a bogey in sight ahead. A few seconds later the forward five-incher opened up slowly and deliberately, then the after gun joined in, then both forties. After that came the cease-fire order, and all was quiet. Wood reported that a single-engine float plane had crossed high overhead from starboard to port. Apparently it was the only one of a six-plane attack group to escape the CVE CAP, and it wisely kept going out of sight.

With all quiet again, it seemed like a good time to go out on deck and look around. It was a cool, gray, windy morning, still overcast, with a lot of dampness to the air. *Abercrombie* was nearly surrounded by small islands rising steeply out of the sea, green but rocky and scrubby with jagged shores and occasional small white beaches. Here and there close by, the sea showed white over a shallow rock or splashed against a dark ledge rising a foot or two above the surface. Among and all around the islands were the ships of the Western Islands Attack Group—rocket

LSMs in closed-up columns making for their assigned beaches, destroyers throwing white water from their bows as they headed for fire-support areas, and others already lying off, close to the shore, methodically firing into the rocky hills. On the horizon astern were the attack transports, waiting until the landing areas had been well worked over before committing their troops. There was no sign of an enemy, until a group of Avengers and Wildcats from the escort carriers arrived and began bombing, rocketing and strafing the silent green hills behind the beaches. Then an occasional puff of AA or a string of tracers would break upward, searching for the planes. The Avengers attacked in about 30-degree dives, firing rockets on the way down, then loosing their bombs just before pull-up. The stubby, blunt-winged little Wildcats flew straight at the faces of the cliffs and hills, let go with rockets, then with .50-calibers, and climbed vertically at the last minute to bank around and come in again.

A few miles to the northward in a kind of strait between the big island of Tokashiki Shima to the east and a group of small islands to the west, a couple of heavy cruisers and a battleship were slamming their big shells ashore. I recognized the battlewagon as the venerable USS *Arkansas* in which I had taken a midshipman's cruise in the last prewar summer of '39. The cruise had been scheduled for Europe, but with the war clouds gathering there, it had been diverted to Quebec, Halifax and Gloucester, much to our disgust and disappointment. The *Arkansas*, commissioned in 1912, was not a new ship in World War *I*, yet here she was at the other end of the world, her dozen twelve-inch rifles still speaking with authority in her country's cause.

Abercrombie's patrol station on that first eventful day (known as Love minus Six or L −6 because the main landings on Okinawa were still six days in the future) was like a fifty-yard-line seat. She steamed back and forth at ten and a half knots on a three-mile east-west line at the southern end of the Kerama Strait just mentioned. The transport area was south of that line, the landing beaches north of it, so that almost everything which went ashore that day passed by—the crowded, noisy LVTs foaming along low in the water; the equally crowded LCVPs, higher in the water and faster, being boats and not amphibious troop carriers; the LCMs, each with its tank and crew; the bigger, broader LCTs, each with several vehicles aboard; then the still bigger, higher LCIs, looking more like ships than the landing barges; and finally the huge, slab-sided LSTs with bow doors gaping and decks jungle-green with troops. But what fascinated *Abercrombie*'s men were the rocket LSMs (LSMRs). The usual vehicle well to port of the off-center conning tower was decked over and sprouted a forest of rocket spindles. And somehow the naval architects had figured out a way to install an entire 5"/38 mount, exactly like those in DE343's main battery, aft of the rocket forest. These strange craft would plow up to their assigned beaches, line up and let go. Each ship seemed to launch hundreds of rockets, which went off with a sustained hissing roar in high-angled lines of flame and smoke. Then, when the flames had gone out and the smoke was beginning to dissipate, the whole target hillside would be blanketed and obscured by a violent blooming of explosions and clustered mushrooms of smoke and dust.

It was 1230 before *Abercrombie* stood down from General Quarters, but one five-inch and one forty-millimeter mount were kept manned. All afternoon, while the CAP buzzed around reassuringly overhead, the landings continued; and by 1700 word came that all except two islands of the Kerama Retto were under U.S. control. Apparently the enemy had not guessed that we had any serious interest in that clump of rocky islands, and they were lightly defended by troops who most often got off a few rounds and scurried back into the hills. The principal Japanese use for Kerama Retto appeared to be as a base for suicide boats. The 77th Division soldiers found 250 of the eighteen-foot, one-man boats armed with two 250-pound depth charges each and promptly smashed them up, thereby saving unknown numbers of U.S. seamen countless hours of anxiety and numerous probable casualties.

At 1735, DE343's battle stations were manned again, the transports formed up, gathered their screen around them and steamed off to the southwest to lose themselves in the night sea. This tactic was called "night retirement" and was designed to deprive enemy pilots of sitting-duck targets in the vicinity of easy-to-find landmarks.

On that first-night retirement, the transport screen consisted of destroyers *Kimberly, Picking, Badger* and *Porter;* DEs *Abercrombie, Suesens, Stern* and *Oberrender;* and APDs *Hopping* and *Gilmer.* It was a spooky night—the first of many—with low patches of clouds, a moderate sea and after about 2200, a bright moon diffusing its light through the clouds. The columns of big transports steamed southwest until midnight, then circled slowly around to the west, north, and finally northeast to arrive back at Kerama Retto at first light. There were bogies on the radar scope almost all night, closing and then opening again, never seen, although a couple of times a destroyer would open up in radar control, firing slowly and deliberately with its main batteries, the quick sparkle of the bursting shells bright under the clouds. The formation zigzagged until it was full dark, and again as the sky began to lighten once more. Shortly after 0600 on the twenty-seventh, the screening ships were released and dispersed to their assigned patrol sectors for another day.

At 0625 *Kimberly* was on the way to her station when a kamikaze found her. The enemy plane, a Val dive bomber with fixed landing gear, bored in through the destroyer's full broadside of five 5-inch guns and all her forties and twenties, slipped, skidded, zoomed and dived to throw off *Kimberly*'s gunners. Smoking from several hits, the plane managed to circle around into the destroyer's wake, where only the after guns could bear, and crashed directly on a still-firing forty-millimeter mount between the number three and number four five-inch guns. Four destroyer sailors were killed, fifty-seven wounded, and two 5-inch and one 40-millimeter mounts put out of commission. *Kimberly* buried her dead, treated her wounded, made what repairs she could, and stayed on station until Kerama Retto was fully secured.

At the same time another Val suicider attacked *Gilmer*, en route to the station adjacent to *Kimberly*'s. The kamikaze came in straight and low on the APD's beam, smashing into the galley deckhouse and bouncing into the sea on the other side. One sailor was killed and three wounded.

About ninety minutes later, at 0755, *Abercrombie* took a near-miss. It was a sunny, breezy morning. I had the deck and Katschinski was on the bridge. DE343's patrol sector was a north-south line off the south end of the big Kerama island of Tokashiki. The ship was at the north end of the line, about half a mile from shore and turning to starboard to reverse course. A division of four Wildcats was passing overhead on a northerly course when the DE was jolted hard by four explosions in the water close aboard, two to port and two to starboard—a perfect straddle. The splashes rose six to ten feet and red-hot balls were visible for an instant underwater. The Captain hit the general alarm. I ordered, "All ahead flank! Right full rudder!" *Abercrombie* came around in a foamy circle to a southerly course to open the land as her crew raced to their battle stations with a special urgency born of those four hammerblows against her hull.

It was never clear what had straddled us. High-angle fire from ashore? Rockets mistakenly fired by one of the Wildcats overhead? A stick of bombs from an unseen aircraft? Each theory had its champions. But for the remainder of that day *Abercrombie*'s turning point at the north end of her patrol was considerably farther from the hills at the southern end of Tokashiki Shima. At noon DE343 went to port and starboard watches, four on and four off for all hands, half the guns continually manned. That day the last two islands of the group were taken and Kerama Retto was ours.

After another night retirement and another day on patrol, on the afternoon of the twenty-eighth *Abercrombie* went into the new U.S. anchorage at Kerama Retto to fuel. There were two tankers in port; a couple of LSTs were dispensing ammunition; a line of buoys marked the channel to the anchorage; several net tenders with their strange beaklike bows were busy laying antisub nets; and LCMs and LCVPs from a newly organized boat pool were charging around the harbor.

But in the hour that *Abercrombie* was alongside the tanker, her men picked up more disquieting news.

On the twenty-sixth the destroyer *Halligan* had hit a mine just to the east of Kerama Retto. Both her forward magazines had blown, demolishing the entire forward half of the ship and killing more than 150 of her crew. The great sub-killing DE *England* had been dangerously near-missed with several bombs. One of the transports on night retirement had been crashed by a kamikaze, unseen and unengaged before it hit. An APD and a destroyer minesweeper had been attacked separately by suicide boats, but had either sunk them or driven them off.

That evening, DE343 took the transports out to sea again, and the next day her men learned that during the night one of the net tenders had been attacked by a suicide boat which fortunately dropped its charge too far away to cause any damage.

All day the twenty-ninth, while on patrol north of Kerama Retto for the first time, the crew of DE343 could see Okinawa, long, low and smoky to the eastward, under the constant pounding of battlewagons, cruisers and destroyers. Occasionally a tower of white smoke would sprout from the island, and minutes later the heavy thump of an explosion would come to us across the water.

During the day thirty big Mariner flying boats came lumbering in, circled over the scrubby islands and landed. Half a dozen seaplane tenders had apparently arrived the previous night. Kerama Retto was now a seaplane base. It was good to see the dark blue, gull-winged Mariners going and coming on their long-range searches. At least there would be no *surface* surprises around Okinawa.

That night's retirement had fewer ships in the screen, so that every time a course change was ordered, *Abercrombie* would have to go to twenty knots and charge across the bow or flank of the formation to maintain her relative position. Just before midnight a group of twin-engine Betty bombers attacked the transports. They were not suiciders but came in one at a time, low on the water, to drop bombs and turn away. From *Abercrombie*'s bridge we could follow the course of each attack by the successive bursts of tracers as individual ships picked up a target visually. There were no hits that we could see, and apparently the Officer in Tactical Command (OTC) thought the Bettys might be dropping mines ahead of the ships, because after each drop, emergency 90-degree turns were ordered.

With only two days to go before the invasion of Okinawa itself, the thirtieth was a clear, sunny day with scattered low, white clouds and a sharp, damp breeze carrying the threat of fog. And all day long the gray ships pounded the target island. But that evening brought a change in *Abercrombie*'s preinvasion routine. With the damaged *Kimberly* and with *Sproston, Isherwood, Stern* and *Suesens,* she went out on night retirement with a group of LSTs at eight knots instead of with the big transports at thirteen. There was a General Quarters on the midwatch for bogies which failed to close, but which kept the crew awake even so.

The strain of four on and four off with several GQs a day thrown in was already beginning to tell. And the combat reports of deaths and damage on other ships was no help. About all there was time for was watch standing, sleeping and eating—and it was unusual to get more than a couple of hours of sleep without being startled awake by the strident, urgent clanging of the general alarm with its message of imminent but unknown danger. Often in those days, running, life belt in hand, to my battle station with all the other half asleep but running men, my heart pounding, ignorant of the nature of the threat—air, sub, surface, or collision—I thought of my young wife, her insistence on the importance of a gentle awakening, and her theory of the dire effects of a rude one on the digestive system and disposition. She would not have thrived off Okinawa.

On 31 March, L Day minus one, for the first time graceful, gull-winged Corsairs from the fast carriers were in sight overhead, patrolling reassuringly in divisions of four. On the afternoon watch I saw Murph's battered old APD go by about a mile away, but there was no chance for an exchange of signals. *Abercrombie*'s patrol station was just north of the long Kerama island of Tokashiki, and from there it seemed that the bombardment of Okinawa, extending all along the eastern horizon, had increased in volume and intensity on this last day before the landings. That night there was no retirement. *Abercrombie* remained on her patrol line southwest of Kerama Retto, steaming east and west at fifteen knots, making all turns outboard (to the south), coordinating the patrol with ships in adjacent sectors, all part of a long oval of fourteen warships enclosing the American-occupied island group. There were bogies on the scope all night, flashes of gunfire, and soaring red balls of tracers to the east, west and north. Tom Parlon's midwatch was especially busy, with the log reading "0205 General Quarters. 0212 Secured from General Quarters. 0234 General Quarters. 0250 Secured from General Quarters." The men whose four hours off fell on that midwatch did not get a lot of sleep.

L Day made little difference to *Abercrombie* and her crew. She continued to steam back and forth, back and forth, along her seven thousand-yard sector south and west of Kerama Retto and out of sight of the Hagushi beaches on Okinawa where the action was. On the bridge and in CIC, the TBS crackled and rasped with scores of unfamiliar voice calls, the fighter director circuits were busy vectoring the CAP after this or that bogey, and the general impression, no doubt reinforced by a knowledge of the Op-Order, was that of a huge naval force being efficiently and vigorously applied.

But while the boldest, most massive invasion thus far in the Pacific war was taking place fifteen or twenty miles away, *Abercrombie* had smaller chores which demanded her attention.

At about 1700 the buzzer from the bridge went off in my stateroom where I was sleeping soundly by way of preparation for another night of bogies and GQs. The voice on the gray phone when I fumbled the instrument out of its clamp bracket was Katschinski's.

"Ed," he ordered, very businesslike. "We've got a couple of enemy bodies adrift out here. Get your boys together and bring 'em aboard. They may have some intelligence value."

Although I was lacking in enthusiasm for this job, I headed for the fo'c'sle, where we inflated one of the rubber rafts while the Captain brought the ship to within about fifty yards of the two floating bodies. With the raft towing gently along the port side forward, Holloway, Manger and I went down knotted handlines to man it. Boats and I rowed, while Manger, strong and quick but a much smaller man, sat in the stern looking forward and providing direction. As we were about to push off, Holloway thought of something. "Captain!" he yelled to the face under the blue ball cap far up on the bridge. "What if these Japs are booby-trapped?"

I could see Katschinski grin. "Just shake 'em a few times, Boats," he called down, "and if nothing happens, bring 'em aboard."

Manger had brought along a coil of light line, and when we got to the first body, he made it fast and we towed it back to the ship. Holloway climbed back aboard to supervise the hoisting arrangements, and as soon as the body was clear of the raft, Manger and I went back for the second one. When we returned, the skipper was getting nervous about being dead in the water for so long. Manger scrambled out, and I was left to secure a line around the remaining body. It was clumsy to handle, and I ended in the water with both arms around the corpse before I could get a bowline around the chest and under the arms for hoisting—a moment which I have come to regard as the low point of my naval career.

By 1725 both bodies were aboard and the ship had resumed patrol.

Both enemy airmen were wearing quilted, dark red kapok life jackets, cheap, coarse wool uniforms, and aviators' leather helmets. Neither wore shoes. Both were carrying a little doll like a Japanese woman in a kimono, and a white stitched belt. The cause of one pilot's death was obvious— a triangular wound about two inches deep in his forehead. He also had a broken leg. The other dead pilot had one arm almost severed at the shoulder by what looked like a twenty-millimeter hit, and two smaller-caliber wounds in his face. The sea had soaked and washed away all traces of blood.

We searched the two bodies, finger-printed them, retained wallets and papers for forwarding to Naval Intelligence, sewed them up in canvas tubes weighted with five-inch projectiles, delivered them back to the sea, and recorded time and position in the log. The time was 1852. The date 1 April 1945, L Day—and Easter Sunday; the position 26°-05' north latitude, 127°-14'-30" east longitude. The incident was over, yet it lingered in the mind and would not be forgotten. The reason, I believe, was a picture in the wallet of one of the enemy airmen. It showed a smiling young Japanese dressed in white shorts and a white polo shirt, and wearing a broad-brimmed white hat rather jauntily on the back of his head, sitting in the sun on the doorstep of a fragile-looking little house with sliding rice-paper doors. The snapshot glowed with sun-filled happiness. But on looking closely at it we could see that the face under the white hat was of the same boy who had lain gray and water-soaked on *Abercrombie*'s deck with that mortal wedge-shaped wound in his forehead, under the casual, curious stare of half a hundred hostile strangers. The contrast cracked the stereotype of the hated enemy that was needed to maintain morale in the war of attrition between the U.S. ships and the Japanese planes off Okinawa. Cracked but did not shatter. However, through the crack for a disturbing moment in the middle of a war came a light like truth which hinted heretically that perhaps it was war itself and not the enemy (specifically not this piteous broken young pilot dead on our decks who had been smiling in the sun even as we would like to be) which was the basic evil.

Before L Day was over, *Abercrombie*'s men were treated to one more evidence of the lurking death and danger that pervaded the seas off Okinawa. A once-beautiful warship was towed past DE343's patrol station on her way to a repair ship in Kerama Retto. She was one of the new 2,200-ton destroyers with six 5"/38s in three twin mounts. This destroyer had been converted to a light minelayer (DM), and her aft twin mount had been removed to accommodate the mines and associated gear. But now that gear was charred and broken, two 20-millimeters normally mounted aft were missing, the stern was almost awash, with after steering obviously flooded and the bow correspondingly and awkwardly high. The number 27 on her bow told us she was the *Adams*. She had been crashed aft by a kamikaze whose two bombs had detonated under her fantail, holing her and disabling both rudders and propellers.

Abercrombie stayed on patrol off Kerama Retto the night of L Day, and the patrol was a repeat of the previous one—General Quarters on the midwatch and low-flying planes on surface- and air-search radars all night. But it was not until full morning that a suicider actually attacked.

The second of April dawned bright and clear with scattered high clouds. The sea was full of ships, the sky filled with planes. *Abercrombie*'s lookouts were kept busy reporting aircraft on almost every bearing and elevation angle, all friendlies—Corsairs, Hellcats, Wildcats, Avengers. Then at 0848 two more planes were routinely reported, quite high and well aft, dodging in and out of high cumulus clouds. Tom Parlon and Rosie put their glasses on them at the same instant and saw the red disks of Japan on their wings.

The general alarm went off simultaneously with the crash of the ready five-incher and the slow hammering of the forty. *Abercrombie* was the only ship shooting. Black five-inch bursts appeared in the blue sky all around the nearest plane, and the tracers of the forty appeared to be whipping past its wings. Discovered and under fire, one enemy pilot seemed to hesitate, dipping his wings first one way, then the other as though looking for the choicest out of the plethora of targets spread out below him. Then with *Abercrombie*'s fire closing in around him and other ships beginning to join in, he banked to the right and slanted down in a fast, shallow glide until he was directly over an escort carrier lying to off the south entrance to Kerama Retto. Apparently the carrier was the target the pilot had selected, because from about one thousand feet overhead, he rolled into a sudden vertical dive straight for her. But it was all for nothing. He missed by about ten yards, fountaining the sea with spray and raising a puff of black smoke just off the carrier's port bow. The other plane stayed high and sped off to the south.

How had those two kamikazes penetrated the heart of the U.S. forces at Okinawa? There had been no warning from any of the scores and hundreds of sea- and shore-based radars, no flash red or even a "flash yellow" (enemy aircraft in the area). Suddenly they were just there, tooling around, taking their time, choosing their targets. The people in CIC thought they knew the answer. They had held a plane on the bearing and at the altitude at which the lookouts had first sighted the suiciders, but on their scope the plane showed the identifying indications of a friendly in trouble—emergency IFF (Identification Friend or Foe). Katschinski checked by signal light with the *Suesens* and the *Oberrender*. They confirmed that one of the hostile planes had been showing friendly IFF.

That afternoon DE343 was relieved in her patrol sector by an APD and ordered to join the screen off Okinawa and escort another group of transports on night retirement. The scene off the landing beaches was truly awesome. None of us had ever seen so many warships at one time. Literally every type of transport, landing craft and minor and major warship in the U.S. inventory was there, usually by the score. The transports and landing craft were massed along the beaches for as far north and south as we could see. Outboard of them, dozens of destroyers, DEs, APDs, gunboats, minesweepers, and PCs patrolled back and forth or hurried along on some mission or other in no discernible pattern or plan, although we knew there was in fact a very careful and thorough one. To seaward of the screening ships steamed several task units of old battleships and cruisers with their escorting destroyers. Two-plane sections of CAP circled overhead. Float planes from battleships and cruisers, and light, insectlike little spotter planes buzzed back and forth low over the smoking land.

Toward evening, out of this apparent chaos came the force of transports *Abercrombie* would screen. Two long columns of big ships almost magically separated themselves from the huddle off the beaches and stood to seaward, serene, majestic, their booms rigged in and the water white at their bows. From the skein of smaller ships offshore, the other escorts assembled and formed in an arc ahead, the two long columns changed smoothly into four shorter ones, and we were off at fifteen knots into the moonlit sea to hide for the night once more. *Abercrombie*'s station was on the starboard bow of the formation.

All night long there were reports of bogies and ships being hit. The condition was "flash red." My watch was the mid. It was fairly rough, with the waning moon glittering on the wave crests and the dark hulls of the transports barely visible astern. There was a turn just as the watch was ending. It was necessary as usual for us to increase speed and change course sharply to maintain our same position relative to the convoy. We had just come back to base course and speed, and Tom was on his way through the pilothouse to relieve me when the noise of several men shouting came unmistakably up to the bridge.

My first thought was that there was an argument going on down on Mount 41; then there was a quality about the shouting that told me what it was: the sound of desperate men making noise frantically and with all their might. The shouting passed rapidly down the starboard side very close to the ship. I ran and looked over and saw small dark figures clustered in the water, disappearing into the white water of our fifteen-knot wake. At the same instant Ralph Rice took a report from Tom Rutters on the starboard K-guns that there were men in the water close aboard.

In such a situation the OOD becomes an extremely busy man with a great many urgent actions to be taken at once.

There was CIC to notify so that they could start the dead reckoning tracer and plot the position of the survivors, there was the Captain to inform, and a man to station to keep constant sight of the men in the water. Twenty or thirty transports were coming up astern at fifteen knots. They had to be warned by voice radio to turn or they would be in danger of running down the men or us or both. A rescue detail had to be readied; and during all this, the ship had to be maneuvered so as to return, in the dark, to the point of sighting and yet not run over the men, or by them, or cut them up with the screws.

Many of these actions were accomplished by simply sounding the general alarm and passing the word "Standby for rescue of survivors." I called the Task Group Commander on TBS and reported, "Survivors in the water directly ahead of convoy. Recommend emergency turn to port." By the time DeCoster relieved me as OOD, we were nearly back to the spot and the men were faintly visible off the starboard bow. Repair I and a few men from the guns had inflated one of our rubber rafts and secured a line to it. When it was launched, I went down a line off the fo'c'sle and into the raft. Chips came down right behind me with a coil of heaving line, the end secured aboard. He sat in the stern and paid out the line as I rowed. It was rough and wet and hard to see, but the guys in the ship helped by pointing as long as we could see them, and then Chips sighted the survivors. In a few minutes we pulled up to them.

There were four men holding on to an empty oil drum, pathetic in their suffering and relief at being saved. One was nearly unconscious, another was conscious but incoherent and very weak. The other two men were rational and fairly strong, but one had both hands badly burned. All were water-soaked and terribly tired. One by one we dragged them into the rubber raft, taking the weakest man first, until at last they lay sprawled and piled up together in the little raft, but at least out of the water. Chips secured his line to the raft and yelled back to the ship. On deck the rescue detail took a strain, and back we went. The Captain had swung the ship toward us as we rowed, and we came close under the sharp, towering bow as the sailors heaved us in.

Once alongside, the problem still was not solved. The ship, dead in the water now, rolled heavily in the seas so that at one moment we were even with the deck, and the next at the base of a sheer steel cliff, wet and dripping in the failing moonlight, with the faces of the men on deck looking down from far above us. Holloway passed down a line, I secured bowlines around each of the survivors in turn, and they were hauled up on deck and carried down to sick bay. Chips and I came up, then the raft, and it was over.

Once again that night we went out in the raft to check a floating object, which turned out to be another empty oil drum like the one the four men had been clinging to. They said there had been others in the water near them, but they must have been lost before we got there.

The previous evening, at about the time that *Abercrombie* was joining the transport screen for retirement, another group of transports and screen was forming up south of Kerama Retto. Among the escorts in the screen were the *Dickerson* (APD21) and the *Bunch* (APD79). *Dickerson*, like Murph's *Humphreys*, was, to put it politely, a veteran ship, commissioned as a destroyer in 1919 and converted to a destroyer transport in 1943. Since then she had delivered her Underwater Demolition Teams to their assigned beaches in five major operations, including Saipan, Guam, Lingayen Gulf and Iwo Jima. *Bunch* had begun life as DE694 in August of 1943 and had been converted to a destroyer transport (APD) a year later. Okinawa was her first combat operation.

When this force was only a few miles out, it was attacked by a group of at least ten kamikazes. One, a Nick fighter, made what appeared to be a strafing run on *Dickerson*—except that he did not fire but dropped a bomb close aboard one of the transports. But apparently he really wanted the *Dickerson*, because back he came in a long, shallow glide, circling around cagily to come in aft where the minimum number of guns could be brought to bear. The Nick tore into the valiant old ship at about 200 mph, slashed off the tops of both her stacks, ripped through the galley deckhouse, toppled the mast, and came to rest in a ball of flame at the base of the bridge. In seconds, flaring gasoline fires were raging the length of the ship. Dozens of men were either knocked overboard or forced to jump to escape the flames. Dozens of others were not so lucky. Fifty-two officers and men were killed instantly, including the skipper, who had been with the ship since reporting aboard as an ensign in 1940, and the Exec. Another fifteen were seriously wounded, as in most kamikaze attacks, by extensive and painful burns.

Bunch, some two miles away, closed at top speed, came alongside with hoses streaming and helped *Dickerson*'s surviving crew to fight the fires. At the same time, *Bunch*'s UDT swimmers went over the side in their rubber rafts and scoured the now darkened sea for survivors, finally recovering about forty. It took nearly six hours to get the fires under control. *Bunch* took twenty five injured men off the charred and battered *Dickerson*, rigged a towing hawser and eased the mortally wounded old man-of-war into the safety of Kerama Retto.

Thanks to *Bunch's* immediate and effective help, the loss of life aboard the *Dickerson* was held to the direct effects of the kamikaze crash. Many of those saved were pulled out of the sea by the sailors of UDT21, but the law of averages and the choppy night sea were against them; they couldn't get them all.

The last four were those found by DE343: a gunner's mate, two firemen and a seaman—William Moore, Delbert Griffin, Raymond Smith and Kenneth Crothers—who by that time had been in the water about nine hours. One man had supported two others for about the last four of those hours. They were four very lucky men. A course error of a couple of degrees by our helmsman would have cut through them with the sharp bow and chopped them up in the screws, and no one would ever have known. If we had not passed close enough to hear the men, the transports probably would have run them down. In any case, at least two could not have survived until daylight.

Somewhere in these United States there are four homes which have reason to remember the USS *Abercrombie*.

At 0936 the following day in Kerama Retto, Moore, Griffin, Smith and Crothers, bandaged but conscious and smiling, were transferred to the evacuation transport *Rixey* (APH3) for treatment of their burns, and another short chapter was closed. But like the recovery and reburial of the enemy airmen, the incident refused to fade gracefully from memory. The memory that lived was of a little cluster of helpless men, soaked, washed over and half submerged in an infinity of ocean, grown men weaker than children, with shaking voices, men with scorched flesh hanging who nevertheless try bravely to thank you for saving their lives when they had given them up as lost.

Abercrombie spent the next two days on patrol off the southwest tip of Okinawa. The nights were dark and quiet but ominous with repeated warnings of mass raids by kamikazes expected within the next two days. Enemy planes dropped eerie greenish flares, but no attacks developed. Then on the morning of 5 April, DE343 was called in from what had become known as the "ping line" and assigned as escort for a score of empty transports going back to Saipan. By 1100 the course was south, the speed thirteen and a half knots, and Okinawa was fading rapidly into the haze astern—to the regret of not one member of the crew. The screen consisted of a destroyer minelayer, the *Fraser*, of the same type as the damaged *Adams*, Two older single-stack destroyers, *Mustin* and *Stack;* a *Fletcher-*class DD, *Bache;* three DEs, *Abercrombie, Oberrender* and a 3"/50 ship, the *Cole;* and an old APD, the *Herbert.*

By late that afternoon, with *Abercrombie* in station number eight, screening back and forth across the long, white wakes of the transports, the expected attacks had not yet developed.

The spirits of *Abercrombie*'s crew seemed to rise in direct proportion to the ever-increasing distance from Okinawa. And they received an additional lift on the morning of the sixth. At 0930 the U.S. Navy's B Squad in the Pacific encountered a portion of the varsity. Steaming slowly northward through the white-capped blue sea, fueling from a detachment of tankers, was one of the elements of Task Force 58, with four carriers, two battlewagons, two large cruisers, four light cruisers and a dozen destroyers.

Two of the carriers were of the new *Essex* class, two were *Independence-*class "light carriers," built on cruiser hulls. The battleships were the newest and best at sea, both of the *Missouri* class. The two cruisers were the *only* "large cruisers" in the world—*Alaska* and *Guam*— really battle cruisers in having traded thickness of armor for speed and fire power. Two of the cruisers were *Atlanta-*class anti-aircraft light cruisers (CLAAs), probably the handsomest warships afloat with their symmetrical pyramids of twin-mount 5"/38s. Over those magnificent gray ships a swarm of blue-winged Hellcats buzzed. Apparently the morning CAP had just been relieved and as the two formations passed, the Hellcats were coming in low and slow, their wheels and hooks hanging, and were flopping down on the decks of the carriers. It was a scene of massive, majestic naval power at rest. At rest, but like an eagle on a crag or a leopard on a limb, the power patently ready for instant use. The long gray guns were trained fore and aft, tampions in their muzzles. The strike groups were out of sight on the hangar decks of the carriers. However, one had only to look to know that when the guns were loaded and trained out and the strike groups launched, no force on earth could withstand them. And this was only one of the four task groups of Task Force 58!

The very next day, 7 April, three of those task groups, including the one which had so impressed the southbound sailors of DE343, converged to smash an enemy surface force bound for Okinawa. Two Mariners from Kerama Retto found the enemy early in the morning and shadowed him for five hours broadcasting his position and homing in carrier strikes. By early afternoon American bombs and aerial torpedoes had put down the battleship *Yamato*—the biggest in the world, armed with eighteen-inch guns—an accompanying light cruiser and four destroyers. Only four damaged destroyers were able to limp back to Kyushu.

But the news from Okinawa was grim. The predicted massive kami-kaze attack had come in on the sixth of April and continued into the seventh. Three destroyers had been sunk, five more and a destroyer mine-sweeper (DMS) badly damaged with many casualties. Kerama Retto had been raided, and two ammunition ships and an LST sunk. One of the sunk destroyers went down under attack by forty to fifty planes. The ships on the antisub ping line had come under heavy attack, with damage and casualties resulting. And all this happened the day after *Abercrombie's* departure. Many of her men thought back to the omen of the visiting man-o'-war bird off Baja that August which seemed so long ago. Just maybe, they thought, just maybe . . .

DE343 steamed into the harbor at Saipan late on the afternoon of 9 April, and it was 2024 when she was finally fueled and anchored in her assigned berth. The next morning she received orders to sail for Ulithi at noon on the eleventh, and took aboard seventy-five bags of mail for delivery to the Fleet Post Office there. There would be no convoy to Ulithi, just *Abercrombie, Oberrender, Mustin, Stack* and *Cole.* It ap-peared that an urgent convoy for Okinawa was awaiting escorts at Ulithi.

Saipan in that spring of 1945 was like no other place on earth. The phrase which kept running willy-nilly through my head was "the eagle's nest. This is the eagle's nest." There was one rounded, shrub-covered, rocky hill overlooking the harbor. Beyond it and on the low, flat island of Tinian only a few miles away were based the B-29 Superfortresses of the Strategic Air Force. Their comings and goings were a fact of life at Saipan much like the trade wind at Ulithi. During the day the planes were silver slivers in the blue sky. At night the small blue flames from their exhausts flickered and sputtered over the anchored ships, their landing lights erased the pictures on the movie screens, and the roar of their engines drowned the sound from the ship's projectors. Unlike the carrier planes DE343's men were used to, they never arrived or departed in formation but always singly to save the fuel expended in circling to join up, fuel they would need for the three-thousand-mile round trips to their targets.

Saipan really *was* the eagle's nest; and the eagles went out on a railroad schedule over a world of water to strike the heart of the enemy Japan. To witness the round-the-clock operations of the B-29s, like natural phenomena in their consistency and predictability, was almost as reassur-ing as the sight of an element of Task Force 58 at sea.

But there was little time for reassurance. *Abercrombie* was under way at 1155 on the eleventh, and she was second ship through the net gates at 1203 behind *Mustin,* with *Oberrender* close astern. Outside the harbor the five escorts formed line abreast, 1,500 yards between ships, and set a southwesterly course for Ulithi at seventeen knots. On the morning of the twelfth, a tow plane came out from the atoll, the ships formed a column, distance six hundred yards, and hammered away at a sleeve target pulled up and down the line. *Abercrombie* expended seventy rounds of five-inch, nearly nine hundred rounds of forty-millimeter and two thousand rounds of twenty-millimeter. At 1632 that day she entered the big lagoon for the second and last time, but this was no rest stop. The seventy-five mailbags were transferred to an LST, which was the Fleet Post Office at Ulithi. Then there was fueling to be done, and the ship remained all night alongside the anchored tanker. The next morning there was ammunition to take aboard, and by 1600, DE343 was on her way back to Okinawa in company with *Oberrender, Cole, Mustin, Gilligan* (DE508), and a mixed group of attack transports and merchant ships fresh from the U.S., speed fifteen knots, course due north.

It was a quiet, calm, warm run back into action, but tension aboard inevitably mounted as the distance to destination shrank. Two pieces of news three days apart increased the tension significantly.

On the first day out of Ulithi came the news of the death of Franklin Delano Roosevelt. For most of *Abercrombie*'s men, he was the only President they could remember. He had been President since I was fourteen. It was, for most of the crew, as though a close and respected relative had died, say, a strong and supportive uncle. On the eve of near and sustained action with a fanatical enemy, there was a feeling of great loss and a loss of confidence, a feeling of "what will happen to us now? Who will make the decisions on which our lives depend? Will they be the right ones?" Sadness fell over the little ship, men spoke less often to each other. Hardly a man had ever even seen the dead President from a distance—yet he had become a part of their young lives, and their grief at his death was real and palpable.

On the day the President died, the day *Abercrombie* departed Ulithi for Okinawa, the Japanese launched 150 fighters, 45 torpedo planes and 185 kamikazes against the U.S. ships around that bloody island. The reports which filtered through to *Abercrombie* as she approached the scene of action were both gory and hard to believe. The destroyers on distant radar picket early warning stations had taken the brunt of the attacks. In picket station number one, fifty miles north, two of them were attacked by thirty Vals and shot down four, but suffered many casualties and damage from grazing hits and near-misses. On another picket station the enemy had used a terrifying new weapon to sink the destroyer *Mannert L. Abele*. It was a piloted, rocket-driven glider called Baka carrying a 2,600-pound warhead and capable of 500 mph. The Baka hit amidships, blowing the *Abele* in half, and she sank in five minutes. Enemy planes then strafed and bombed the men in the water. In another action a kamikaze had flown straight into a quad forty-millimeter mount manned by Marines on the battleship *Tennessee*, wiped out the gun crew, killed a total of twenty-three officers and men and wounded another hundred. Of more personal interest to *Abercrombie's* people was a report that the *Walter C. Wann* had narrowly averted disaster when a kamikaze dived at her from the starboard beam, banked vertically so close overhead that several antennas were severed, and crashed and exploded only twenty feet from the port bow, showering the ship with airplane parts and bomb shrapnel. Two other DEs on the ping line had not been as lucky as the *Wann*. One, the *Whitehurst*, shot down two Vals, but a third smashed through her crowded CIC, killing thirty-seven men. The other, the *Riddle*, had destroyed two attackers, but one had landed so close aboard that its bomb tore through the ship, killing one man and wounding six.

During that Ulithi-to-Okinawa passage, belated reports also came in of attacks on two other ships well known to *Abercrombie's* crew. Destroyer *Charles J. Badger* had been disabled by a suicide boat on the Hagushi beaches on 9 April. The same day *Hopping* (APD51) had lost two killed and eighteen wounded to a direct hit by a coastal battery.

The day before *Abercrombie's* task unit arrived back at Okinawa, the desperate enemy threw another 165 planes against the naval forces there. Another picket destroyer was sunk; two others, two destroyer minesweepers and an APD, were badly damaged; a total of two hundred officers and men were killed and hundreds more gravely wounded, usually with ghastly burns. According to a report received aboard DE343, one of the damaged destroyers should by any rational standard have been sunk, and the circumstances of her survival sounded so fantastic that many of us doubted the report (which later was confirmed in every respect).

The report said that the destroyer *Laffey* in radar picket station number one (apparently directly on the track of enemy planes from Kyushu) was attacked by at least fifty bombers and kamikazes starting at about 0830. She had CAP overhead, which accounted for several of the enemy planes before they came in range of *Laffey's* guns. But in the next eighty minutes, the destroyer was attacked twenty-two times by planes diving at her from every possible direction. Weaving and circling at flank speed, her gunners sticking to their guns and firing continuously, she shot down eight, but was crashed by six kamikazes, hit with four bombs, strafed, and near-missed by another bomb and another suicider. When the surviving enemy planes finally retired, *Laffey* had lost thirty-one killed and seventy-two wounded, what guns could still shoot could do so only in local control, she was badly flooded aft, and her rudders were jammed hard over. But with the help of a couple of salvage tugs she made it back to Kerama Retto for repairs.

On the afternoon of the seventeenth, *Abercrombie* fueled from the *Nantahala,* and when the first dogwatch came on duty, she was back on patrol, part of the ping line off smoldering Okinawa. On the way to her station she passed the *Suesens,* which flashed cheerfully, "Grease up yer shootin' irons." A few minutes later over the TBS came an announcement by an unknown destroyer, "We are proceeding for repairs with one Zeke, I spell Z-E-K-E, lodged in a large hole in the starboard side."

For the USS *Abercrombie* now began the most dangerous and deadly two months of her short existence. She was part of a sea battle like no other in history, one in which naval forces were denied the freedom of movement and surprise provided by the open ocean, and were required instead to remain in a closely restricted area well known to the enemy in order to protect and support ground forces ashore. From late March until late June the Japanese knew exactly where to find the concentration of U.S. warships upon which the battle for Okinawa depended. And they also knew, whatever their propaganda, that defeat on Okinawa would eventually and inevitably mean defeat on the sacred home islands themselves. So they threw everything they had at that ring of gray ships—the *Yamato* and her escorts, the Baka, and kamikazes by the hundreds in wave after bloody wave—and the American men-of-war, supported by carrier- and land-based air patrols, fought back with bitter, stubborn courage— for eighty-seven days. The result was the longest and costliest naval campaign of the greatest of all wars, a campaign in which casualties afloat rivaled those ashore, in which U.S. losses of destroyer-type warships were so heavy that at times the issue hung in the balance.

During most of her ordeal at Okinawa, *Abercrombie* occupied one of the patrol stations of a chain of thirty-nine known as the Outer Screen. Inside that ring of ships were battlewagons, cruisers and destroyers providing fire support to the soldiers and marines ashore, the transports and supply ships unloading over the beaches, and the logistical, repair and seaplane base at Kerama Retto. Outside, at distances of from eighteen to ninety-five miles, were fifteen radar picket stations occupied by destroyers with fighter director teams aboard and CAP assigned, whose job it was to provide warning of incoming raids and initial opposition to them.

In the Outer Screen, or ping line, *Abercrombie* most often seemed to draw the northwest corner, where the loop ended with the high-numbered stations just a mile or so from the little outlying island of Ie Shima with its airfield and its six hundred-foot volcanic pinnacle like a miniature Iwo Jima. Perhaps because of their proximity to that prominent landmark, those stations, A34A to A38A, received a disproportionate amount of attention from enemy pilots following the chain of islands down from Kyushu. It was station A38A, just off Ie Shima, to which DE343 was assigned on her return from Saipan and Ulithi. Elements of the 77th Infantry Division had landed on the little island on the previous day and were driving the enemy garrison back toward a final stand on the slopes of the volcanic peak. *Abercrombie* was just offshore on 18 April when news came that gentle little Ernie Pyle, the soldiers' and sailors' war correspondent, had been killed there by a burst of machine-gun fire as he followed close behind the attacking troops.

For the next few days, life aboard DE343 settled into a deceptively tranquil routine. The tactics of the patrol itself were spelled out with great exactitude in the Op-Order and they became second nature to the three OODs (still Parlon, DeCoster and Stafford) and the watch in CIC. Speed was fifteen knots (230 rpm). The length of the patrol line was seven thousand yards. Turns to reverse course were always outboard (away from the land). The ship passed through the center of the sector (3,500 yards from each end) clockwise with regard to the periphery or circumference of the whole screen, on the hour and half hour, counterclockwise on the first and third quarter hours. All the ships in the chain of stations synchronized their movements, changing course at the same time, thus maintaining constant distance between ships, minimizing the danger of collision and sonar interference from adjacent wakes. At dusk and dawn and when warned of imminent attack in daylight, ships in adjacent stations joined up, closing to one thousand yards, to double the volume of fire on the enemy. Under attack at night, each ship remained in its own sector and maneuvered as necessary, first to avoid detection and then, if detected, to destroy the attacker.

The ping line around Okinawa that violent spring was almost a geographical feature—a chain of slim gray ships, as predictable in their arrangement and positions as the lumpy little islands around them. No ship left the line unless it was relieved on station, sunk or incapacitated by damage—and in the last two cases it was immediately replaced. Every third or fourth day a tanker came down the line, refueling each ship in turn. On different days but with about the same frequency, an LCI made the same run, delivering and picking up mail. Mail service off bloody Okinawa was the best afloat in the Pacific—a major blessing in an accursed place. Every couple of weeks, on a rotational schedule, each ship went into the anchorage at Kerama Retto or Hagushi for dry and fresh provisions, ammunition, and repairs beyond the capabilities of the crew. And as a welcome break in the dangerous drudgery of the patrol, frequently there were odd jobs to be done.

Abercrombie was assigned one on 20 April. After being properly relieved and taking 28,000 gallons of black oil from the big tanker *Atascosa* late in the afternoon, she steamed southwestward, past the crowded Hagushi anchorage to a point about seven miles off the south end of Okinawa. On the Op-Order diagram this was shown as a circle with a diameter of three miles labeled "Killer One." This area was one of four antisub, hunter-killer stations strategically located around the island, and was continuously occupied by teams of two ships whose job it was to investigate any sub contact made in the vicinity, locating and destroying the sub if possible. DE343's teammate in Killer One was none other than DE635, the most accomplished subkiller of them all, the USS *England.*

At 1250 the next day a Mariner sighted a periscope about fifteen miles off the west coast of Okinawa, and *Abercrombie* and *England* were ordered to the scene. Since it would be about six hours after the sighting before the two ships could arrive, they planned a retiring search in the form of an expanding square, speed fifteen knots, *Abercrombie* being 3,500 yards on *England*'s starboard beam at the start, initial course due east, since the sub could be assumed to be approaching the island. En route to the initial point, the TBS crackled a warning from the task force commander, "Expect raids on outlying stations tonight, expect daylight attacks tomorrow."

The two DEs began the search at 1815, and twenty-five minutes later *Abercrombie* picked up a sonar contact and went to General Quarters. Excitement was high as the ship nosed in toward the unseen target. Cy DeCoster's first team was tense and businesslike at stack and recorder, hedgehogs armed and ready, depth charges set and ready to roll. *England* circled, her sonar passive, listening, ready to assist and regain the contact if it were lost. But the echo turned mushy and broke up; Cy disgustedly reported it as nonsub, and the expanding square resumed.

At nine-thirty that night came a report that the DE which had relieved *Abercrombie* in A38A was under air attack.

At the beginning of the midwatch, another solid echo came clanging back into the sound shack, but it, too, broke up and spread out; apparently it was a school of fish.

The two ships continued the search plan until the afternoon of the twenty-second, and then returned to Killer One. If it had been a periscope the Mariner crew saw, the sub had made good its escape.

That afternoon the expected attack came in. On the ping line, destroyer *Isherwood* took a kamikaze which exploded her depth charges and killed forty-two of her crew, but she made it into Kerama Retto. A big minesweeper, the *Swallow,* in another ping line station was crashed and sank in seven minutes.

At noon on 23 April, DE343 was detached from Killer One to take up patrol across the entrance to a deep, enemy-held bay, Shimu Wan, on the west side of Okinawa. Assisting to shoreward of *Abercrombie*'s patrol line were two LCIs on the lookout for suicide boats and swimmers. The enemy made no attempt to use the sheltered waters of the bay and the patrol was blessedly uneventful.

But the next day *Abercrombie* was refueled and back on the ping line. Then on Friday and Saturday, 27 and 28 April, the Japanese hurled 115 more planes against the ships off Okinawa. DE343 was patrolling in station A34A. Saturday night would have been a beautiful one almost anywhere else and in almost any other April. At Okinawa in April of 1945 it was, for the U.S. sailors on the ping line, as bad as it could be—calm, with a bright full moon in a nearly cloudless sky, a night for kamikazes, a night for men to die. Tom Parlon had the midwatch. Katschinski was on the bridge. With several bogies on the scope, flash red was in effect. At 0314, without warning came the sound of an aircraft engine approaching fast from astern. In a few seconds the bridge watch had the plane in sight, a single-engine fighter, flying straight and level at about five hundred feet, elevation angle about 35 degrees. The ready five-inch and forty-millimeter mounts opened up with a crash and a heavy pounding. The red forty-millimeter tracers clipped at the planes' wings, and five-inch puffs bloomed in the moonlight around it. Tom estimated the range to be about one thousand yards. The five-incher got off six rounds, the forty-millimeter 150 rounds before the enemy passed out of sight and out of range ahead. The pilot never varied course or speed as he flew low and fast right down the ping line, passing over or close to each ship in turn. It was as though he were counting them, scouting the line for future attention.

As if that were the case, one of his countrymen found and attacked the *Abercrombie* in earnest when darkness next fell on the ping line.

All day on the twenty-eighth, there were raid warnings: flash yellows, flash reds, flash whites and back to flash red again. CAP from the fast carriers, Corsairs and Hellcats, were busy overhead, orbiting high in the clear sky, then lining out at high speed to the north and northwest. The air was full of reports of bogies splashed all around the island. As dusk came on, enemy activity increased. The small white blips of bogies began to appear around the edges of *Abercrombie*'s own scopes. At 1605 her tired and sleepy sailors manned their battle stations. They stayed there for two and a half hours with mess cooks bringing sandwiches and coffee to the guns, secured at 1852, ran back to General Quarters at 2037, secured at 2100, manned up again at 2135, and secured at 2204. Then twenty minutes before midnight, a blip popped up on the SA (Air Search) scope just a mile back on the port quarter, closing fast. Katschinski hit the general alarm and swung the ship to port to unmask the forward forty-millimeter, and Tom Parlon, who had the deck, released his guns. Mount 52 buzzed and jerked, training around to the danger bearing provided by CIC. Fred Manger, the Mount Captain, was first to spot the enemy, a Jake fighter 750 yards out, coming in straight and level at about five hundred feet. The five-incher shook the ship as the first round slammed out, adding urgency to the clanging alarm as the exhausted men below tumbled from their bunks. Jim Payton on the forward forty was on target a second later, and the red tracer balls stabbed down the port side toward the fast-approaching enemy as the after twenties joined with their rapid hammering. Tracers from the forty and the twenties laced around the Jake as he roared overhead, some ahead, some behind. The five-incher was able to get off seven rounds, the last two pursuing the plane out into the darkness to starboard. Just as the Jake crossed the ship, the sea erupted off the port quarter, and the thudding explosion of a near-miss by a single bomb hammered against the hull.

On 29 April it was *Abercrombie*'s turn in Kerama Retto for fuel and food. But even in the relative shelter of that harbor, with the high islands on three sides and smoke boats providing protective cover, there was little rest. DE343 fueled and provisioned in the afternoon, and anchored for the night near the midpoint of Kerama Strait in the lee of a coastal peak on the west side of Tokashiki Shima. Enemy planes circled and probed all night, and *Abercrombie* manned her guns for an hour or more on every watch. In addition, a special watch was set against enemy swimmers, about whom warnings had been received—a man posted at the bow, another at the stern, and one on each side, all armed with carbines. Sometime during the midwatch, the man on the starboard side shattered the night and brought the topside sleepers scrambling to their feet with a burst from his carbine. His target turned out to be only a drifting mattress soaked into lumps that in the dim light of the anchorage resembled a man.

In Kerama Retto the scenery was appalling and all the news was bad. On the busy TBS circuits at Okinawa, the voice call of the task group commander in Kerama Retto was "Wiseman," and the code for the harbor and repair base under his command was "Wiseman's Cove." But as April wore on along the ping line, the latter designation had been altered somewhat irreverently to "Wiseman's Junkyard." Now *Abercrombie*'s sailors knew why. Alongside the repair ships and tenders in the crowded little harbor was a fleet of twisted, listing, holed and broken warships, almost all destroyer types, most of them the *Fletcher*-class DDs with which DE343's men had operated, and which they had come to respect as the big brothers of the Pacific. *Isherwood* was there, a former companion on night retirement, her whole stern a tangle of charred wreckage; *Bryant* with her bridge structure where thirty-four men had died, demolished; *Harding,* a big new DMS with a gaping hole in her deck and a twisted keel; *Rathburne* with her bow smashed and scorched; and half a dozen others. As bad as the looks of the broken ships was the appearance of the men still aboard. They stood at the lifelines staring vacantly across the harbor or wandered mindlessly along the twisted decks to disappear through a blackened, doorless hatch back into the superstructure.

Before *Abercrombie* left the junkyard at 0715 next day to return to the ping line, word came that *Haggard* of Taffy 2 had been smashed by a kamikaze at the waterline and was under tow back to Kerama Retto badly flooded and without power.

Even worse and truly horrifying was the news that a kamikaze had crashed the superstructure of the hospital ship *Comfort.* Fully lighted, painted snow-white with huge red crosses in accordance with the Geneva Convention, she was heading for Saipan under a full moon with a capacity load of wounded. According to the news report, the suicider had demolished the ship's surgery, where operations were in progress, killing all hands there, including seven patients and six Army nurses, for a total of thirty killed and forty-eight wounded, including four more nurses and ten patients.

Silently and privately I prayed that my small, warm, forever anonymous friend of the DesPac Café was not one of those nurses.

That night DE343 was back on the line; her station A33A. I had the first watch, the 20–24. Condition was flash red, with bogies all around. We could see the nearest one on the little repeater scope on the bridge. He appeared to be circling around about six or eight miles on our starboard bow. Katschinski was on the bridge, but had not called GQ in the hope of allowing his exhausted crew a few more minutes of rest. All the ready guns which could bear were trained out on the danger bearing. The ship was easing through the calm moonlit sea at five knots to reduce her wake and thus her visibility. Every few minutes a burst of firing out to starboard showed that either someone had sighted the enemy or a destroyer had opened up with a radar solution. All eyes, all guns were trained out on that starboard bow. Men spoke in whispers, tense and excited. Then out of the darkness and the silence came the close, angry, loudening buzz of an aircraft engine *from astern and to port.* We whirled as the buzz built quickly to a roar, and saw a plane coming straight at us from the port quarter, *below* the level of *Abercrombie*'s low bridge, already so close that we could see the whirling disk of the prop, the plane's long "greenhouse" canopy and inside it the dark blob of the pilot's head. *This*, I thought, *was how you died by kamikaze*. This was the last thing you saw and heard before the crushing and the burning—the onrushing plane growing to monstrous size, the spinning prop, the deafening crescendo of the engine. For one terrible second, Captain, OOD, talkers, lookouts, signalmen stood frozen, an instant from death. But the enemy pilot was not ready to die. He must have been as startled as we were. The plane flipped into a vertical left bank in the last split second before collision, exposing its whole underside with the tucked-up wheels and the great red balls on the wings. A man on the bridge could have hit it with a rock. One portside twenty-millimeter gunner recovered from his surprise in time to hammer out a stream of tracers, which cast an eerie green light on the bottom of the plane and followed it back out into the darkness; the gunner angrily expended the whole sixty rounds of a single magazine in relief, frustration and fear.

Now at General Quarters and making twenty knots, *Abercrombie* tracked the enemy plane, a Jill, as it circled, climbed, and came back in to attack in a safer and more conventional manner, so high as to be invisible in the night sky, but dropping a bomb, which whistled into the sea uncomfortably close to the port side, jarring the ship, hurling buckets of water on her decks, but doing no damage.

The damage was to the nerves of the crew. It was unnerving to know that such a thing could happen. There had been nothing to indicate the proximity of the Jill until its engine was heard on the bridge, no radar contact, no warning from adjacent ships, not even the blue sparkle of exhaust. It was impossible not to picture the results had that pilot been a kamikaze. The awareness that such an attack was a constant, ever-present possibility placed an additional strain on men already acutely short of sleep who had not been out of their clothes for weeks or eaten a hot meal with time to digest it. Added to that uncomfortable awareness was the recent graphic illustration in Kerama Retto of what just such attacks could do—and to bigger, faster, better-armed ships than theirs.

The increasing strain affected men differently. Some grew morose and uncommunicative. Others snarled and snapped at their shipmates. Others were reluctant to go below, afraid of being trapped and drowned. Still others remained in the vicinity of their battle stations, resolved to survive by killing the enemy before he killed them. One young sailor drove his mates from a mess table by catching flies, mixing them with his meal and devouring them with apparent relish.

DE343 celebrated the first anniversary of her commissioning steaming back and forth at fifteen knots on A33A. At 1530 a PC boat came alongside with a dozen bags of mail and the change in mood was instantly apparent.

May was a nightmare of sleeplessness, fatigue, flash reds, bogies, General Quarters and single combat on the ping line, occasionally relieved by a short escort job, a hunter-killer mission or a day or two at anchor, but building to a climax of swift and violent action toward the end of the month.

On the morning of 4 May, on radar picket station number twelve, sixty miles west northwest of Okinawa, the destroyer *Luce,* which had been part of the screen with *Abercrombie* from Manus to Lingayen, was crashed by two kamikazes and sunk with heavy casualties—149 killed or missing, another 57 wounded.

The same morning another 153 destroyermen died and another 108 were wounded when *Morrison* on picket station number one, fifty miles north, took four suiciders and went down.

Both losses were the result of a fifth wave of attacks, this one by 125 enemy aircraft. With the coming of darkness, that wave broke across the ping line.

For *Abercrombie* it was another grimly alert and anxious night at flash red, with a dozen raids reported in sequence on the warning net, all picked up well to the north, all closing. "Raid five, three five zero, ninety, closing." "Raid five, now three five five, seventy-five, closing"—and so on at sixty, fifty, twenty and ten miles. At the first warning, night fighter Hellcats roared off from Yonton Field, climbing fast to the northward, their distinctive amber taillights visible for several minutes. As each raid approached to within about ten miles, it broke up, and from DE343's quiet and darkened bridge, the watch could see firing as first, AA batteries ashore and then ships on the northern end of the line opened up.

Abercrombie was in A34A the night of 4 May, her men at battle stations. Just after 0300 her SL radar picked up a fast-moving blip coming down the ping line from Ie Shima, fifteen miles to the northeast. As it drew opposite the first ship, in A38A, tracers broke the darkness on that bearing, sailing out nearly horizontally from port to starboard. A minute later came another, closer cluster of tracer streams as the second ship, in A37A, sighted the enemy. Even without radar the picture would have been clear: a single attacker, very low, coming straight down the line about one thousand yards inside. In *Abercrombie,* bridge watch, lookouts and gunners stared intently into the darkness ahead while the ship slipped silently along to the northeast—dead slow, guns loaded and trained out —fingers curled around firing keys, eyes pressed into sights or binoculars.

In CIC a radarman called out bearings and ranges, another marked each range and bearing, making a small black cross with a grease pencil on the surface plot.

"Bogey bearing zero four two, range seven miles."

"Bearing—zero four zero, five miles."

The deadly little white blip passed straight down the sides of the next two ships—in A36A and A35A. Topside in DE343 they watched and waited for more firing, but none came. Either the two ships didn't see the plane or chose not to draw attention to themselves.

"Bearing zero five zero, *one mile.*"

Ten seconds later there it was, a twin-engine Frances bomber, flat on the water off the starboard bow, not flying down the side at all, but boring straight in as though the enemy pilot had finally selected his target. Before the guns could get on it, the Frances released a torpedo. From bridge and guns *Abercrombie*'s men could see the long, shiny fish glint in the moonlight as it dropped, and the sheet of white water that sprang up as the torpedo entered the sea.

"Right full rudder!" roared Katschinski. "All ahead flank!"

The bow swung to starboard and the ship surged forward, picking up speed, but only the forward twenties had time to get on target. The Frances pulled up sharply to clear bow and bridge, and the twenties slammed their explosive tracers into it at point-blank range.

"Meet her!" Katschinski yelled into the voice tube. "Steady as you go!" *Abercrombie* was now on a course exactly opposite to that of the torpedo. It was the tactic rehearsed so many times off Pearl Harbor—"comb the wakes," present the DE's narrow beam to the incoming fish, not her 306-foot length. All through the surging, racing ship, men who had heard "torpedo in the water" braced themselves for the hit. Many prayed, some blessed themselves. Thirty seconds went by. A minute. The ship began to breathe again. A minute and a half. The fish had missed. Somewhere under the dark water it had bubbled down the side parallel to *Abercrombie*'s course and gone on astern. About three minutes after the drop, a heavy underwater explosion to port shook the ship. Either the torpedo had a self-destruct device or it had fired on a wake.

The Frances disappeared into the darkness aft. Radar picked it up again half a mile away, and saw it pass down the port side of the ship in A33A and move on toward the next station. Neither ship fired. But as the plane drew abeam of A32A, there was a blooming of red flame in the sky, then a burst of fire curving downward, then a brief pool of flame on the sea, then nothing as the night closed down again on the ping line.

But there were still bogies in the area, and an hour later *Abercrom-*

bie's guns spoke again as another Frances followed the ping line southwest from Ie Shima. But this one was not interested in DE343. It flew straight overhead from forward aft, with five-inch bursts and tracers lighting its underside while *Abercrombie*'s men waited for a bomb that never came. The Frances continued on course and disappeared astern.

The same afternoon, like a reward for the crew which had been at battle stations all night, an LCI delivered a fat bag of mail. Sleep was forgotten. Exhausted sailors sat on the deck or leaned in corners all over the ship, reading intently and delightedly. Afterward, buddies shared letters, and pictures were passed around. When the inevitable GQ sounded again, men ran to their battle stations actually smiling. I heard one machinist's mate mutter as he ran past, "Damn Japs, no regard for a guy, I got three letters to read yet."

DE343 stayed on A34A until 7 May, then dropped her anchor for the first time among the scores of ships off the Hagushi beaches for four days of fueling, provisioning, ship's work and restocking of ammunition.

Late on the evening of the seventh, with two thirds of her crew sleeping soundly for the first time in weeks, Ray Shiel on signal watch received the following message by flashing light from the yardarm blinkers of *Mount McKinley*, the force flagship:

> To Task Force 51. From Commander, Task Force 51. News bulletin. Communiqué. Radio news. Germany has surrendered unconditionally to Western Allies and Russia. Surrender took place at General Eisenhower's Command Post. Surrender was signed by Colonel General Jodl, German Chief of Staff.

It was good news. But it didn't have much meaning for the combat-weary officers and sailors of the *Abercrombie*. They were too close to the trees to consider the forest. They were glad that no more men would die in Europe. They knew that in time more ships, more planes, more weapons would come to help in the Pacific. In time. But after how many more days and nights on Able Thirty-something Able? After how many more GQs, how many more bombs, torpedoes and kamikazes, how many more operations after Okinawa? For *Abercrombie*'s men at Okinawa in early May, squinting at the world through a fog of fatigue, the only reality was the DE herself, mess hall, bunk and battle stations, the other gray ships, the sea, the rocky islands and the enemy. Home was a fading dream of love and warmth, achingly distant and eons in the past. Far in the clouded future they could glimpse another rosy dream of peace and happiness. But all that was real and tangible was this operation, the last one, and those to come, whatever they would be—rehearse, invade, fight, withdraw, rehearse, invade, fight and withdraw again, ever more northward, ever more difficult, ever more deadly, *ad infinitum.*

But they did get some rest in the Hagushi anchorage. There were even two nights without a GQ, although not consecutive.

On 9 May the kamikazes got *England* and *Oberrender.*

England, the queen of the sub killers, was in station A28, a few miles northwest of Kerama Retto, her men at battle stations for evening twilight, when three Vals came slanting down from the north with a two-plane section of CAP hot on their tails. To the cheers of the DE gunners, the CAP smoked two into the sea. But the third kept coming. *England* went to flank speed, turned to unmask her broadside and opened fire with everything she had. The Val began trailing smoke, a wheel was blown off, the cockpit canopy shattered—the pilot had to be dead. The plane swerved and faltered, thoroughly shot up. For a few seconds it looked as though it would miss. But it didn't. It fell burning into *England's* deck just abaft the bridge; its bomb demolished the wardroom, CIC, radio shack and pilothouse, and flames engulfed the open bridge. Thirty-five of the DE's men were killed, another twenty-seven wounded. It took more than an hour, with help from other ships, to put out the fires. *England* joined the other hulks in Wiseman's Junkyard. Her combat career was over. Even so, in the bloody ledger of the war, the balance was heavily in her favor—thirty-five Americans against some four hundred Japanese —the crews of six submarines blasted to the bottom by *England's* unerring hedgehogs while *Abercrombie* was still shaking down at Bermuda.

Even more personal for *Abercrombie's* men was the ordeal of her sister ship, *Oberrender* (DE344), commissioned just ten days after DE343 and with us on nearly every mission since Aruba. *Oberrender* was patrolling good old A34A, and by a freakish coincidence was hit at the same instant as *England* a few stations down the line, precisely at 1853.

At 1844 the "Obie" 's TBS sounded a familiar warning. "Bogey bearing three zero zero, range thirty-four." Her own SA radar picked up the incoming raid at 298 degrees, 16 miles, and tracked it in until lookouts and gunners picked it up visually—a single fighter, high in the western sky above the setting sun, estimated altitude 18,000 feet, range 9,000 yards. At the instant of first sighting, the kamikaze pushed over into a 35-degree dive straight for *Oberrender,* coming in on the starboard bow. At flank speed the DE turned hard to port and opened fire with her main battery. At a range of four thousand yards the forties joined in and immediately began making hits. A mile out a close five-inch burst jolted the enemy plane and the left wing began to flop. At 1,500 yards the starboard twenties began firing, the tracers from five guns converging on the target. The kamikaze seemed to be diving through a torrent of fire, flaming and smoking heavily and that wing flopping grotesquely. At 250 yards the wing ripped off, and it looked as though the "Obie" 's gunners had saved the day. But both wing and burning plane kept coming, and both smashed into the ship. The wing hit just aft of the stack and dented the uptake from the after fireroom. But the kamikaze itself flew straight into twenty-millimeter number five, which was still pouring out lead at the moment of impact, killed the three-man crew and demolished the gun tub. That would have been bad enough. But the dead pilot had been carrying a delayed action five hundred-pound bomb. It tore through the main deck inches inside the gunwale and exploded in the starboard fireroom, blowing every man there to bits, blasting a hole ten feet by twenty-five feet in the ship's bottom, wrenching twenty-five feet of her keel out of shape and nearly breaking the ship in two. The force of the bomb's explosion raised a four-foot-high bulge in the main deck over the fireroom, and buckled and twisted the whole bridge superstructure. The fireroom, the adjacent engine room aft of it and the big living compartment forward all flooded instantly, and *Oberrender* settled in the sea until her freeboard was only two feet amidships. Four fuel tanks forward of the hit were ruptured and the heavy black oil mixed with the seawater in the flooded and demolished spaces. All the shrouds supporting the mast were snapped and the mast whipped so violently that the SA radar's big bedspring antenna was torn from its mountings and catapulted into the sea. The whaleboat was blown overboard and sunk.

Eight of *Oberrender*'s men died, five in the fireroom, of whom only bloody shreds were ever found, and the crew of the number five twenty-millimeter. Another fifty-three were wounded. Ted Gruhn's old ship, the destroyer *Farenholt,* and a PCE came alongside to help put out fires created by the kamikaze's gasoline. A big fleet tug, *Tekesta,* came foaming out of Kerama Retto and towed DE344 back in.

Oberrender never went to sea again. Naval engineers found her to be damaged beyond repair. Half her crew was sent home. The other half remained in the junkyard to help with the dismal task of cannibalizing her for the benefit of other ships. When that job was over, she was towed to sea and sunk by gunfire. Thus died the second ship of Escort Division 69.

Two aspects of the loss of DE344 bothered the crew of DE343. First, there was personal grief for the killed and wounded, many of them friends of *Abercrombie*'s sailors. Second, there were the discouraging circumstances of her fatal damage. Attacked by a single kamikaze on a station to which *Abercrombie* was frequently assigned, DE344 had done everything right—flank speed, a tight turn, heavy, sustained, accurate shooting by all guns. She had made hits, set the enemy ablaze, killed the pilot, smashed his engine, even torn off a wing. Still it had not been enough. Still men had been blown apart, crushed and burned. Still the fine fighting little ship had been lost. Could *Abercrombie*, an identical ship, with a crew that had received identical training, do any better?

It would be two more weeks before the fortunes of war would bring the answer to that question. In the interval there were more patrols to be made, an assortment of odd jobs to do—and scores of GQs to run to. In that interval also *Abercrombie*'s men were witnesses to events that temporarily diverted them from the nagging concerns about the kamikazes.

On the tenth of May, while DE343 was still anchored at Hagushi, the Japanese sent a Nick fighter across the anchorage on a photo reconnaissance mission. It was a clear morning, and the Nick was so high it was only a bright speck in the vault of the sky. It seemed ironic that a single enemy pilot could send a hundred ships and thousands of men to their battle stations, depriving them of the rest they so badly needed or their ships of the work they were forced to abandon. Ironic and infuriating. A CAP of four Marine Corsairs out of Kadena Field on Okinawa was in the air; and although the high-flying Nick was well above the service ceiling of his Corsair, one of the Marines asked for and received permission to go after the enemy. At full power, the Corsair clawed its way up, up and up in pursuit, keeping the Nick in sight. After an hour and a half, at a frigid 38,000 feet, the Corsair pilot was finally on the enemy's tail and squeezed the triggers of his .50-calibers. Nothing happened. The guns were frozen tight. It had been a long, cold, miserable flight, and this Marine was angry. He closed in on the Nick, chewing at its rudder and elevators with his big four-bladed steel prop. He made three passes, knocking off more and more of the enemy's empenage each time. After the last pass, the Nick did not have enough control surface left to maintain flight, and all the way down the sky it tumbled, fluttering and spinning for more than eight miles vertically into the sea. On all the ships at Okinawa, listening on the fighter net, men cheered and laughed and pounded each other on the back as though the home team had scored a winning touchdown in the final seconds of play.

But the Marine Lieutenant, Robert R. Kunoman by name, was in trouble. There were holes in the plane's wings and engine cowling that had been punched by debris from the Nick, he was out of oxygen, and on the way home the engine quit at ten thousand feet. But he made a safe dead-stick landing at Kadena, the most beloved man at Okinawa.

On 11 May the naval flight-training program opened up for married officers under age twenty-seven with at least one year of sea duty; I sent in my application.

Three times in the following ten days, *Abercrombie* was able to escape from Okinawa and the ping line for brief but welcome intervals.

On the fourteenth she joined with the brand-new destroyer *Compton* (DD705) to escort the old battlewagon *Texas* twenty-four hours steaming to the south. The three ships sailed from the Hagushi anchorage at noon. *Abercrombie* reversed course at noon the next day and returned to Okinawa the following noon at the center of an eight-ship destroyer squadron in circular formation, making nineteen knots.

After two nights of GQs and bogies on A33A, she went out at midnight on a similar mission. With an APD, the *Loy*, she steamed 250 miles south to join the screen for an ammunition ship and escort her back to Kerama Retto.

At 0600 on Sunday, 20 May, she was pulled off patrol in the Inner Screen for the Hagushi anchorage and ran south for twelve hours to assist a destroyer in screening the battleship *Idaho* inbound to Okinawa from the eastward. By 1700 next day she was anchored again off Hagushi.

The men enjoyed the variety of those short voyages away from the bloody island, short as they were. Each provided a break in the deadly patrol routine and an opportunity for a few hours of unbroken sleep, a shower and some hot, uninterrupted meals. The majestic old battlewagons, bristling with guns, broad of beam with wide torpedo blisters along their sides, bright colors and signal flags flying as in pictures on recruiting posters, were stirring to see and lifted the spirits. And tired as they were, *Abercrombie*'s men could feel that now she was what she had been intended from the beginning to be—an efficient, effective unit of the fleet, routinely accomplishing whatever mission she was assigned with precision and dispatch, frequently complimented by seniors afloat. Each rendezvous, each ETA was made on the button; on each join-up with a new formation, DE343 sliced through the sea to her assigned position, spun on her heel, slowed and fell precisely into her slot, instantly conforming to whatever zigzag plan or tactical maneuvers were in progress. The growing, unspoken pride officers and men felt in their ship and their shipmates was the most effective antidote to the sinkings and the casualties that continued to occur all around them.

It was eerily symbolic that on the evening of the twenty-first, as the DE screened ahead of the mighty *Idaho*, westbound for Okinawa, the horizon was dark with clouds, smoky with curtains of rain, and smeared with the dark, blood red of the smothered sun, while astern the sky was a clear, pale blue and a few early stars sparkled daintily.

One night on patrol in A38A adjacent to Ie Shima, *Abercrombie* was treated to a few moments of high drama. The condition was flash red, the cause a single enemy plane flying high across the little island just a couple of miles away. Although CIC held it on the SA radar, the plane was invisible at first. Then the Army's newly installed ninety-millimeter AA batteries on Ie Shima opened up in radar control. The heavy guns fired slowly in a precise and deliberate way, and we could see the flashes on the island and then the single white tracers soaring up and bursting with a little sparkle one after the other in an evenly spaced horizontal line. After about the tenth round, a moving speck of light appeared close to the last burst at the end of that line. The moving speck of light continued on a straight and level course and grew brighter. Several bursts now flashed very close to the brightening light, which suddenly began to fall, its color changing to a flaring red. A few hundred feet above the sea it broke apart, the two pieces fell separately for a few seconds, and then both red lights winked out at the same instant.

During those days of trial by kamikaze and fatigue, there was not a man in *Abercrombie* who would have traded his lot, as bad as it was, for that of a soldier or Marine ashore. News bulletins from the radio shack told almost daily of the stubborn enemy resistance in difficult terrain, of Japanese strong points fanatically held and interconnected with tunnels, of heavy U.S. casualties. On warm days we could see the dust of combat rising through the trees. On infrequent (but very welcome) days of rain, we could imagine the muddy foxholes, the sodden uniforms, the flooded latrines ashore. On shipboard, unless or until the moment his ship was hit, a man lived in acceptable comfort—with a clean, dry bunk, clean, dry clothes, hot showers, and, usually, three hot, nourishing meals a day. For the officers, again for as long as they stayed afloat, living conditions, compared to those ashore, were almost sinfully comfortable. Most enjoyed the privacy of a conveniently furnished stateroom of their own. Once a week their laundry was taken aft and returned washed and ironed the same day. Meals were served on china by white-jacketed steward's mates and eaten with silver implements set out on a linen cloth. At sea, although injury and death could come at any time, while a man lived and his ship was under him, he lived well.

In the two days from the twenty-third to the twenty-fifth of May, 165 more kamikazes came swarming down the island chain from Kyushu. On Friday the twenty-fifth, elements of that swarm gave DE343 the busiest night of her life. It was perfect kamikaze weather, clear and with the full moon that *Abercrombie*'s men had learned to dread. The DE was in station A38, a five-thousand-yard sector of the Inner Screen about halfway between Ie Shima and "Point Bolo" on Okinawa, steaming at ten knots on courses 078 and 258 degrees. With bogies all over the scope, the ship was fully buttoned up and every weapon manned. A defensive system was in effect which had been developed under the unprecedented and peculiar circumstances of warfare in the waters off Okinawa, a situation in which warships were tethered for long periods to fixed locations in close vicinity to prominent landmarks where they could be readily located and attacked. Although *Abercrombie* had a main director which could aim and fire both five-inch guns from the bridge, and a director for each forty-millimeter, all guns were in local control with gunners ordered to open fire as soon as they could see the target. To help them find that target as quickly as possible, the sound-powered phone circuits were cross-connected so that the gunners could hear the ranges and bearings of the enemy reported by the radar operators in CIC. Most often the SA radar would pick up the bogey first and track it in until it appeared on the surface-search (SL) gear. The Captain and the OOD could then watch it on the small remote radar scope on the bridge and maneuver the ship to keep the enemy on the beam where all but the offside twenties could bear.

At about 0140 on the midwatch, one of the bogies which had been circling off to starboard apparently sighted DE343. On radar the little white blip suddenly straightened out and began closing rapidly on a steady bearing. The engine order telegraph jingled, a puff of dark smoke belched from the stack, the turbines began to whine and the ship surged forward, ready for battle. On the bridge scope it looked as though the plane were circling to come in astern—the same tactic used with fatally successful results on *Kimberly*, *Dickerson* and others. Katschinski, his eyes fixed on the scope, kept turning to starboard, swinging the stern away, keeping all guns clear. But the speed differential—20 knots to 180—was against him, and when the twin-engine Betty bomber popped into sight in the flash of a single three-inch round from the DE astern, it was well back on the starboard quarter.

Gunner's mate third Bob Hawthorne, Gun Captain on Mount 41, saw it first through a set of binoculars he had borrowed from quartermaster Howard Amos for exactly this purpose. It was a sight to make a strong man quail—the big bomber close and boring straight in, the two props whirling with blue exhaust flames sputtering behind them, the roar of the engine building, the nose aimed directly at him, the whole mass seeming to be driving right down his throat. But Bob Hawthorne didn't quail at all. Since neither Harry Hensler, the trainer, nor Red Henderson, the pointer, had yet seen the plane, Hawthorne pushed Hensler out of the trainer's seat and took over, spinning the wheel to bring the twin muzzles around to the target bearing, and yelled across to Henderson, "Down a little, Red, down, down, a little more." Then Hawthorne hit the firing key, and the forty began hammering out its two-pound high-explosive rounds, cherry-red balls lancing out into the dark, nearly three a second. "Up a little, Red, now down a little," Hawthorne coached; and steady in train, raising and lowering slightly in elevation, the twin forties banged away straight into the teeth of the enemy.

After the first few tracers Henderson picked up the target and needed no more coaching. Both men now held the nose of the incoming plane on the X at the dead center of their cobweb sights. Its barrels level with the water, so low was the kamikaze, Mount 42 stood its ground in the face of what looked like imminent obliteration. Close above and behind Hawthorne and Henderson, Tom Rutters and Sloan Duncan jammed four-round clips down into the slotted loaders, while Chicken Clinedinst, Al Deaton and Jim Hensley kept them supplied with clips from the ready-ammunition locker. With the forty-millimeter tracers pointing out the target, the two aft twenties on the starboard side got into action. But it was Hawthorne's forty on which life or death depended. He and Henderson watched a couple of red balls clip close above the plane, then two went under, tearing into the sea below it. Then another hit the water, bounced up and detonated on the enemy's right engine, which exploded with a blinding white flash. For an instant the plane kept coming. Then the right wing broke off at the engine, flipped up and back into the night sky; the plane rolled right, the stub of the wing dug into the sea, the bomber cartwheeled in a fountain of spray, came to rest and settled out of sight ten yards from *Abercrombie*'s stern. Buckets of seawater splashed onto the main deck aft. Hawthorne and Henderson thought they could make out two heads in the white water where the plane had been. In the sudden silence of the guns, from topside fore and aft, from engine and firerooms and after steering, from repair party stations in passageways and living spaces, from CIC and radio and pilothouse, DE343 rang with shouted cheers of relief and deliverance as the tension broke. If it had been up to *Abercrombie*'s crew that night, Bob Hawthorne would have been elected President of the Universe for Life.

But that bloody night was not yet over. Bogies swarmed across the scope like flies scouting for carrion. Four times DE343's radarmen watched as fast-moving blips closed and merged with the slower ones of ships, and on the bridge at the moment of merge, they could see bursts of fire as another ship was crashed. Antiaircraft fire, explosions, patches of flame, and a couple of huge, flaring fires marked the vicinity of Yonton Field; and the next day we learned that the enemy had sent five Sally bombers with suicide teams to make belly landings and destroy parked planes and fuel supplies. Four had been shot down, but one team had destroyed some planes, damaged others and fired seventy thousand gallons of aviation gasoline before being exterminated.

An hour after shooting down the Betty, *Abercrombie's* guns opened up on a similar plane, which crossed astern, low and slow, apparently in search of a juicier target.

Then just at the end of the midwatch it was *Abercrombie's* turn again. The second attack began in the same way as the first, with a circling bogey suddenly closing straight and fast from starboard. This time, Katschinski was able to keep it broad on the beam. In the midships closet and passageway of Repair II, we heard radar report the plane one mile out— then, "one five double oh," then "one oh double oh." Under our bottoms, as we sat on the steel deck, we could feel the turbines pick up speed and hear the pitch of their humming rise. The deck slanted as the rudder was put hard over to starboard. "Range eight double oh." "Range five double oh." In another second or two came the heavy hammering of the forties from fore and aft, next the faster chattering of twenties, hideously noisy because number five was almost directly over our heads, and tough on the nerves because when the twenties opened up, we *knew* the attacking plane was close. And when they kept firing in a sustained, steady way, we knew he was still on his way in.

Then came the unmistakable roar of an aircraft engine so close overhead that we all instinctively ducked. The forties and twenties went silent, but in a moment the ship shook with the booming of the forward five-inch, firing repeatedly and at equal intervals of about ten seconds.

"He's circling the bow," Don Wood reported from under his big talker's helmet. "Fifty-one is firing at his exhaust flames. Looks like he's coming in again."

As tough as it was for the men topside, directly exposed to the impact of the kamikaze, and for the engineers below the waterline, surrounded by pipes full of scalding steam, I think this kind of action was hardest on the men of the repair parties. Topside and below a man had things to do —search, aim, load, fire, pass magazines or clips, steer, watch the radar, turn a throttle wheel, open a valve. Even the men in the handling rooms for the five-inch guns, under dogged-down doors and hatches far below the waterline, surrounded by explosives, passing their fifty-four-pound projectiles and twenty-eight-pound cases up through scuttles to the mount, had something to do, something to occupy hands, body and mind. A man in a repair party had nothing to do, his job began only when the ship was hit. Until then he had simply to sit deep inside the hull, water-tight doors and hatches closed around him, ventilation off, blind except for the eerie glow of red battle lights, wait, and try to piece together from the sounds of the ship and the fragmentary reports of a talker, the events outside on which his life depended.

Thus, below decks, we waited in tense silence for the kamikaze to attempt again to sink us, ordering our minds not to think of what we knew had happened to other ships like ours and other men like us in situations much like this.

The second attack was a nearly exact repetition of the first. Again the kamikaze (now identified as a single-engine Hamp) came in low and fast from the starboard beam. Again the forties opened up, then the twenties, but earlier this time since the gunners knew what they were looking for. Again came the crescendo of engine sounds close overhead and even louder than before. However, now there was a difference. A clattering of twenties broke out along the port side, lasted for perhaps fifteen seconds, and stopped. Dead, suspenseful silence after all the firing. Then from above our heads came another burst of unrestrained, profane cheering. Forty minutes later, with the scopes at least temporarily clear, General Quarters was secured and we found out what had happened. After the first attack and as the kamikaze was beginning his second run, Tom Parlon had ordered the port twenties to elevate to their maximum angles, pointing nearly straight up at the zenith, and be ready to open fire as (and if) the plane passed over again. On his first pass, the Hamp had just missed the top of the stack, nearly clipping the mast with his right wing. The second time he was even lower, skimming across the torpedo tubes between the stack and Mount 42, and burning from half a dozen hits. But that time the port twenties were waiting for him, laced his belly full of high explosive rounds at point-blank range as he went over and followed him unmercifully into the darkness until he tumbled into the sea a few hundred yards away. A short-lived pool of burning gasoline fell rapidly astern and flickered out. Score: *Abercrombie* three, kamikazes zero.

But that was not a final score. The deadly game continued.

After the clear, moonlit night, daylight brought a heavy, low overcast and occasional rain, the kind of weather that the sailors on the ping line prayed for. But despite the weather, bogies reappeared on the fringes of the radar scopes, and after a respite of three and a half hours, DE343 went back to General Quarters. At 0800 she joined up with two other ships for mutual protection, and the three steamed back and forth on the patrol line in column with three hundred yards between ships—*Abercrombie*, *Roper* (APD20) and *Gosselin* (APD126). At 0925, with flash red in effect and with *Abercrombie* leading the little column on a course of due south, the starboard lookout reported a single-engine enemy plane, a Zeke, on the starboard quarter (bearing 300 degrees true) about four miles away and closing. The guns on all three ships were on him instantly, but before a single round was fired, it appeared that shooting would not be required. Right on the Zeke's tail appeared two Marine Corsairs pouring bullets into the enemy. We could see the red blinking of the .50-calibers along the Corsairs' wings and the gray smoke streaming back. The Zeke began to smoke. It looked as though the plane would go down at any second. It seemed to falter, but caught itself and steadied. The pilot banked right, then left, weaving and skidding, the Corsairs still blazing away. It was up to the Marines. None of the ships could fire for fear of hitting them. A mile out the Zeke was headed straight for *Abercrombie*'s stern, but by then she was doing better than twenty knots and pulling away to the plane's right. It tried to turn right to follow, but one of the Corsairs was close on its right wing, firing. The Zeke leveled its wings again and flew straight into the starboard bow of the *Roper*, three hundred yards astern. A gout of thick black smoke sprang up at the APD's bow, red flame at its base. It blew away in a few seconds, leaving a thin column of gray-white smoke and a jagged round hole about four feet in diameter. Flames flickered redly inside the hole. There was no sign of the crew of the forward three-inch gun.

Abercrombie circled back, looking for survivors, found none, and pulled alongside the wounded APD with all hoses led out and full fire main pressure at their nozzles, ready to help with the fire fighting. But *Roper*, thirty-odd years young and, in a previous incarnation as a destroyer, a veteran of the Battle of the Atlantic, needed no help. With *Abercrombie* escorting her just to be safe, she retired slowly to the Hagushi anchorage to tend to her wounds and her wounded.

By 1100 *Abercrombie* was back on patrol in the Inner Screen for the anchorage, and late in the afternoon she moved out to A39A northeast of Ie Shima.

In those final days of May the enemy never relaxed his pressure on the ships off Okinawa. The kamikazes surged down from Kyushu in waves a few days apart, but even between the waves there was no respite, with just enough attackers to keep the U.S. crews at their guns—and out of their bunks. In *Abercrombie* and the other DEs, APDs and destroyers on patrol, sleep became the most valued and desired commodity in life. Men slept wherever and whenever they could, fully clothed with life jacket and helmet close at hand. All the officers and chiefs and many of the men wore life belts twenty-four hours a day. The belts could be inflated by a single firm squeeze, which released the contents of two CO_2 capsules. In the water the belts would ride up under the armpits. Many of us had personally designed small watertight packages that attached to the belts. They contained shark repellent, a signaling mirror, a dye marker, and whatever other small items we thought might assist us to survive if we were suddenly blown overboard.

The crew smelled bad and looked worse—soiled and rumpled, red of eye and unshaven. Between calls to General Quarters, most hung around their battle stations. And the weeks under the continuous threat of surprise attack by kamikazes took their toll in a variety of ways. Sociable, affable firecontrolman first Ralph Rice ceased to smile or joke and left his battle station at the main director on the open bridge only momentarily for calls of nature; he slept curled around its base, his life jacket as a pillow. Little George Ferroni, *Abercrombie's* laundryman and Rice's talker at General Quarters, kept him provided with sandwiches and coffee. Jim Garland, torpedoman first class, with the crafty ingenuity of the marginally rational, located what he considered to be the best-protected location in the ship (a belowdecks passageway), squatted there in helmet and life jacket, and with a kind of wild-eyed tenacity adamantly refused to move —even to man his battle station. Chief Engineer Gus Adams took to wearing his .45-caliber pistol night and day, apparently the victim of a pressure-induced paranoia in which he saw his long-standing personal unpopularity as a threat against his life. Even tough, resilient bo'sun's mate Fred Manger suffered from occasional moments of irrationality, as when he leaped down from the superstructure one day to grab and shake a shipmate doing a routine chore. His friends thought the fact that he had sliced an ear from one of the enemy airmen as a souvenir before burying him at sea was weighing on Manger's mind, adding to the burden of the kamikazes shared by all.

Instinctively the men found ways to relieve the pressure. In the chiefs' quarters the chief pharmacist's mate issued liberal (and illegal) doses of medicinal alcohol whenever the ship was at anchor and under smoke. In the number two engineroom, a still, ingeniously constructed and concealed by Jim Triplett, provided the same kind of relief in the form of a potent but palatable supply of raisin jack for a select group of engineers in the know. Back aft, the snack-bar-deli in the carpenter shop flourished. Some men worked with their hands—like Steve Stephens who made watchbands for his mates out of pieces of enemy aircraft salvaged at Saipan. Whenever possible, the routine of the ship's services went on and there was comfort in that. On the prescribed days, first the port and then the starboard watch, then the chiefs and officers sent their soiled clothing back to Ferroni's laundry; storekeeper Ken Eidemiller opened his little shop to dispense cigarettes, candy and toilet articles; H. C. Eckroad kept cutting hair; Sparks Martrildonno cranked his sheets of mimeographed news reports out of the radio shack; Frank Grout continued to process and distribute the blessed mail.

Once in a great while there was even a good laugh to break the mood of tension and anxiety. One night in Kerama Retto, the white smoke protectively thick overhead, a movie was shown in the mess hall, crowded as usual for the occasion. In one scene a luscious brunet actress in a thigh-length tennis skirt was perched on a wrought-iron chair in a garden, her legs demurely crossed. The camera showed her close up from head to toe in all her female glory. She occupied the entire picture. In the course of the action she moved languorously, uncrossing and then recrossing those long, slim legs. Stocky, blue-stubbled little Dago Paiva was sitting all the way up front, directly below the screen, and at that point he stopped the show with a wild yell, jumping up in the darkened compartment so that most of the picture was projected on his wildly gesticulating body. "I seen it!" he yelled. "I *seen* it! I tell ya I *seen* it!" It was necessary for movie-operator Bob Wachter to stop his projector and turn on the lights before Dago and the laughter of his mates could be quieted. Even then, he settled back below the screen muttering, "Goddamnit, I tell ya, I seen it!"

One bright morning off Kerama Retto, the men of DE343 had a laugh on themselves, but it was a laugh with a potential for disaster. The air warning condition was flash red. Lookouts, gunners, bridge watch—all scanned the skies for the first sign of enemy aircraft. After some minutes there came a shout, "There he is! High overhead. Bearing zero nine zero. Elevation angle seventy." There was a whirring and buzzing as all the guns trained around and elevated to that bearing and angle. The little speck of brightness high in the clear sky was hard to see with the naked eye, but in a while all guns were on, or said they were. Then nothing happened. The enemy aircraft must be very high indeed. And it didn't seem to be moving. Someone with binoculars, probably Tom Parlon, found that the object had the shape not of an aircraft but of a tiny disk. Quietly the order went out to the guns: "Train in and stand by." The enemy aircraft was Venus. A ripple of embarrassed laughter rolled across the ship. But if a real attack had developed, a kamikaze or a torpedo bomber had come in, low on the water, while all the DE's guns were pointing at a planet, there would have been no chance to laugh.

Occasional laughter did help, and in those last days of May when she had to be to survive, DE343 was as effective a warship for her size as had ever sailed the seas. The process which had begun at Orange and been accelerated at Bermuda and Pearl, and honed and tested at Leyte and Lingayen, was now complete. Two hundred and sixteen officers and men and 306 feet of steel hull crammed with ordnance and machinery had been welded into a single lethal weapon as responsive to the will of the United States of America as a saber in the hands of a swordsman. One of more than 500 DEs flying the Stars and Stripes, *Abercrombie* still was unique, a composite product of her crew, her training and her experience, a weapon with a personality. Given a job, she would do it with dispatch, persistance, some dash, and a blessedly disproportionate but consistent quota of plain good luck. Routinely her battle stations were now manned in under two minutes. In action the characters, capabilities and training of individual crewmen melded into a dynamic, coordinated flow akin to that of a steeplechaser or a high hurdler.

On gunner's mate Jim Payton's forward forty, G. P. McMillan of the Galveston birthday party, and the sailor whose indiscretion in the aptly named handling room on commissioning day had so startled the invited guests, were two of the loaders. In Ed Schuh's Mount 51, Fred Manger was Gun Captain; and Buckets Bowers and Jack Green and Foch Costner of the whaleboat adventure at Leyte, deeply Southern Jack Dempsey Blackwell, and Pappy McAleer, who had helped splice the shroud after the carrier collision, handled projectiles and cases and worked the gun. Bill Watkins of the great accordion caper was port lookout, while his partner in crime, Tom Rutters, loaded clips passed to him by Chicken Clinedinst into one of the twin forties of Bob Hawthorne's Mount 42. Sparks Martrildonno with the tattooed rose kept the ship in touch with others from the radio shack. Bo'sun's mates Pete Kish and Pop Deatherage operated Mount 52. And below them, young seaman Curt Foley from Rice's hometown of Roanoke, Virginia, led a gang of five men in the handling room, sending a steady supply of cases and projectiles upward to the mount. Harry Miles stood by with Butch in after steering to handle any emergency involving the rudders. Frank Grout, the mailman, manned part of the sonar gear. Chief Albert Lee Murphy Holloway and Doc Bour were forward in Repair I where Bob Zuzanek was the talker. Ph.D. candidate Cy DeCoster was OOD, Howard Amos was on the wheel, his station since Galveston. Tom Parlon controlled all guns from aft on the port side of the bridge, and Hicks was in charge one level down in CIC.

As diverse a crew in terms of regional and cultural backgrounds, education, religion and even age as perhaps had ever sailed, at this one time, in this place where the needs of the nation had sent them, they were a lethally effective element of American seapower, which could, and did, keep the sea and do the job despite the best efforts of a desperate enemy over many weeks.

During the night of 27 May to 28 May, the enemy redoubled its efforts with another scourge of more than one hundred suiciders. In raid after raid, all night long, they came winging down from the northward in clusters of a dozen or more which broke up eight to ten miles north of Okinawa and scattered to buzz and circle just above the water, looking for targets. *Abercrombie* started that perilous night in station B-29 in the northwest sector of the Inner Screen for the Hagushi anchorage, steaming back and forth at 10 knots on a line 5,000 yards long, running 062 and 242 degrees. Flash red was signaled at 1920. DE343 went to General Quarters and stayed there all night. The air was full of warnings, and bogies crossed back and forth across the SL scope, circling, opening, closing, attacking. Occasionally under the red lights and among the tools and gear at Repair II, it seemed there would be some respite. Raid twenty had been tracked in for forty miles out, and scattered; there had been some firing, a ship or two had been hit, and all was quiet. We began to think we might be able to grab a couple of hours of sleep after all. Then Don Wood would shake his head and repeat what he had just heard. "Raid twenty-one, three five three, thirty-seven miles, closing," and it would begin all over again—the gradual closing of the range, a few splashes by the night CAP, then "Raid twenty-one breaking up." In a few minutes there would be reports from *Abercrombie's* own CIC. "Bogey three one zero, five, closing, bearing steady." Then would come the orders to helm and engines, the slamming of the five-incher, the rhythmic pounding of the forties, the quicker, louder hammering of the twenties, the rush of an engine overhead. The men below felt limp and wet after each attack, and personally angry when still another raid would be reported.

At 2330 that night, DE343 opened up on a suicider that came in astern, flew up the port side close aboard, and continued straight ahead to crash the stern of the APD on the next station, the USS *Rednour*. In the red glare of the resultant fire, *Abercrombie's* gunners could see the APD on the far side of *Rednour*, and knew uncomfortably that their own ship was equally conspicuous. Either the kamikaze was not carrying the usual bomb or it had failed to detonate, because *Rednour* quickly doused her fires and *Abercrombie* escorted her into Hagushi to tend to her casualties and damage.

Shortly after midnight DE343 shifted her patrol to the Outer Screen, station A34A. And true to its reputation, that station saw her come under attack twice more in the next hour. The first enemy made a single run from port to starboard, met a storm of fire and continued on out of range, presumably to immolate himself on a less resistant target.

The second attack was as bad as it could get.

At first, it looked like a burning plane skimming in just above the surface on the port quarter, a horizontal stream of fire shooting from its tail. But it was coming faster than any airborne object the men topside had ever seen. The speed and the fire stream told Tom Parlon what it was —a Baka. Twenty-six hundred pounds of rocket-propelled, high-explosive warhead attacking at 500 mph under the most accurate of all guidance systems—a human pilot. In April an identical weapon had blown a picket destroyer in two. There was no time to maneuver the ship, barely time to train a gun or two in the general direction of that onrushing stream of fire. But one of those guns was Mount 52. Gun Captain Pete Kish, his head protruding from the top of the mount, had the Baka in his sights. The gun swung rapidly around, its long barrel parallel to the deck, as pointer and trainer matched the markers on their dials with those sent down by Kish's sights. The instant they were on, Kish gave the order "Commence firing!" and two rounds blasted off ten seconds apart. With the second round, the fire stream angled abruptly downward and winked out, and a moment later the DE's stern was lifted and hurled to starboard by a booming underwater explosion like a dozen depth charges set on shallow and going off together. Scratch one Baka and another suicide pilot. Add the name of Pete Kish to that of Bob Hawthorne in the special Valhalla of the USS *Abercrombie.*

Three things had saved DE343—the speed with which an alert gun captain had swung his mount on target, good (and lucky) shooting, and the proximity or VT fuse in the so-called "AA Special" ammunition which was used. This highly classified antiaircraft fuse put out a radio signal which detonated the projectile within killing range (sixty feet) of the target without requiring a direct hit. It accounted for most of the enemy aircraft shot down by U.S. ships in the Pacific.

General Quarters, which had been called at 1920 on Sunday, was not secured until 0528 on Monday. A passage from *Abercrombie's* action report for that night is a classic of understatement:

> It is regretted that, due to the large numbers of bogies constantly in the area and the large numbers of friendly ships engaged, that a clear and comprehensive picture of the night's action cannot be rendered. Several vessels were seen to be struck by kamikazes in our immediate vicinity, among them the USS *Rednour* (APD102). A total of 32 rounds of 5"/38 AA Special and 175 rounds of 40-mm HET was expended. No damage or casualties were suffered.

Monday was DE343's day to fuel. She was relieved on A34A at 0530 and escorted an oiler into the Hagushi anchorage, arriving at the same time as a single enemy Zeke, which was shot down in a thunderous barrage of fire and spiraled smoking into the sea half a mile off the port bow.

The next day *Abercrombie* lost her Captain.

The first hint came in a visual message to the task group commander at Hagushi after fueling on the twenty-eighth. "Commanding Officer would appreciate chance to see a doctor if possible."

The same afternoon, with the ship at anchor, the whaleboat took Katschinski across to the flagship. On his return he announced in a most matter-of-fact way that he was to be transferred for hospitalization due to high diastolic blood pressure, that Hicks was to relieve him as C.O. and to choose between Tom and me for Exec. Since Tom was a month or so my senior, and my orders to flight training were expected any day, Hicks selected Tom. The next morning, with *Abercrombie* still anchored at Hagushi, Katschinski simply left. No ceremonial mustering of the crew at quarters. No reading of orders. No words of farewell or good luck. Not even a personal good-bye to anyone. He left that little man-of-war and its crew of over two hundred which had never known another captain, as a man would leave his home to mail a letter or walk his dog.

The effect on the crew was traumatic. Although not everyone had liked Katschinski, nearly everyone had confidence in his ability to lead and see them through. Now, without warning, in hostile waters, in the face of the enemy, bright, impatient, acerbic, competent, familiar Katschinski was gone. Who would take care of them now? Make the right tactical decisions out in A34A? Give the right orders to helm and engines at the right times? Hicks?

Although Hicks had been Executive Officer from the start, he was largely an unknown quantity to the crew. Katschinski was most to blame. His lack of confidence in his Exec had been embarrassingly obvious. It was rare that Hicks had been allowed to handle the ship. Half the crew at one time or another had witnessed their skipper's profane, insulting and unresisted castigations of the Exec. Inevitably the Captain's attitude had rubbed off on the crew, reinforced by Hicks's unfortunate appearance. Uniformly from wardroom to berthing spaces, he was known as "Tubby" or "Chubby," or more disparagingly as "Jelly Belly."

Now "Tubby" Hicks was Captain. On the ping line at Okinawa.

Nor was it auspicious that when he called the crew together on the fantail and climbed up on a blower housing to announce the change of command, tears were rolling copiously down his cheeks.

Yet so solidly had the months of training and pressures and tensions of the war at sea welded and formed the weapon which was *Abercrombie*, that not even a loss of leadership could break or even dull it. The ship held together. The organization worked. Watches were well stood, the ship's work well done. If the men were uneasy, it did not affect the performance of their duties. If the officers were worried, they mentioned it to no one.

That afternoon DE343 steamed out to Kerama Retto to load ammunition and anchor for the night. The next day, still at anchor, she collided with an LST in an adjacent berth "due to unusual swinging of both vessels" (according to the log). The port depth-charge racks on the stern were bent out of shape. A crew from the tender *Hamul* came aboard and repaired them.

· At 1711 on the last day of May, in company with *Walter C. Wann*, *Abercrombie* went back on patrol. As Exec, Tom Parlon was off the watch bill; the OODs were now Wheeling, DeCoster and Stafford.

During the first few days of June, enemy air attacks around Okinawa fell off to only one or two a day, and although the tired American sailors welcomed the respite and made the most of it, the consensus was that the Japanese were husbanding planes and pilots for another big assault of one hundred or more kamikazes. During those days, *Abercrombie* patrolled the transport area and the outer screen, fueled, and one dark night steamed five miles south of Kerama Retto to escort in a Mariner seaplane which had made a forced landing and could taxi but not fly. At 0300 on 3 June in patrol station B-14, fourteen miles north of Kerama Retto, DE343 came under attack again.

The night was dark and overcast, the first warning a fast-approaching blip on the SL scope five miles on the port quarter. With flash red in effect, all battle stations were manned. The guns trained out on the danger bearing and waited, the gunners strained their eyes into the darkness for that first glimpse that would let them fire, and listened tensely for what seemed like the hundredth time as radar reported the rapidly closing ranges, the steady bearing. The Zeke roared into sight three to four hundred yards out, flat on the water, wings level, the hub at the center of the whirling prop like a bull's-eye, and all guns opened fire at the same instant, the tracers ripping the darkness to shreds. The sudden fountain of fire erupting out of the night must have startled and disoriented the enemy pilot because he banked sharply to the right, climbed, pursued by strings of tracers, and disappeared in the direction from which he had come. In CIC they watched as the little blip reappeared out of the disk of light in the center of the scope which was the ship, saw the blip circle out to about four miles, turn—and start another run. Back came the Zeke, this time from the port beam, fast and straight in. Again the guns opened at four hundred yards and hammered away steadily, lighting up the sea to port, the acid powder smoke blowing across the decks, the tracer streams from fore and aft converging ever more sharply as the kamikaze closed. This time the pilot did not turn away. It was evident from his unwaveringly straight flight path at minimum altitude that he had made up his mind to die for his Emperor on the deck of this small ship, which put out such a surprising torrent of gunfire. At a hundred yards, the twenties were chewing into his wings, but they couldn't stop him. This was it. Yet no man ducked, jumped or took cover. At five twenties and at both twin forties, the crews were like machines, loading and firing now at point-blank range with steady precision, the onrushing aircraft huge at the end of the barrels, the hot, empty brass cascading onto the deck. At the final instant, when fiery death seemed certain, the Zeke flashed overhead and was gone. He had simply missed.

Why? How?

Because a darkened ship at sea at night is hard to hit with an airplane. Doubly so if she is blessed with the low silhouette of Abercrombie's class, and trebly so if she is moving fast and firing, with all those guns flashing and the tracers scorching past. To get low enough to hit her means getting low enough to fly into the water by accident and thus die not gloriously but stupidly with no loss to your enemy. To crash a warship which is maneuvering and fighting back at night takes more than courage and determination and self-sacrifice. It takes experience and proficiency as a pilot. Abercrombie survived that midwatch of the third of June because thanks to Midway and the Solomons and the Marianas "turkey shoot" and other actions, Japan was just about out of such pilots.

And this particular Zeke driver, with a shot-up airplane to worry about, decided to call it a night. In Abercrombie's CIC, radar watched him continue straight ahead and vanish from the scope.

The action with the Zeke demonstrated that the abrupt change of command had not affected the ability of DE343 to take care of herself out on the line, and the sagging spirits of the crew noticeably revived. But two days later they took another body blow.

Early on the fifth, Abercrombie was ordered into Kerama Retto for repairs to her ailing sonar. While maneuvering in the crowded anchorage to come alongside a destroyer tender, Hicks misjudged his turning radius and brought the ship's stern dangerously close to the bow of an anchored destroyer, the Dyson (DD552). Although close, the situation was still salvageable. Abercrombie's stern, moving slowly, was close under the Dyson's starboard bow. Backing the port engine and going ahead on the starboard with left rudder would have swung the stern clear. But Hicks, nervous and unsure of himself through lack of experience, gave precisely the opposite orders, and before they could be corrected, the DE's stern crunched heavily into the destroyer's bow. Abercrombie's port K-gun racks were bent and twisted, and the hull dished in at that location. Dyson's bow was deeply dented. Both ships required two days alongside the tender for repairs.

Shiphandling is the most public demonstration possible of a naval officer's professional competence and, rightly or wrongly, his reputation and that of his command are affected in direct proportion to his demonstrated ability. There is no hiding poor shiphandling, especially in harbor. Nor can any amount of modesty disguise or diminish its opposite. The Captain is high up on his bridge, as prominent as a bronze statue in a park; he has to be because he must have an unobstructed view in all directions. His every order as he handles his ship is relayed and repeated. The entire operation is performed in full view of—as a minimum—the whole deck force of his own ship, usually the deck force of one other ship as well, and often those of several others. Success or failure and degrees of both are as apparent to even the dullest observer as the success or failure of a driver parallel-parking at a curb. There is the ship. There is the dock, or the other ship. There is the water in between. The ship either closes that water gap and comes alongside smoothly, expeditiously and with a minimum of shouted orders, jingling bells and swirling currents at the stern—or it doesn't. A crew will forgive their Captain a multitude of sins, be he only a sharp shiphandler. But if he is not, be he ever so wise, kind, lenient and even brilliant in all other aspects of his profession, he will have an uphill battle to maintain the morale of his men.

Thus *Abercrombie* was not a happy ship as she lay in Wiseman's Junkyard while the cutting and welding went on for two days.

But life in that crowded little anchorage among the battered blackened ships was far less dangerous than on the ping line. The general alarm still clanged at night and men rushed to the guns, but no longer was it single combat. At the first warning of flash red, LCVPs and LCMs with smoke generators opened their valves and ran back and forth upwind until the entire harbor was under a white, protective blanket. Ships were ordered not to fire even if the enemy was sighted through the smoke, since the gunfire would only reveal their locations and provide a point of aim. So on all the ships the men stood or sat at their battle stations, breathed in the oily white airborne chemicals swirling around them and waited in frustration while enemy engines droned maddeningly back and forth overhead and finally, no doubt with equal frustration, flew away. Often the enemy was only a single plane, with a single pilot, whose mission presumably was simply to keep the Americans awake, but to attack if the opportunity arose.

From the junkyard *Abercrombie* returned for a day to Hagushi, then on the morning of 8 June she joined a tanker and her screen to refuel before returning to the line. It was a calm morning with a high overcast as DE343 eased up along the starboard side of the big fleet oiler *Sebec* (A087) on a northwesterly course at seven knots, got over the fueling rig in what by now was an operation as routine and familiar as anchoring and unanchoring, and began taking on fuel. The time was 0751. By 0810 she had received 27,600 gallons of black oil. At that moment fueling was abruptly terminated by the all-too-familiar bonging of the general alarm. Over the horizon dead ahead, low on the calm, lead-colored sea, spread out in line abreast as regularly spaced as in an air show, came four enemy aircraft straight for the fat tanker and her customers. With an APD fueling from her other side, scores of men on the decks of all three ships, oil flowing in torrents to port and starboard, most doors and hatches open to expedite the fueling process, the *Sebec* and both her customers were terribly vulnerable. The chance that the ships' gunners, taken by surprise, could account for all four of the attackers was remote. A major disaster was in the making.

Abercrombie's deck force leaped into action to cast off the fueling rig and clear the tanker's side as the guns were manned. On *Sebec* they slacked the ten-inch manila towing hawser, and two deck hands on the DE flopped the eye off our towing bitts and overboard. The tanker began to reel in the two fueling hoses, but they were lashed into the DE's trunks. I ran through the athwartships passageway to cut the lashings at the forward trunk, but Fred Manger, always fast and alert, beat me there. A quick slash severed the line, and the fuel hose swung clear, spurting black oil as the ships separated and surged forward.

As *Abercrombie* pulled ahead to shield the tanker, the enemy formation was still boring in, now only a couple of miles away and coming fast. The forward guns were on and about to open fire when almost magically, because although visibility was good no one had seen them before, two four-plane divisions of CAP appeared behind and above the enemy, swooping down on them like hungry hawks. One division was composed of heavy-looking, blunt-nosed P-47 Thunderbolts, the other of sleek, gull-winged F4U Corsairs. I saw one Thunderbolt kill two kamikazes in about five seconds, one as he came diving down, the other just as he leveled off. In the same few seconds the Corsairs got the other two, and in an instant what had been a prospective disaster was dissipated into four, equally spaced thin columns of black smoke rising from the surface of the sea ahead. The eight fighters, in tight formation, roared overhead, the two leaders rocking their wings, then climbed away, brisk and businesslike, to look for other prey.

That night DE343 was back off Ie Shima in A38A, in condition flash red. General Quarters sounded at 2340, 0155 and 0447. It was dark with a high overcast, but the enemy overcame those disadvantages with a seldom-used tactic. At times coinciding with those calls to battle stations, he strung the sky with floating white flares—fifteen the first time, nine the second and five the third, as though he were running short. Each group of flares must have been sewn by a single plane because they appeared in sequence and in line with equal spacing, floating down so slowly that they burned for five full minutes, shedding a ghastly, ghostly pale and greenish light across the ping line. Perhaps the Japanese had acquired the flares from their Axis allies because I had seen, and come to hate, identical ones in 1943 at Bizerte, Gela, Palermo and Salerno. But although she was uncomfortably visible and bogies shuttled across the scope all night, *Abercrombie* was not attacked.

At 0825 on the morning of 10 June, with DE343 still plying back and forth from northeast to southwest on A38A, destroyer *William D. Porter*, with which she had arrived at Okinawa back in mid-April, went down at her radar picket station thirty-five miles to the northward. A single Val, diving out of a low overcast, caught her men away from their battle stations, their ship open below. He missed her stern by inches, but his bomb went off under the fantail like a mine, opening her seams and breaking the legs and ankles of scores of her crew. The resultant flooding could not be controlled, and she sank at 1119.

The following day *Abercrombie* was relieved in A38A, fueled from the oiler *Tallulah*, and was dispatched to a new patrol line fifteen miles long off the southwest tip of Okinawa. This was where all the action was now. The enemy garrison had been driven to the southern end of the island and was holding out there, making maximum use of the hilly, rocky, heavily wooded terrain. But the Japanese had more to worry about than the Marines and Army troops pressing down from the north. En route to her new station, *Abercrombie* passed the battleships *Idaho* and *New Mexico* and four heavy cruisers steadily slamming their big shells into the small area into which the enemy had been squeezed. One of the heavies, the *Louisville*, looked strangely truncated with her forward stack missing —amputated the week before by a kamikaze. Rocket-firing Wildcats and Avengers circled and dived over the same area, and about the time DE343 arrived on station, her men were treated to the sight of a score of Corsairs burning the enemy out of hillside fortifications with napalm. The hillside faced the sea. Each plane in turn circled out over the water to the right, picked up speed in a shallow power glide, and swept in low across the hill. From *Abercrombie*'s decks we could see two long, narrow, blunt-ended objects separate from the plane, tumble end over end and burst in a roaring smear of flame as they hit the ground, igniting the trees and shrubs all around.

Close by, a group of Avengers was using delayed-action bombs on the face of a very steep, rocky hill. They would fly in over the water directly at the face of the hill and pull straight up at the last instant. The bombs raised little puffs of dust as they hit, but a few seconds later, where each puff had been would come a fountain of smoke, dust, and flying earth and rocks, the thud of the explosions following by almost half a minute.

Early on the morning of the twelfth, after all her close calls on the line, *Abercrombie* nearly lost an officer, and the enemy had nothing to do with it. At about 0645 the man on watch on the fantail noticed wisps of white vapor issuing from one of the smoke generators. He assumed the valve was not fully closed, but when he tried to close it, it would not move. So he went below for a pipe wrench, applied it to stop the leak—and broke the valve clean off the generator, sending clouds of acrid FS smoke gushing across the deck. On the bridge we saw what was happening and quickly turned the ship south, upwind, so the smoke would clear the ship. It was fifteen minutes before the broken generator was empty and patrol course could be resumed. From the bridge it seemed an annoying incident was over.

But on the bridge we didn't find out about Otto Braunsdorf until later. Otto and Mert Olson had been sleeping the sleep of the truly exhausted in the after officers' quarters. Before the ship could be turned, the intake ventilation blowers aft had sucked in a choking cloud of FS smoke and discharged most of it into the little space where they slept. Mert woke at the first whiff, grabbed his gas mask and dashed from the room, thinking the ship was under gas attack and not even aware that Otto was there. But Otto was sleeping more soundly, and by the time he awoke, his lungs were already full of the stuff and he was hallucinating. In the light of the single bulb above him, the thick white smoke looked yellow and liquid, and his first thought was that the ship had been sunk and he was already several fathoms down. He rolled from his bunk, coughing and retching, but he was half blind, too weak to walk. On hands and knees, panting, eyes streaming, Otto crawled out into the more open crew's berthing space and collapsed on the deck, where he was quickly found and carried to sick bay. Otto coughed wrackingly for a week but eventually recovered completely. Medical officers who examined him six days after the incident said that another minute or two of inhaling that smoke could well have killed him.

At 1114 on the fourteenth, *Abercrombie* steamed back around the south tip of the island and up to the Hagushi anchorage to await orders. At 1340, with APDs *Rednour, Sands* and *Badger* she formed a screen for four lumbering AKAs and three merchantmen, took departure with tangents on a couple of small islands, and set a course of 155 degrees for Saipan.

The long nightmare of Okinawa was over.

4. The China Sea

WITH THE DAWNING OF 15 June it was as though *Abercrombie* had sailed out of purgatory into a sunlit summer sea. The blue vault of the sky held not a shred of cloud and was reflected in the mirror-calm Pacific. The six big ships, with the arc of the screen before them, drew straight white lines southward toward peace and rest. The little convoy ran a simple zigzag plan. Twice during that day and the identical days that followed, the ready guns fired at five-inch bursts put up by the screen commander. In the early mornings one of the escorts left the screen to pull twenty miles or so ahead, then came back in with frequent course changes, simulating an approaching skunk, to provide practice in radar tracking—all by now rather elementary, certainly not demanding. The passage south to Saipan was, after the sixty-eight days and nights at Okinawa, despite the drills and training, a virtual pleasure cruise. The little things were what the crew relished the most. Time to take a hot shower and shave. To sleep *in* a clean bunk in just their skivvy shorts, and to sleep all night or until the next watch or scheduled morning GQ. Hot, hearty meals below and time to enjoy them. Release from ever-present anxiety, and from the vicinity of a battle station.

Saipan had not changed since our one-day visit in April.

The big silver planes thundered back and forth overhead, the beach and harbor glittered with lights at night while blue-white searchlights swept the rocky hill for enemy holdouts who still managed to sneak down in the darkness to steal clothes drying on the lines, or food, or water. The harbor was jammed with small craft of the little Navy I used to be in, PCs, SCs, and YMSs. There was a lot of work, some of it arduous, to do, but no one seemed to mind. Gus's boys rebricked the boilers. Tom's gunner's mates overhauled all the guns. Ralph Rice and his helpers worked over the directors and fire-control equipment. The radarmen, sonarmen and radiomen, with the help of radio technician Yates, tuned and checked over their gear. The deck force repainted the ship. In one twenty-hour *tour de force,* with the ship awkward and precarious-looking in a floating dry dock, all hands (every officer and man on the ship except for the cooks and mess cooks who kept them fed) turned to to scrape and repaint her long, slim bottom, clean and polish her twin screws, and work over her twin rudders.

Arrangements for the crew's liberty, regulated by the SOPA, was not appropriate either as a reward for the hardships on the ping line or as compensation for the hard work in Saipan. With rare exceptions, liberty was restricted to a beach area known as Mitscher Point, a sort of "poor man's Mogmog," where each man was allowed two beers and a Coke. But with a little scientific padding of the liberty lists so as to get more men ashore, a couple of predictably popular Red Cross girls serving coffee and doughnuts, some noisily competitive softball games, good movies *(To Have and Have Not, Going My Way, Stormy Weather, Hollywood Canteen)* in the soft open air of the fantail, and a truly great Seabee band which came aboard one afternoon, the men managed to enjoy themselves anyway.

The officers had it better. The club was big and airy and pleasant with lots of ice-cold beer. After the months at Okinawa it was unbelievably good to sit at a table under a palm tree, legs stretched out comfortably, the cool breeze blowing, a cold beer at hand, and talk with friends from other ships and other places. There I met a fraternity brother from college, the brother of a high school classmate, and a fellow subchaser skipper from the Med, with whom I had celebrated the birth of my son in a wineshop in Palermo in another war and another age.

On 21 June word came that the Okinawan campaign was over. Organized resistance by the enemy had ended. The island was secure.

All the while in Saipan I was waiting and hoping to receive the expected orders to flight training. On the twenty-fifth of June, a flashing light message from ashore requested an officer to pick up an official dispatch. Otto went over for it. I had the deck when he returned. He brushed by on his way to deliver the message to Hicks, saying offhandedly, "How does it feel to be standing your last watch?" *This has to be it,* I thought, but because if it were true it would be second only in importance to the arrival of my first son, I clamped down on my eager imagination and would not let myself believe it. It was just as well. In a few minutes Hicks called me up to his cabin. He held the dispatch in his hand. It was orders all right—orders sending Katschinski home, orders making Hicks C.O., and orders designating me as Exec.

A little later Hicks, Tom and I had a conference and decided that in view of the expected arrival of my orders to Pensacola, Tom would continue to perform the actual duties of Exec, while I signed the log and other official papers in that capacity. In that way we would avoid the turmoil of two turnovers in a few days or a week. At the same time, to cover himself in the event my orders did not come through, Tom would submit a letter to the Bureau of Naval Personnel, requesting a relief on the basis that being required to serve under an officer junior to him created an awkward and embarrassing situation aboard.

Abercrombie lost its number one helmsman at Saipan when Howard Amos was transferred to the naval hospital there. He had been suffering for months with a stubbornly recurrent abscess at the base of his spine, but Katschinski would not spare him. Hicks, more considerate of his men, let him go.

A few days before *Abercrombie*'s scheduled departure, a message came aboard that demonstrated in a formal but rather refreshing way that naval logistics in the Pacific war, as efficient as they normally were, still were devised by humans who made occasional miscalculations. It was from the Naval Supply Depot ashore. The depot, it said, "has excess of *four hundred thousand pounds* of wiping rags. Request ships present draw this item to capacity" (the emphasis is mine).

At the end of the month another dispatch came which raised eyebrows (and DE343's prestige) all around the harbor. It was from none other than Vice Admiral Jesse B. Oldendorf, the hero of Surigao Strait, now commanding naval forces at Okinawa. It said, in effect, "Advise earliest possible ETA *Abercrombie* at Okinawa. Urgently required."

Ashore and aboard the tenders and repair ships at Saipan, *Abercrombie*'s work took top priority and was completed in record time. A convoy short of escorts was scheduled to leave for Okinawa on 2 July. DE343 was ordered to sail alone and direct on the first.

When she steamed into Kerama Retto on the Fourth of July, it was as though having survived her trial by fire on the ping line, rested, restored and refurbished, she had been promoted to the Big Time. If it was not the starting lineup of fast carriers and new battleships, it was at least the second string, the first replacements. Within two days she was part of a screen of seven destroyers and six DEs around a potent battle group of three battlewagons—*(California, Nevada* and *Tennessee)*, three heavy cruisers *(Chester, Salt Lake City,* and *Wichita)* a light cruiser *(St. Louis)*, and four escort carriers *(Cape Gloucester, Fanshaw Bay, Lunga Point* and *Makin Island)*. Among the other DEs in the screen were *Abercrombie*'s old friends and fellow survivors from the ping line, *Wann* and *Suesens*.

This was Task Force 32. Its mission was to cover a massive minesweeping operation under way in the East China Sea. The CVEs, now flying

Corsairs and Avengers, would provide CAP for the sweepers. The battlewagons and cruisers with the seven destroyers as screen were to intercept and destroy any surface force attempting to interfere, while the DEs escorted the carriers.

Rumors were rife in Kerama Retto that the next operation would be landings on both Kyushu and the China coast. It looked as though the minesweepers and their covering force were engaged in the preliminaries.

Abercrombie's first job on joining up was to pass mail to the rest of the force, which had already been at sea for a week. Between 1400 and 1950 she made *Tennessee, California, Chester, Wichita, St. Louis,* two destroyers, and the *Wann.* Each passing was performed with precision and dispatch. Hicks was learning how to handle the ship, and the line handlers on the fo'c'sle were quick and unerring.

Abercrombie operated with Task Force 32 for three weeks, and she was at the top of her form, a salty, versatile, veteran ship. Although the days were demanding, they passed quickly. Station keeping was simplified by the large number of escorts, which permitted a circular screen. Course changes required no rush to reorient, no quick calculation in CIC, just a simple turn to the new course as the whole great circle of warships moved off in a different direction. It was a busy, constructive, dramatic time. Three times the force practiced dividing into attack dispositions, with the cruisers and three destroyers racing off to intercept a theoretical enemy surface force, the battlewagons with a four-destroyer screen moving into position to block his retreat, and the DEs forming protectively around the carriers as they launched against the "enemy."

Abercrombie and the other DEs of the force were ships-of-all-work. They sank floating mines and empty oil drums, investigated unidentified drifting objects, plane-guarded the CVEs, and escorted the flagship on a couple of special missions. Once, DE343 picked up an empty U.S. life raft. On another day she blew up a mine and suffered her lone casualty of the war thus far when a piece of shrapnel whizzed aboard and struck a young gunner in the backside. Although he hollered as with a mortal wound, investigation showed only a red spot in the affected area with the skin unbroken, and the young man returned to duty somewhat shamefacedly to the ribald comments of his mates.

It is surprisingly difficult to sink or explode a mine from a small ship like a DE. The mine floats very low in the water, exposing only a quarter sphere of rusty metal. It bobs up and down in the chop or swell, and frequently disappears in the trough. The ship is also moving with the sea but with a different frequency, and it rolls. Added to the difficulty is the fact that the guns themselves are only a few feet above the water so that the angle of fire is necessarily highly acute. Nor can the problem be solved by simply closing the range, because where many mines simply bubble and sink when hit and others merely pop and frizzle, a high percentage go off with a high-order explosion, spraying shrapnel which can cause far more damage than a scary whack on the backside.

Task Force 32 seemed to be looking, asking for trouble. Every other day an Avenger would tow a sleeve around the force for target practice. On other days Corsairs from the CVEs would make mock attacks on the ships to give guns and directors tracking practice. Often those drills would be quickly secured, and the ships would go to General Quarters in earnest as a bogey approached, but although we sometimes saw the vapor trails of high-altitude snoopers overhead, and the CAP shot down an occasional Betty or Dinah out on the fringes of visibility, no enemy ever came close enough to shoot at during daylight. Once or twice at night, a bogey would close to two or three miles, but turn under the threat of airborne night fighters or radar-controlled five-inch fire from the heavy ships.

On the order of once a week, the force would steam back into the big harbor on the west coast of Okinawa, which used to be Nagagusuku Wan but was now called Buckner Bay in honor of the U.S. Lieutenant General commanding the forces which conquered the island who was killed in action four days before their final victory. The ships fanned out to tankers, ammunition and supply ships in the bay, and stayed just long enough to be refueled and resupplied and to pick up their mail, usually about eight hours. And even during those eight hours they were under orders to be ready for sea in two.

Then back to sea again in that circular formation, the bristling battlewagons at the center, the potent, graceful cruisers next, the protective ring of fast, slim ships and off five or ten miles, the high, square little carriers under their circling planes. On *Abercrombie's* bridge, Paul Fry, Red Shiel, Tom Skoko, Paul McMillan and the quartermasters were kept busy with flag hoists and twelve-inch lights and semaphore, because most of the maneuvering during daylight was by visual signal to prevent enemy interception.

Of all the odd jobs DE343 was assigned during those weeks, the one the deck force liked best was plane guard. We never tired of watching the blue planes drop down out of the sky to circle and land, suddenly extending wheels, flaps and hooks like hawks returning to the nest. We were eager for an opportunity to put our little organization to work. The inflatable boats were ready to launch, cargo nets rolled at the gunwales and ready to drop, wire Stokes stretchers on deck, our best swimmers standing by with harnesses on and lines attached, and a foolproof plan of action, in which all hands had been well drilled, ready for any contingency. But as seems to happen so often when all is in readiness, none of that was needed. Not once did the CVE pilots avail themselves of our services.

Once, *Abercrombie* was selected as the sole escort for the force flagship *Tennessee* on a quick run into Buckner Bay and a quick return to sea. Looking back at the great old ship, with Admiral Oldendorf's three-star flag rippling at her truck, it struck me why battleships are always described as "bristling" with guns. It is not hyperbole or any other figure of speech. It is literally true, a simple, accurate description. Battlewagons' silhouettes from ahead or astern are those of towering fortresses, with elevated gun barrels protruding at every level, not just the long rifles of the main battery, which are trained fore and aft, but five-inchers, forties and twenties seemingly beyond count, poking up symmetrically on both sides.

In that little task unit of *Tennessee* and *Abercrombie*, the Navy of reserve crews and small, mass-produced ships and the Navy of professional regulars, tradition, and the proud "ships of the line" had been fully integrated. Here there were no more regulars or reserves. Here were just two gray U.S. warships teamed up to do a job, each with its own differing functions in the team but fully comparable in its ability to perform those functions. It made no difference that the battlewagon had been commissioned in 1921 and the DE in 1944, or that the battleship's skipper was a regular captain who no doubt would make Admiral, while the Captain of the DE was a reserve lieutenant who, if he were lucky, would one day make civilian. In the China Sea in the summer of '44, they were simply two warships on a mission.

On 25 July, Task Force 32 reentered Buckner Bay and remained for an unprecedented thirty hours. When the force got under way again the next day, although it was composed of exactly the same ships, it was no longer Task Force 32 but Task Group 95.3, no more a "heavy covering force," but a "heavy striking force." As we steamed back out to sea, six more heavies joined up; large cruisers *Alaska* and *Guam* in the lead, with their nine twelve-inch guns and reputed thirty-five knots of speed; followed by light cruisers *Cleveland*, *Columbia* (which we had seen crashed at Lingayen), *Denver* and *Montpelier*. *Alaska* and *Guam* were awesomely beautiful, as long as battleships and nearly as heavily gunned, but with slim, sweeping cruiser lines.

The cruiser force had its own screen of destroyers and did not join the circular formation of the former Task Force 32. Both groups headed due north, with the cruisers pulling away as night came on. The next day the cruisers appeared again, a destroyer from our screen went alongside the *Guam* with orders from the flagship, and they disappeared over the horizon once more.

On the twenty-eighth, one hundred miles southeast of Shanghai, the carriers turned into the wind to launch a strike against enemy forces and installations in and around that city. Up from the short flight decks of the CVEs struggled the TBFs, heavy and slow with their loads of bombs and torpedoes and rockets, to circle, roaring, as the Wildcats hopped briskly up to cover them. Then both groups formed up in neat geometrical patterns and bore off to the northward—fifty-six planes, we counted them. While the planes were away, the cruisers appeared again from a nightlong sweep of the China Coast and reported disgustedly by TBS, "Very poor hunting." Later in the day the TBFs and F4Fs came back . . . fifty-six . . . we counted them again, light and easy now with their bomb bays and rocket launchers empty, no doubt to the confusion of the enemy around Shanghai.

After two days of resupply in Buckner Bay, the two groups went back to Shanghai and stayed almost a week, mounting daily strikes from the CVEs.

Abercrombie sank a few more mines and oil drums, did some more plane guarding and fueling at sea, went to battle stations four or five times, sighted some more vapor trails high in the sky, picked up a couple of bogies on radar, watched the constant flights of TBFs, Corsairs and Wildcats leaving heavy and returning light.

In the early days of August *Abercrombie* hit the heaviest weather of her life when a typhoon sideswiped the striking force in the China Sea. It began on the midwatch of the first when the wind picked up to forty knots from the northeast and the cloud cover began to increase. By that afternoon the wind had backed around into the northwest, the sky was totally obscured by heavy, dark cumulostratus clouds at around four thousand feet, and the seas had built up to thirty to forty feet from trough to crest. The task group slowed to ten knots, spread out in cruising disposition, and headed into wind and sea, the ships rearing and plunging violently, the battleships and cruisers repeatedly burying their heavy bows and sending Niagaras of solid water sluicing down their decks. The escorts bobbed and thrashed with a quicker, sharper motion, exposing yards of red bottom paint, their propellers occasionally racing, clear of the water. It got worse the next day with the wind over fifty knots and the seas ten or twenty feet higher, jumbled and confused so that it was no longer possible to take them consistently on the bow. Now the little ships began to roll as well as pitch and plunge. Men were catapulted from their bunks, and those on watch slammed into assorted unyielding metal structures all over the ship. *Abercrombie's* mess hall was secured. It was hard even to make a sandwich, and just as hard to eat it, given the necessity for constant bracing and hanging on with at least one hand. In the wardroom on the first day, the stewards had loyally rigged fiddle boards with holes for plates, glasses and silver; but at the first meal the filled plates leaped from their holes like prairie dogs and undulated down the long athwartship table, easily clearing the low partitions and distributing their loads along the way. The officers went on sandwiches along with the crew.

The watch during those days was continually drenched with salt water, eyes smarting, binoculars useless. Most men below were sick in varying degrees, and all were miserably tired and uncomfortable. But it was toughest on the engineers. In the engine rooms they held tight and watched the clinometers as the ship rolled—40 degrees, then 45, then 50. On the midwatch of the third, she rolled down to starboard 54 degrees, paused ominously, then snapped back across the vertical and down to 50 degrees to port. In the engineering spaces, temperatures rose to over 120 degrees because the ventilators had to be closed to keep out the sea. Down there if a man lost his grip he could be thrown into solid-steel machinery, which was not only hard but also hot enough to sear the skin. Nor was it comforting to remember that in the typhoon of mid-December in 1944, three destroyers had been capsized and sunk with very heavy loss of life: on the *Monaghan,* only six of the crew survived. On all three destroyers, the entire watch below was lost. Of more comfort was the knowledge that *Tabberer,* a DE of *Abercrombie's* class, although dismasted, had not only survived but had been able to rescue most of the destroyermen who made it into the sea.

On one of the worst days I had the morning watch. I was holding tightly to the cluster of voice tubes at the center of the open bridge, keeping an eye on the lubber's line as the helmsman tried to stay within about 20 degrees of the ordered course, and could feel the toss and heave of the ship and the periodic rumbles as the propellers raced out of water. The watch was tiring but tolerable. Then as the first light began to spread from the cloudy east, I felt a massive, moving presence high above my left shoulder, on the port quarter as I was facing forward. I turned to look and . . . my God, it was a wave! A great, black mountain of a wave, with white caps along its crest and towering twenty feet above the bridge, bearing down on the little ship. I braced both feet, circled the voice tubes with a full-arm grip that should have bent the brass, and yelled to Rice and Shiel to take cover. Just when it seemed certain that the whole huge hill of water would come crashing down to drive us to the bottom, *Abercrom-*

bie rose like an express elevator and the thing slid harmlessly away below her keel. At that point I felt very foolish because I realized that similar mountainous seas had been coming up from astern all night; they had just not been visible in the Stygian darkness of the overcast night sea.

It was not until the afternoon of the fourth that the storm moved off to the northward, wind and sea began at last to abate and the sky to clear. Then on 7 August the operations in the China Sea were over.

A message about those operations was received aboard at the height of the typhoon; now it could be appreciated:

> To all who participated in and supported the minesweeping operation. The arduous and difficult task which you have just completed will give increased safety and greater freedom of action to our mobile forces for the tasks which lie ahead of them. Well done. Nimitz.

While DE343 had been in the China Sea, her men knew the first team was off Japan, bombing and shelling, withdrawing a couple of hundred miles to fuel and take on ammunition, and coming back to paste the enemy again. It looked as though the rumors about China and Kyushu were right. The men pushed the thoughts of what those operations would be like to the backs of their minds as best they could, and concentrated on the good feelings of confidence and competence imbued by a solid month of well-conducted fleet operations.

Then on the way back to Okinawa from Shanghai, down from *Abercrombie's* radio shack came news of the atomic bomb. The first reaction aboard DE343 was simple disbelief. The news report must have been garbled in transmission. Twenty thousand *tons* of TNT? Pounds maybe, but not tons. Four-thousand-pound "blockbusters" had been used in Europe, and a five-fold increase seemed plausible—and a really devastating weapon. But twenty thousand *tons?* Impossible! In Buckner Bay we learned the opposite. The report had not been garbled. For an immediate reaction by one of *Abercrombie's* officers, three weeks past his twenty-seventh birthday, here is an unexpurgated, unedited journal quote written at the time:

> When I could finally believe it I was frankly scared. I am not at all sure humanity itself has grown up enough to handle a force like that. I keep thinking of what it could do in the hands of a man like Hitler or the Japanese militarists. They could obliterate literally in a few weeks all that man has built so painfully in thousands of years.

A statement like that should not be true but it seems it is. Is it possible to keep the secret? If not, is it possible to control the production in any way? I would like to know what steps are being taken to keep this Frankenstein controlled.

It is more responsibility than man has ever had before. Sometimes I think it would almost be best to decorate and memorialize the men who discovered this thing and no doubt won the war in a hurry, saving thousands of American lives, and then burn the plans, destroy the products and, in a suitable ceremony, execute all the men involved. Then I am ashamed because this is the kind of old-woman talk that has always tried to put the skids under every advance in history.

Back in Buckner Bay two new officers reported aboard, and Tom's orders to other duty were waiting for him, to take effect as soon as a relief arrived.

One of the new officers was an ensign, Don Samdahl, straight from Reserve Midshipmens' School who was welcomed heartily by George Quinn, now no longer junior officer aboard. The other was Lieutenant (j.g.) Ted Barber, assigned as Assistant Gunnery Officer. Not only did he have lots of gunnery training behind him, but he came from a year and a half in a corvette in the North Atlantic, tough and valuable experience that should qualify him quickly as OOD. Ted was an exceptionally likable and conscientious officer, hailing from Fairfield, Connecticut, and he fitted into *Abercrombie*'s little wardroom at once. He went on the watch bill with me to be trained as OOD. His only deficiency in that job was a lack of experience in naval formations, tactics and signals, since all his time at sea had been with merchant convoys, but he was a quick study and a good seaman and qualified in short order.

Barber was sincerely glad to be aboard. It had been six months since he had left his last ship, almost all of the time spent in transit—chasing DE343 around the Pacific. His orders, which were required to be endorsed by each ship or activity to which he reported en route, were fat with seventeen such endorsements. Even on this last day he had been in the harbor for five or six hours looking for the ship. *Abercrombie* was the farthest to seaward, and he came aboard after dark only hours before she sailed once more.

Ted billed himself as the "Dove of Peace," alleging that no ship to which he had ever reported had fired a shot in anger after his arrival.

And so it turned out, although for a while it didn't seem that it would. There were two GQs in Buckner Bay on the midwatch of 8 August, and the CAP was reported to have splashed an approaching Tony. *Abercrombie* was under way at 0730 that morning, with APDs *Hopping* and *Tollberg* screening *Nevada* and *Columbia*, bound south for Leyte.

The next day another A-bomb was dropped on Nagasaki. On the first watch during the night of the tenth to the eleventh, while we were running down the coast of Samar, the first news came of Japanese negotiations to end the war. Nothing was definite or official, but it seemed obvious, with the two terrible bombs added to the loss of their whole stolen empire, including Okinawa and the fire raids and carrier strikes on the home islands, that Japan was beaten at last.

I had the watch with Ted Barber when the news came in, and we passed the word on the PA system as each new development was received. There was some cheering from the ready guns and down in the living compartments, but no violent, consuming outbursts of joy. The news was too important, too good. The officers and men of DE343 had to let it sink in, had to readjust the mind-sets of years, let down the barriers to thoughts and dreams about the future. The first feeling was relief, as though a heavy pack had been lifted from our backs. Then came an incredibly joyous realization—there would be no next operation this time, not in China, nor on Kyushu, nor anywhere. That meant assured survival, that there really *would* be a future, not of dreams but of reality. There really *would* be that long-dreamed-of-but-pushed-away homecoming, and a life to live in peace, ashore, with wives, families, children, beloved people. We were young. Our lives had been given back to us. That was a lot to think about. It took time. Maybe the cheers would come later. Someone broke out a couple of boxes of apples and passed them around, and that was the way the first news of peace was celebrated in the USS *Abercrombie*.

BOOK · III

1. Korea and Japan

Abercrombie ARRIVED IN LEYTE at 1000 the next day, and after fueling and provisioning, the crew went to work repairing the wear and tear of the month of intensive operations in the China Sea.

On 13 August, to Tom's unmitigated joy, his relief reported aboard. Lieutenant Lloyd Parker was a quiet, smart, soft-spoken Southerner from Memphis with a year of sea duty on an Atlantic Fleet destroyer and a year of instructing in gunnery ashore. Like Ted Barber, he became an integral part of the ship's company at once, both professionally and socially. It took Lloyd less than three days to take over as Gunnery Officer—and Tom was off for home, the first one after Katschinski to go, and the most deserving.

The same day I assumed the duties of Executive Officer to which I had been ordered in late June.

As it turned out, Tom was only the first of many to go. Some we had been trying to get transferred for months for medical or other reasons. First among those was bo'sun's mate Pop Deatherage, the unofficial father of the Second Division of the deck force. Pop had been in World War I, but enlisted right after Pearl Harbor at age forty-four, served some fairly rugged duty on a sailing ship being used for inshore patrol, and joined DE343 as a cox'n at Orange. He earned his nickname aboard, not just because of his lined and craggy face and gray hair, but because he really took the teenage kids in his division under his wing, taught them, helped them, kept them out of trouble, cared about them. He was always first to volunteer for any job, always on hand when needed, always willing, hardworking, kind, polite. The ever-changing personality of the ship was altered when Pop was no longer aboard with his friendly, sunburned old face, Kentucky laugh and bony knees under hacked-off working shorts.

It would have been better for us if the loss of men had stopped there, but it didn't. No sooner were the Japanese surrender terms accepted, with no peace treaty signed and no occupation forces in Japan, than demobilization orders arrived. By the time *Abercrombie* left Leyte on 20 August, she had orders to transfer most of her key men, including Holloway, Gruhn, chief yeoman Larkin, chief gunner's mate Ramsey, chief water tender Elliot, leading signalman Fry and half a dozen of her veteran first class petty officers. A few new men were ordered aboard as numerical replacements only.

It was in Leyte in mid-August that we got word of the boot riots in San Francisco on VJ Day. Women were raped, people killed, buildings burned—all by callow kids who had had nothing to do with the victory they were "celebrating." No words can express the disgust and contempt of the war-weary DE sailors upon hearing this news.

On the morning of 20 August *Abercrombie* steamed out of Leyte Gulf, bound back to Okinawa in the screen of a task force of four battleships and two light cruisers escorted by one destroyer, one DE (343), and seven APDs. The voyage was my first off the watch bill since commissioning, and I reveled in the change. I enjoyed the challenge of navigating and the satisfaction which comes when the observed altitudes of celestial bodies, processed through neat columns of reduction computations and translated into lines of position on the chart, result in a tiny triangle whose coordinates in latitude and longitude closely agree with those promulgated by the force commander.

Abercrombie's OODs were now DeCoster, Wheeling and Olson.

Okinawa was a different island than in the bad old days of the ping line. Even though peace was not yet confirmed, and U.S. planes were still being fired on over Japan, and though the enemy airfields were not yet occupied or the kamikaze pilots disarmed, the ships in Buckner Bay remained brightly lighted all night. About half showed movies on deck. This made us nervous. Japan had begun the war with treachery. Some of her die-hard warriors might well choose to end it the same way, with gloriously bloody crashes on conveniently illuminated American ships. But our fears were unfounded. None did.

The radio news in those days was full of the prospect of the formal Japanese surrender in Tokyo Bay followed by the actual occupation of Japan. In *Abercrombie* we fully expected to be part of both operations. We were only half right. When the instrument of surrender was signed on 2 September, DE343 was still swinging around her hook in berth L-66, Buckner Bay, Okinawa. And except for a day of gunnery practice and a couple of days on patrol off Hagushi, she remained there until the morning of the tenth.

On the fourth of September, *Abercrombie*'s officers were relieved of a time-consuming and distasteful chore when censorship of personal mail was cancelled. But on the same day the ship lost three key men. Chief bo'sun's mate Albert Lee Murphy Holloway of the Tri-Cities, bo'sun's mate first Fred Manger and chief pharmacist's mate Bailey, all regular Navy petty officers, were sent home to other duty. I was especially sorry to see Holloway and Manger leave. I had come to depend on them, and despite the required barriers of rank, rate and duty, we had become friends.

Almost every day during that period, warships steamed out of Buckner Bay with their long, homeward-bound pennants flying. And increasingly from that time on, the thought of returning home became more and more obsessive. With the Japanese surrender, all emotionally convincing and sustaining rationales for separation dissolved. For a while some ships would be required to assist the occupation, but this seemed trivial and inconsequential. The obsession with going home in actuality reflected and was part of the national mood and temper. The departing shipmates, the destroyers and other ships steaming out of harbor homeward bound were all part of the process of demobilization which was taking place worldwide (with the exception of the Soviet Union), and nowhere as rapidly as in the armed forces of the United States.

But on the tenth of September, *Abercrombie* did not go home. Instead she sailed for Jinsen (now Inchon), Korea. It was a strange voyage in that never-never time between war and peace. I picked up the orders and routing instructions from the little Port Director's shack on Brown Beach. *Abercrombie* was to escort an ancient tanker, the *Stonewall* (with no gyro and no radar), and two tiny and heavily laden Army oilers called TYs. Our speed of advance would be six to seven knots. In paragraph three, the orders read "Enemy submarines have been sighted in this area and all precautions should be taken." In paragraph seven, they read "All ships will burn navigational lights at full brilliancy." When I pointed out the discrepancy, the Lieutenant in charge just shrugged. "It's odd all right," he said, "but those are the orders." When I returned to the ship and plotted the route on the chart, I found it took us right through a known minefield and skirted the corner of another. With the skipper of the tanker, who was OTC, we agreed to use our joint discretion. We replotted the route and darkened ship at night.

On the morning of departure, *Abercrombie* lost another key man, Paul Fry, now signalman first class, the former long-haul truck driver who had manned the helm from Orange to the Gulf of Mexico the first time she was ever under way, and who had led the signal gang ever since. He had been good company on maybe a thousand watches; and so I lost another friend.

It should have been a short run to Jinsen, but at seven knots it took five long, wet, rough, uncomfortable days. *Abercrombie*, with her gyro and radars, navigated for the little convoy, patrolling back and forth at ten knots 3,500 yards ahead of *Stonewall*. In the rough weather, the well decks of the little TYs were awash so constantly that from the DE's bridge each looked like a small ship. At noon on the twelfth we sank a floating mine with the forties and twenties. All day the fifteenth, with *Abercrombie* in the lead, the four-ship column picked its way up the seventy-mile channel between scores of small, high islands toward Jinsen. Nearly every other island had a lighthouse, but unlike any we had seen. They were white and walled and battlemented like castles, high on the tops of sheer cliffs at the water's edge. On the way up that distant channel, the *Suesens* overtook us and passed ahead, screening the big destroyer tender *Hamul*, which had mothered the shaking-down DEs at Bermuda half the world and a war away.

Abercrombie and *Suesens* anchored for the night fifteen miles below the city, moved up and reanchored the next day. I will not soon forget that fifteen-mile voyage. Hicks had gone up to Jinsen in the morning, sightseeing with the skipper of the *Suesens* and the Division Commander. Orders to bring the ship up arrived at 1300. It was my first time in acting command, my first opportunity to handle the ship in the manner in which I felt in my bones and blood she should be handled. We were under way precisely on time with a single command to the engines as soon as the anchor was clear of the water—"All ahead standard." We departed at fifteen knots with no more bells, no dozen rudder orders, no having to wait for *Suesens* and follow her because the Division Commander might like that. At each turn of the channel, the ship spun on her heel and came smartly to the new course with a single order, "Right standard rudder. Come to course zero one zero." We passed a tug, with a solid blast of the whistle and no hesitation. At the anchorage we slowed, steamed directly to our ordered berth, stopped, backed down momentarily and dropped the hook. I felt cleansed, refreshed, renewed.

At 0540 the two DEs stood down the channel to sea in column at fifteen knots, distance five hundred yards, and after some gunnery and tactical drills, we arrived off Okinawa at noon on the nineteenth. This was typhoon season in the western Pacific. There was nearly always one on the chart somewhere, spinning dangerously, something to be carefully watched and studiously avoided. One had hit Okinawa in our absence, blowing down shore facilities, wrecking and grounding ships. Twenty miles off the harbor entrance there was solid evidence of the typhoons' destructive force. Two huge, yellow outboard-powered pontoon barges were adrift in the still heavily rolling sea. The Division Commander in

Suesens directed that each ship take one in tow. Ours was loaded with about sixty anchors of assorted sizes and types. We maneuvered alongside and put a couple of machinist's mates aboard to try and start the huge outboards, but in a few minutes they reported the motors were too soaked with salt water. By 1435 we had the thing in tow. It took five hours at four knots to enter Buckner Bay and anchor, still with the barge astern. At ten the next morning, a yard tug came out and returned it to its moorings.

Abercrombie stayed in Buckner Bay just long enough to lose another batch of key men, including yeoman first Bob Strike and yeoman second Jesse Miller, chief gunner's mate Jim Ramsey, ship's cook first McFaul and ship's cook second Dave Allen, machinist's mates first Kella Turner and Jim Triplett, ship's barber (and still seaman second) Hibbert Eckroad, sonarman first Joe Taylor, and signalman third Tom Skoko.

In all departments a lot of frantic reorganization and rewriting of watch bills was required to hold the ship together and keep her functioning after losses like those. Some slots could be filled by well-deserved promotions, others not as well by strikers. The ship's office, where demobilization was causing more paper work than ever, was especially hard hit. When *Abercrombie* sailed again from Okinawa, the office staff had been reduced from a chief, a first class, a second class and a third class to one second class (the original third) and two brand-new strikers who had just reported aboard.

On the evening of 22 September, DE343 sailed from Okinawa for the U.S. occupation of Japan. The transition to peacetime operations at sea was now complete. The five DEs in company *(Suesens, Abercrombie, Wann, Foreman* and *Gendreau)* steamed in a staggered column, with *Suesens* leading, at fifteen knots, not zigzagging, burning navigational lights, hatches open. The next night, for the first time ever, *Abercrombie*'s crew watched a movie on the fantail, under way. It was *In Old California,* starring John Wayne.

After a day of flag-hoist and signal drills and of brisk tactical exercises, with the ships switching from columns to various lines of bearing and swapping positions, the high coast of the Japanese home island of Honshu came in sight on the starboard bow at dawn on the twenty-fourth. All that morning the little formation steamed northward into the Kii Suido between Honshu and Shikoku to the south. It was hard to believe that five U.S. destroyer escorts were entering the home waters of Japan unchallenged. But shortly after noon when the ships scattered to fuel and anchor, the fact became believable. At anchor off the adjacent communities of

Wakayama and Wakanoura, on the south shore of Honshu, was a fleet of familiar gray ships with blue union jacks forward and the Stars and Stripes at their sterns. The signal gang identified and logged two battleships, three light cruisers, nine destroyers, eight minesweepers of various types, two amphibious group command ships, a tanker, two seaplane tenders and a hospital ship. The battlewagons, cruisers, destroyers and newly arrived DEs were to provide "fire support" for the occupation forces scheduled to go ashore the next day.

Abercrombie anchored off Wakanoura, which seemed to be just a fishing village. Farther up along the coast, the stacks and chimneys of what was left of industrial Wakayama were visible. She lay there all day the twenty-fifth while the actual landings took place. It was an assault landing in peacetime. A column of the familiar attack transports steamed past up the channel and lowered their boats off Wakayama. As the LCVPs loaded with troops chugged ashore, columns of LSTs and troop-laden LCIs came in. Corsairs from a couple of CVEs swept protectingly back and forth across the beaches. The "fire support" ships with a hundred barrels lay just offshore. But the ships had been putting small sightseeing parties ashore all morning, and when the troops in full combat gear dashed up the beaches, they ran into groups of grinning sailors in liberty whites with their arms full of souvenirs.

It seemed a farce, but it had to be done that way to assure that no last-minute enemy treachery could thwart the occupation. It made no sense to take chances at this point.

Abercrombie operated out of Wakanoura Wan for a month. For the remainder of September, she simply lay at anchor, awaiting orders and sending liberty parties ashore, until by the end of the month every man had made a liberty in Japan or been offered the opportunity. Around the twenty-ninth, Jim Russell and I went ashore together. Although looking back it seems absurd, we both carried loaded .45s in the waistbands of our trousers, covered by our field jackets. "Japanese" and "enemy" had been synonymous for too long, and enemy treachery too often warned against to take any chances now. For nearly a year and a half, the closest any of us had come to a Japanese was in hoisting a corpse from the sea or in the rush of a kamikaze overhead, the only sight the sodden dead or a helmeted face in the sight of a gun. I found the weight of the pistol and the feel of its barrel against my stomach entirely comforting.

It was a strange and unfamiliar world we walked into ashore. It was hard to get used to seeing Japanese soldiers close up, in ragged olive drab and short-visored cloth caps with a star on the front. It was a crowded world of small people who walked with a rocking motion on wide wooden sandals that made a kind of shuffling clatter unlike anything we had ever heard. Most of the civilian men were thin and stooped, although a few older boys looked well fed and husky. Almost all the men wore parts or remnants of uniforms. The women we saw were in no danger from us. To our young American eyes, influenced by memories and movies, they seemed like flat-chested dolls, an effect emphasized by bright red spots on the cheekbones of many of the younger ones. Most wore kimonos of once-bright but now faded patterns, although there were a few drab Western-style dresses. Mothers carried their children rather casually on their backs, where some of them slept, heads lolling and small feet swinging below. There were a few automobiles that looked like old American models with right-hand drive and bulky devices on the back to convert them for charcoal fuel, and a lot of slow and noisy charcoal-burning tricycles. The town of Wakanoura was crowded with U.S. sailors in whites, loaded down with brightly colored cloth and fragile lacquered articles they had bartered for with soap, gum, candy or cigarettes. The sailors reported that a few cigarettes would buy almost anything, including colored scenic postcards with English captions.

Jim and I caught a ride in a U.S. Army truck up to nearby Wakayama, where it was a different story. The B-29s had worked it over one morning with incendiaries. There wasn't much left. We walked down an untouched, modern, four-lane concrete street that led through a plain of rubble. On both sides for blocks there was nothing but broken masonry, plaster and tiling, masses of rusted metal twisted into odd shapes, nothing standing more than two or three feet above the ground. The inhabitants were clinging to the tiny squares of land that had been their homes, living in huts made of scrap lumber and rusty corrugated iron like hovels in a junkyard in the States. That's what Wakayama looked like—a well-tended junkyard. In many places the broken tiling had been raked aside to bare square plots of earth in which were planted neat rows of vegetables. Here and there, in the middle of these gardens which had been houses, stood an especially rugged safe, rusted and charred and battered, but standing solidly on its concrete foundation with vegetables growing around it.

Thousands must have died in the destruction of the town only a few weeks before, and I would not have been surprised to have been fired on or stoned or at least cursed at from the huts that were standing where a city had been. But the inhabitants were not angry, or if they were they concealed it amazingly well. They smiled and did business readily with the souvenir hunters, learned English phrases and taught Japanese words, then went home for the night to that field of ruins. What kind of people are they? we asked ourselves. Do they think of the war as impersonal and inevitable like a typhoon or an earthquake? Do they fail to identify the cocky Army pilots with the high silver wings of the B-29s that wiped out their city? We guessed that was it, and let it go at that.

Abercrombie, the other DEs and several CVEs spent the first half of October at sea in uniformly dirty weather, searching for an Admiral and a Captain who had disappeared on a surveillance flight in preparation for the occupation of Kure. There were typhoons all around the search area, and while we avoided the highest winds, it was rough enough to dip the high carrier decks into green water and make life on the escorts truly miserable. Even after all their recent time at sea, dozens of *Abercrombie's* men were sick, and those who were not felt subnormal, headachy and tired from the constant necessity to hold on to something, even in their bunks where they tried to sleep on their stomachs with their feet jammed down over the bottom corners of the mattress and their hands gripping the tops. The only man aboard apparently unaffected was Buckets Bowers.

One typhoon caught the search group in port, unable to get to sea because that way lay the center of the storm. *Abercrombie* put out all the chain she had, 180 fathoms, in 22 fathoms of water, and kept steam to the boilers and an underway watch on deck in case she dragged. It was a wild night, the ship plunging and rolling as though she were at sea, sailing back and forth on the long chain through some 70 degrees, sheets of spindrift driving down across the bay and slamming in sheets against the superstructure, ninety knots of wind blasting down the decks so that no man could venture out. In the darkness, nearby anchor lights changed suddenly to running lights as ship after ship dragged her anchor and was forced to pull it up and find another berth, groping on radar around the bay through the howling night.

We got under way again the next day with five CVEs and six other DEs in weather so rough that one ship signaled, "Pardon me, but your sonar is showing". We stayed out four more days, but no trace was ever found of the lost officers or their plane.

By the fourteenth the search was over, and back at Wakanoura, under a new directive, the men aboard who had three or more children were transferred for discharge. There were only three. They went to a destroyer, part of the screen for the *Tennessee* and the *California,* which were headed home via Singapore, Calcutta, Capetown and Rio, and due in Boston on 15 December.

Also on 14 October, both Hicks and I were promoted by directive to Lieutenant Commanders in the reserve, to date from the first of the month. I had never expected to make that rank, but it felt good. It was rumored among the crew that Hicks wore his new gold oak leaves on his pajamas.

As though the long grind of the Pacific war had worn down their resistance, and now with the pressure off the symptoms surfaced, Jim Russell and Cy DeCoster both fell ill and had to be transferred for treatment. (Tom Parlon, too, had taken to his bunk with a bad digestive malfunction for a week or so before his departure.) Jim's appendix suddenly ruptured, and he had to be sent over in a breeches buoy to the CVE *Lunga Point*, a hairy operation in heavy seas. He became so sick so suddenly that he was unable to sign the pay records and wind up his job as Supply and Disbursing Officer—a fact which caused no end of difficulty, delay and complications later.

At the end of that transfer, which had come after the completion of fueling, Hicks received the seagoing equivalent of his diploma from the hard school of experience in shiphandling. A message came over from the *Lunga Point* that was a mirror image of the one sent to Katschinski from *Manila Bay*—"Your shiphandling during the difficult fueling operation was excellent. Well done."

Cy came down with what he thought was a bad cold and was confined to his stateroom for three days while *Abercrombie* plane-guarded a CVE as she searched once more for that lost plane on the first leg of her trip home. Back in Wakanoura on 20 October, we loaded Cy, looking drawn and pale, into the whaleboat with all his gear and delivered him to the hospital ship *Hope* with a full-fledged case of pneumonia. Don Ervin, the division doctor, assured us that Cy, despite his frightening appearance, would be perfectly okay, and in fact would probably beat us home, since the *Hope* was scheduled to sail any day. But Cy's departure felt hollow, like the end of something. Perhaps it was the wartime *Abercrombie* that had gone; where Parlon, DeCoster and Stafford rotated the top watch endlessly under way in that order, interrupted only and frequently by calls to General Quarters, when the ship was fully manned, when there was no past and no future, when the war was the only fact of life that mattered and the "next operation" was always just around the corner. Now Parlon and DeCoster were gone, Stafford was navigating instead of standing watch, and other signatures appeared in sequences of three in the underway log each day. How many times, in how many places, in how many kinds of weather and circumstances of routine or urgency had I relieved Cy as OOD? How many times had I come up out of CIC to the bridge and onto the little elevated platform where Cy stood, sometimes helmeted, more often bareheaded, with the glasses around his neck, and after a look around and a brief conversation, had spoken the ritual words "I relieve you, sir"? And how many times in port had we sat in rare moments of quiet and leisure, discussing with candor and at length war and love and death and life and all the questions for which each man has or seeks his own answer?

As if that date were truly an end and a beginning (a beginning of the end?), the day of Cy's departure brought the first firm news of going home and a new Supply and Disbursing Officer, Ensign Willis Leon McGill to replace Jim Russell. The expected date of departure was 5 November, the route through Pearl, ETA San Diego, 5 December. The news came just in time. By the end of October it would have been necessary to hold men aboard who were eligible for discharge simply to be able to operate the ship (we had already lost the ability to fight her effectively). Now those men could take her home. The definite nature of the news was a blessing. It reduced the crew's vulnerability to each new rumor or piece of scuttlebutt that came along, and it allowed them at last to place a finger on the calendar and say with certainty, "*There* on *that* date I shall be home."

Meanwhile, there was still work for *Abercrombie* to do, and as though to help her do it, to reinforce this beginning of the end, she received another new officer on 24 October. He was Harry Sello, an exceptionally bright twenty-four-year-old ensign, just commissioned, but with a master's in physical chemistry and an immediately obvious desire and ability to learn. He was quickly assigned a dual responsibility as assistant in both communications and gunnery.

The next day DE343 got a new job. Her men thought when they towed in the barge load of anchors at Okinawa that she had had them all. Wrong. She was to act as the Harbor Entrance Control Post (HECP) at the principal entrance to the Inland Sea of Japan, the north-south strait between Shikoku and Kyushu called the Bungo Suido.

She arrived there, after an all-night coastal run from Wakanoura, just at daylight on the twenty-sixth. Another DE, the *McGinty* (365), was already on duty there. Keith Wheeling and I went aboard for a conference and discovered what an HECP, or at least this one, was supposed to do. Essentially it consisted of determining the identity, port of departure and destination of each ship or group of ships entering the Inland Sea through Bungo Suido, logging the exact time and date of that passage, and providing entering ships with charts and port instructions when necessary. Thirty to forty miles inside the narrowest point of the straits were the major ports of Kure and Hiroshima (of recent fame), so there was a lot of traffic, most of it related to the U.S. occupation. The job was made easier by the fact that the channel had been recently swept; it now abounded with floating mines and therefore should be used only during daylight. This meant that almost all inbound traffic passed through before early afternoon. *Abercrombie* quickly fell into the routine recommended by the *McGinty*: patrolling slowly back and forth across the straits until noon, performing the duties just described, then after lunch anchoring in a quiet little cove on the Shikoku side for the afternoon, watching the strait visually and by radar, and communicating with any passing ships by radio or twenty-four-inch signal light. The little cove was snug and sheltered in a semicircle of 1,200-foot green hills whose steep slopes must have continued beneath the sea, since the bottom was 53 fathoms down. At night there were movies on the fantail, their variety maintained by judicious swapping with a group of minesweepers operating out of an adjacent cove. At 0545 each morning the DE would be under way and back on sentry duty.

Thus for five days the USS *Abercrombie*, late of Orange, Texas, manned out of the cities, small towns, high schools, farms and factories of all America, watched over the Bungo Suido, gateway to the vitals of Japan. If she had been there (and somehow invisible) in the fall of 1941, her men would have seen *Akagi, Kaga, Shokaku, Zuikaku, Hiryu, Soryu* and their attendant battleships, cruisers and destroyers steaming out (in twos and threes to aid in deception), bound for the Kuriles and the Sunday assault on Pearl Harbor. Had she been there in the fall of 1944, her men could have watched carriers *Zuihu, Zuikaku, Chitose, Chiyoda* and the strangely awkward half-carriers, half-battleships *Hyuga* and *Ise* going out sacrificially to bait Halsey into running north; this had left San Bernadino Strait unguarded and resulted in the battle off Samar. And if she had been there just the past spring on the sixth of April, her men could have watched (as those of the USS *Threadfin* did through their periscope) the beautiful but doomed *Yamato* plow bravely down the straits at twenty-five knots with her escorting cruiser and eight destroyers, a mammoth seagoing kamikaze on her way to Okinawa and the bottom of the China Sea.

On the afternoon of 29 October the message came which *Abercrombie*'s men had been waiting for since the Bomb. It came buzzing in in the rapid, high-pitched little pellets of sound that make sense only to radiomen. It was from Commander, Fifth Fleet, to the task force commander at Wakayama/Wakanoura, and it read "When ready for sea, detach and sail CortDiv 69 plus *Gendreau* (DE639) to Yokosuka to report ComFifthFleet for further routing. Available Magic Carpet."

Those last three words were the key. "Magic Carpet" was the worldwide operation that was bringing American servicemen home. "Available Magic Carpet" meant available to take people home!

The next evening the *McGinty* came up the strait to relieve us, sent a boat over containing her Engineering Officer, our first homeward-bound passenger, and at 2030 *Abercrombie* was on her way.

However, she had a long, long way to go, and nature was not cooperating. As she came out of the lee of Shikoku and turned northeast for Kii Suido and Wakayama, the DE ran into thirty to forty knots of head winds and truly mountainous head seas. She came around the corner out of the Bungo Suido at an eager and impatient seventeen knots, but after slamming into the head sea for half an hour, hurling solid water over the bridge, feeling as though she would break apart, she slowed to fifteen, then twelve, then ten, where she stayed most of the night. Even at ten knots the motion was extreme, a long, swift rise of the bow, a pause, and a shuddering, pounding drop endlessly repeated. With the slightest moderation of the sea we cranked on a few more turns; back to eleven knots at 0637, to twelve ten minutes later, thirteen at 0700, fifteen by 0735.

2. Homeward Bound

Abercrombie PULLED INTO WAKANOURA WAN at 1300. *Suesens, Wann, Stafford* and *Gendreau* were waiting, not very happily. The head seas had delayed us and cut short our time in port. Orders called for all five ships to be under way for Yokosuka by 1430. In that ninety minutes we had to take on 36,000 gallons of fuel, locate and get aboard 1,200 pounds of flour (we had none), transfer five men to other ships, take aboard two officers and twenty-eight men as passengers, and make up and mail a list of those passengers and the Separation Centers to which they were ordered. Somehow, incredibly, it all got done, and by midafternoon the five DEs were standing out of Wakanoura Wan at sixteen knots, column open order, distance five hundred yards. *Suesens* was in the lead, *Abercrombie* number three astern of *Stafford*, bound for Tokyo Bay.

The last night of October was still rough because of the storm that had delayed *Abercrombie* en route up from the Bungo Suido, but not rough enough for the five homeward-bound DEs to reduce speed. November the first dawned clear, the sea was down to a rolling swell, and blue in the haze but capped with snow, broad on the port bow, seventy-five miles away, loomed Fujiyama, the sacred mountain of Japan, shown on the chart as Fuji San. All morning the column of DEs threaded through the high green islands with their white lighthouses on the approaches to Tokyo Bay, then through the mass of anchored shipping off Yokosuka and Yokahama. By signal the Division Commander in *Suesens* changed the uniform of the day to undress blues with white belts; and now on all five little ships, the crews stood in orderly lines along the decks, and the four colored flags of their international call signs rippled bravely at the yardarms. At 1300 exactly, *Suesens* passed slowly abeam of the USS *New Jersey* and rendered honors, her PA system ordering, "Attention to starboard!," then the blast of a police whistle as her officers faced starboard and saluted, and two blasts to end the salute. Each DE in turn saluted the battleship and the four-star flag of Commander, Fifth Fleet, which fluttered at her truck. She was awesomely impressive lying there at anchor under Fujiyama in the home waters of the enemy she had helped defeat. She was sleek and crisply shipshape, radiating power, a floating symbol and the essence of victory and triumph. And as though to emphasize that symbolism by the starkest of contrasts, not a thousand yards astern of *New Jersey* lay a *Nagato*-class Japanese battleship, the last one left afloat, her pagoda superstructure mangled and bent, her turrets scorched and rusted. The Union Jack flew at her bow, the Stars and Stripes from her stern. On her battered after turret was a large sign with yellow letters, "No Visitors Allowed." Armed U.S. sailors patrolled her decks to reinforce that message.

The little formation of DEs filed slowly into the narrow cove of the Yokosuka Naval Base. Just before 1500, *Wann* picked up a mooring buoy there, and *Abercrombie* moored to her port side.

Every man on all five ships was hoping on that November first that they would fuel, provision and sail at once for home. But it was not to be. The next morning they all shifted to anchorages outside the base, *Abercrombie* anchoring this time with *Stafford* (DE411). That afternoon orders arrived to sail on the fourth, direct to Pearl, so there was a full day to waste. First priority was to get as many of the men as possible ashore on liberty. That turned out to be impossible to do through normal procedures, so after several hours of frustration and with the afternoon wearing on, five cases of beer convinced the crew of a nearby LCT that they should get under way and take our liberty party ashore.

Most of the officers took the train from Yokosuka up to Tokyo and returned later with colorful tales of the luxuries of the Imperial Hotel and of the telegrams they had been able to send home. Rosie's report was more relevant. He had ferreted out the fact that souvenir enemy weapons might be available for all hands if a truck could be arranged to drive fifteen to twenty miles north of Tokyo to pick them up. He had even tentatively arranged for that truck.

The project was very tempting. I knew at once how much it would mean to the young sailors in the crew to come home with such tangible evidence of their wartime service. I discussed it with the Exec of the *Stafford* (who turned out to have been one of my students at a Reserve Midshipmen's School in 1942) and decided to try the next day to get enough for all five ships. And there began a genuine adventure.

That night we organized a working party of five men from each ship. From DE343 we picked the most deserving and reliable—chief machinist's mates Puddy and Larby, chief commissary steward Glidewell, gunner's mate first Schuh, bo'sun's mate first Pete Kish and yeoman second Mitchell. Mert Olson went along to give me a hand, and Lloyd Parker came just for the ride to Tokyo.

We left in the whaleboat at 0700 and met the people from the other ships at the Naval Base headquarters ashore. There we discovered that the five ships had been assigned one ten-wheeler Army truck, which could carry twenty or twenty-five men or 1,100 or so rifles, but certainly not both. So we had to cut the working party to three men per ship, turning the others loose on liberty in Yokosuka. From *Abercrombie* I picked Don Puddy who was her senior chief, Jim Larby who ran the other engine room, and Pete Kish who had a brother stationed somewhere in the Tokyo area.

I rode in the back of the truck with the working party. There was a velvety carpet of cement dust on the truck's deck left over from its last job. It was a long, dusty ride over terrible streets and roads, first through downtown Tokyo and then through what had been its industrial suburbs. We skirted the Imperial Palace and drove through the heart of the city. The damage was shocking. On a street comparable to, say, Fifth Avenue, each block had several piles of rubble where major buildings had once been. Even in the department stores open for business there was no glass in the upper stories and there were holes in the roofs visible from the street. Most of the traffic was bicycles and American military vehicles with a sprinkling of charcoal-burning cars. There were a lot of recently installed signs in English pointing the way to this or that Army unit or headquarters. The crowds were colorless, shoddy, threadbare. The people were not hostile, nor did they seem to be attempting to ignore us. They acted as though this was the way things had always been. In the streets of small towns little kids beside the road would grin and wave and shout, "Hallo!" as though we were their own victorious army returning from having just secured for all time the Greater East Asia Co-Prosperity Sphere.

But the seeds of the future were already evident. One U.S. soldier crossed the street ahead of the truck with a Japanese girl on his arm who really got the men's attention. She was cute and petite with black hair in a pageboy to her shoulders, and she was dressed the way a smart young lady in the States would be—in a tailored suit, silk stockings and high heels.

Grinding around one corner in Tokyo, we encountered General MacArthur, in a long black Cadillac with five silver stars on a red background for a license plate, and directly astern another car labeled "Imperial Household."

The suburbs were like Wakayama multiplied a hundred times, acres and miles of broken masonry, plaster, tile and red, rusty, twisted metal. The tallest objects were the safes and the corrugated iron and wood shacks, some with earthen roofs.

As we stopped at one of the many checkpoints to show our papers and identify ourselves, one of the MPs, a tough-looking, husky soldier, fully armed, was tending a huge potted sunflower nearly as tall as he was. This rough character had a K-ration can squeezed together to make a spout and filled with water. Solemnly and carefully he watered the big yellow flower, not just in the pot, but all up and down the long stalk, tenderly pouring over the big yellow head as though he were washing a baby. He grinned a little sheepishly as he felt our gaze, and then quickly became stern and military as the next truck approached for him to check.

After three or four hours we arrived at our destination, which turned out to be the headquarters of the First Cavalry Division. We had the name of a major we were supposed to see there, and it didn't take long to find his office. In the next five minutes it appeared that our trip had been for nothing. The Major had an inner office. In the outer office there was a very suave, pleasant captain who was very sorry and sympathetic. He would be "glad to get rid of the stuff," but there absolutely "was no more." The last had gone out yesterday. All that remained, still unchecked and guarded at the original turn-in points, of course couldn't be touched, was probably booby-trapped, and so forth.

We were disgusted, disappointed and ready to go. Then I remembered that the First Cavalry was the outfit of my best friend in high school, Jim Farquharson. Although I hadn't heard from Jim in more than a year, I asked the smooth Captain if he were still around. He dialed the phone on his desk, handed it to me, and there was noisy old Jim yelling, "Where the hell are you?" He said I should turn left outside the building and keep walking, and he would meet me. My friends were invited to lunch on the Army, and on top of this miracle, when I hung up and turned around, the Major came out of his office and announced that we could have the rifles after all, that we should meet him here at 1300, and he would take us back down into Tokyo where they were stored.

In the next minute, there was my old buddy, big, deep-voiced, warmly friendly, seemingly not changed one iota by his uniform or the railroad tracks of a Captain or the war he had just been through (the "First Cav" had taken the Admiralties and Manus, we had escorted its transports to Leyte and Lingayen, and the division had been first into Manila and Tokyo—all according to Jim). We talked all during lunch, and the trip would have been well worthwhile to me if we had not acquired a single rifle.

The Major was as good as his word, and our truck followed his jeep on the long ride back into town and to a police headquarters on one of the main avenues. There we found a huge, second-floor storeroom—completely filled with neat stacks of captured and confiscated weapons, rifles, bayonets, carbines, machine guns, swords and sabers of all Japanese makes and vintages. Each stack was about six feet high, four or five wide, and about thirty to forty feet long. The Major pointed out the piles from which we could take our booty, assigned a Second Lieutenant to make certain our working parties kept to their instructions, and a Sergeant to keep an account of the equipment we took out. We went to work. It was a big job and it took a long time, even with the officers and the driver joining in.

Although one of the stacks of weapons consisted entirely of samurai swords, we were told that they were not for issue. But after a lot of persuasion, assisted by a canteen of bourbon, which Mert had brought along for just that sort of contingency, and after we had pointedly observed an officer from General MacArthur's staff pick up twenty swords for the General to give away, the Major relented and allowed us four swords per ship.

While the officers were negotiating, Puddy and Larby had applied themselves to the problem in a more direct and practical way, with Larby outside under a window near which Puddy in his official capacity was selecting the weapons to be loaded. Their efforts roughly doubled the quantity of swords that finally made it into the truck.

It was nearly dark when I signed a receipt for 2,300 rifles, 1,200 bayonets and 20 swords, and we took leave of the Major and his men and set off with the working party perched uncomfortably atop the jiggling, rattling load of weapons.

Since one of the ships was anchored off Yokohama, that city was to be our first stop, but when I gave the orders to the driver, he sorrowfully announced that he had no idea where we were at the moment nor did he know the route to Yokohama. Without a road map, route signs, or the local language, that posed quite a problem. However, we knew the general direction, the bright stars helped a little, and in a couple of hours we unloaded the loot for one ship and their working party. On the way back to Yokosuka we passed Olson's famous but badly depleted canteen up to the freezing men on top of the cargo, where it noticeably improved morale.

It was 2300, dark, cold and windy, when we backed the truck out onto the same pier at which we had landed about 0800. An LCVP was waiting to pick up the gear and the men for two of the other ships, but since they were anchored in the opposite direction from *Abercrombie* and *Stafford*, this was of no help to us.

While the men unloaded the truck, I went to the transportation shack to arrange a boat. The cox'n on duty informed me that the Commandant of the base had ordered that none of the transportation-pool boats could go outside the breakwater at night. Since *Abercrombie* and *Stafford* were about four miles outside, this was quite a blow. I asked the cox'n what people did who *had* to get out to their ships at night and had no boat. He answered, perfectly respectfully, that either they got the personal permission of the Commandant—which was hard to do since he had no phone, lived three miles away, and had never been known to grant this permission to anyone under his own rank, which was that of Captain— or they waited until daylight.

I pictured Escort Division 69, *Abercrombie* included, homeward bound, pennants streaming, steaming out of Tokyo Bay at daylight, and me and my working party with the truckload of rifles and swords degenerating into psycho cases there on the beach. I wandered out onto the dock wracking my brain for a solution. Out in the harbor but well within the breakwater were two LSTs. They had LCVPs in their davits. Back I dashed to the transportation shack and found that a scheduled round trip to the LSTs was due to shove off that moment. In less than five minutes, I was saluting the OOD on the nearest one and relating my sad story. He was a pleasant enough young officer, and after I promised him and his boat crew a rifle or carbine in good condition for their trouble, he arranged immediately to lower away an LCVP and turn it over to me.

It took nearly an hour before we loaded the six hundred rifles for the two ships and were headed out into the bay. It was crowded with ships, and very rough, very dark and very cold. The blunt high bow of the LCVP threw each little breaking chop eight or ten feet in the air, whence it fell onto the working party and their cargo. In ten minutes all were so wet and so cold that everything afterward made no difference because it was impossible to be any more miserable.

After about forty minutes of this, we picked up the two adjacent pairs of red truck lights belonging to the *Stafford* and the *Abercrombie*, and in a few minutes more we were alongside. By this time it was around 0100, but it was necessary to break out big working parties on both ships to get the gear aboard. It was a major task because the little LCVP rose and fell like a runaway one-story elevator, parting line after line and repeatedly taking whole seas aboard over rifles and men alike. The touchy matter of dividing the spoils evenly between the two ships was handled by having a chief from the *Stafford* count the gear unloaded for *Abercrombie* and vice versa. Finally it was done, the LST boat crew collected its well-earned reward, with a cup of hot coffee thrown in, and shoved off. After stationing a watch on the rifles until they could be distributed in the morning, I turned in. It was 0230 and no bunk had ever felt so good.

But the next morning felt even better. All five ships were underway at 0635, streaming their long homeward-bound pennants from the truck, one foot of white over red bunting for every day out of the States. *Abercrombie*'s had been laboriously but lovingly pieced together on the signal bridge's little manual sewing machine by signalman Tom Skoko, and a man had to be stationed atop Mount 52 to hold the end and keep it out of the sea. It was a clear, calm morning after the rough night, and once outside the offshore islands, the Division Commander put the ships in line abreast, five hundred yards between ships, speed sixteen knots (the maximum economical speed that would get them to Pearl unrefueled), and that was the way they steamed, with minor variations, two thirds of the way across the Pacific.

On that first morning the rifles and bayonets were distributed. A hat filled with numbered slips of paper was taken around, and each man drew a slip. Because there were only one third as many bayonets as rifles, every third slip had the word "bayonet" written on it. All the gear was spread on the fo'c'sle, and when the word was passed, the men formed a line leading up there in order of the number drawn. Number one man got first choice. If a man was on watch, the line was held up until he was relieved and made his selection. The lucky ones with slips for bayonets picked them at the same time. A similar deal was run for the passengers after all our own crew had chosen, the assumption being that their own ships had taken care of them previously and that we had to look after our own men first. The crew was as pleased as kids with the souvenirs, and for days there was much cleaning, sanding, polishing and oiling all over the ship.

The first night out, we called all the passengers down into the mess hall (we had received eight more off Yokosuka) and told them about the ship's routine and regulations and what would be expected of them. A few who held critical rates we had to put on watch, especially quartermasters, electricians and firemen. A gang of motor machinist's mates went to work under Stephens putting the heaters back in the ventilation system. My new roommate, a jaygee named Charley Royce, was made Passenger Division Officer, and he picked a sharp first class bo'sun's mate as leading petty officer. They were assigned a quarters-for-muster parade on the torpedo deck and required to report their muster each morning with the other divisions.

Charley Royce had had an interesting war. He had been skipper of an

LCT, really just a beamy, flat-bottomed tank barge with a bow ramp. His must have been a more advanced model than the ones I had shepherded around the Med or that we had seen at Lingayen and Okinawa, because he had arrived out in the western Pacific not on the deck of an LST or a cargo ship, but on the LCT's own bottom as part of a flotilla of identical craft—from Panama to Pearl to Saipan to Leyte to Okinawa at six knots, through two typhoons, on a barge!

It was a beautiful and deeply satisfying sight in those days to look out to port and starboard and see the other DEs slashing along, the sea passing between them like a sixteen-knot river, to know that their course was east, in a great circle toward home, and that this time they would stay on that course, except for the brief stop at Pearl, until they arrived. I would go up to the bridge every hour or so for a few minutes between jobs just to watch the five ships at the end of their white sea ribbons, their sharp bows biting into the swells, and to glance at the gyro-repeater, where the lubber's line stood around 083 degrees. I always went back to work with a wonderful, warm feeling, as though I had had a big swallow of strong, sweet wine. The only flaw in that sight and that feeling was the memory of the two identical DEs which should have been there but were not, which lay smashed and broken instead on the sea floor off Samar and Okinawa, *Samuel B. Roberts* and *Oberrender.* And the *Stafford,* out there all trim and salty, had almost joined them, losing two men and half her engineering plant in her duel with the kamikazes off Lingayen. But after several months of major repairs and modernization in the States, she had come back to the war just at the end of the Okinawa operation and was now in the best shape of all.

Navigation on that joyful passage took on an unaccustomed interest. We posted a big chart of the Pacific from China to the U.S. West Coast on the bulletin board in the fore-and-aft passageway. Each day when the noon mean position was signaled, quartermaster Henry Beattie would plot it in with red pencil and join it to the last one with a red line. There was always quite a crowd around by the time he was ready with the new day's position. Of course, he was subject to the usual heckling, especially since on a chart of that scale our little four hundred or so miles a day was not a very impressive advance across the great blank expanse of paper. Nor did all the men understand the principle of the great circle, which when plotted on a Mercator chart gives the impression of a considerable detour. "What we goin' way the hell up there for, Hank? Pearl's down here, see?" And "Come on, Beattie, get it up. Latitude goes this way and longitude that way [pointing]." "Jeez, is that all the farther we've come since yesterday? We ain't got the oil aboard to make it at that rate."

The last speaker was not the only one aboard to be worried about the fuel. The Chief Engineer, the Captain and the Exec were a little anxious, too. *Abercrombie* was using much more fuel than the other ships, as shown by the daily reports, and Gus couldn't find out why. It looked as though we would be very, very short if we made Pearl at all. The Commodore didn't like it, either. We received several visual messages elucidating that fact in some detail and suggesting that corrective measures be taken at once. Gus was using only one boiler at a time, and he tried everything he knew, even coming up to the foreign territory of the bridge to complain that the erratic courses being steered by the helmsmen were at least partially responsible. But our track was a ruled line across the chart relative to those of *Suesens* and *Gendreau*, both of which were using much less fuel. The mystery continued unsolved.

Late on the fifth, a report came in of a drifting mine a few hundred miles to the north and east of our position. At daylight the next morning, we changed course to look for it, much to the highly vocal disapproval of all hands on the fuel-short, homeward bound, impatient *Abercrombie*. Nevertheless, the five ships criss-crossed that spot in the Pacific for about six hours, found nothing and continued on toward Pearl.

The seventh of November was a navigator's dream. Morning and evening twilight were perfect, with the first-magnitude stars bright points of light, each by itself in the clear, blue-gray dusk, the horizon a clean, ruled line between sea and sky, calm, pleasant. It was not hard to get up around 5:00 A.M. on that kind of morning. All during daylight there was not a cloud, morning and afternoon sun lines cut in perfectly, latitude at Local Apparent Noon came out right on the nose.

That evening we expended most of our excess pyrotechnics. It was better than any Fourth of July, the five slim ships in line abreast at sixteen knots, and the red, green and white clusters of fire balls breaking overhead and drifting toward the sea. Each exploding display threw a strange, dim light over the line of DEs, then fell slowly astern and went out. After the big charges came the short colored arcs of the Very stars. Then the night closed down, leaving only the red and green side lights of the moving ships and an occasional white disk or rectangle from an open port or door.

At 1400 on the twelfth, the lookouts could make out the high, blue mass of Kauai on the starboard bow. Radar reported it forty miles away. That evening the ships shifted smartly into column formation and turned south to pass through the Kaulakahi Channel between Kauai and Niihau, then eastward again to Oahu and Pearl. All night the smell of flowers and warm earth permeated the sea air and brought smiles to the faces of sleeping men below.

At Pearl they must have forgotten that the war was over. At the crack of dawn out came the familiar yellow B-26 towing its red target sleeve, and for an hour and a half the ships blasted away at it. It was the first time that all of *Abercrombie*'s guns had spoken together since last they did in deadly earnest back in A38A. As soon as the exercise was over, the Commodore ran up the signal to make the uniform undress whites for the crew, ties and jackets for the officers, and then the column of DEs headed for the entrance to Pearl Harbor.

Abercrombie was in Pearl just twenty-eight hours and forty-five minutes. The first thing she did was fuel. Of the 96,000 gallons with which she had sailed from Yokosuka, exactly 3,000 of usable oil remained. Still no one knew why so much had been used, why DE343 had come so close to the ignominy of "running out of gas" on the high seas. We learned that our destination had been changed from San Diego to San Pedro. Then there were provisioning and mail to see to, and the ever-present problems of transfers and passengers to be solved. Two Marine pilots came aboard as passengers. We managed to keep almost all our remaining crew aboard, since we were the fastest way they could get home. All but two.

Orders came from ComDesPac to transfer two second class machinist's mates to a new destroyer bound west for six more months. We had only two aboard, both members of the commissioning crew who had been through the whole thing from Orange to the Bungo Suido. I went over to DesPac Headquarters and protested, pointing out the injustice, inequity, hardship and just plain rotten deal those sailors were getting. The Captain I talked to was sympathetic but adamant. The ships of the occupation and policing forces in Japanese waters had to have men to operate them, and *Abercrombie* had to furnish her share. I came back to the ship, called up the two men and told them. It was the hardest thing I ever had to do. They went below pale and grim-faced to pack up. But the next day when the time came for them to leave, one could not be found. I was afraid that in his bitterness and disappointment, he had gone over the hill, but he had not left the ship. It took several hours to find him. Just before sailing he was located, pathetically hiding deep in the bilges of the space in which he worked.

On the morning of the fourteenth, with departure scheduled for 1600, by the sheerest accident the riddle of excessive fuel expenditure was solved. The bow hook of the whaleboat, returning after one of its many trips, noticed something under the surface close to the side of the ship. He poked it with the boat hook. The object was solid, metallic. Investigation showed that it was a thirty-foot section of the port bilge keel, apparently torn loose and bent back in the pounding head seas between Bungo and Wakanoura. All the way across the Pacific it had been dragging broadside, deep enough to be out of sight, but acting as a huge underwater brake on the progress of the ship, Gus and his gang were vindicated, and his relief was marvelous to see.

But now we were in trouble. Normal procedure called for dry-docking and repair, about a three-day job assuming a dock was available right away. But this was not a time for normal procedure. No report was made. Olson and I made an immediate trip to a nearby tender. The Repair Officer understood. We returned with a diver and an underwater cutting torch. In about ten minutes the former bilge keel was settling permanently into the bottom mud of Pearl Harbor.

With the amputation of the bilge keel, all doubts about sailing on schedule should have been removed, but at the last minute one more arose. Fifteen minutes before sailing time, with the crew in whites at Special Sea Details and the lines singled up, Hicks came back from the Officers' Club feeling no pain whatever. He was not bad enough to be obviously out of control, just revealingly and abnormally casual, cocky and loudly authoritative. To clear the anchorage and enter the channel called for some fairly tricky maneuvering, and the bridge watch collectively held its breath as we backed out. I didn't even want to look. But he was either lucky or his hard-earned ability as a shiphandler overcame the fumes in his head because with only a couple of close shaves, he managed to back clear into the channel, wait for the *Suesens* to do the same, and follow her out to sea.

All hands expected that from here it would be a straight and simple run, directly to San Pedro. But the Commodore still had a few tricks up his sleeve. He scheduled us to fire hedgehogs at a bank about thirty miles off Oahu that evening. The ships ran parallel to the ten-fathom shoal, then executed simultaneous port turns, slowed to attack speed and approached in line. We picked up the bank on sonar, and each ship made its attack on a point directly ahead of it, except that the hedgehogs were trained for maximum port deflection to avoid possible damage from ships passing over their own exploding charges. It was a clear, moonlit night, so we could follow our own projectiles as they streamed up and out over the sea in successive pairs, each pair departing with the unique, half sputter, half bang that only the hedgehog makes. The black powder smoke and wadding drifted back over the bridge, and we waited long seconds for the reports. They came in a jarring rumble, as though a big pneumatic hammer had been turned for a second against the bottom of the ship. We could hear the other ships firing and feel the detonation of their projectiles. We reloaded, turned around, fired another pattern at the edge of the shoal, and finally swung east for San Pedro.

For two days the line of small ships stood eastward under a solid overcast, no stars, no sun for position, but on the third day the morning stars showed that arrival in San Pedro would be on the morning of the twenty-first. On the ensuing nights the remaining pyrotechnics were fired and then the excess twenty-millimeter ammunition. The night firing of the twenties was dramatic and enjoyable now that it could be watched without ducking. The tracers lanced out over the sea in bright, short strings, some ricocheting up at sharp angles and disappearing, others glowing red hot for an instant when they hit the water.

As *Abercrombie* ran down her easting, you could feel the tension building. Most of the men who would leave for discharge on arrival had packed two days early, their bulging seabags stacked below their bunks, their lockers empty. Appetites fell off, many men stayed up late and rose early, unable to sleep in the turmoil of anticipation.

All night on the twentieth, the islands off southern California were in sight, and the navigators were kept busy timing the lights and taking bearings.

Then when daylight came, San Pedro came into view, its buildings gleaming white in the thin morning haze across the calm sea. It was a sight never to be forgotten. This was the States which we had so often wondered if we would ever see again. This was the sight, the day, nearly the hour of a thousand dreams. *Abercrombie*'s crew was tense and silent in a way I had never seen. It was as though they were waiting for something to happen. The senses were abnormally alert, all nerve endings seemed open, receptive, vulnerable. The mind seemed to idle down, totally aware and waiting, ready to register in color and three dimensions everything that happened on this long-awaited magic morning.

Before reveille I had borrowed a dash of after shave from Charley Royce. Now, even after forty years, a whiff of that particular brand brings back the pungent, smoky chill, the gleaming buildings, the silent men in blues lining the rail, the morning when DE343 came home.

At 0641 we passed through the Sea Breakwater off San Pedro. Six minutes later the pilot came aboard. The buildings ashore grew taller. The dock we were to make came into sight, then the people on it. It was hung with bunting and signs which read: "Welcome" and "Well Done." As we drew closer, there were Red Cross girls with cartons of milk and boxes of doughnuts, and booths from which free telegrams could be sent.

The working uniform was undress blues for only the second time since Boston, because the smoky California air had a real chill in it. The passengers and crew scheduled for discharge crowded the fantail in their dress blues, their seabags piled around them, their orders in their hands. At 0722 the first line was on the dock. Ten minutes later the *Wann* tied up to starboard—the *Wann* with which we had first sailed from Galveston to Bermuda so long ago. At 0810 the men began to file ashore, first the passengers and then the crew. I watched as they went over—Don Wood of Repair II, Ed Schuh of Mount 51, Jimmie Allen, perennial cox'n of the whaleboat, Pappy McAleer, Chief Don Puddy, Tom Rutters of the accordion caper, Ralph Rice, sharer of a year of watches on the bridge and probably the best-loved man aboard; quiet, capable, make-anything, fix-anything Charles Stephens of the C and R gang, and a couple of dozen others after I found the watching too hard to do.

Besides, there was work to be done. There was line handling to supervise as the *Wann* came alongside and a truck to arrange for hauling the departing men's baggage to the local receiving station where they were to be discharged. Then a call came in from Operations ordering us to clear our berth in fifteen minutes for an arriving transport.

At 0900 first *Wann* and then *Abercrombie* were under way, short-handed and missing many familiar faces, and an hour later we anchored at our assigned berths out in the harbor.

In the few minutes of calm and quiet after the starboard anchor splashed down onto U.S. bottom again, I felt I would explode with the need to get the hell ashore and find my wife. The thought that she might even now be watching the little ship from *that* pier or the window of *that* hotel was almost maddening. But I could not go yet. Still the ship was first.

We had to know how much liberty we could grant and to how many men, when we could shove off our leave parties, when our speed run was scheduled, how long we were to be anchored out like this, what was to happen to us anyway. It was my job to go ashore and find out.

I went in the whaleboat and in a bus and on foot. I talked to WAVE Lieutenants, USN Captains and Operations yeomen. I think I was military and respectful and alert, the young DE Exec back that day from the Pacific. I returned to the ship, turned over what I had learned to the Commodore and Hicks, and organized the liberty in the ship's office. But all the while I was a hollow man. My heart was somewhere ashore, searching. At last it was all over, everything that had to be done that day was accomplished. I was in my fresh khakis and new stripes and back in the whaleboat going ashore, no longer a hollow man.

I ran up the dock into the officers' waiting room and into a phone booth to start my search. But as I entered the booth, Mert Olson tapped me on the back and handed me a note. It was in my wife's writing and it said, "I am waiting for you at the landing. You will know me by my favorite color." I went back onto the landing with my heart slamming in my dry throat, my eyes scanning back and forth for a glimpse of red. There it was at the lunch stand, the back of a girl's red suit. She was sitting on a stool at the counter, wearing a tallish black hat. It was she. The glass door nearly broke as I burst through it. Somehow the black hat ended up on the floor, but then I could feel her, slender and strong and feminine, in my arms after all this terrible time. I could smell her lovely, familiar scent, hear her low, exciting voice in my ear, taste the eager warmth of her mouth—and for one reserve officer in one small warship of the United States, the war was really over at last.

Epilogue

FOR A FEW DAYS after the return of DE343 to the country of her birth, her remaining crew lived in a kind of golden aura of happiness and satisfaction, suffused with the joyous awareness that the war was over and they were back in the States. In the euphoria of those few days, the distinctions and barriers of rank and rate thrown up by naval discipline, and absolutely necessary to the operation of the ship and her survival, began to appear to many as simply partitions between friends; ashore the differences eroded comfortably, at least partially, and were replaced by the liking and mutual respect engendered by the shared experiences of a year and a half. San Pedro and adjacent Long Beach were not Manus or Leyte or Ulithi with their Officers' Clubs, chiefs' clubs and enlisted recreation areas. The reserve officers and reserve sailors, civilians before the war and shortly to be civilians again, met in warmly congenial groups to eat and drink and enjoy the homecoming together.

On the evening of the second day of this new era, some of us met for dinner in the Sky Room of the Long Beach Hilton. We sat at a single long table that overlooked the harbor, and out there, far below in the dusk and the distance, we could make out the little ship, slim and gray, which had taken us to war and brought us home again. Mert Olson was with us, and Ted Barber, and quartermaster Fran Wall, and Pete Kish, and Ed Schuh, and Steve Stephens (who had not left yet for home), and Bob Hawthorne whose cool gunnery had saved us all, and others whose names the years have erased. The talk, of course, was exclusively of the ship which was the bond between us, and which was visible far below even after dark, her red truck light glowing and yellow light spilling from a couple of open hatches. From that collective conversation, most of us realized for the first time how consistent and unvarying *Abercrombie's* good luck had been.

Six DEs had sailed to war as Escort Division 69. Of those six, two had been sunk, three hit and hurt. DE343 alone, although she had shared fully in every action, came home with no combat damage and no casualties. The string of luck challenged belief, but as we talked, we realized:

- She could well have been assigned to Taffy 3 off Samar where *Roberts* was lost—but she was not.
- She could have been anchored in the vicinity of the *Mount Hood* with *Oberrender* in Manus—but she was not.
- Off the beach at Lingayen the kamikaze which hit *Columbia* had aimed at her but turned away.
- That first week at Kerama Retto she could well have missed or killed *Dickerson's* four burned and wounded sailors—but she did not.
- She could have been on the ping line that first week in April when the first mass attack by kamikazes had sunk so many ships—but she had left for Saipan the day before.
- If she had arrived back at Okinawa on 16 April, she would have been in time for another attack by 165 suiciders—but she had arrived on the seventeenth.
- The mysterious four-round straddle and either of the bomb near-misses at Okinawa could just as well have been hits—but they were not.
- The Jill coming in from the port quarter, which caught her cold with no gun on it, could have been a kamikaze—but it was not.
- The torpedo that had been dropped so close by the Frances could well have hit—but it did not.
- It could have been DE343 instead of DE344 in A34A the night the "Obie" was hit—but *Abercrombie* was anchored off Hagushi.
- Bob Hawthorne's forty, in the few seconds available, could very easily not have stopped that inbound Betty—but it did.
- The Zeke which had tried twice to crash us and simply missed could have had a better pilot—but it did not.
- The other Zeke which had flown into the *Roper's* bow would have flown into *Abercrombie's* stern had that Marine Corsair not been riding its right wing—but the Corsair was there.
- The Thunderbolt and Corsair CAP could have been somewhere else the day she was fueling from *Sebec*—but it was there.

Just at the end of dinner that evening, an officer at a nearby table rose and came over. I recognized him as the skipper of one of the destroyers with which we had operated off Okinawa. He was a full Commander, and his Naval Academy class ring was prominent. I would have risen, but he held me down with a hand on my shoulder.

"I don't want to intrude on your evening," he said, looking down the table, "and I'm glad to see you enjoying yourselves, because you sure as hell deserve to! I couldn't help hearing that you're from the *Abercrombie*. We operated with you a couple of times out west and there's something I want to say." He paused, and he had the whole table's attention. "You DE sailors," he went on, "did one hell of a job out there. Don't you *ever* take a back seat to *anyone* as far as fighting that war is concerned." (That last sentence was spoken like an order.) "You went out there right out of civilian life, most of you right out of school or your parents' homes, with a minimum of hurried training, in little ships that could have been better armed and equipped, and you did damned near everything we did with bigger, better, faster ships and a hell of a lot more training—and you did it just as well, sometimes better. I'm proud as hell of you and I want you to know it!"

The next morning after quarters I called the whole crew back on the fantail and repeated that little speech as best I could, being especially careful to cite its source. No man who heard it at either first or second hand has forgotten it. I like to think that it was because it had the ring of sincerity—and truth.

In the ensuing weeks, life aboard DE343 went on according to the normal routine of a warship in port. She could have been in Boston or San Diego in the summer of 1944. The ship's work went forward. Liberty was granted daily. The married men (but not the shackmasters) were allowed ashore all night. As was normal, Harry Miles came back half an hour late from liberty. There were movies on the fantail for those who stayed aboard.

But the clock was running down on *Abercrombie*. Word came that she was to be deactivated—decommissioned and mothballed. All sense of mission or urgency vanished with that news. The ship's work became a dirty chore leading nowhere, a drudgery of chipping, scraping, cleaning, priming, preserving, accompanied by reams of equally uninspiring but rigidly required paper work.

On Saturday the twenty-fourth, Mert Olson and Rosie saluted and left the ship forever. A week later, on Friday the thirtieth, the log of the 16–20 watch bore this entry:

> 1700 Lieut. Cmdr. Edward P. Stafford (D), USNR (102590), detached as per orders of ComDesPac dated 29 September 1945 ... to report to Commanding Officer, U.S. Naval Receiving (Intake) Station, San Pedro, California, for separation.
>
> [Signed] W.L. McGill, Ensign, USNR

Early in the new year, with her propulsion system deactivated, *Abercrombie* was towed down to San Diego, where the Reserve Fleet of mothballed ships was located; there the work of cleaning and preserving continued.

On the first of May, the second anniversary of DE343's commissioning, little Butch, Harry Miles's friend, survivor of fifteen months of war, met his end under the wheels of a laundry truck on the dock beside the ship.

On 15 June, a message from the Commander, San Diego Group Pacific Reserve Fleet, informed the Chief of Naval Operations (CNO) that the *Abercrombie*, along with several other ships, was placed "Out of Commission in Reserve." Since she was no longer habitable, the few members of the crew remaining were moved to the *Suesens*, reporting each day to DE343 to complete her deactivation.

Young Harry Sello, one of the final officers to leave, took with him the last ensign to be flown by the *Abercrombie* before decommissioning, carefully folded in a neat Navy blue bag. On his way to his home in Chicago, he made a stop in Salt Lake City. There, in the lobby of a downtown hotel, he met Mr. and Mrs. C. W. Abercrombie and presented the flag to them. Events, and the life of a warship, had come full cycle from that winter day in Orange when Mrs. Abercrombie had smashed the champagne against the stern of the hull named for her dead son. Both Abercrombies wept and hugged Harry as though he were the reincarnation of the big, quiet young aviator who always wanted to know how far he was from Kansas City.

On 14 August 1946, her deactivation completed, DE343 turned in with the long, quiet rows of her sisters and went to sleep. Once when war blazed up again, in Korea, they roused her and overhauled her, and it looked as though she might be needed again. But back to sleep she went, and the whole decade of the fifties rolled over her and receded into history. Sometime during that decade she was towed up to Bremerton, Washington, but it was just a change of resting places. Most of the sixties went by.

Then in March of 1967, with the war in Vietnam heating up, someone took notice of her again. A memo passed from one naval office in the Pentagon to another. In paragraph one it said, *"Abercrombie,* an inactive ship, is recommended for striking and disposal primarily because of her extensive hull deterioration."

After that, events moved quickly.

On 3 April 1967, the CNO and the Secretary of the Navy decreed that "The USS *Abercrombie* is unfit for further naval service and shall be stricken from the Naval Vessel Register" as of the first of May.

On that date she became the "ex-USS *Abercrombie.*"

On 18 April instructions went to Bremerton to begin stripping her of any and all machinery and equipment that could be used by other ships or that had significant salvage value.

That process took almost all the remainder of 1967. In November a big fleet tug, the *Tatnuk,* hauled her back south to San Diego, where she was turned over to Commander, First Fleet, the officer charged with the training and readiness of warships based on the West Coast and in Hawaii.

On 6 January 1968 another tug, the *Mataco,* took her in tow. At the end of a long hawser, she passed again under Point Loma and continued westward to sea, bobbing high in the water as when she had first been launched, but now blind and comatose, bereft of sensors, crew and weapons, and thus no longer a ship, only a hull as she had been at Orange when I first saw her. And yet . . . and yet, does a ship which has belonged to men, in which men have lived and fought, a ship which men have loved, ever lose all vestige of them? If something in the thin steel of her sides and decks itself has not changed, then something at least of her men is left, despite the decades and the stripping—a sock sucked into a ventilator in George Ferroni's laundry, a final can of contraband beer under a bolted plate in Ted Gruhn's carpenter shop, part of a letter between bunk and bulkhead in Tom Parlon's stateroom, an undiscovered vial of medicinal alcohol in the chiefs' quarters, a torn playing card in the wardroom pantry. Something of the men, something of their spirit, some imprint must be left.

But the hull which had been *Abercrombie* knew nothing of that; and late in the afternoon, men from *Mataco* climbed aboard to throw off the towing hawser. The tug reeled it in and steamed back eastward, leaving its tow to roll unsteadily, drifting with the currents and the winds.

That evening the target practice began. A task force consisting of the nuclear cruiser *Long Beach,* the light cruiser *Oklahoma City,* the carrier *Bonhomme Richard* and eight destroyers came up over the sea horizon to conduct a scheduled training exercise. The destroyers were first, steaming in a column twelve thousand yards away. They were of a type *Abercrombie* had never seen, taller, larger, their guns firing faster. They did not use explosive ammunition but inert projectiles in order to prolong the training exercise and derive maximum benefit. When they had finished, Marine gun crews on the *Long Beach* opened up with World War II vintage 5"/38s. *Abercrombie* would have understood those guns. Then the cruiser let go with a weapon which would have astounded the crew of DE343: Terrier surface-to-air missiles, depressed at launch for surface-to-surface use. Swift and silent they came, flat on the sea, supersonic, the driving rockets glowing white hot at their tails. Next came the light cruiser, firing her six-inch turrets slowly, one at a time, also using "blind loaded tracer" ammunition.

The next morning the practice resumed, and now the carrier attack squadrons got in their licks, speedy little A-4F jet Skyhawks swooping down, with a whistle never heard by *Abercrombie*'s men, to fire heavy rockets and drop long, pointed bombs. They came back again with missiles, Bullpups remotely guided to the target by the pilot working a little joystick from the cockpit, and a Walleye with its television nose like a human eye to take it unerringly into any target it could see.

The air strikes did it.

At 1135 exactly, on 7 January 1968, riddled and perforated, with gaping holes in her sides from the missiles and in her decks from the bombs, fifty miles due west of San Diego, in nine hundred fathoms of water, what had once been the USS *Abercrombie* (DE343) rolled quietly to port and vanished under the waves of the Pacific.

Vanished. The old hull gone. But not the name, neither that of the man at Midway, nor of the ship which wore it proudly up the far Pacific to Japan. That name stays. It is engraved forever on the honor rolls of war. And it will live in human hearts while one man remains of those who served in her.

Itinerary and Chronology of Significant Events

14 January 1944	USS *Abercrombie* (DE343) launched at Orange, Texas
3 March 1944	First officers and men report to Precommissioning Detail
24 March 1944	Lieutenant Bernard H. Katschinski reports for duty as prospective Commanding Officer
21 April 1944	The bulk of the crew, 5 officers and 160 men report for duty
1 May 1944	USS *Abercrombie* commissioned
9 May 1944	Under way from Orange for builder's trials in the Gulf of Mexico and overnight at Sabine Pass, Texas
10–19 May 1944	Fitting out and loading at Galveston, Texas
19–25 May 1944	Under way from Galveston to Bermuda
25 May–23 June 1944	Shakedown training at Bermuda
23–25 June 1944	Under way from Bermuda to Boston
25 June–6 July 1944	Post-shakedown maintenance at Boston. Leave for the crew
6–7 July 1944	Under way from Boston to Norfolk, Virginia
7–13 July 1944	Under way from Norfolk to St. Nicholas, Aruba, Dutch West Indies
15–17 July 1944	Under way from Aruba to Cristóbal, Canal Zone
18–22 July 1944	Antisubmarine patrol out of Cristóbal
23–28 July 1944	Under way from Cristóbal to Windward Passage to Aruba
30 July–1 August 1944	Under way from Aruba to Cristóbal
1 August 1944	Transited Panama Canal to Balboa, Canal Zone
3–11 August 1944	Under way from Balboa to San Diego, California
11–22 August 1944	Loading stores, training and maintenance in San Diego
22–29 August 1944	Under way from San Diego to Pearl Harbor, Hawaii
20 August–19 September 1944	Post-shakedown advanced training out of Pearl Harbor

19 September 1944	Under way from Pearl Harbor to Seeadler Harbor, Manus, Admiralty Islands
23 September 1944	Crossed the 180th meridian, international date line
29 September 1944	Crossed the equator
30 September–14 October 1944	In port, Manus, Admiralty Islands
14 October 1944	Under way with escort carriers to cover the liberation of the Philippines
23 October 1944	Rescue of Lieutenant Gerald Lee Bridge
25 October 1944	Battle off Samar, loss of *Roberts*, *Hoel*, and *Johnston*
26 October 1944	Collision with USS *Manila Bay* (CVE61)
3 November 1944	Return to Manus
10 November 1944	Explosion and destruction of USS *Mount Hood*, damage to *Oberrender*
3–28 November 1944	In port, Manus
28–30 November 1944	Under way from Manus to Bougainville, Solomon Islands
30 November–19 December 1944	Invasion rehearsals at Bougainville and Huon Gulf, New Guinea
19–22 December 1944	Under way from Huon Gulf to Manus
22–27 December 1944	In port, Manus
27 December 1944	Under way from Manus to Lingayen Gulf, Luzon, Philippine Islands
5 January 1945	USS *Stafford* (DE411) attacked and damaged by kamikazes
9 January 1945	Amphibious landings at Lingayen Gulf. Under way for Leyte, Philippine Islands
10 January 1945	Rescue of three young Philippine men from capsized outrigger
12–18 January 1945	Provisioning and antisub patrols at Leyte
18–22 January 1945	Under way from Leyte to Biak, Schouten Islands
22 January–2 February 1945	Antisub patrol and sonar repairs at Biak
2–6 February 1945	Under way from Biak to Leyte
7–9 February 1945	Under way from Leyte to Mindoro, Philippine Islands
10–12 February 1945	Under way from Mindoro to Leyte
13 February 1945	Summary Court Martial of Harry Miles
15–19 February 1945	Under way from Leyte to Ulithi Atoll, Caroline Islands
19 February–3 March 1945	Provisioning, maintenance and painting ship, Ulithi
3–6 March 1945	Under way from Ulithi to Leyte
6 March 1945	Arrived at San Pedro Bay, Leyte. Provisioning and antisub patrol

12 March 1945	Whaleboat wrecked and beached
19 March 1945	Whaleboat recovered
21 March 1945	Under way for invasion of Okinawa
26 March 1945	Arrived at Kerama Retto off Okinawa
27 March 1945	*Abercrombie* straddled by rounds from unknown source
1 April 1945	Recovery of dead enemy pilots
3 April 1945	Rescue of four survivors of USS *Dickerson* (APD21)
5–9 April 1945	Under way from Okinawa to Saipan, Marianas
11–12 April 1945	Under way from Saipan to Ulithi
13–17 April 1945	Under way from Ulithi to Okinawa
20–23 April 1945	Antisub operations with USS *England* (DE635)
28 April 1945	Near-miss by bomb from Jake fighter
30 April 1945	Near-miss by Jill
5 May 1945	Torpedo attack by Frances. Frances shot down
9 May 1945	*Oberrender* (DE344) mortally damaged by kamikazes. *England* seriously damaged
14 May 1945	Escort for USS *Texas* (BB35)
20 May 1945	Escort for USS *Idaho* (BB42)
26 May 1945	Betty bomber shot down, Hamp fighter shot down, Zeke misses *Abercrombie,* hits *Roper* (APD20)
28 May 1945	Baka bomb shot down
29 May 1945	Katschinski detached, Hicks assumes command, Parlon becomes Executive Officer
31 May 1945	Two near-misses by Zeke kamikaze
5 June 1945	Collision with USS *Dyson* (DD552)
8 June 1945	Fueling group under attack
12 June 1945	Failed smoke generator nearly asphixiates an officer
14–18 June 1945	Under way from Okinawa to Saipan
18 June–1 July 1945	Rest, maintenance, painting ship at Saipan
1–4 July 1945	Under way from Saipan to Okinawa
6 July–8 August 1945	Task force operations in the China Sea
24–25 July 1945	Escort for force flagship, USS *Tennessee* (BB43)
1–3 August 1945	Typhoon in the China Sea
6 August 1945	News received of atomic bombing of Hiroshima
8–11 August 1945	Under way between Okinawa and Leyte
10 August 1945	First news of Japanese surrender negotiation
11–20 August 1945	In port, Leyte, upkeep and maintenance
14 August 1945	News of Japanese surrender
16 August 1945	Parlon detached, Stafford takes over as Executive Officer
20 August 1945	First demobilization orders received

20–23 August 1945	Under way between Leyte and Okinawa
23 August– 10 September 1945	In port, Buckner Bay, Okinawa
4 September 1945	Mail censorship terminated
10–15 September 1945	Under way between Okinawa and Jinsen, Korea
17–19 September 1945	Under way between Jinsen and Okinawa
22–24 September 1945	Under way between Okinawa and Wakayama, Honshu, Japan
26 September 1945	First liberty for crew in Japan
3–8, 11–13, 17–20 October 1945	Search and rescue operations out of Wakayama
10 October 1945	Typhoon hits anchorage at Wakayama
25–26 October 1945	Under way between Wakayama and Bungo Suido, Japan
26–30 October 1945	Harbor Entrance Control duties at Bungo Suido entrance to Inland Sea of Japan
30–31 October 1945	Under way between Bungo Suido and Wakayama
31 October–1 November 1945	Under way between Wakayama and Tokyo Bay
3 November 1945	Souvenir weapons received for crew
4–13 November 1945	Under way between Tokyo Bay and Pearl Harbor, Hawaii
14–21 November 1945	Under way between Pearl Harbor and San Pedro, California
1 May 1946	Butch dies under wheels of laundry truck on the dock
15 June 1946	*Abercrombie* placed "Out of Commission in Reserve"
7 January 1968	DE343 "Expended as a target"

Crewmen Contributors

THE FOLLOWING officers and men of the USS *Abercrombie* assisted in various ways with the writing of this book:

James E. Allen	Electrical contractor
Howard W. Amos	Retired federal employee
Floyd E. Apple	Barbershop owner
Charles A. Bailey	Industrial records specialist
Bruce D. Baker	Farmer
J. E. Barber	Machine tools salesman
Jack D. Blackwell	Fireman
Rufus L. Bond	Retired appliance store owner
John D. Boudreaux	Oil field worker
Harold E. Breeling	U.S. government employee
Christian I. Carpenter	Retired printer
Ray J. Clift	Animal caretaker leader
Jack C. Cochran	Municipal employee
Roe C. Combs	Automobile mechanic
Glenn W. Craig	Community college instructor
Cyrus C. DeCoster	College professor
Sloan B. Duncan	Retired textile worker
Kenneth L. Eidemiller	Building maintenance man
Earl C. Evans	Retired oil company executive
Thomas W. Ferris	Waste-water treatment plant operator
George A. Ferroni	Building maintenance man
Curtis W. Foley	Retired retail druggist
Paul R. Fry	Retired truck driver
Graham Fulcher	Retired chief petty officer, U.S. Navy
Robert T. Glynn	Retired electrical foreman
Jack M. Green	Printer
Martin T. Grider	Builder/cabinetmaker
Theodore E. Gruhn	Construction estimator
Clester P. Hawley	Millwright
Joseph L. Henderson	Truck driver
Harold E. Hensler	Experimental machinist
William H. Hobson	Industrial maintenance man
Albert L. M. Holloway	Retired chief petty officer, U.S. Navy
Charles A. Holston	Church administrator
Joseph Kowalski	Retired postal service worker
Clarence B. Krause	Freight agent
Homer Lynn	Plastic products manufacturer
Merle McBurney	Retired federal employee
Fred B. McLean	Retired electrical engineer

Gilbert P. McMillan	U.S. government employee
Frederick Manger	Carpenter/retired chief petty officer, U.S. Navy
Vernon Millsaps	Aluminum worker
Wilbur Morris	Machinist
Glen W. Moth	Retired toolmaker
Charles R. Nelson	Truck driver
E. Merton Olson	Retired petroleum executive
Travis Pair	Retired autoworker
V. Lloyd Parker	Stockbroker
Thomas N. Parlon	Retired materials handling equipment dealer
"J C" Parnell	Textile supervisor
James E. Payton	Lineman electrician
George S. Peters	Salesman
Nick Pratchenko	Retired airline mechanic
A. P. Presnell	Retired federal employee
George D. Quinn, Jr.	Commander, U.S. Navy (Retired)
James A. Ramsey	Retired chief gunner's mate, U.S. Navy
William F. Ressler	Grocery store owner
Lew A. Reynolds	Retired telephone company employee
Ralph R. Rice (now deceased)	Railroad communications supervisor
Melvin I. Rosenberg	Retired retail clothing store owner
Thomas M. Rutters	Retired postal service worker
John Sawyer	Retired food packaging worker
Harry Sello	Engineering consultant
Raymond J. Shiel	Retired master chief quartermaster, U.S. Navy
Thomas Skoko	Policeman
Charles L. Stephens	Retired cabinetmaker/carpenter
Lester A. Strampher	Retired television field engineer
James A. Triplett	Distillery worker
Kella Turner	Retired master chief machinist's mate, U.S. Navy
Robert M. Wachter	Truck manufacturing worker
William W. Watkins	Restaurant owner
L. W. White	Retired moving and storage manager
Harry Whitworth	Retired dental technician
Henry J. Wilcoxson	Metals manufacturer general foreman
Donald C. Wood	Retired paper company executive
Lawrence E. Wright	Retired railroad engineer
Robert J. Zuzanek	Industrial sales manager

Bibliographical Notes

FOR THE NINETY percent or so of this book which deals exclusively with the *Abercrombie*, there were five basic sources: the ship's Deck Log, her official Action Reports and War Diaries, the visual signal log, my own personal journal, and written and oral material supplied by the officers and men who served aboard.

For the activities and adventures of other ships, I have used their logs, Action Reports and official histories where available, supplemented by interviews with former crew members. In this category, the accounts of individual ship actions described in *United States Destroyer Operations in World War II* (Naval Institute Press, 1953) have also been most helpful. In the special case of the *Samuel B. Roberts*, I was fortunate to have an unpublished account of her final gallant action entitled *The Spirit of the "Sammy B,"* written by her Commanding Officer in that engagement, then Lieutenant Commander Robert W. Copeland, with Jack O'Neill, as well as an excellent official report by her Gunnery Officer, William S. Burton.

For historical perspective, the big picture, I have relied primarily on the patron saint of all U.S. naval historians, Samuel Eliot Morison, whose *History of the United States Naval Operations in World War II*, Volumes XII *(Leyte)*, XIII *(The Liberation of the Philippines . . .)*, and XIV *(Victory in the Pacific)*, was indispensable. For the same purpose but to a lesser degree, I have also used *Triumph and Tragedy*, Volume VI, of Winston Churchill's *The Second World War;* and *Return to the Philippines* and *The Road to Tokyo* of the *Time-Life* series on World War II.

As a ready reference to the names, numbers, characteristics and ultimate fate of U.S. warships generally, *The Ships and Aircraft of the United States Fleet*, war edition, by James C. Fahey, has been invaluable.

The details of ping line and radar picket stations off Okinawa and the tactics prescribed for the ships assigned to them are contained in the Operation Order, COMPHIBSPAC OP Plan A1-45, then top secret but now declassified. Tactics to be used against the kamikaze are spelled out in a formerly secret pamphlet entitled *Counter-Measures Against Suicide Planes*, published by Amphibious Group Seven, and kindly furnished by *Abercrombie's* Gunnery Officer, Thomas N. Parlon.

There are also some useful and interesting Japanese data on the kamikaze at Okinawa and elsewhere in *The Divine Wind*, by Rikihei Inoguchi, Tadashi Nakajima and Roger Pineau (U.S. Naval Institute, 1958).

Index